EXPERIMENTAL SLIPS AND HUMAN ERROR

Exploring the Architecture of Volition

COGNITION AND LANGUAGE
A Series in Psycholinguistics • Series Editor: R. W. RIEBER

Recent Volumes in this Series

A Continuation Order Plan is available for this series. A continuation order will bring delivery of each
new volume immediately upon publication. Volumes are billed only upon actual shipment. For further
information please contact the publisher.

EXPERIMENTAL SLIPS AND HUMAN ERROR

Exploring the Architecture of Volition

Edited by

BERNARD J. BAARS

The Wright Institute
Berkeley, California

Plenum Press • New York and London

Library of Congress Cataloging-in-Publication Data

Experimental slips and human error : exploring the architecture of
  volition / edited by Bernard J. Baars.
        p.   cm. -- (Cognition and language)
    Includes indexes.
    ISBN 0-306-43866-6
    1. Speech errors. 2. Will. 3. Psychology, Experimental.
  I. Baars, Bernard J.   II. Series.
  P37.5.S67E97 1992
  401'.9--dc20   92-23100
                                                                  CIP

ISBN 0-306-43866-6

© 1992 Plenum Press, New York
A Division of Plenum Publishing Corporation
233 Spring Street, New York, N.Y. 10013

Printed in the United States of America

Contributors

BERNARD J. BAARS, The Wright Institute, 2728 Durant Avenue, Berkeley, California 94704.

JACK W. BERRY, The Wright Institute, 2728 Durant Avenue, Berkeley, California 94704.

LAWRENCE BIRNBAUM, The Institute for the Learning Sciences, Northwestern University, Evanston, Illinois 60201.

GORDON H. BOWER, Department of Psychology, Stanford University, Stanford, California 94305-2130.

JENN-YEU CHEN, Department of Child Psychiatry, New York State Psychiatric Institute, New York, New York 10032.

JONATHAN COHEN, Department of Psychology, Carnegie-Mellon University, Pittsburgh, Pennsylvania 15213.

GREGG COLLINS, The Institute for the Learning Sciences, Northwestern University, Evanston, Illinois 60201.

GARY S. DELL, Department of Psychology, University of Illinois at Champaign, Champaign, Illinois 61820.

DONALD G. MACKAY, Department of Psychology, University of California at Los Angeles, California 90024.

MARK E. MATTSON, Social Sciences Division LL916, Fordham University, New York, New York 10023.

DONALD A. NORMAN, Department of Cognitive Science, University of California at San Diego, La Jolla, California 92093.

JAMES T. REASON, Department of Psychology, University of Manchester, Manchester, M13 9PL, United Kingdom.

RENEE J. REPKA, Department of Psychology, University of Rochester, Rochester, New York 14627.

ABIGAIL J. SELLEN, MRC Applied Psychology Unit, 15 Chaucer Road, Cambridge CB2 2EF, United Kingdom and Rank Xerox Ltd. Cambridge Euro-PARC, 61 Regent Street, Cambridge, CB2 1AB, United Kingdom.

JOSEPH PAUL STEMBERGER, Department of Communication Disorders, University of Minnesota, Minneapolis, Minnesota 55455.

Preface

Whereas most humans spend their time trying to get things right, psychologists are perversely dedicated to error. Errors are extensively used to investigate perception, memory, and performance; some clinicians study errors like tea leaves for clues to unconscious motives; and this volume presents the work of researchers who, in an excess of perversity, actually *cause* people to make predictable errors in speech and action.

Some reasons for this oddity are clear. Errors seem to stand at the nexus of many deep psychological questions. The very concept of *error* presupposes a goal or criterion by comparison to which an error *is* an error; and goals bring in the foundation issues of control, motivation, and volition (Baars, 1987, 1988; Wiener, 1961). Errors serve to measure the quality of performance in learning, in expert knowledge, and in brain damage and other dysfunctional states; and by surprising us, they often call attention to phenomena we might otherwise take for granted. Errors also seem to reveal the "natural joints" in perception, language, memory, and problem solving—revealing units that may otherwise be invisible (e.g., MacKay, 1981; Miller, 1956; Newell & Simon, 1972; Treisman & Gelade, 1980). Thus errors show how the nervous system copes with failures of its own goals and constraints; they clearly reveal the limits of our immediate memory and conscious capacity, but they also show the price to be paid for the many *un*conscious automatisms that come to the fore when people are absent-minded or distracted (Reason, 1982, 1983, 1984, 1992). In the world outside the laboratory, human error is thought to be a major contributor to industrial disasters, airplane crashes, medical malpractice, and automobile accidents. And even in the psychology clinic, dysfunctional symptoms appear as persistent, unwanted errors in the actions, thoughts, and perceptions of clinical patients (see Baars, 1988, and Chapter 1, this volume; also Spitzer, 1979).

These points are especially applicable to inadvertent errors, or *slips,* which are generally defined as errors that violate their own governing intentions. Such errors are *known* to be errors by the person who commits them, but they are made nonetheless. Slips differ from errors made out of ignorance or forgetfulness of a goal; they are especially revealing of the control problems we encounter in carryng out our voluntary intentions.

SLIPS IN MODELS OF LANGUAGE

It may seem obvious that an adequate theory of language should explain speech errors as well as fluent, correct speech. But this view is not universally held. For example, Chomsky's widely accepted goal for linguistic theory (1957, 1965) is to generate *"all and only* the grammatical strings" of a natural language like English. This definition excludes errors. It has taken some time and effort to persuade modern linguists that nongrammatical utterances are worth studying (Fromkin, 1968, 1973). Even today few proposals in the Chomsky tradition venture to account for errors (but see Fay, 1980; also Chen & Baars, Chapter 9, this volume).

Likewise, some artificial-intelligence language simulations do quite a good job of analyzing and generating meaningful sentences, but they do not make humanlike errors (e.g., Winograd, 1972). Of course one could always *add* an error-generating mechanism to these models, but that would be artificial and unparsimonious. To simulate real human speech, a model should produce both correct and erroneous output in a natural way, without extraneous theoretical baggage.

A third type of theory has begun to fill this gap. Parallel distributed processors (PDPs) treat the cognitive system as a society of specialized networks, in which activation can spread from node to node in a parallel-interactive fashion. Dell (1985, 1986) has developed a model of sentence production in which several levels of representation exist, including phonemic and lexical. Activation numbers are assigned to lexical and phonemic nodes, and the activation spreads to adjacent nodes both within and between levels. (In "true" PDP models, connections between the nodes are also assigned strength levels, a very important theoretical modification.) When simulations are run with a range of plausible parameters, it appears that this type of network generates correct lexical output as well as spoonerisms and displacements of single phonemes. The model demonstrates the same preference for lexical over nonsense spoonerisms that has been shown to exist in both induced and spontaneous slips (Baars, Motley, & MacKay, 1975; Dell, 1986). Along similar lines, MacKay (1982, 1987) has proposed a spreading-activation model of the serial order issue in speech and action. The general properties of PDPs have been worked out in considerable detail by Grossberg, Rumelhart, McClelland, and others, and the PDP approach has been used quite successfully to model other well-studied phenomena in perception, memory, language learning, and action control (Grossberg, 1982; Hinton & Anderson, 1981; Rumelhart, McClelland, & the PDP Group, 1986; see also Arbib, 1980; Baars, 1980a,b, 1983, 1987, 1988; Gel'fand, Gurfinkel, Fomin, & Tsetlin, 1971; Greene, 1972).

Distributed models suggest a new way of thinking about human beings. We normally think of ourselves as guided by an executive "self": "we" have control over our actions. But distributed systems are strongly decentralized. The intelligence of such systems resides in its independent components and in the interactions between them, so that the whole system behaves much like a market economy, in which thousands of individual transactions take place without centralized intervention, and fundamentals like supply, demand, and price emerge from the system as a whole. Details of processing are generally handled by specialized networks in the processing "society." A decentralized system does not *rule out* executive control, just as the existence of market forces does not rule out a role for government. But it limits the purview of executive systems and creates possibilities for a reciprocal flow of control between executive and subordinate elements. Such systems have some distinct virtues (e.g., Greene, 1972).

Thus, there has been notable progress in understanding and modeling both correct and erroneous language. However, almost no current theory attempts to explain the *involuntary* character of slips, an issue that is explored in some detail in Chapters 1 and 4. Indeed, it is argued in Chapter 1 that "local" theories of speech and action are *in principle* unable to explain some of the core issues raised by slip phenomena, such as the clear psychological differences between voluntary and involuntary acts (viz. Baars, 1988, and Chapter 4, this volume).

PRACTICAL ASPECTS OF SLIPS

While the study of slips is contributing to scientific theory, it also has important practical implications. Inadvertent errors can apparently cause serious accidents. Reason (1984, 1992) has analyzed several catastrophic accidents in which fatalities were apparently caused by slips: a London bus driver who crashed a double-decker bus into a low overpass, killing 6 passengers (perhaps because he was in the habit of driving the same route in a single-decker bus); a train collision killing 90 people because the driver made a habitual turn, but this time onto the wrong track; and the notorious runway collision on the island of Tenerife in 1977, in which a KLM Boeing 747 taxied into the path of a landing jumbo jet, killing 577 passengers and crew. The very senior KLM pilot failed to obtain clearance from the control tower before takeoff, perhaps because he had just finished a different assignment involving hundreds of hours of training pilots in a cockpit simulator, in which runway clearance was not required. In all three cases, Reason suggests that the fatal errors may reflect a "habit intrusion," that is, an inadvertent substitution of a highly habitual and automatic action for the correct one (see also Langer, 1989).

A similar pattern of accidents may have occurred in flight training with the B-29 bomber in World War II. The B-29 was a four-engine aircraft designed to fly on only one engine in an emergency. As a routine part of flight instruction, three of the four engines were shut off in midflight, to prove to student pilots that the aircraft would indeed continue to fly on just a single engine. For this demonstration to work, the fourth engine had to be kept running, however, to generate the electrical power needed to restart the others. With *all* engines turned off, electrical power would be inadequate to restart any engine, and the aircraft would simply lose altitude and crash. Several training flights came to grief when pilots and instructors inadvertently turned the fourth engine *off,* rather than turning a second engine *on.* Norman (1976) points out that, in emergencies like this, panic may serve to degrade rather than improve effective action, by interfering with conscious/limited-capacity processing.

SLIPS AND PSYCHOPATHOLOGY

Perhaps the most unusual point I will make here is the close connection between slips and the symptoms of clinical psychopathology. Clinical symptoms may be viewed as *recurrent, uncontrollable slips* in speech, action, emotion, imagery, or thought (Baars, 1988, pp. 246–344). This observation exactly fits the operational definition of slips suggested in Chapter 1, as errors that occur *even though* they are quickly recognized to be errors when we pay attention to them. Thus, catastrophic mental images in phobias, compulsive behavior, tics, stutters, obsessive thoughts, or excessive and upsetting emotions are quickly recognized by their victims as unwanted and unintended. They are nevertheless difficult or impossible to stop. All of the "Axis I" dysfunctions in the current American Psychiatric Association *Diagnostic and Statistical Manual* (DSM-III-R; APA, 1987)—the so-called ego-dystonic syndromes—involve such sliplike symptoms (Spitzer, 1979). Thus, the pattern of normal slips also fits a great deal of psychopathology. The main difference is, of course, that clinical symptoms are repetitive, unlike ordinary slips, and may not disappear over time. Nevertheless, the study of slips may yield some new leads toward understanding such clinical phenomena.

In sum, slips are more than amusing curiosities. They have already begun to contribute to current theories of speech production and may play a rather grim role in serious accidents, unwanted habits, and psychopathology.

PRIMARY AIMS

This book has three primary aims.

1. The first is *to present current theory* on the control of speech and action, based on modern experimental studies of slips. Parts I and II are devoted to this aim.

2. The second goal is *to provide a single, complete, easily accessible source for the methodology and results of a 15-year-long research program on the laboratory induction of slips,* which now enables us to study a wide variety of these errors experimentally. We now have two different experimental methods for eliciting spoonerisms; several methods for obtaining predictable word-exchanges in compound sentences; and methods for obtaining predictable word-

blends, errors in verb tenses, phonological feature errors, predictably false answers to simple questions, typing errors, errors in hand and arm movements, and object-exchange errors. This new methodology is discussed in Parts III and IV; it allows us to explore a number of questions that were previously untestable.

3. The third and final aim of this book is to explore the implications of slips in *understanding the overall architecture of voluntary control*. This aim is addressed in Chapters 1–5 and 11. (See also Norman & Shallice, 1980; Reason, 1983; Shallice, 1978.)

BERNARD J. BAARS
Berkeley, California

REFERENCES

American Psychiatric Association (1987). *Diagnostic and statistical manual of mental disorders*, 3rd ed., rev. (DSM-III-R). Washington, DC: Author.

Arbib, M. A. (1980). Perceptual structures and distributed motor control. In V. B. Brooks (Ed.), *Handbook of physiology* (Vol. 3). Bethesda, MD: American Physiological Association.

Baars, B. J. (1980a). The competing plans hypothesis: An heuristic viewpoint on the causes of errors in speech. In H. W. Dechert & M. Raupach (Eds.), *Temporal variables in speech: Studies in honour of Frieda Goldman-Eisler*. The Hague: Mouton.

Baars, B. J. (1980b). On eliciting predictable speech errors in the laboratory. In V. A. Fromkin (Ed.), *Errors in linguistic performance: Slips of the tongue, ear, pen, and hand*. New York: Academic Press.

Baars, B. J. (1983). Conscious contents provide the nervous system with coherent, global information. In R. Davidson, G. Schwartz, & D. Shapiro (Eds.), *Consciousness and self-regulation* (Vol. 3, pp. 47–76). New York: Plenum Press.

Baars, B. J. (1987). What is conscious in the control of action? A modern ideomotor theory of voluntary control. In D. Gorfein & R. R. Hoffman (Eds.), *Learning and memory: The Ebbinghaus Centennial Symposium*. Hillsdale, NJ: Erlbaum.

Baars, B. J. (1988). *A cognitive theory of consciousness*. New York: Cambridge University Press.

Baars, B. J., Motley, M. T., & MacKay, D. G. (1975). Output editing for lexical status in artificially elicited slips of the tongue. *Journal of Verbal Learning and Verbal Behavior, 14*, 382–391.

Chomsky, N. (1957). *Syntactic structures*. The Hague: Mouton.

Chomsky, N. (1965). *Aspects of the theory of syntax*. Cambridge: MIT Press.

Dell, G. S. (1985). Positive feedback in hierarchical connectionist models: Applications to language production. *Cognitive Science, 9*, 3–23.

Dell, G. S. (1986). A spreading-activation theory of retrieval in sentence production. *Psychological Review, 93*, 283–321.

Fay, D. (1980). Transformational errors. In V. A. Fromkin (Ed.), *Errors in linguistic performance*. New York: Academic.

Fromkin, V. A. (1968). Speculations on performance models. *Journal of Linguistics, 4*, 47–68.

Fromkin, V. A. (Ed.). (1973). *Speech errors as linguistic evidence*. The Hague: Mouton.

Gel'fand, I. M., Gurfinkel, V. S., Fomin, S. V., & Tsetlin, M. L. (1971). *Models of the structural-*

functional organization of certain biological systems (C. R. Beard, trans.). Cambridge: MIT Press.

Greene, P. H. (1972). Problems of the organization of motor systems. *Journal of Theoretical Biology, 3,* 303–338.

Grossberg, S. (1982). *Studies of mind and brain.* Boston: Reidel.

Hinton, G. E., & Anderson, J. A. (1981). *Parallel models of associative memory.* Hillsdale, NJ: Erlbaum.

Langer, E. J. (1989). *Mindfulness.* New York: Addison-Wesley.

MacKay, D. G. (1981). Speech errors: Retrospect and prospect. In V. A. Fromkin (Ed.), *Errors in linguistic performance* (pp. 319–332). New York: Academic Press.

MacKay, D. G. (1982). The problems of flexibility, fluency, and speed-accuracy trade-offs in skilled behavior. *Psychological Review, 89,* 483–506.

MacKay, D. G. (1987). *The organization of perception and action: A theory for language and other cognitive skills.* New York: Springer.

Miller, G. A. (1956). Human memory and the storage of information. *IRE Transactions on Information Theory, IT-2* (Vol. 3), pp. 128–137.

Newell, A., & Simon, H. A. (1972). *Human problem solving.* Englewood Cliffs, NJ: Prentice-Hall.

Norman, D. A. (1976). *Memory and attention.* New York: Wiley.

Norman, D. A., & Shallice, T. (1980). *Attention and action: Willed and automatic control of behavior.* Unpublished paper, Center for Human Information Processing, University of California at San Diego, La Jolla.

Reason, J. R. (1983). Absent-mindedness and cognitive control. In J. Harris & P. Morris (Eds.), *Everyday memory, actions and absentmindedness* (pp. 113–132). New York: Academic Press.

Reason, J. T. (1984). Little slips and big disasters. *Interdisciplinary Science Reviews, 9*(2), 3–15.

Reason, J. T. (1992). *Human error.* London: Cambridge University Press.

Rumelhart, D. E., McClelland, J. L., & the PDP Research Group. (1986). *Parallel distributed processing: Explorations in the microstructure of cognition: Vol. 1. Foundations.* Cambridge: MIT Press.

Shallice, T. (1978). The dominant action system: An information-processing approach to consciousness. In K. S. Pope & J. L. Singer (Eds.), *The stream of consciousness: Scientific investigation into the flow of experience.* New York: Plenum Press.

Spitzer, R. L. (Ed.). (1979). *Diagnostic and statistical manual of mental disorders* (3rd ed.— DSM III). Washington, DC: American Psychiatric Association.

Treisman, A. M., & Gelade, G. (1980). A feature-integration theory of attention. *Cognitive Psychology, 12,* 97–136.

Wiener, N. (1961). *Cybernetics: On control and communication in the animal and machine.* (2nd ed.). Cambridge: MIT Press.

Winograd, T. (1972). A program for understanding natural language. *Cognitive Psychology, 3,* 1–91.

Acknowledgments

I am grateful for support from the National Science Foundation (Grant No. BNS-7906024) and from the National Institutes for Mental Health (Grant No. 1R03MH3333401), which made possible the studies reported in Chapters 1, 6, 9, 11, and 12. A Cognitive Science Fellowship in 1980–1981 from the Alfred P. Sloan Foundation at the Center for Human Information Processing, University of California at San Diego, made possible a good deal of reflection and interaction with others, notably Donald A. Norman. The research reported in Chapter 11 was supported by the John D. and Catherine T. MacArthur Foundation, through the Program on Conscious and Unconscious Mental Processes, directed by Mardi J. Horowitz, in which the editor served as Visiting Scientist in 1984–1985. Finally, the Wright Institute and its president, Peter Dybwad, were extremely helpful in supporting the completion of this book.

All modern research on speech errors owes a special debt to Victoria A. Fromkin and Donald G. MacKay, the modern pioneers in the study of speech errors, who made the topic scientifically respectable and valued in linguistics and experimental psychology, respectively. We are happy to acknowledge this common debt.

I am also grateful for crucial assistance in the compilation of this volume to Dr. Katie McGovern and to Chris, Andrew, and Megan McGovern.

Contents

Part III: Methods for Inducing Predictable Slips in Speech and Action

Part IV: Findings and Theory Derived from Induced Slips

Part V: Commentary

I

INTRODUCTION

The first chapter sketches a framework for slips and the closely related issue of voluntary control. The framework accounts for many empirical findings, including the necessary conditions for most slips, by means of a general architecture for the nervous system. In this architecture, voluntary actions are controlled by a conscious limited-capacity system, operating in the distributed "society" of intelligent, autonomous, and unconscious processors.

The Many Uses of Error

Twelve Steps to a Unified Framework

Bernard J. Baars

INTRODUCTION

Human activity is rife with momentary control problems: hesitations, dysfluencies, false starts, memory lapses, and errors. This seems rather strange, because normal human action also tends to be effective, complex, adaptive, and fast. Clearly our action control system is the product of many millions of years of evolution: Why then is it so prone to control problems? This is a paradox that emerges most clearly in the case of inadvertent *slips*, which may be defined as actions that reveal a mismatch between a reportable intention and overt performance (Baars, 1988; MacKay, 1987; Norman, 1981; Reason, 1979). Such a mismatch has several clear implications:

First, it suggests the existence of a *momentary dissociation* between the governing intention and its execution. After all, if the intention were properly connected to the action, the slip would not occur.

Second, slips are events that *would have been avoided* had the actor somehow managed to keep control. The error would have been corrected had it been detected in time.

Third, when we become conscious of the flawed action, the momentary

BERNARD J. BAARS • The Wright Institute, 2728 Durant Avenue, Berkeley, California 94704.

Experimental Slips and Human Error: Exploring the Architecture of Volition, edited by Bernard J. Baars. Plenum Press, New York, 1992.

dissociation between intention and performance seems to disappear. *Consciousness of the action* seems to be a sufficient condition for recognizing that the slip *is* indeed a slip (Baars, 1988, and Chapter 4, this volume; Levelt, 1983; MacKay, Chapter 2, this volume; Mattson & Baars, Chapter 11, this volume). Since a slip may violate any one of many very complex levels of control, this ability to recognize the error *as* an error is no small accomplishment.

Fourth, since slips are avoided whenever possible, they *tend to cause surprise* when they become conscious. "Surprise," of course, involves all the varied and extensive aspects of the orienting response, both autonomic and central.

Fifth, *errors tend to violate not just a single level of control, but multiple levels,* including our general intention to communicate and our desire not to appear ridiculous or incompetent.

Sixth and finally, *true slips tend to be disavowed* as soon as they are detected, as if people attributed their flawed action to some agency *other than* themselves.

Evidently, then, these trivial-seeming errors touch on some surprisingly deep issues, issues like voluntary control, momentary dissociation between cognitive "modules," the role of consciousness in the detection and repair of errors, and the conditions under which people accept or disavow control over their own actions (Mandler, 1975; Weiner, 1986). However, we will begin in the simplest way, with the basic notion that *slips are in essence a mismatch between intention and performance.* Given this concept, we can define slips operationally as *"actions that people quickly recognize as unintended, once they become aware of them."*[1] This is a convenient, practical, and easily observable criterion for judging whether some particular action is a slip.

Tables 1 and 2 show the main points covered in this chapter. We begin by drawing some essential distinctions between "slips," "mistakes," and "automatisms." Next, we explore 12 scientific implications of slip research. The first 7 of these points focus specifically on the control of speech and action (Table 1). One might expect slips to be completely understandable at this level, but after contemplating these phenomena for some 15 years, I (and others) have been forced to conclude that *slips are not sufficiently explained by local theories of speech and action.*

This point is easy to demonstrate; no current theory, for example, can account for the elementary fact that people can repeat their own slips voluntarily. Yet speech errors are often repeated spontaneously, as when someone says, "Did I say X? I really meant Y!" Note that the slip and its voluntary imitation are behaviorally identical—but psychologically they are vastly dif-

---

[1]Many slips can be consciously *recognized* to be in error, even if one cannot consciously *describe* the error. Indescribable errors may involve the complex, *un*conscious regularities of syntax, phonology, and the like. However, even these errors can be consciously recognized. Our operational definition of slips covers both cases: consciously describable errors and the more common case where the error and its correction are merely consciously recognizable.

TABLE 1

Implications of Slips for Theories of Speech and Action

Definitions

Conceptually, slips are actions that mismatch their own guiding intentions.

Operationally, slips may be defined as actions that people quickly recognize to be unintended when they become aware of them. They are quite distinct from other types of mistakes and automatisms.

Implications for speech and action

1. Slips are exquisitely sensitive to the many factors that shape normal speech and action.
2. Slips decompose speech and action into underlying *units* and *accommodation mechanisms*.
3. Such units and accommodation mechanisms may be viewed as highly specialized *automatisms*, which are relatively autonomous and context-free when they are not guided by an active goal structure.
4. Studies of slips also suggest that *goals* and *subgoals* may be autonomous and underspecified at certain times.
5. A great variety of specific slips can be elicited in the laboratory by *creating competition between mutually incompatible output plans*, while *limiting the time available* to resolve the competition. The resulting elicited slip is usually some "regularized combination" of the two competing plans.
6. Slips can also help reveal mechanisms of *self-monitoring, editing,* and *repair* in speech and action.
7. Slips seem to reflect a three-way trade-off; between the risks of making an *unintended error* and the benefits of increased *speed* and *flexibility*.

---

ferent. Not a single one of the six properties of slips listed above applies to the voluntary repetition of the slip. Yet no current theory of error even attempts to explain this difference.

The difference between the two behaviorally identical utterances evidently has something to do with the fundamental question of voluntary control. If that is true, then our psychological theories will be badly incomplete until they can address this basic question. Therefore, the first set of seven points discussed below will deal with the "local" implications of slip studies (Table 1) and the second set of points will sketch out a broad new framework for understanding voluntary control (Table 2). This new framework may come close to an emerging consensus in the field, as parallel ideas have been proposed by several other researchers (e.g., Bower & Cohen, 1982; MacKay, 1981, 1987, and Chapter 2, this volume; Norman & Shallice, 1980; Reason, 1983, 1992; Shallice, 1978. For further details, see Baars, 1988, and Chapter 4, this volume).

Tables 1 and 2 present a quick overview of the chapter. The reader may wish to read them first, to make the chapter as a whole easier to grasp.

We will begin by distinguishing slips from other kinds of errors, and from the automatic components of normal speech and action.

TABLE 2
Implications of Slips for the Issue of Voluntary Control

---

1. In the most general case, a slip represents a *loss of voluntary control* rather than a *rule violation.*
2. Slips seem to reflect the two operating modes found in all human mental processes: *One* mode, associated with consciousness, is flexible and has quite limited capacity, and the *second* operating mode involves unconscious automatisms that are inflexible but very efficient, with high parallel-processing capacity (Table 3; Figure 2).
3. *Where conscious access is needed.* Conscious access may be needed at *nonroutine and underdetermined choice points* in planning, control and error-detection, i.e., those points where novel resources must be mobilized to help make the correct choice.
4. *Two necessary conditions for slips.* Slips seem to be *activated automatisms that are liberated from a goal structure.* This may happen when two factors coincide: *First,* some unintentional automatisms are activated by priming, habit, or the influence of competing goal systems; *second, there is some degree of interference with the conscious access needed to resolve critical choice points in planning, control, and error detection.*
5. *The competing-plans hypothesis.* One common source of these two necessary ingredients is *competition* between two goal systems, each *actively working to gain limited-capacity access,* in an attempt to control voluntary action. As a result:
   a. Competition between the two alternative plans, each contending for limited-capacity access, may overload the limited-capacity system momentarily, thereby interfering with the conscious access that is needed to resolve underdetermined choice points.
   b. The two plans interact in an automatic way to produce a regularized combination of the two competing plans.
   c. If plan competition last long enough, error detection via the limited-capacity system is also blocked, and the error is allowed to be made overtly.

THE NATURE OF INADVERTENT SLIPS

Our first point defines the topic: *Conceptually, slips are actions that mismatch their own guiding intentions. Operationally, they may be defined as actions that are quickly* recognized to be errors as soon as we become aware of them. *Defined in this way, slips are seen to be quite distinct from other mistakes and from automatisms.*

A mistake caused by ignorance of the correct action is not considered a slip, nor are judgment errors that are caused by systematic biases, such as halo effects or the effects of differential conscious availability (e.g., Reason, 1992; Tversky & Kahneman, 1973). A perceptual illusion is not a slip, nor are memory lapses usually considered slips. A slip is an error that is quickly *recognizable* as an error, yet is nonetheless carried out. It is an act that mismatches its own governing goal structure (Norman, 1981).

Many slips are never caught by the person who makes them, perhaps because people simply cannot direct their attention continuously to any stream of events (including their own actions) without lapsing (e.g., Reason & Mycielska, 1982). MacKay (1981) showed that even subjects who are instructed to listen for tape-recorded slips miss quite a few of them. Undetected slips are nevertheless genuine slips, by the operational definition given here, because they are quickly recognized to be in error when people *do* direct their attention to them (Baars, 1977; Levelt, 1983).

There are some striking similarities between slips and automatisms—the overlearned, complex, and generally very efficient building blocks of voluntary action (LaBerge, 1980; Shiffrin & Schneider, 1977). The bulk of any voluntary action is, of course, not conscious. It is made up of many routine, unconscious components that may have been conscious at one time, but that have been overlearned and made automatic by dint of long practice. What is conscious in any given voluntary act is likely to be only those aspects that are novel, conflictual, or especially significant (Baars, 1988, and Chapter 4, this volume; Norman, 1976). Reason (1984a,b) has observed that many spontaneous action slips appear to be "habit intrusions," in which more habitual and automatic components of one action take the place of less habitual parts of the intended act. Thus, automatisms can be separated from their contexts, ending up as slips (LaBerge, 1980). Further, many slips occur when conscious control is lost because of momentary distraction or absentmindedness; this occurrence, too, is reminiscent of the way automatisms tend to run on blindly when "just paying more attention" would prevent the problem (Langer, 1989; Reason & Mycielska, 1982).

Slips and the automatic components of voluntary actions thus have close similarities. Indeed, many automatisms can actually be *turned into* slips of a kind, if they are simply resisted voluntarily after they have already started. Thus, the reader can simply look at a word on this page and try *not* to read it; or one can *try* to stop automatic word search in a memory-scanning task (Sternberg, 1966); or one can read a phrase like "Eeny, meeny, miny, ... " and try *not* to fill in the final word. If these examples seem artificial, consider the case of *unwanted habits,* which behave much like voluntarily resisted automatisms. Informal observation suggests that almost everyone has at least one unwanted habit. Some habits, like smoking or overeating, may have a physiological basis, but even then, the physiological craving is accompanied by numerous overpracticed automatisms, such as reaching automatically for a pack of cigarettes or opening the refrigerator door. Most of the time, one can stop any *specific* occurrence of the unwanted automatism, but doing this apparently takes up attentional capacity: when we are preoccupied or distracted, we tend to lose the ability to resist the unwanted act.

In the normal case, of course, the automatic components of an action operate *in the service of* reportable, voluntary goals. This, indeed, seems to be the true difference between automatisms and slips. Automatisms typically do not violate their governing intention, whereas slips do (Baars, 1988). Nevertheless, the similarities between slips and automatisms are interesting and important. We will argue below that it is useful to view slips as "liberated automatisms," that is, errors that result from a *partial decomposition* of a voluntary act into its automatic components.

SPEECH AND ACTION

1. Slips are exquisitely sensitive to the many factors that shape normal speech and action.

In Reason's compelling phrase (1984a), slips are "not a sign of incompetence, but of *misplaced* competence" (p. 515). This is especially clear in the case of certain spontaneous action slips, where part of one action intrudes into another, for example,

   a. "As I approached the turnstile on my way out of the library, I pulled out my wallet as if to pay—even though I knew no money was required" (Reason, 1982, p. 20).
   b. "I went up to my bedroom to change into something more comfortable for the evening, and the next thing I knew, I was getting into my pyjama trousers" (Reason, 1984b, p. 5).

What is striking—and sometimes very funny—about such slips is precisely their air of smooth competence in contrast to their obvious violation of their guiding intentions.

The case for real competence shining through the error can easily be made for verbal slips as well. Any speech act conforms to a great number of very precise and demanding constraints, all at the same time. A single sentence in a normal conversation obeys simultaneous regularities in the standard linguistic levels of *phonology, motor control, morphology, vocabulary, syntax, semantics,* and *pragmatics;* it must also fit the rules of *intonation* and *stress, discourse regularities, rhetorical style, dialect,* and *anaphoric reference;* it obeys social conventions such as *brevity, relevance, informativeness, conversational turn taking, politeness,* and *credibility;* and finally, a speech act is shaped even by purely acoustical considerations, having to do with *voice loudness* and *spectral distribution, background noise, the reverberant quality of the acoustical space,* and the *distance between the speaker and the listener.* Changing any of these conditions will cause corresponding changes in the speech act. Figure 1 illustrates these multiple levels of control on a single utterance.

A typical slip of the tongue modifies only one level of this multileveled control system, but this single change generally violates the constraints of higher levels. Consider the standard linguistic structural hierarchy (Figure 1): an error at any one level necessarily violates the levels above it, but not those below. For example, we have induced slips like "nook bice—book nice," which violate the adjective–noun order of English (Motley, Baars, & Camden, 1980). This syntax error does not violate the lower levels of vocabulary, morphology, phonology, and motor control. But at higher levels, rules are violated: the semantics of such slips is indeterminate, to say the least, and the pragmatic goals of the speaker are hard to fathom as well. Thus, a change in syntax violates no levels below syntax, but it does mismatch all levels above the syntactic level.

For another example, consider a semantic error such as the one below (elicited by Baars & Mattson, 1981; see Chapter 6, this volume, for details):

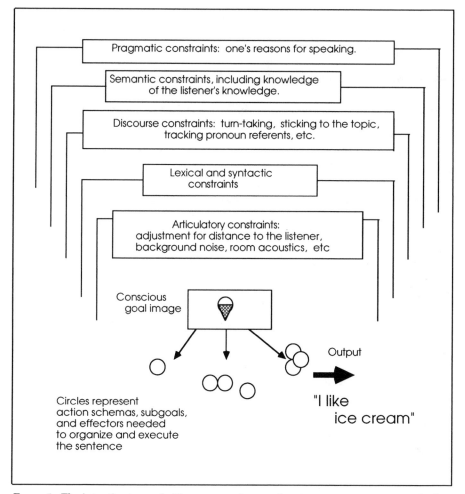

FIGURE 1. The intention to speak. Many unconscious goal systems cooperate to constrain the articulation of a single sentence.

Question: Is the gray sky below the blue sea?
Answer: No, the blue sky is below the gray sea. (False slip.)

This slip is correct at all levels below semantics, including syntax, but it violates semantic truth conditions and pragmatic considerations, such as the normal aim people have to communicate credibly.

These observations suggest that slips are often actually *correct at many levels of control.* Indeed, slips that are insulting or tactless, or those that reveal a secret the speaker wishes to hide, violate no semantic or linguistic rules at all. A memorable example from Freud's *Psychopathology of Everyday Life* (1901/1938, p. 81) may be cited to make this point: it concerns the ambitious young medical student who met the famous Dr. Virchow (alas, no longer famous nine decades later) and said, in effect, "How do you do, Professor Schmidt, *I'm* Dr. Virchow," instead of "How do you do, Professor Virchow, I'm Dr. Schmidt." Freud attributes the error (which has been slightly changed in this example) to the young doctor's ambition, whereas we know today that we can elicit errors of this exact kind in the laboratory, merely by creating confusion about the order of two of the phrases in the intended sentence (Chapter 6, this volume). Whatever the cause, the slip contains no linguistic rule violation at all. It is purely semantic and pragmatic.

There is more evidence for the sensitivity of slips to the normal constraints on speech and action. All other factors being equal, "good" (more normal) slips are made much more often than "bad" slips. This is easy to demonstrate in the laboratory, because there we can set the *a priori* probability of "good" slips to be equal to the *a priori* probability of "bad" slips. Under these conditions, we have found that good slips occur far more often than bad ones, at all the levels tested so far.[2]

Specifically, Baars, Motley, and MacKay (1975) showed that lexical spoonerisms, such as "darn bore—barn door," occur several times more often than very similar nonsense slips, like *dart board–bart doard,* when the *a priori* probability is set to 50%. Likewise, semantically well-formed slips occur more often than semantically anomalous slips, syntactically correct slips more frequently than matched nonsyntactic slips, truthful slips happen more often than false slips, socially appropriate ones more often than socially embarrassing slips, and easy-to-pronounce slips more often than hard-to-pronounce slips (Baars, 1977; Baars & MacKay, 1978; Baars & Mattson, 1981; Dell, 1985; Mattson & Baars, 1985; Mattson & Baars, Chapter 11, this volume). The lexical preference found by Baars *et al.* (1975) has now been verified for spontaneous spoonerisms as well, indicating that even slips *tend* to fit the regularities of language and usage as much as possible (Dell, 1986).

Thus slips are not *just* errors; on many levels of control, they are quite regular, shaped by precisely the same criteria that govern normal speech and action. They appear to provide as much evidence for the persistence of control factors as they do for failures of control. Slips are "not a sign of incompetence but of *misplaced* competence" (Reason, 1984a, p. 515).

2. Slips decompose speech and action into underlying units and accommodation mechanisms.

One goal of science is to "carve nature at the joints"—to decompose the flow of events into natural underlying units. This strategy has worked very

[2]Unfortunately, Fromkin (1980) misinterpreted these results as claiming that "good" slips *occur more often in absolute numbers* than "bad" ones, forgetting that spontaneous spoonerisms are *a priori* more likely to be bad than good. Of course, that claim is not intended: "Good" slips are predicted to occur more often compared to the *a priori* probability of good slips, whereas the opposite relation is predicted for "bad" slips. See Chapter 11.

well in cognitive science over the past few decades, and it is quite productive in the study of slips. Spontaneous slips of the tongue almost always reflect known linguistic units—phonological, morphemic, and syntactic (Fromkin, 1968, 1973; MacKay, 1981). The same holds true for experimentally evoked slips (Stemberger, Chapter 8, this volume).

Spoonerisms, for example, decompose words into phonemes or phoneme clusters:

1. fried soup—side froop
2. feel good—gheel food
3. key band—be canned

These spoonerisms can be obtained in the laboratory either by priming with words that sound like the error, or simply by the so-called ordinal-conflict effect (OCE), which involves conflicts between the order of two words. Specifically, presenting a series of word pairs and then demanding a quick reversal of the order of the last word pair will cause spoonerisms. Likewise, creating uncertainty about the order of two multisyllabic words with similar stress patterns will result in *syllable exchanges.* Thus:

4. horrible miracle—mirable horricle
5. interfacing homophone—homofering interphone
6. dignified monastery—monafied dignistary

Word exchanges between two phrases are easily elicited by order competition between them:

7. She (*touched* her nose) and (*picked* a flower)—She (*picked* her nose) and (*touched* a flower).
8. He (*talked to* the woman) and (*looked at* the baby)—He (*talked to* the baby) and (*looked at* the woman).
9. He (*found* his trousers) and (*dropped* his watch)—He (*dropped* his trousers) and (*found* his watch).

These errors illustrate the claim that slips decompose actions and speech into underlying units and accommodation mechanisms. First, they always move and replace natural units: phonemes, syllables, words, gestures, and so on. These natural units are by no means simple or "merely physical" events. They are physically quite complex and are executed differently in different contexts (Liberman, Cooper, Shankweiler, & Studdert-Kennedy, 1967). The spoonerism "feel good"—"gheel food," for example, involves quite different formant transitions between /g/ and the following vowel when the initial /g/ moves from *good* to *gheel*. In *good,* the formant transition /g/ loops downward, while in *gheel,* it loops upward. Further, the two formant transitions start at different points on the frequency spectrum. Acoustically, therefore, the two /g/'s are quite different and indeed nonoverlapping physical events. Nevertheless, they are *perceived* to be quite normal /g/'s.

Similarly, in spoonerisms, syllable-initial consonants always exchange with other initial consonants, final consonants with other final consonants, and medial vowels with other medial vowels. The moving phonemes always follow the regularities of phonemic sequencing. For all of these reasons, our first major point is that, in most slips, *abstract units move from place to place in a fashion that maintains their perceived identity, even if changes must be made at other levels of control* for this to occur.

Note that these abstract units may be viewed as *automatisms:* the unconscious, overpracticed components of voluntary action. Indeed, we will make the case below that the slips may be viewed as "activated automatisms" that have been liberated from their normal goal structures.

The second part of this claim involves the *integration* of the moving units into their new surroundings. Whenever possible, the migrating units will move to similar contexts; when this is not possible, they will take along or create anew (more rarely) the appropriate contextual surround. That is to say, the moving units are very sensitive to the manner of their integration into their new contexts: in the vocabulary of linguistics, the movement of units is highly constrained by *accommodation mechanisms* (Berg, 1987; Garrett, 1980). The nasalization in "key b*and*"—"be c*anned*" is a case in point. The italicized phonemes are nasalized, and in the slip, the nasal formant spreads to the initial consonant /k/ by coarticulation, even though the initial consonant is integrated into its new articulatory context, and becomes nasalized when that is required, or "denasalized," when that is appropriate.

Likewise, it appears that moving syllables tend to migrate only between similar phonetic, syllabic, and stress contexts. Migrating words invariably move into the correct syntactic positions, taking along the proper prepositions if necessary. We rarely observe syntactic errors such as:

10. "He *talked at* the baby and *looked to* the woman."

Instead, the correct prepositions tend to migrate along with the moving words, to produce:

11. "He *talked to* the baby and *looked at* the woman" (Baars, 1977; Baars & MacKay, 1978).

Thus, accommodation mechanisms work to integrate migrating units into their new surroundings; and it seems likely that they also act to keep the "liberated" units away from inappropriate new positions.

In this connection, an interesting point can be made about Error 1 above: "*f*ried soup"—"side *f*roop." Notice that the cluster /fr/ tends to move as a unit. English phonotactics do not allow /sr/ in a word-initial position, as in *sride foop,* and this error is *never* observed in the laboratory when slips are elicited involuntarily. However, when, in a pilot study, we simply asked subjects to *voluntarily create spoonerisms,* they did give responses like "sride foop." This is consistent with the idea that our voluntary actions are, in a real sense, "out of touch" with the subtle and complex rules of English phonetics. Voluntarily, we sometimes create non-English errors. Involuntarily, we almost always stick to the subtle, complex, and unconscious regularities of natural language.

These observations all support the general claim made above that slips always decompose a complex action into its *natural units,* and that these units are integrated into a smooth, normal-seeming action by means of *accommodation mechanisms.*

3. *Such units and accommodation mechanisms may be viewed as* specialized automatisms, *which are relatively context-free when they are not guided by an active goal structure.*

Notice how *complex, rule-governed,* and *unconsciously produced* the units and accommodation mechanisms discussed above are. These are characteristic properties of automatisms (LaBerge, 1980). Automatisms are highly overpracticed skills that have become unconscious in their detailed functioning. As pointed out above, phonemes are not simple acoustic or articulatory elements: they are quite abstract, complex, and regular. But they are unconscious in detail: What normal person knows, after all, how to produce an /r/ or /g/ or any other class of speech sounds? Accommodation mechanisms are similarly unconscious, and not under voluntary control.

The role played by habit and automaticity is so compelling that Reason (1984a) has proposed that most action slips are due to the migration of more habitual and automatic units into the place of less automatic units. He therefore has suggested a law of error, as follows:

> Whenever our thoughts, words, or deeds depart from their planned course, they will tend to do so in the direction of producing something that is more familiar, more expected and more in keeping with our existing knowledge structures and immediate surroundings, than that which was actually intended. (p. 184)

Reason's law of error appears to be a good rule of thumb in analyzing spontaneous action slips. From the viewpoint of experimentally elicited slips, a somewhat different perspective emerges because plan competition is the primary means for eliciting specific errors. From this point of view, the law of error helps to explain the final *form* of slips, but not their primary *cause.* Indeed, much of the evidence for other causal factors derives from Reason's other research. For example, he has shown (1983, 1984b) that *overloading* of the limited-capacity system is an important factor in many slips. We also know that "priming" or *recency* will increase the probability of slips (see Chapter 6, this volume; Harley, 1984). The vast research literature on memory retrieval suggests that recency *and* frequency (habitualness) are both likely influences; both may serve to activate abstract action units (Anderson, 1983; Norman, 1981). Later in this chapter, we will suggest that the combined effects of *plan competition, activation,* and *overloading of the limited capacity system* provide the necessary and sufficient conditions for slips to occur. Of these factors, *plan competition for access to the conscious/limited-capacity system* may be the one that can easily trigger the other factors at the same time. We will propose, therefore, that plan competition is causally primary in most cases.

Point 3 also claims that automatic units and accommodation mechanisms are "relatively context-free when they are not guided by an active goal structure." What evidence is there for this proposal? One primary source is the scientific literature on automaticity. The standard sources, indeed, define automatic skills as "unavoidable, without capacity limitations, without awareness, without intention, with high efficiency, and with high resistance to modification" (LaBerge, 1980, p. 53). This is obviously similar to slips themselves, which always show some degree of "blindness" or "dissociation" from the hierarchy of constraints shown in Figure 1. Indeed, it is tempting to view slips as nothing but automatisms that have been "liberated" from their controlling goals.

The multileveled control system shown in Figure 1 can be viewed as a goal hierarchy, part of the control system for every English utterance. "Intentions," as they are defined here, clearly involve such multileveled goal structures (Baars, 1988, Chapters 6 and 7). Pragmatics, the top-level goal system, specifies the reasons for performing the speech act; these goals must be embodied in some semantic form, which in turn requires syntactic and lexical expressions, and these in turn must be carried out with appropriate phonetic, suprasegmental, and articulatory control. Thus, each lower level may be viewed as providing subgoals for carrying out the goals of the higher levels, and slips may be viewed as actions that are partly dissociated from this complex goal structure because they violate higher levels of control.

We will argue below that conscious involvement is needed at *underdetermined choice points* in such a goal hierarchy, and that overloading the conscious/limited-capacity system blocks the conscious access necessary to resolve such choice points in action planning, control, and error detection (see also Chapter 4, this volume, and Baars, 1988).

In summary, a voluntary act apparently involves many specialized units and accommodation mechanisms—automatisms—that work together in the service of a certain goal structure. A slip may be viewed as an accidental decomposition of such a voluntary act into its preexisting automatic components. In slightly different words, we can view slips as *automatisms that have been liberated from their normal, guiding goal structures.*

4. Some slip studies suggest that goals and subgoals are also autonomous *and* underspecified *at certain times.*

If the components of speech and action are often automatic, what about the goals that serve to organize those components? There is evidence that goals, too, can behave like modular, automatic units. Consider the following spontaneous slips cited by Reason (1984a, p. 576), in which a consciously accessible part of the intention is apparently lost:

1. "I went upstairs to the bedroom and stopped—not remembering what I had gone there for."
2. "I went into my room intending to fetch a book. I took off my rings, looked in the mirror and came out again—without my book."
3. "I went to the bathroom to clean my teeth. When I got there I picked up a towel and walked out again, without brushing my teeth."

A speech analogue of these action errors might be the case of forgetting what one was going to say (Baars, 1988; Luborsky, 1988). Reason (1984a, p. 518), called this class of slips "lost intentions" and separated them from "detached intentions," such as:

4. "I intended to place my hairbrush in its usual place by the bookcase. I put my boyfriend's lighter there instead."
5. "I had an appointment at the dentist's, but went to the doctor's instead."

These errors involve substitution of goals. They suggest that goals may themselves be quasi-autonomous, at least at some point in the production process, just like the units and accommodation mechanisms discussed above. Goals and subgoals may be able to combine and recombine rather freely, before they meld into the specific hierarchy that is needed to control a single, coherent action (Figure 1). This is indeed the case that is made on functional grounds by Birnbaum and Collins (this volume, Chapter 5; see also Greene, 1972). Norman (1981) and Reason (Chapter 3, this volume) have also argued that goals may be only partly specified much of the time, and the ideomotor theory has similar implications for conscious goals (Chapter 4, this volume).

These examples raise an interesting conundrum about our operational definition of slips: If we claim that all slips violate their intentions, what is being violated if the intention itself is "lost" or "detached"? In fact, this is not a difficult problem if we view the detached or lost intention in the context of its own *superordinate* goal hierarchy. Thus, Slip 5 above is a lost intention at the level of "going to the dentist." But it surely exists in its own higher goal context of "I must do something about this toothache," or even "I want to be healthy and have an attractive smile." Those higher level intentions are indeed violated even when the specific local goal is lost. This point suggests that *local* intentions operate generally in the service of some enduring life goals, such as survival, maintaining one's health, learning, career development, maintenance of social alliances, and even a lifelong commitment to a certain amount of relaxation and entertainment.

In any case, the slips cited above support the notion that goals themselves may be *modular,* that is, able to undergo insertion, deletion, and substitution in a larger goal structure. This evidence, like that cited earlier, has a strongly "distributive" flavor. It seems to fit contemporary notions of localized, intelligent, often parallel processors, which may combine for some time into larger, more global structures. The fine details of processing may remain local and widely distributed throughout the system.

5. A great variety of specific slips can be elicited by creating competition between mutually incompatible output plans, while limiting the time available to resolve the competition. The resulting slip is often a "regularized combination" of the two competing plans. The same ingredients of plan competition and time pressure *seem to play a role in many spontaneous slips as well.*

Over the past 15 years, we have learned to elicit a great many very specific slips in the laboratory, always by creating competition between competing plans given to the subjects, and then demanding a quick response. The types of slips so elicited include the humble tongue twister, and also two different techniques for eliciting spoonerisms, several methods for inducing word movements in a sentence, word and action blends, putative "transformational" sentence errors, finger exchanges in typing errors, hand and arm movement slips, and place-setting errors on a dining table. Chapter 6 presents these methods in detail. (See also MacKay, 1981, 1987.)

It is important to point out that many of these slips do not resemble *obvious* fusions between the two competing plans. Rather, they are a "regularized combination" of the two plans; they combine components from the two plans in an automatic but highly rule-governed way. Consider just a few examples of slips that do not resemble the two competing plans that created them. The slips cited below were chosen from a list of "transformational errors" collected by Fay (1980), who argued that these sentence errors may reflect a failure or misapplications of a grammatical transformation, along Chomskian lines. However, Chen and Baars (Chapter 9, this volume), show that all of the presumed transformational errors can be elicited in the laboratory, by the simple creation of competition between two plausible paraphrases of the intended sentence. Thus:

1. The error *"What could have I done with the check?"* was obtained by creating competition between two near-paraphrases: "What could I have done with the check?" and "What have I done with the check?"

2. *"Where do you suppose are they?"* was obtained by creating competition between "Where do you suppose they are?" and "Where are they, do you suppose?"

3. *"They didn't actually withdrew the needle"* was obtained by creating competition between "They almost withdrew the needle" and "They didn't actually withdraw the needle."

In retrospect it may seem obvious that many of these errors reflect competing sentence plans—but this was not at all obvious to Fay and others, who explained them by faulty syntactic transformations. There are numerous other examples of slips whose origin is not obvious on the surface, but that emerge quite naturally from laboratory-induced competition between normal plans (Chapters 6–9, this volume). As we pointed out above, we have found that creating order competition between higher level constituents can induce movements of lower level elements. Competing words can induce phoneme exchanges (spoonerisms), competing phrases word exchanges, and competing actions automatic component exchanges. Competition at one level of control may therefore *propagate downward through the structural hierarchy,* resulting in overt slips at a lower level. Indeed, there are few spontaneous slips that cannot be explained as some sort of plausible plan combination (Baars, 1980a,b).

How likely is it that the two critical ingredients of *plan competition* and *time pressure* occur naturally? Plan competition may occur quite often in spontaneous speech. Consider, for example, the fact that there are almost

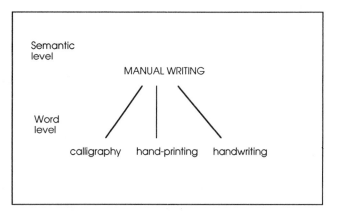

F<small>IGURE</small> 2. The one-to-many relationship between semantic codes and nearly synonymous words and paraphrases.

always several ways to express a single thought. In very careful writing or speaking, we may find ourselves consciously selecting among alternative words and idioms with various shades of meaning. But the same process may occur quickly and more automatically in normal, spontaneous speech. We can model this process by showing an abstract meaning representation such as a logogen (Morton, 1970), which maps into three slightly different words (see Figure 2). In order to clothe the meaning representation with words, we must choose one of the alternatives in the figure. Plan competition may occur if two of the synonyms seem equally well suited.

Another scenario for plan competition involves the execution of a basic sentence frame, with a late-coming adjective rushing to be inserted in its proper place, even as the syntactic train is leaving the station. Thus, one may be all prepared to say, "Oops! I really made a goof!" and decide at the last moment to add an adjective for emphasis, in order to say, "I really made a *bad* goof." If the insertion is made too late, "goof" and "bad goof" may compete with each other, creating exactly the kind of order competition described above, which has been shown to produce spoonerisms in the laboratory (Baars & Motley, 1976). The sentence might come out therefore as "Oops! I really made a gad boof!"

Evidently, one plausible source of competition is the "one-to-many mapping" between a higher level and lower levels in the linguistic structural hierarchy (Figure 1). This kind of relationship is exactly parallel to the problem of ambiguity in perception and comprehension, which creates one-to-many mappings between levels of input representation. There are, of course, numerous sources of ambiguity in input: one-to-many mappings between sounds and phonemes, between phoneme strings and lexical items, between words and their meanings, and between syntactic groupings and semantics (e.g., Baars, 1988, pp. 147). Ambiguities, in general, create *choice points* in the flow of *input,* just as plan competition creates choice points between alternative *output* paths. Any comprehensive theory of action must represent such choice points and must suggest mechanisms for resolving them.

What about the second ingredient of induced slips, the factor of time pressure? Does it exist in spontaneous speech? Indeed, all speech and action are rhythmic. English is pronounced with *rough*ly *al*ternating *stress*ed *syll*-ables, as the reader can verify simply by pronouncing this sentence with exaggerated emphasis. The pattern of alternating high and low stress clearly creates temporal expectations, which may serve to pace and synchronize the many components of speech production. Rhythmic expectations may well create time pressure for various components of speech production to be ready to go "on time," as in the "gad boof" example discussed above. When the components of an action begin to go out of synchrony, we can always speak slower or pause, of course. But we seem to prefer regularly paced speech and action. Therefore, some time pressure seems inherent in normal speech production.

At the end of this chapter, we propose that plan competition and time pressure may cause the majority of spontaneous slips. The central importance of competition has been suggested by Butterworth (1980; 1982) and others as well. However, we will also suggest a *third* necessary ingredient, namely *a momentary overloading of the limited-capacity system* (Broadbent, 1958). This third factor is required to explain why the error is made overtly, rather than being avoided or caught before execution. Although this third factor may seem to complicate matters somewhat, there is good evidence that it can result from the same process of plan competition that leads to the error in the first place (see Chapter 4). Thus, plan competition may cause both the *form* of the slip, *and,* by blocking the limited-capacity system, *the slip's being allowed to escape control.*

6. Slips also help reveal mechanisms of self-monitoring, editing, and repair in speech and action.

Consider a rather obvious but very significant observation: When we *consciously* hear ourselves say a sentence containing an error at *any* level of linguistic control, we can quickly detect and correct it—even though we are never conscious of the criteria by which it is judged to be an error, or of the mechanisms by which it is corrected. Although this fact is well known, its implications are generally ignored. The unconscious regularities of phonology, morphology, and syntax that may be violated by an error are exceedingly complex, and the task of detecting and correcting errors by these rules is computationally impressive. Yet we bring these unconscious rule systems and mechanisms into play merely by becoming conscious of the flawed output.

Having many very complex, unconscious systems interact with a conscious "target" may require a specially tailored system architecture (see Chapter 4). Rather surprisingly, this architecture is also found in real-world engineering systems, such as the control of a NASA rocket launch. In both cases, multiple simultaneous constraints must be satisfied *before* the point of no return in the launch. In both cases, there may be a large penalty for making an error in even a single critical constraint. NASA deals with this problem by having multiple "observers"—both humans and computers—simultaneously monitoring a large set of rocket engine parameters. More than 100 engineers sit at their terminals at launch time, each able to stop the countdown if necessary. Thus, each observer has veto power over the launch if the monitored parameter exceeds certain limits. This is a "parallel-interactive" monitoring system, and in Chapter 4, considerable evidence is cited that sentence production involves a similar parallel-interactive system, for much the same reasons (Baars, 1988; Marslen-Wilson & Welsh, 1978).

Notice that we are reversing the commonsense point of view here. Normally, we may speak of "conscious checking" of some plan, meaning a conscious review of a conscious plan. However, we argue in Chapter 4 that the more frequent case by far involves *un*conscious checking of conscious plans. This is plausible, first of all because the unconscious rule systems are much more detailed and efficient than any consciously expressible version of those rules, and second, because there is much compelling evidence for a system architecture in which multiple unconscious system can monitor, halt, and repair conscious plans (Chapter 4; Baars, 1983, 1988).

7. *Slips seem to reflect an evolutionary trade-off between the risks of* unintended error *and the benefits of increased* speed *and* flexibility.

Errors can exact painful penalties. A rabbit pursued by a fox may die by zigging rather than zagging at a critical moment, and the fox may risk starvation by underestimating the length of a leap. In some cultures, a tactless slip of the tongue may lead to social disgrace, and slips in driving a car, flying a plane, hunting, or warfare may be fatal (Norman, 1976; Reason, 1984ab). Thus, from an evolutionary point of view, errors represent a threat to survival and reproductive success. Nevertheless, they occur remarkably often. Why, then, over eons of evolution, did an error-free control system not develop?

One possibility is that the risk of errors trades off against some other, desirable property of the action control system. Evolutionary biology shows many hundreds of examples of such trade-offs between the costs and benefits of certain traits (Gould, 1982). In the research literature on slips, two proposals have been made for a trade-off in which the benefits of an error-prone action-control system may outweigh its obvious drawbacks. A third trade-off will be suggested below, based on well-established evidence.

The Speed–Accuracy Trade-Off

The first proposal appeals to the very general phenomenon of *speed–accuracy* trade-offs in human performance (MacKay, 1987). There is robust and widespread evidence that increasing the speed of an action will decrease its accuracy, whereas demanding greater accuracy will tend to decrease its speed.

Models of speech production by Dell (1986) and MacKay (1982) demonstrate such a speed–accuracy trade-off. These models propose networks of phonemes and words, in which formulating a correct response takes time; further, more careful or detailed formulation takes more time. Forcing a rapid response tends to cut short the time needed to produce an error-free action. Presumably, then, an animal could trade off errors against time if it needed to leap very quickly to evade a predator, risking an error to achieve greater speed. Such a risk may be justified given the near-certain alternative of being caught and killed. But in a less pressing situation, the animal could take more time to act, thus reducing the probability of error.

The Trade-Off between Flexibility and Accuracy

A second class of proposals claims that slips are the price that is paid for the great *flexibility* of the human control system, that is, its ability to select among numerous degrees of freedom. We know, of course, that flexibility in action and thought is closely connected with the functioning of the limited-capacity system associated with consciousness (Baars, 1988). This might be called a *flexibility–accuracy* trade-off. It reflects the fact that highly over-learned skills are both more accurate and less flexible, and that novel or voluntarily controlled actions may sacrifice efficiency and error-free accuracy in favor of greater flexibility. Reason (1979) stated this point well by referring to slips as "the price of automaticization."

Several models have been proposed to explain the flexibility of human action. Norman and Shallice (1980) suggested that action schemata may compete for the limited capacity system. Similarly, Reason (1983) suggests that schemata in a general domain called the *board* may compete for the conscious/limited-capacity "blob." My own publications work out in considerable detail the implications of a global workspace, containing conscious material, in a distributed system of unconscious automatisms (Baars, 1983, 1987, 1988, and Chapter 4, this volume). In effect, all three approaches overlap and may be considered variations on a theme. However, the global workspace theory gives a specific reason *why* it is important for alternative plans and goals to compete for the limited-capacity system: The reason is that consciousness is intimately associated with a "broadcasting" capability. Any goal system that is able to reach consciousness can broadcast a message able to recruit and control numerous subgoals and effectors that can carry out its goal. This may be the only functional explanation currently available for competition between goal systems.

The Trade-Off between Speed and Flexibility

Logically, the two trade-offs explored above imply a third: a trade-off between *speed* and *flexibility*. This trade-off is not usually discussed under such a heading, but it is actually well known and easy to observe: it is the fact that choice reaction time is slower than simple reaction time. The more choices we have, the slower our response will be, as psychologists have known since the 19th century. This classical finding completes the empirical evidence supporting the notion of a general three-way trade-off, among *speed, accuracy, and flexibility* in human action. These trade-offs may help to explain the curiously high rate of slips in human performance.

Notice, by the way, how the theme of the conscious/limited capacity mechanism has begun to appear at several points in our discussion. We will try to clarify this theme as we turn to the implications of slips for the broad architecture of cognition.

CONSCIOUSNESS AND THE ARCHITECTURE OF VOLUNTARY CONTROL

We began this chapter by noting that local theories of speech and action are unable, so far, to explain the difference between behaviorally identical slips and voluntary actions. This inability implies that a new approach is needed, to place specific models of speech and action in the larger context of a theory of voluntary control. This section explores one such approach. In particular, we will develop arguments that large, unconscious goal systems must gain access to the conscious/limited-capacity system in order to control the voluntary musculature. Only by placing a goal image in consciousness can these goal systems recruit the subgoals and effectors that enable their goals to be carried out (for details, see Chapter 4, this volume, and Baars, 1987, 1988). If more than one goal system attempts to gain limited-capacity access, competition results, which can, under the proper circumstances, lead to specific overt slips. Thus, the present approach emphasizes not merely the idea of plan competition in general, but specifically the role of *plan competition for access to the conscious / limited-capacity system* (see Butterworth, 1982).

We start with a fairly radical claim, one that is at odds with the standard post-Chomsky approach to speech errors:

1. In the most general case, a slip represents a loss *of voluntary control rather than a* rule violation.

At the beginning of this chapter, we posed the following problem: Imagine repeating a slip of the tongue you have just made. The slip itself is experienced as involuntary; its repetition is voluntary. And yet the two isolated actions are hard for any outside observer to tell apart . Some famous slips by the Reverend A. W. Spooner illustrate the point:

1. Instead of "our dear old Queen," "our queer old Dean."
2. Instead of the hymn, "Conquering Kings Their Titles Take," "Kinquering Congs Their Titles Take."
3. Upon dismissing a student, he intended to say, "You have wasted two terms, and you will leave by the down train," but he actually said, "You have tasted two worms, and you will leave by the town drain."

Let us suppose the Reverend Spooner actually made these slips (there is some doubt—see Fromkin, 1980). Now imagine that Spooner *repeated* each slip immediately after making it, as exactly as possible, so that it was said again by the same speaker, in the same tone of voice, at the same rate of speaking, and so on. What is the difference between the slip and its voluntary repetition? Surely, there is no basic physical difference nor any real linguistic difference. The main difference is psychological. In the first case, the utterance is involuntary and unwanted; in the second, it is voluntary (Baars, 1987, 1988).

But what a difference this invisible difference makes! In the first case, the speaker fails to execute his intention. If he becomes conscious of his error, he will experience surprise at his own utterance. In that case, we should be able to observe the whole panoply of physiological reactions that make up the orienting response. He may be embarrassed and apologetic. Having failed to carry out his intention, he may try again. If, like Spooner, he is also head of one of the Cambridge colleges, he may become a figure of fun in student folklore. If he makes involuntary errors so often that he can no longer function effectively, he may lose his position, be examined for neurological problems, and so on.

None of these consequences flow from doing physically identical, voluntary imitations of these slips. If Spooner were voluntarily making the slip to amuse his audience, or if someone quotes a slip in a discussion of voluntary control, none of these consequences follow, nor is the speaker going to be surprised by the "slip." Thus, two identical actions may be psychologically quite distinct, but not because of a difference in complexity, as the early behaviorists thought. Voluntary actions are not just agglomerations of simple reflexes. Involuntary components put together do not result in a voluntary act. Something else is involved in volitional control.

These considerations have some important consequences. In the approach we are developing here, it is *not* the rule violation itself that defines a slip. An erroneous utterance may be intentional and thus would *not* constitute a slip psychologically. Conversely, a tactless slip of the tongue that reveals a secret or unmentionable fact is perfectly rule-governed linguistically but is nonetheless psychologically involuntary.

Of course, most slips in speech do violate general regularities of the lexicon, of phonology, morphology, syntax, or semantics. The study of slips can certainly reveal properties of these systems. But local theories of speech and action do not account for the fundamental distinction between slips and their voluntary imitations: They have no mechanism for showing how an error could be intentional, or how a generically correct phrase could, in principle, be unintentional. A complete account of slip phenomena must be able to represent this difference.

This observation sets the stage for all of the following points (Table 2).

2. *Slips seem to reflect the* two operating modes found in all human mental processes: *One mode, associated with consciousness, is flexible and has quite limited capacity, and the second operating mode makes use of unconscious automatisms that are inflexible but very efficient, and have high parallel-processing capacity (Table 3).*

Cognitive psychology has dealt since its inception with the limited capacity of conscious and voluntary mechanisms (e.g., Broadbent, 1958; Neisser,

1967; Wundt, 1912, 1973). More recently we have rediscovered the important role of unconscious, largely automatic, but very efficient information-processing systems (LaBerge, 1980). Modern conceptions of syntax, of visual processing, of motor control, and the like postulate many such automatic systems, which are highly specialized and interfere very little with conscious or voluntary tasks (e.g., Baars, 1983, 1988; Rumelhart, McClelland, & the PDP Group, 1986). These are the two outer poles of human mental functioning: On the one hand, conscious processes are slow and very flexible and have a great range of possible contents; on the other, unconscious automatisms are fast, efficient in their specialized tasks, and rather inflexible.

It is not surprising that slips seem to involve *both* sides of this polarity. Reason (1979, 1992, and Chapter 3, this volume) reports that many action slips can be viewed in terms of highly habitual action schemata that intrude and substitute for less overlearned units. On the other hand, slips are also associated with interference with the limited-capacity system, due to absentmindedness or lapses of attention (Reason & Mycielska, 1982). Table 3 shows the

TABLE 3

The Many Involvements of the Conscious/Limited-Capacity System in Slips

1. Slips can be operationally defined as actions that are quickly recognized to be errors as soon as we *become aware of* the output. Hence, conscious review of the output is already part of our operational definition (Tables 1 and 2). However, the criteria by which the errors *are* identified as errors are, of course, largely unconscious.
2. Mere consciousness of actual or anticipated output seems to facilitate the error detection, stopping, and repair mechanisms, all of which are *un*conscious in their details (Chapters 4 and 11).
3. A three-way trade-off seems to exist among the probability of errors, speed of execution, and flexibility (Point 7 in Table 1). But flexibility—the ability to choose between alternative output plans—is strongly associated conscious access to plans, as well as conscious feedback from the action. Conversely, the more automatic and *un*conscious the action, the less flexible it will be in the face of new conditions (Point 3 in Table 1).
4. Slips often occur in states of absentmindedness, in which there is a lapse of conscious access to normally conscious aspects of action (Reason & Mycielska, 1982, Figure 1.3).
5. There is a strong commonsense relationship between consciousness and voluntary control. When someone makes many mistakes, we are likely to remind them to *pay more attention*—to be more consciously involved in the details of planning and controlling the action (Reason & Mycielska, 1982).
6. Some slips seem to reflect plain forgetting of consciously available goals (Reason, 1984; Point 4 in Table 1).
7. Some slips may be induced by phonemic primes, that is, by presenting repeated *conscious* stimuli resembling the slip (Chapter 6). The rate of such errors can be increased by adding conscious semantic primes (see Chapter 11). Conscious perceptual intrusions have also been observed to trigger some spontaneous slips (Harley, 1984).
8. In Chapter 4, a modern ideomotor theory is developed, suggesting that conscious goal images are required to recruit and trigger nonroutine actions, which are made up of mostly *un*conscious automatisms and constrained by a mostly *un*conscious goal hierarchy.

many ways in which *the limited-capacity system and conscious experience* are involved in slips, and how they interact with *unconscious / parallel automatisms.*

Figure 3 provides a striking illustration of the effect of conscious attention directed to the output. Baars (1977) elicited a number of word-exchange slips resulting in *semantic anomalies* (marked with an asterisk), such as:

1. The hunter [*looked for* his partner] and [*cleaned* his prey]. Error: The hunter [*cleaned* his partner (*)] and [*looked for* his prey].
2. She [*touched* her nose] and [*smelled* a flower]. Error: She [*smelled* her nose (*)] and [*touched* a flower].

Compare the above to very similar slips that are *semantically acceptable:*

1a. The hunter [*looked for* his partner] and [*found* his prey]. "Error": The hunter [*found* his partner] and [*looked for* his prey].
2a. She [*touched* her nose] and [*cut* a flower]. "Error": She [*cut* her nose] and [*touched* a flower].

As Figure 3 shows, the order of the two phrases was vitally important to the error rate: if the semantic anomaly occurred in the first phrase of the slip, the error was made much less often than when it occurred in the second

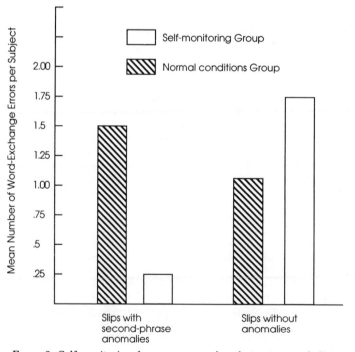

FIGURE 3. Self-monitoring decreases anomalous but not normal slips.

phrase. By itself, this result suggests the operation of a limited-capacity system, which is normally set to scan only a single phrase at a time—probably sufficient to avoid errors in most sentences (Bever & Abrams, 1969).

The fact that second-phrase anomalies occurred almost as often as semantically acceptable phrases created the opportunity for a new experiment: What would happen to these second-phrase anomalies if the subjects were made to pay more attention to their speech? To test this, we inserted a number of self-report trials in the task, in which experimental subjects were cued after a response to report whether it was correct or not. By calling attention to possible errors, such self-report trials presumably encouraged the subjects to monitor their speech more closely. Now a striking change appeared in the error rate: Semantic anomalies, even in the second phrase of the error, dropped to zero, while semantically acceptable slips remained at the same level (Figure 3). This result strongly suggests that people can allocate increased attention to their own speech, thus inhibiting the production of obvious semantic errors. It gives another reason to suspect the intimate involvement of the conscious/limited-capacity system in error detection and control.

Table 3 also reminds us of the *dissociation* of intention and performance that is revealed by slips, often demonstrably accompanied by absentmindedness—a state of decreased conscious involvement in the intended action (Reason & Mycielska, 1982). One intriguing possibility is that the fleeting dissociation of intention and performance is actually *caused by* momentary blocking of the conscious/limited-capacity system. This is explored in the following point.

3. Where conscious access is needed. *Conscious access may be needed at nonroutine and underdetermined choice points in planning, control, and error detection, that is, those points where novel resources must be mobilized to help make the correct choice.*

Traveling home along familiar streets, we may remind ourselves to buy cat food at the local grocery story. To get there, we may have to turn from our usual route on the daily trip. But being preoccupied with other thoughts, we pass the critical choice point and arrive home to face the wrath of a hungry cat. This type of error is not just commonplace; it may also be paradigmatic of many other errors in which a *nonroutine choice point* in a habitual series of actions is missed because the conscious/limited-capacity system is overloaded at the critical moment.

We have previously considered two specific examples of such underdetermined choice points in speech production (Table 1). One is the one-to-many mapping between a semantic representation and the many paraphrases that could express it. Such paraphrases are readily available to people, as shown by the fact that when asked to repeat a recently heard sentence, people typically produce a *paraphrase* of that sentence. Second, we have cited the case of a sentence plan that is about to be executed, even while an additional word is trying to catch the "syntactic train" as it is leaving the station. Third, especially at the pragmatic, semantic, and lexical levels of control, one may encounter competing goals and plans as part of the normal act of speech planning and production. Many of these choice points become conscious when we proceed slowly, as in writing an essay, or in carefully rehearsing a speech to deliver on an important occasion. We have previously shown how such choice points can lead to actual slips, and we have pointed out that all of the dozen or so laboratory methods available today for eliciting slips make use of such competing-plans techniques (Chapter 6).

Further evidence of the need for conscious involvement in underdetermined choices comes from the study of hesitation pauses in speech, which are known to occur at points of high uncertainty (Goldman-Eisler, 1972). Increased conscious involvement may lead to hesitation pauses because previously fast and parallel automatisms must now be channeled through the limited-capacity bottleneck. There is also evidence for limited-capacity-loading events at junctures in the flow of speech, such as clause and sentence boundaries (Abrams & Bever, 1969; Levelt, 1983). These junctures are likely to be points of high uncertainty, of course.

Chapter 4 suggests that the conscious/limited-capacity system is closely associated with a global workspace, a "blackboard" that can broadcast conscious goal images able to mobilize novel knowledge sources. This capability is required to resolve new and uncertain choices in the production process. In general, underdetermined choice points in the flow of control need to be made conscious (see Baars, 1988). If this claim is true, it implies that *interfering* with conscious access at the critical choice points can produce errors.

Errors of Omission and Commission

Missing a choice point in planning or executing action would seem to produce deletions, that is, errors of omission rather than of commission. For example, Reason (1984a) cited a spontaneous slip in which the subject went to her bedroom to put on some earrings, became absentminded, and left without her earrings. This seems to be a case of pure deletion of a unit controlled by a choice point in the flow of action, as shown also by "telescopic errors" in speech (Fromkin, 1973). Most slips, of course, are errors of *commission;* that is, they involve insertions, fusions, or exchanges as well as deletions. It would seem that, by itself, the mechanism of overloading the conscious/limited-capacity system at nonroutine choice points can account for deletions, but such overloading does not seem to completely explain errors of commission. Overloading of the conscious/limited-capacity system may be a necessary but not a sufficient condition for those slips.

Coincidence of Plan Competition and Overloading of Limited Capacity that Seems to Create Slips

It seems likely that overloading of limited capacity occurs not just in the case of absentminded errors, but momentarily in all errors; after all, if the error-producing plan were conscious long enough, the slips would not be made. That is, from our previous considerations, it seems that bringing consciousness to bear on the error is guaranteed to create recognition of the slip *as* an error and will also trigger unconscious stopping and repair mechanisms (Table 3). If that is true, how could such errors occur at all? If they are known to be errors, why is this knowledge not brought to bear on the formulation of the action plan?[3]

We can bring these puzzles down to three basic questions: (1) What causes errors? (2) What shapes their form? And finally, (3) what causes the evident blocking of conscious access to the error, allowing it to be made overtly? Notice that lack of conscious access *by itself* does not explain the *form* of the slip. Likewise, if there are plans that have already been *activated* (by frequency, recency, or plan competition), the activated automatisms may blend and "fire off." This may help to explain the *form* of the slip, but not the failure to detect and stop it before execution.

These considerations lead to the following generalization:

4. Two necessary conditions for slips. *Slips seem to be activated automatisms that are liberated from a goal structure. This liberation may happen when two factors coincide:* First, *some incorrect automatisms are activated, by priming, habit, or conflict between alternative goals or plans;* second, *there is some degree of interference with the conscious access needed to resolve critical choice points in planning, control, and error detection.*

As we have noted above, the dozen or so techniques for the experimental induction of specific speech errors consist entirely of different ways of creating competition between alternative speech plans. By itself, this induced competition yields errors like blends, spoonerisms, phoneme anticipations and perseverations, word-movement errors in sentences, and various action errors (see above and Chapters 6 and 7). Above, we have also developed the argument that normal voluntary actions consist largely of unconscious automatisms, which may become "liberated" from their voluntary goal structures because of plan competition.

But why should competing plans "just happen" to coincide in time with a limited-capacity overload that prevents the detection and editing of the slip? Surely, it is too much to expect these separate events to happen at the same moment merely by chance—unless, that is, the competing plans *both* create the overload *and also* provide the raw material for the error itself. If this is true, it implies that the process of competition is not just located among the competing unconscious automatisms; rather, *plan competition is itself primarily competition for access to the conscious / limited-capacity system.* Chapter 4

---

[3]Notice our implicit commonsense belief that, *once* knowledge of the correctness or incorrectness of a plan is consciously recognized, this knowledge can be brought to bear on the process of stopping and repairing the error. This is one of many arguments for a close relationship between conscious availability and voluntary control (Table 3). There is direct experimental evidence to support this commonsense view (e.g., Baars, 1988, pp. 266–267; Langer & Imber, 1979).

suggests why goal systems may need to gain access to consciousness: because access by a plan to the conscious/limited-capacity system creates the ability to recruit and control effector systems that can carry out the winning plan.

If this is true, competing plans, working to gain access to the limited-capacity system, have the side effect of *overloading* this system for a few hundred milliseconds, at precisely the right moment to interfere with conscious access to the competing choices. There is direct evidence that induced slips take approximately 200–300 milliseconds longer to execute than closely matched correct responses in the same subjects (Baars, 1977). This response delay may be caused by the limited-capacity-blocking effect of the competing plans. We know, of course, that different conscious (or limited-capacity-loading) events will interfere with each other (Baars, 1988; see Chapter 4), and this rather long delay in the case of slips may be due to this kind of interference.

Of course, plan competition may not be the only cause of errors. We have noted above that errors or omission (deletions) may occur simply when some underdetermined choice point in the production process is blocked to conscious/limited-capacity access. In addition, Harley (1984, p. 194) cites a very interesting set of *perceptual intrusion* slips. For example:

1. Slip: Why not a bee?
   Intended: Why not a plain white dress?
   Context: The speaker was talking to someone about dress making.
   The other person was turning the television off; just as she did so, a program named "Bee in My Bonnet" was verbally announced.
2. Slip: Is that box heavy or /slo/?
   Intended: Is that box heavy or light?
   Context: The speaker was helping to move a box marked with the words "SLO-Cooker."
3. Slip: What about tomatoes?
   Intended: What about bananas?
   Context: The speaker was in the supermarket standing beside and looking at the tomatoes.

These slips seem to be induced by accidental perceptual intrusions; *prima facie,* Harley's slips would seem to contradict the general competing-plans notion. Curiously enough, these apparent exceptions can be used to argue in favor of competing plans as the most general case: after all, *by definition,* perceptual slips involve competition for access to the conscious/limited-capacity system; hence, they can clearly compete with the intended utterance, and the result is a regularized combination of the two inputs.[4] Thus, perceptual

[4]Harley's perceptual intrusions resemble the priming phenomena in induced slips, in which priming has the effect of increasing the rate of related slips (see Chapters 6, 11, and 12, this volume). "Priming" usually implies conscious access, of course, and the competition between different plans is for access to the conscious/limited-capacity system. In the theoretical framework developed in Chapter 4, once the winning plan gains access to consciousness, it is able to broadcast a conscious goal, which serves in turn to recruit the subgoals and effectors that can carry out the winning plan (Baars, 1988, and Chapter 4, this volume).

slips seem to present the two essential features of competition and limited-capacity loading as well. Because humans are surely confronted with *internal* plan competition far more often than with *external* perceptual intrusions, the more general hypothesis of plan competition for the conscious/limited-capacity system is actually strengthened.

These considerations lead to our final hypothesis of the genesis of slips:

5. The Competing-Plans Hypothesis.[5] *A common source of internal interference is the presence of two goals,* each actively working to gain access to the conscious/limited-capacity system, in an attempt to control the forthcoming action. This process of competition may create both *of the necessary conditions for slips suggested above (Point 4).*

We have already described some evidence for competing-output plans above (Baars, 1980a,b and Chapters 4, 6, and 11, this volume; see also Butterworth, 1982). There is the fact that dozens of spontaneous slip types in speech and action can now be reproduced in the laboratory by means of competing-plans techniques. In addition, we know that spontaneous language generation often poses a choice between alternative versions of abstract plans. These are points in favor of a general Competing-Plans Hypothesis (CPH). Nevertheless, the fruitfulness of competing-plans techniques in the laboratory does not *prove* conclusively that spontaneous slips are evoked by competing plans. Because we cannot directly observe the conditions that trigger spontaneous slips, we must look to inferential evidence.

The strongest argument for CPH as a general explanation of spontaneous slips is the need, elaborated above, to have *both* the internal error *and* the limited-capacity overload *coincide in time.* This seems too much of a coincidence to happen by chance, *unless* some single factor causes both at the same time. That single factor may well be competition between goal systems attempting to gain limited-capacity access in order to recruit and control actions. Such competition is actually required in the theory of voluntary control described in Chapter 4 and elsewhere, so that there is a major *functional role* for the CPH. Competition for limited-capacity access may plausibly cause *both* a momentary overload *and* the error itself.[6]

---

[5]The current statement of the Competing-Plans Hypothesis supersedes my previous version (Baars, 1980a).

[6]The reader may well wonder how the Competing-Plans Hypothesis relates to other general hypotheses. In general, my claim would be that most other general accounts explain the form, and perhaps part of the process, of slip formation, but not the proximate cause. For example, Reason (Chapter 3, this volume) has proposed the Incomplete-Specification Hypothesis for spontaneous slips (see also Norman, 1981). In Reason's words, "When cognitive operations are underspecified, they tend to default to contextually appropriate, high-frequency responses" (this volume). This statement is very plausible but does not answer the question: How is it that the cognitive operations were underspecified? In principle, we might say that it is because there was an attempt to execute them before they were ready; and indeed, sheer speeding of speech does produce errors. However, I know of no evidence that slips *in general* are associated with hurried speech or action, although there is good natu-
(continued)

We can flesh out the Competing-Plans Hypothesis with points made earlier in this chapter. Specifically:

a. *Two competing plans, each contending for limited-capacity access, may produce a response consisting of an automatically regularized combination of the two plans.*

This is merely a generalization from the dozen or so "competing-plans" slip-induction techniques described above and in Chapter 6 (Table 1). We can use explicit plan competition to induce in the laboratory a great variety of slips, including blends, spoonerisms, syllable exchanges, word exchanges, slips in typing, in gestures, and in simple actions.

b. *Competition between two alternative plans may also* overload *the limited-capacity system momentarily, thereby interfering with the conscious access that is needed to resolve nonroutine choices caused by the competing plans.*

These arguments were made above (Table 2) and are elaborated in Chapter 4 and Baars (1988). We have already cited the finding that induced slips take longer to produce (by 200–300 msec), than very similar correct responses. This surprisingly long lag time for slips may be caused by the mutual interference of contending goal systems, each of which needs the conscious/limited-capacity system in order to be executed. Because the limited-capacity system is also needed to make the optimal choice between the competing plans themselves, all of these functions begin to interfere with the others. Like all competing attention-loading tasks, they are impaired in quality and speed.

c. *If plan competition lasts long enough, error detection via the limited-capacity system is also blocked, so that the error is allowed to be made overtly.*

It appears that the conscious/limited-capacity system is also needed by systems able to detect and correct errors. One argument in favor of this supposition is simply that errors are *by definition nonroutine* and hence require limited-capacity involvement to detect and repair (Chapters 4 and 11, in Figure 1 above; also see Table 3, Figure 3, and Baars, 1988).

Thus, the Competing-Plans Hypothesis emerges from all the points dis-

---

ralistic evidence that they are associated with absentmindedness or momentary distraction, that is, overloading of limited capacity (Reason & Mycielska, 1982). Thus, although high speed may account for some errors, and general absentmindedness for others, competition between plans aiming to gain access to consciousness seems to be the most general explanation of (1) the form of the error; (2) its proximate cause; (3) the failure to detect, stop, and repair the error before execution; and (4) an explicitly stated relationship to a general theory of voluntary control (see Chapter 4, this volume, and Baars, 1988, Chapter 7).

Dell (1985, 1986) has worked out the most explicit model of speech generation that also generates one class of slips in a principled way. This model, indeed, has a competition parameter, which allows the model to choose between two activated nodes and to execute the one with the highest activation. In addition, the model exhibits a kind of "incomplete specification" effect, when the flow of activation is cut off before it has been allowed to circulate to all relevant nodes and to come to equilibrium. In a sense, therefore, Dell might accept both incomplete specification and competition as contributory causes to slips. However, Dell's work currently does not attempt to model conscious/limited-capacity processes and, in that sense, does not represent the current CPH (Mattson, 1987).

cussed so far. It makes sense theoretically (Chapter 4) and has empirical backing from almost all of the current laboratory work on slips (Chapter 6). It is arguably responsible for the great majority of spontaneous slips and provides a clear and testable target for future research.

SUMMARY AND CONCLUSIONS

The reader may wish to reexamine Tables 1 and 2 in order to review the main points of this chapter. Here, we will simply summarize the flow of the arguments and their conclusions.

1. Slips are not so much "errors" as emerging, preexisting automatisms, which make up the greater part of any normal voluntary action. Slips violate their own governing intentions and thus suggest the existence of a momentary dissociation of the intention and the performance.

2. Slip studies suggest that many automatic components of speech and action have a degree of autonomy from unified, voluntary control, at least for some brief moments in the production process.

3. A functional trade-off appears to exist between the *risk of making a slip* and two other, desirable properties of action, namely, *speed* and *flexibility*. The Global Workspace architecture developed in Chapter 4 can work to optimize these trade-offs.

4. Competing plans that attempt to gain access to the limited-capacity system, in order to control action, may have three effects: First, competition may momentarily *block* the necessary conscious access to nonroutine choice points in the intended plan, thus liberating automatisms from the plan. Second, competing plans may also shape the *form* of the error, as shown by the large set of laboratory techniques discussed in Chapter 6. Third and finally, plan competition may block the limited-capacity system long enough to interfere with error detection, thus allowing the slip to emerge overtly.

In general, then, it seems that an action may be influenced by goals that are not dominant at the moment, but that are actively competing for access to the limited-capacity system.[7] Such competition is required, because conscious access allows the winning goal system to recruit subsystems and effectors able to carry out its goal (see Chapter 4). Competition may also be especially common when people face true dilemmas, or situations in which impulses urge one course of action, while mature reflection points to another. The most obvious and easily observed examples of this kind of competition can be found in efforts

---

[7]The Competing-Plans Hypothesis has an interesting resemblance to the general Freudian Slip hypothesis (Chapter 12). After all, the importance of the everyday slips and lapses cited by Freud (1901/1938) was not the phenomena themselves but the way in which they seemed to reveal the existence of hidden conflicted motives. Such conflicted motives correspond closely to the competing plans of the CPH; or rather, CPH presents a way in which largely unconscious motivational systems may compete for the privilege of controlling voluntary action. Several implications of this similarity are explored in Baars (1988).

to control unwanted habits such as overeating and cigarette smoking. But there are many other examples.

The theoretical framework that has been developed here to account for slips has far broader implications. These could not be pursued in detail in the current chapter. Readers who are curious about this broader framework are referred to Chapter 4 of this book and Baars (1988, Chapter 7).

REFERENCES

Abrams, K., & Bever, T. G. (1969). Syntactic structure modifies attention during speech perception. *Quarterly Journal of Experimental Psychology, 21,* 280–290.

Anderson, J. R. (1983). *The architecture of cognition.* Cambridge: Harvard University Press.

Baars, B. J. (1977). *The planning of speech: Is there semantic editing prior to speech articulation?* Doctoral dissertation, University of California at Los Angeles, Department of Psychology.

Baars, B. J. (1980a). The competing plans hypothesis: An heuristic viewpoint on the causes of errors in speech. In H. W. Dechert & M. Raupach (Eds.), *Temporal variables in speech: Studies in honour of Frieda Goldman-Eisler.* The Hague: Mouton.

Baars, B. J. (1980b). On eliciting predictable speech errors in the laboratory. In V. A. Fromkin (Ed.), *Errors in linguistic performance: Slips of the tongue, ear, pen, and hand.* New York: Academic Press.

Baars, B. J. (1983). Conscious contents provide the nervous system with coherent, global information. In R. Davidson, G. Schwartz, & D. Shapiro (Eds.), *Consciousness and self-regulation* (Vol. 3, pp. 47–76). New York: Plenum Press.

Baars, B. J. (1987). What is conscious in the control of action? A modern ideomotor theory of voluntary control. In D. Gorfein & R. R. Hoffman (Eds.), *Learning and memory: The Ebbinghaus Centennial Symposium,* Hillsdale, NJ: Erlbaum.

Baars, B. J. (1988). *A cognitive theory of consciousness.* New York: Cambridge University Press.

Baars, B. J., & MacKay, D. G. (1978). Experimentally eliciting phonetic and sentential speech errors: Methods, implications, and work in progress. *Language in Society, 7,* 105–109.

Baars, B. J., & Mattson, M. E. (1981). Consciousness and intention: A framework and some evidence. *Cognition and Brain Theory, 4*(3), 247–263.

Baars, B. J., & Motley, M. T. (1976). Spoonerisms as sequencer conflicts: Evidence from artificially elicited errors. *American Journal of Psychology, 89,* 467–484.

Baars, B. J., Motley, M. T., & MacKay, D. G. (1975). Output editing for lexical status in artificially elicited slips of the tongue. *Journal of Verbal Learning and Verbal Behavior, 14,* 382–391.

Berg, T. (1987). The case against accommodation: Evidence from German speech error data. *Journal of Memory and Language, 26,* 277–299.

Bower, G. H., & Cohen, P. R. (1982). Emotional influences in memory and thinking: Data and theory. In M. S. Clarke & S. T. Fiske (Eds.), *Affect and cognition* (pp. 291–331). Hillsdale, NJ: Erlbaum.

Broadbent, D. E. (1958). *Perception and communication.* New York: Pergamon Press.

Butterworth, B. L. (1980). Some constraints on models of language production. In B. L. Butterworth (Ed.), *Language production: Vol. 1. Speech and talk.* London: Academic Press.

Butterworth, B. L. (1982). Speech errors: Old data in search of new theories. In A. Cutler (Ed.), *Slips of the tongue.* Amsterdam: Mouton.

Dell, G. S. (1985). Positive feedback in hierarchial connectionist models: Applications to language production. *Cognitive Science, 9,* 3–23.

Dell, G. S. (1986). A spreading-activation theory of retrieval in sentence production. *Psychological Review, 93,* 283–321.

Fay, D. (1980). Transformational errors. In V. A. Fromkin (Ed.), *Errors in linguistic performance* (pp. 111–122). New York: Academic Press.

Fodor, J. A. (1983). *The modularity of mind: An essay in faculty psychology.* Cambridge: MIT Press.

Freud, S. (1901/1938). The psychopathology of everyday life. Trans. A. A. Brill, in A. A. Brill (Ed.), *The basic writings of Sigmund Freud.* New York: Basic Books.

Fromkin, V. A. (1968). Speculations on performance models. *Journal of Linguistics, 4,* 47–68.

Fromkin, V. A. (Ed.). (1973). *Speech errors as linguistic evidence.* The Hague: Mouton.

Fromkin. V. A. (Ed.). (1980). *Errors in linguistic performance: Slips of the tongue, ear, pen, and hand.* New York: Academic Press.

Garrett, M. F. (1980). The limits of accommodation: Arguments for independent processing levels in sentence production. In V. Fromkin (Ed.), *Errors of linguistic performance: Slips of the pen, tongue, and hand* (pp. 263–271). New York: Academic Press.

Goldman-Eisler, F. (1972). Pauses, clauses, and sentences. *Language and Speech, 15,* 103–113.

Gould, S. J. (19820. *The panda's thumb: More reflections on natural history.* New York: Norton.

Greene, P. (1972). Problems of organization of motor systems. *Journal of Theoretical Biology, 3,* 303–338.

Harley, T. A. (1984). A critique of top-down independent levels models of speech production: Evidence from non-plan-internal speech errors. *Cognitive Science, 8,* 191–219.

LaBerge, D. (1980). Unitization and automaticity in perception. In J. H. Flowers (Ed.), *1980 Nebraska Symposium on Motivation* (pp. 53–71). Lincoln: University of Nebraska Press.

Langer, E. J. (1989). *Mindfulness.* New York: Addison-Wesley.

Langer, E. J., & Imber, L. G. (1979). When practice makes imperfect: Debilitating effects of overlearning. *Journal of Personality and Social Psychology, 37*(11), 2014–2024.

Levelt, W. J. M. (1983). Monitoring and self-repair in speech. *Cognition, 14,* 41–104.

Liberman, A. M., Cooper, F. Shankweiler, D., & Studdert-Kennedy, M. (1967). Perception of the speech code. *Psychological Review, 78*(2), 130–140.

MacKay, D. G. (1981). Speech errors: Retrospect and prospect. In V. A. Fromkin (Ed.), *Errors in linguistic performance* (pp. 319–332). New York: Academic Press.

MacKay, D. G. (1982). The problems of flexibility, fluency, and speed-accuracy trade-off in skilled behavior. *Psychological Review, 89,* 483–506.

MacKay, D. G. (1987). *The organization of perception and action: A theory of language and other cognitive skills.* New York: Springer.

Mandler, G. A. (1975). *Mind and emotion.* New York: Wiley.

Marslen-Wilson, W. D., & Welsh, A. (1978). Processing interactions and lexical access during word recognition in continuous speech. *Cognitive Psychology, 10,* 29–63.

Mattson, M. E. (1987). *Sources of competing activation in action errors.* Doctoral dissertation, Department of Psychology, State University of New York, Stony Brook.

Mattson, M. E., & Baars, B. J. (1985). *Competition in activation networks: A test using laboratory-induced action blends and spoonerisms.* Paper given at the Eastern Psychological Association, Boston, MA.

Morton, J. (1970). A functional model of memory. In D. A. Norman (Ed.), *Models of human memory.* New York: Academic Press.

Motley, M. T., & Baars, B. J. (1976). Semantic bias effects on the outcomes of verbal slips. *Cognition, 4,* 177–187.

Motley, M. T., & Baars, B. J. (1978). Laboratory verification of "Freudian" slips of the tongue

34　　　　　　　　　　　　　　　　　　　　　　　　　　　**Bernard J. Baars**

as evidence of pre-articulatory semantic editing. In B. Ruken (Ed.), *Communication Yearbook 2*, New Brunswick, NJ: Transaction.

Motley, M. T., & Baars, B. J. (1979). Effects of cognitive set upon laboratory-induced verbal (Freudian) slips. *Journal of Speech and Hearing Research, 22*, 421–432.

Motley, M. T., Baars, B. J., & Camden, C. T. (1979). Personality and situational influences upon verbal slips. *Human Communication Research, 5*, 195–202.

Motley, M. T., Baars, B. J., & Camden, C. T. (1981). Syntactic criteria in prearticulatory editing: Evidence from laboratory-induced slips of the tongue. *Journal of Psycholinguistic Research, 10*(5), 503–522.

Neisser, U. (1967). *Cognitive psychology*. New York: Appleton-Century-Crofts.

Norman, D. A. (1976). *Memory and attention*. New York: Wiley.

Norman, D. A. (1981). Categorization of action slips. *Psychological Review, 88*, 1–15.

Norman, D. A., & Shallice, T. (1980). *Attention and action: Willed and automatic control of behavior*. La Jolla: Center for Human Information Processing, University of California at San Diego.

Reason, J. T. (1979). Actions not as planned: The price of automatization. In G. Underwood & R. Stevens (Eds.), *Aspects of consciousness: Vol. 1. Psychological issues* (pp. 67–89). London: Academic Press.

Reason, J. T. (1982, June). Learning from absent-minded mistakes. *SSRC Newsletter, 46*, 19–26.

Reason, J. T. (1983). Absent-mindedness and cognitive control. In J. Harris & P. Morris (Eds.), *Everyday memory, actions and absentmindedness* (pp. 19–26, 113–132). New York: Academic Press.

Reason, J. T. (1984a). Lapses of attention in everyday life. In R. Parasuraman & D. R. Davies (Eds.), *Varieties of attention* (pp. 515–549). New York: Academic Press.

Reason, J. T. (1984b). Little slips and big disasters. *Interdisciplinary Science Reviews, 9*(2), 3–15.

Reason, J. T. (1992). *Human error*. Cambridge: Cambridge University Press.

Reason, J., & Mycielska, K. (1982). *Absent-minded? The psychology of mental lapses and everyday errors*. Englewood Cliffs, NJ: Prentice-Hall.

Shallice, T. (1978). The dominant action system: An information-processing approach to consciousness. In K. S. Pope & J. L. Singer (Eds.), *The stream of consciousness: Scientific investigation into the flow of experience*. New York: Plenum Press.

Shiffrin, R. M., & Schneider, W. (1977). Controlled and automatic human information processing: 2. Perceptual learning, automatic attending, and a general theory. *Psychological Review, 84*, 127–190.

Sternberg, S. (1966). High-speech scanning in human memory. *Science, 153*, 652–654.

Tversky, A., and Kahneman, A. (1973). Availability: An heuristic for judging frequency and probability. *Cognitive Psychology, 2*, 207–232.

Weiner, B. (1986). *An attributional theory of motivation and emotion*. New York: Springer-Verlag.

Wundt, W. (1912/1973). *An introduction to psychology*. London: G. Allen. (Reprinted, New York: Arno Press.)

II

THEORETICAL APPROACHES

Four theoretical chapters are presented in this section. Donald G. MacKay pioneered the modern psycholinguistic study of speech errors (along with Victoria A. Fromkin in linguistics) and has been for many years the most prolific and influential cognitive theorist on speech production and errors. His current chapter extends his spreading activation model of speech production (MacKay, 1987) to problems of speech perception and the issue of awareness. Awareness is addressed by postulating two different types of activation, one concerned with automatic (unconscious) readiness to respond (called *priming*), and the second (called *activation*) with the likelihood of some element in the network's reaching consciousness. Some such distinction is necessary to solve the paradox that practicing a predict task generally leads to automaticity, after which the task is performed *more readily* under the proper triggering conditions, but also *less consciously*. Thus, "conscious access" and "readiness to respond" show an inverse relationship. It is therefore very unlikely that they can both be explained by a single activation mechanism.

Whether MacKay's proposed solution is adequate remains to be seen. The "dual activation solution" raises questions about the *functional* difference between the two proposed systems; otherwise, it becomes merely a labeling distinction. (A dual activation system was also proposed by Freud in his "Project for a Scientific Psychology" 1885/1976, in terms of two kinds of neurons, one being conscious and the other unconscious; but this appears to be merely a labeling solution to the problem.) In spite of these concerns, MacKay is to be commended for working to incorporate the issue of consciousness, which is, indeed, one of the principal problems raised by the existence of unintentional slips (see Chapter 1).

Like MacKay, James T. Reason (Chapter 3) has worked to incorporate the issues of conscious access and limited-capacity mechanisms into a wider model of action control (see Reason, 1979, 1984a,b). He has suggested an "architectural" solution to the problem of consciousness resembling the approaches of Shallice (1978), Norman and Shallice (1986), and Baars (1983, 1988). All of these approaches suggest that "distributed" goals and plan components must compete for access to a limited-capacity mechanism before they can be executed. A distributed architecture implies that these components have a good deal of autonomy. In such an architecture, executive systems may command a goal that is not entirely specific in its details, which are worked out by relatively autonomous effectors. In a similar fashion, an army general might command his troops to capture a strategic point without telling them which foot to put in front of the other. If this design strategy obtains in human action, the issue of "underspecification" discussed by Reason as a source of error becomes quite important (see also Norman, 1981). Indeed it is natural in such a system for executive systems to issue only underspecified commands, whose details are worked out locally. Underspecification may also be reflected in the point made in Chapter 1 that conscious goal images may be quite variable and even superficially "irrelevant" to an action, and still act in an executive capacity, to recruit, organize, and trigger automatic plan components to carry out the action.[1]

In Chapter 4, I explore a fortuitous connection between the Global Workspace (GW) theory (Baars, 1983, 1987, 1988) and William James's ideomotor theory of voluntary control (1890). GW theory attempts to work out an architectural solution to the question of consciousness and its functional role in the nervous system. It is similar to Reason's architectural concepts and to Norman and Shallice's (1986), but it assigns an explicit function to a global workspace to broadcast messages very widely, in order to recruit, organize, and execute actions made up of distributed components. There is a remarkable fit between James's very sophisticated observations about voluntary control, made a century ago, and the system architecture suggested by GW theory.

Finally, in Chapter 5, two artificial intelligence theorists, Lawrence Birnbaum and Gregg Collins, provide a functional argument for the relative autonomy of goals; it shows a satisfying fit with the thinking explored in the preceding theoretical chapters. They begin from the premise that there are such things as Freudian slips; as we show in Chapter 12, the evidence for this premise is still unresolved. However, if we assume that Freudian slips exist, Birnbaum and Collins show the theoretical implications, namely, that humans need an *opportunistic* planning system, one that is able to modify actions in progress in order to take advantage of unexpected opportunities. If humans are to be able to do that, goals that are desirable but not in control of current actions must somehow remain available.

This seems again to imply a system architecture in which different goal systems can compete for the privilege of controlling action; even if they appear to lose this competition at some point, they may nevertheless remain active and able to influence the flow of activity "opportunistically," in the future (Baars, 1988). Thus, in terms of the models advanced in the preceding chapters, goals can be viewed as relatively autonomous systems that may compete for access to the limited-capacity system, where they can control normal vol-

---

[1]Reason's theoretical position is further developed in his recent book, *Human Error* (1992).

untary action. But even if they fail to win access to the conscious/limited-capacity system, they may still "keep trying," and if the right opportunity arises, they may successfully influence action.

REFERENCES

Baars, B. J. (1983). Conscious contents provide the nervous system with coherent, global information. In R. Davidson, G. Schwartz, & D. Shapiro (Eds.), *Consciousness and self-regulation (Vol. 3,* (pp. 45–76). New York: Plenum Press.

Baars, B. J. (1987). Biological implications of a global workspace theory of consciousness: Evidence, theory, and some phylogenetic speculations. In G. Greenberg & E. Tobach (Eds.), *Cognition, language, and consciousness: Integrative levels* (pp. 209–236). Hillsdale, NJ: Erlbaum.

Baars, B. J. (1988). *A cognitive theory of consciousness.* New York: Cambridge University Press.

Freud, S. (1885/1976). Project for a scientific psychology. In Karl H. Pribram & Merton M. Gill (Eds.), *Freud's "Project" reassessed: Preface to contemporary cognitive theory and neuropsychology.* New York: Basic Books.

James, W. (1890). *The principles of psychology.* New York: Holt.

MacKay, D. G. (1987). *The organization of perception and action: A theory for language and other cognitive skills.* New York: Springer.

Norman, D. A., & Shallice, T. (1986). Attention to action: Willed and automatic control of behavior. In R. J. Davidson, G. E. Schwartz, & D. Shapiro (Eds.), *Consciousness and self-regulation: Advances in research (Vol. 4).* New York: Plenum Press.

Reason, J. T. (1979). Actions not as planned: The price of automatization. In G. Underwood & R. Stevens (Eds.), *Aspects of consciousness: Vol. 1. Psychological issues.* London: Academic Press.

Reason, J. T. (1984a). Absent-mindedness and cognitive control. In J. Harris & P. Morris (Eds.), *Everyday memory, actions, and absent-mindedness.* London: Academic Press.

Reason, J. T. (1984b). Lapses of attention. In R. Parasuraman & D. Davies (Eds.), *Varieties of attention.* New York: Academic Press.

Reason, J. T. (1990). *Human error.* London: Cambridge University Press.

Shallice, T. (1978). The dominant action system: An information-processing approach to consciousness. In K. S. Pope & T. L. Singer (Eds.), *The stream of consciousness: Scientific investigation into the flow of experience.* New York: Plenum Press.

2

Errors, Ambiguity, and Awareness in Language Perception and Production

Donald G. MacKay

Three interrelated puzzles have been haunting my work on speech errors, almost since it began in 1965. The awareness puzzle is one, and it consists of two parts. Part 1 of the awareness puzzle concerns relations between awareness and the "adjustments" or accommodations that often follow the production of errors. For example, the speaker who *misproduced* "cow tracks" as "track cow*z*" (Garrett, 1980; see also MacKay, 1979) selected the appropriate context-dependent plural *unconsciously* from among the three alternatives that English allows (/z/, /ez/, and /s/) for the transposed word *track*. The unconscious nature of these "context-sensitive accommodations" indicates that speakers can choose unconsciously among alternative outputs, contrary to the proposal of Reason (1984) and others that unconscious processes are inflexible and that only conscious processes are sensitive to context and capable of choice. Context-sensitive accommodations also undermine Marcel's proposal (1983) that choice among actions can serve as a criterion for consciousness. The puzzle is how these unconscious choices are made.

The awareness puzzle, Part 2, is how unconscious perceptual factors give rise to production errors. In particular, how do unconsciously processed ambig-

DONALD G. MACKAY • Department of Psychology, University of California at Los Angeles, Los Angeles, California 90024.

Experimental Slips and Human Error: Exploring the Architecture of Volition, edited by Bernard J. Baars. Plenum Press, New York, 1992.

uities cause speech errors in sentence completion tasks (as in MacKay, 1966, 1969, 1970) where a subject is presented with a sentence fragment, thinks up a relevant completion, and produces the entire sentence aloud as quickly as possible? After a series of, say, 100 recorded sentence completions, the experimenter asks the subject if any of the sentence fragments seemed unusual or ambiguous and then goes over each sentence with the subject, reading aloud the subject's completion and asking the subject whether his or her completion seems grammatical and relevant to the fragment. The experimenter then informs the subject that some of the fragments were ambiguous (e.g., "Having a ball with his case, Perry Mason ... "), and that others were unambiguous (e.g., "Having a pencil with his case, Perry Mason ... "). (Unambiguous versions were formed by changing a single word in an otherwise identical ambiguous sentence, and a counterbalanced design ensured that no one subject received both versions of the same sentence.) The experimenter next announces the two meanings for each ambiguous fragment and asks the subjects whether they had seen both of these meanings while thinking up the completion, and if not, which meaning they saw. By these measures, subjects almost invariably fail to notice any of the ambiguities: they report awareness of only one meaning and claim to be unaware of the other meaning when completing the ambiguous fragments.

However, significantly more ambiguous than unambiguous fragments evoked speech errors, and the nature of these errors indicates that the unseen meaning had an unconscious or subliminal effect on how the subjects completed the sentences. For example, one subject produced the sentence, "After stopping arguing in the court [fragment], Wimbleton was perjured, I mean, disqualified" but reported being unaware of the meaning "court of law," despite its obvious connection with the error, *perjured*. Deepening the puzzle, whole classes of errors such as stuttering (segment repetition) that bore no direct relation to the unseen meanings also occurred more frequently for ambiguous than for unambiguous fragments. The awareness puzzle, Part 2, is how the unseen meanings of ambiguous sentences can trigger speech errors, both directly and indirectly.

Puzzle 2, the practice puzzle, is why no simple relation exists between prior practice and the probability of speech errors at various levels. Prior practice (repetition over the course of a lifetime during everyday speech) reduced the probability of errors and is confounded with the level of a unit in the speech production system (see MacKay, 1982): during everyday speech, phoneme units receive more practice than syllable units, which receive more practice than word units, which receive more practice than phrase units. Logically, then, errors and level in the hierarchy should be highly correlated: errors involving phonemes should be least likely, and errors involving phrases should be most likely. However, no such pattern is observed. Phrases participate in fewer errors than do words, and syllables participate in fewer errors than do phonemes (see Garnham, Shillcock, Brown, Mill, & Cutler, 1982). Why are naturally occurring errors distributed in this way with respect to level and prior practice? The suggestion of Dell (1986) and Shattuck-Hufnagel (1983) that phrases and syllables do not exist as speech production units augments rather than resolves Puzzle 2; after all, the fact that syllables and phrases *sometimes* participate in errors must surely be explained in terms of production units.

Puzzle 3, the error detectability puzzle, also comes in two parts. Part 1 is why the level or focus of awareness shifts following self-produced phonetic and phonological errors. As adults, we are normally aware of the higher level aspects of a conversation, but not of the phonemes or phonetics of pronunciation, in either self-produced or other-produced speech. However, a self-produced phonetic error such as a slurred speech sound will immediately bring our awareness down to the phonetic level. The error detectability puzzle, Part 1, is how such errors shift the level of awareness to the phonetic level.

The error detectability puzzle, Part 2, concerns a difference in the detectability of self-produced and other-produced errors. *Self-produced* word substitutions are detected and corrected with fairly high frequency (60%), as in "Moses, I mean, Noah built the ark." However, otherwise similar errors *produced by others* are detected with relatively low probability: even when warned of possible errors, subjects under no time pressure whatsoever rarely detect other-produced "errors," as in "How many animals of each kind did Moses bring on the ark?" (Eriksen & Mattson, 1981). This is the error detectability puzzle, Part 2: If self-produced and other-produced speech are represented via the same system (a reasonable assumption; see MacKay, 1987, pp. 14–140), why are self-produced errors easier to detect than other-produced errors?

ORGANIZATION OF THE CHAPTER

The main point of the present chapter is that these and other related puzzles are no longer puzzles. They follow logically from a recently developed theory of language perception and production (MacKay, 1987, 1988). I originally developed the theory[1] not just to explain speech errors or even language production, but to address much more general issues: the mechanisms underlying sequencing and timing in behavior, the effects of practice on behavior, the speed–accuracy trade-off in the perception and production of skilled behavior, asymmetries in the ability to perceive as opposed to produce skilled behavior, the perception of ambiguous inputs, the use of perceptual feedback in monitoring skilled behavior, and the effects of delayed and amplified auditory feedback on the production of speech and other cognitive skills. However, the theory also ended up making numerous claims about errors, including error-correction errors, bumper-car errors, haplologies, dysgraphia, omission errors in speech and typing, internally generated errors, tongue twisters, stuttering, perceptually based production errors, experimentally induced per-

---

[1]The reader is referred to MacKay (1987) for a more extensive discussion of the original theory, its supporting data, and its relations to other theories, such as that of McClelland, Rumelhart, and the PDP Research Group (1986).

ceptual errors, and relations between slips of the tongue and slips of the ear.

In what follows, I briefly summarize this theory and then extend it so as to explain consciousness and its relation to error perception and production. As soon as is feasible in developing the theory, I show its bearing on the puzzles discussed above.

BASICS OF THE NODE STRUCTURE THEORY

Nodes, the basic components of the theory, fall into three classes, depending on the nature of their connections with one another: muscle movement nodes, sensory analysis nodes, and mental nodes. Sensory analysis nodes represent patterns of input, registering, say, speech inputs via the basilar membrane and associated auditory pathways, for example. Muscle movement nodes represent patterns of muscle movement for the respiratory, laryngeal, velar, and articulatory organs, among others. Mental nodes represent neither sensory experience nor patterns of muscle movement, but higher level cognitive components common to both perception and production. Mental nodes for speech include phonological nodes representing segments and syllables and sentential nodes representing words and phrases. These shared perception–production units send "top-down" outputs to muscle movement nodes for use during production and receive "bottom-up" inputs from sensory analysis nodes for use during perception (including the perception of self-generated feedback), and they send symmetrical top-down and bottom-up signals among each other. Mental nodes become active during perception, production, and cognition, as when we perceive a sentence and produce it, either aloud, or within the imagination (internal speech).

Nodes represent not just intersections in a descriptive parsing tree (as in, say, Anderson, 1983), but theoretical processing units (as in, say, Wickelgren, 1979). All nodes respond in the same way to basic variables such as practice (repeated activation) and share a set of relatively simple and universal processing characteristics: activation, priming, self-inhibition, linkage strength, and satiation.

The Distinction between Activation and Priming

The distinction between activation and priming is fundamental to the node structure theory, but it derives from the original use of these terms by Lashley (1951), rather than from current uses of the same terms. Node activation is an all-or-none process that is self-sustained, like neural activation; it lasts for a specifiable period of time, regardless of whether the sources that led originally to activation continue to provide input. Unlike neural activation, however, node activation can—and, in the case of mental or perception–production nodes, usually does—involve more than one neuron. Neurons and nodes also differ greatly in how long they remain activated and in how long they take to recover from activation: isolated neurons require only a few milliseconds to recover from activation, whereas nodes can take over a hundred milliseconds to recover (see MacKay, 1987, pp. 141–157).

Node activation also differs from the concept of spreading activation in propositional network theories such as Anderson's (1983). Node activation never "spreads," and its intensity never changes; unlike spreading activation, node activation remains constant with "distance," fatigue, and the number of other nodes connected to an activated node. Also unlike spreading activation, node activation is terminated by a brief period of reduced excitability known

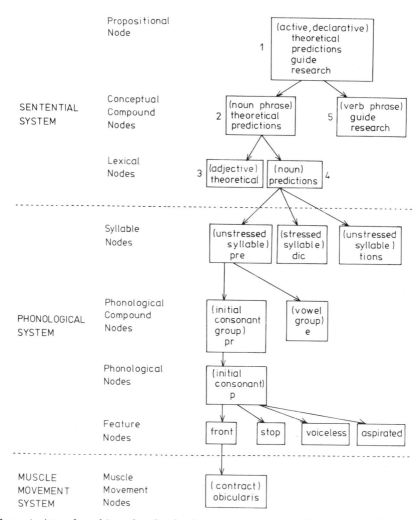

FIGURE 1. A top-down hierarchy of nodes for producing aspects of the sentence "Theoretical predictions guide research." The numbers represent the order in which the nodes become activated during production (from MacKay, 1987).

as *self-inhibition* (discussed below). Finally, node activation is sequential and nonautomatic in nature; a special activating mechanism (sequence node) must become engaged to determine when and in what order different nodes will become activated. By way of illustration, the numbers in Figure 1 represent the typical order in which the nodes for a sentence become activated during production.

During the period of self-inhibition following activation, the level of priming of a node falls below normal or resting level (see Figure 2). Then follows the recovery cycle, during which priming first rises above and then returns to resting level (see Figure 2). The mechanism underlying self-inhibition is an inhibitory collateral, or "satellite," that connects with and receives a connection from its "parent" node. The inhibitory satellite has a very high but otherwise standard threshold and becomes activated only after a set amount of input from its activated parent. Once activated, the satellite inhibits and deactivates its parent, thereby deactivating itself and enabling recovery to begin. This self-inhibition mechanism helps explain a variety of empirical

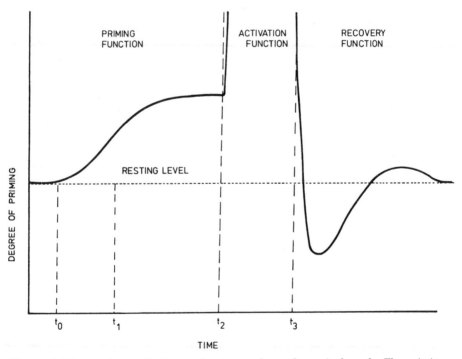

FIGURE 2. The priming, activation, and recovery phases for a single node. The priming function shows how priming summates to asymptote following the onset of priming at $t0$. The activation function illustrates the multiplication of priming and self-sustained activation until time $t3$. The recovery cycle that follows the termination of activation shows how priming first falls below resting level (self-inhibition), rebounds (the hyperexcitability phase), and then returns to resting level.

phenomena, for example, pathological stuttering and the effects of delayed and amplified auditory feedback (see MacKay, 1987, pp. 178–193). This chapter argues that self-inhibition also plays a central role in awareness and error detection.

Priming refers to a transmission across an active connection that, in some respects resembles the automatic spread of activation in other theories such as those of Dell (1986) and McClelland, Rumelhart, and the PDP Research Group (1986). However, priming is necessary to prepare a connected node for possible activation *as defined above:* In order to become *activated,* nodes must receive priming during the period of self-sustained activation of a directly or indirectly connected node. An activated node primes its connected nodes most strongly (first-order priming), and an unactivated node receiving first-order priming primes its connected nodes less strongly (second-order priming), and so on, up to n^{th}-order priming, where n is currently unknown (see below), and $n + 1^{th}$-order priming does not alter the resting state.

Priming summates both spatially (across two or more simultaneously active connections to the same node) and temporally (during the time that any given connection remains active). However, summation of priming cannot by itself cause a connected node to become activated: priming accumulates only to some subthreshold asymptotic level (see Figure 2). Moreover, priming does not self-sustain but gradually decays as soon as input into its connected nodes stops. Also unlike activation, priming is not followed by a period of self-inhibition and recovery and is order-free or parallel in nature; an active source primes its connected nodes simultaneously, and no special triggering mechanism is required to determine when and in what order the nodes become primed.

Activation Hierarchies. The structure of connections between nodes can be described as hierarchic with respect to activation and heterarchic with respect to priming (see MacKay, 1987, p. 23). Figure 1 illustrates aspects of an activation hierarchy, specifically, the hierarchy of top-down connections between nodes for producing the sentence "Theoretical predictions guide research." Following MacKay (1982), I designate each node by a two-component label: the content that the node represents appears in italics, followed by its sequential domain (explained below) in parentheses. Thus, the highest level node representing the entire thought underlying this particular sentence has the *content "Theoretical predictions guide research,"* occurs in the domain (active declarative), and is labeled *theoretical predictions guide research* (active declarative). Activating this particular node primes two phrase nodes top-down: *theoretical predictions* (noun phrase) and *guide research* (verb phrase) (see Figure 1). Activating *theoretical predictions* (noun phrase) primes two lexical nodes, *theoretical* (adjective) and *predictions* (noun). These lexical nodes prime specific phonological nodes, representing syllables (e.g., *pre*), phonological compounds (e.g., *pr*), segments (e.g., *p*), and features (e.g., the one representing the frontal place of articulation of *p*). The reader is referred to

MacKay (1972, 1973, 1978, 1979, 1987) and Treiman (1983) for evidence supporting the particular units and connections illustrated in Figure 1, which omits the more complex but otherwise similar hierarchy of nodes underlying the control of muscle movements.

Linkage Strength

Linkage strength is a relatively long-term characteristic of connections that determines how rapidly they can transmit priming per unit of time. The initial slope of a priming function is sensitive to differences in linkage strength (see MacKay, 1982): highly practiced connections have a steep slope, whereas unpracticed connections have a shallower slope. Linkage strength also influences how much priming a connection can transmit before hitting asymptote. Connections with high linkage strength transmit priming more rapidly and up to a higher asymptote than do connections with low linkage strength.

Practice (the frequency with which a node has been primed or activated via a particular connection in the past) increases linkage strength, an effect known as *engrainment learning* (MacKay, 1988, after James, 1890) that helps explain a wide range of practice effects in the psychological literature.

Satiation

Satiation refers to a process in which nodes become less responsive to priming as a result of continuously repeated activation over a prolonged period of time. Like activation, self-inhibition, priming, and engrainment learning, satiation is an extremely simple process if taken by itself, as in the above discussion. However, each of these processes interacts with the others in complex ways that depend on the current state of the node and on its history of activity over the course of a lifetime. Satiation varies with the extent and duration of repeated activation and manifests itself in reduced rebound and prolonged self-inhibition following activation. Activating a node increases the linkage strength of its connections and causes its connected nodes to become primed. Linkage strength influences how much and how rapidly priming can be transmitted across a connection. Finally, priming is necessary for activation and influences the probability of activating a node in error (see MacKay, 1982). As discussed below, the *mechanisms* likely to underlie these basic processes are also quite complex.

SEQUENCE NODES: THE ACTIVATING MECHANISM FOR CONTENT NODES

The nodes in the preceding discussion are known as *content nodes* because they represent the form or content of action, perception, and thought. A different type of nodes, known as *sequence nodes,* constitute the nonspecific activating mechanisms that activate content nodes according to a "most-primed-wins principle." As discussed below, sequence nodes also organize content nodes into domains and determine the serial order in which content nodes become activated.

Domains

Sequence nodes are connected to and activate not individual content nodes, but categories or domains of content nodes, where a domain consists of a set of nodes that share the same sequential properties (see MacKay, 1987, pp. 50–55). I use capital letters to denote sequence nodes and parentheses to denote the corresponding domain of content nodes. For example, content nodes in the domain (vowel) all share the same sequential properties or privileges of occurrence in the syllables of English or any other language and are activated by the sequence node VOWEL. Nodes in the domain (color adjective) likewise all share the same sequential properties or privileges of occurrence in English and are activated by the sequence node COLOR ADJECTIVE.

Multiplication of Priming

When activated, a sequence node multiples the priming of every node connected with it by some large factor within a relatively brief period of time. This multiplicative process has no effect on unprimed nodes, but it soon serves to activate (i.e., bring to threshold) the content node with the greatest degree of priming in its domain. For example, COLOR ADJECTIVE is connected to and, when activated, multiplies the priming of the dozens of content nodes in the domain (color adjective).

The Most-Primed-Wins Principle

The "most-primed-wins" activation principle follows directly from the nature of the connections between sequence and content nodes. Once a sequence node becomes activated, it automatically and simultaneously multiplies the priming of the entire domain of content nodes connected with it, increasing their level of priming rapidly over time. Normally, however, one node in a domain has more priming than all the others, and this "most-primed" node reaches threshold first and becomes activated.

During production, content nodes generally achieve their most-primed status via priming "from above." In producing the adjective *green,* for example, a superordinate node such as *green apples*(noun phrase) becomes activated and strongly primes *green*(color adjective) (see Figure 3). Being most primed when its activation mechanism begins multiplying its priming, this primed-from-above node reaches threshold sooner than other "extraneous" nodes in its domain and becomes activated.

Content nodes can achieve their most-primed status "from below" as well as "from above." For example, visual perception of the color green or the printed word *green* will prime *green*(color adjective) from below. *Green*(color adjective) then passes second-order priming to its connected sequence node (see Figure 3), enabling COLOR ADJECTIVE to become activated, and in turn activating the most primed content node in its domain, that is, *green*(color adjective) itself. This most-primed-wins principle is the basis for all node activation (see MacKay, 1987, pp. 49–55).

Quenching

The term *quenching* refers to a threshold mechanism that, if exceeded, causes content nodes to inhibit rather than prime their sequence nodes. This process enables an activated content node to quickly quench, or deactivate, its corresponding sequence node. Quenching is necessary to prevent reverberatory reactivation via the return connection between an activated content node and its sequence node (see Figure 3) and to ensure that only one content node becomes activated at any one time: without being quenched, a sequence node could potentially activate every node in its domain, causing behavior to break down.

Timing Nodes: The Activation Mechanism for Sequence Nodes

Timing nodes control the rate of perception and production by determining how rapidly sequence nodes become activated. They connect with and activate sequence nodes in the same way that sequence nodes connect with and activate content nodes, so that sequence nodes within a system (e.g., the phonological system and the sentential system; see Figure 1) can be considered a domain of nodes sharing the same sequential function. Timing nodes "self-activate" according to an endogenous rhythm, and timing nodes for different systems exhibit different endogenous rhythms. Each activation of a timing node multiplies the priming of connected sequence nodes and activates the most primed one, following the most-primed-wins principle, just as for content nodes.

How Sequence Nodes Code Sequential Rules

Connections between sequence nodes represent sequential rules that resolve the sequencing conflict that occurs when two or more sequence nodes have received simultaneous priming. The sequence nodes COLOR ADJECTIVE and NOUN, for example, are connected in such a way as to represent the

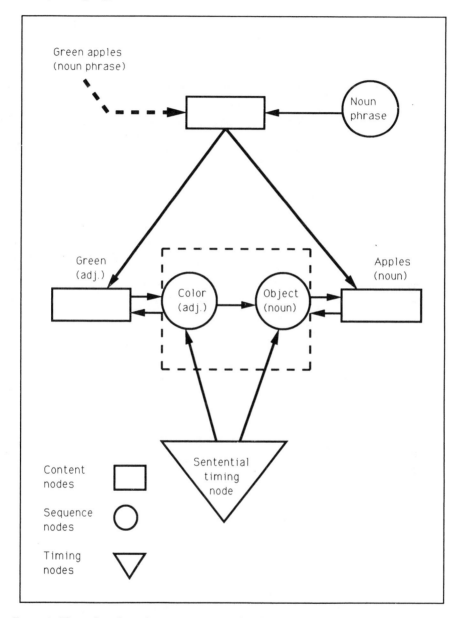

FIGURE 3. The order of top-down processes (in brackets) underlying the activation of the content nodes (in circles) and the sentential timing node for producing the noun phrase *green apples*.

rule that color adjectives precede nouns in English noun phrases.[2] Similarly, the sequence nodes INITIAL CONSONANT GROUP and VOWEL GROUP are connected in such a way as to represent the rule that initial consonants in a syllable precede the vowel and the final consonants.

Inhibitory connections determine the order relation among sequence nodes: Whenever two or more sequentially organized sequence nodes receive simultaneous priming, the sequence node that must be activated first inhibits its connected sequence nodes, so that it can become activated first under the most-primed-wins principle. Quenching this first sequence node releases the other sequence nodes from inhibition, and the most primed of these becomes activated next, and so on. For example, when COLOR ADJECTIVE and NOUN receive simultaneous priming from noun phrase constituents, COLOR ADJECTIVE inhibits NOUN, dominates in degree of priming, and becomes activated. However, once COLOR ADJECTIVE is quenched, NOUN is released from inhibition, dominates in degree of priming, and becomes activated. This process thus determines the sequence for this and any other noun phrase consisting of a color adjective and a noun.[3]

SPEECH ERRORS UNDER THE NODE STRUCTURE THEORY

As discussed in MacKay (1982, 1983, 1985, 1987), activation via the most-primed-wins principle serves a variety of important functions but is susceptible to error. Specifically, substitution errors occur when an "intended" or primed-from-above node fails to achieve the greatest priming in its domain when the most-primed-wins activating mechanism is applied, and some other "extraneous" node receiving more priming becomes activated. This explains why the substituted and substituting components in these errors almost in-

---

[2]Rules such as (color adjective + noun) are of course needed for producing adjectives in preferred sequences such as *fast red car*. However, it remains to be determined whether specific rules such as (color adjective + noun) can be "inherited" from a more general rule such as (adjective + noun), so that a color adjective content node connects with and is potentially activated by both ADJECTIVE and COLOR ADJECTIVE.

[3]Sequential rules such as (color adjective + noun) bear a surface resemblance to the phrase structure rules of Chomsky (1957) and Gazdar (1981) such as Noun Phrase → Adjective + Noun, where the arrow stands for "is rewritten as." Like phrase structure rules, sequential rules are nontransformational and refer to categories of units—in this example, the set of all adjectives and all nouns. There are many differences, however. For example, there is no sense in which the sequence node NOUN PHRASE is "rewritten" as COLOR ADJECTIVE + NOUN in the node structure theory (see also MacKay, 1974). Rather, the lexical content nodes connected to some particular noun phrase node simultaneously prime their respective sequence nodes, which happen to be NOUN and COLOR ADJECTIVE. The node structure theory also postulates new rules and new sequential domains, such as (initial consonant group + vowel group), which were unforeseen in phrase structure grammars. See MacKay (1987, p. 51) for other differences in the detailed nature of phrase structure categories and sequential domains).

variably belong to the same sequential class (the sequential class regularity; see MacKay, 1979, 1987). At the sentential level, nouns substitute for other nouns, verbs for verbs, and not for, say, nouns or adjectives; at the morphological level, prefixes substitute for other prefixes, suffixes for other suffixes, and never prefixes for suffixes; at the syllabic level, initial consonant clusters substitute for other initial clusters, final for final, but never initial for final; and at the segment level, vowels substitute for vowels, consonants for consonants, and never vowels for consonants. Substitution errors result from a most-primed-wins competition between priming of content nodes, rather than from competition between activating mechanisms (because the same activating mechanism activates both the correct and the incorrect nodes), or from competition between plans (which correspond to a preformed hierarchy such as the one in Figure 1; see MacKay, 1982). The sequential class regularity should also hold statistically for other errors, including paradigmatic errors such as blends (see MacKay, 1972, 1973), because an activating mechanism (sequence node) can activate and misactivate nodes only within the same sequential domain as the appropriate or intended-to-be-activated node, but the theory also predicts exceptions to the sequential class regularity under special circumstances exhibiting regularities of their own (see MacKay, 1987, pp. 60–61).

The automatic integration of top-down and bottom-up priming can also give rise to blends, phonologically similar word substitutions, and "Freudian" errors, including Freudian slips of the ear (see Dell, 1980; MacKay, 1973, 1987). Indeed, errors in general are largely attributable to the automatic manner in which mental nodes integrate priming from heterogeneous sources. However, mental nodes also make the relatively infrequent errors that do occur especially easy to detect and correct (see below).

The Level-within-a-System Effect

As noted in the introduction, phrase nodes participate in fewer errors than do lexical nodes, and syllable nodes participate in fewer errors than do segment nodes. This frequency distribution can be explained in terms of speed–accuracy trade-off: lover level nodes are activated at a faster rate than higher level nodes in the same system, so that the probability of error is reduced for higher level units. That is, nodes at lower levels in a hierarchy are more numerous and become activated at a faster rate than higher level nodes. For example, segments are produced much faster than syllables: a syllable node is activate every, say, 400 milliseconds on the average, whereas a segment node is activated every, say, 150 milliseconds on the average. This faster rate allows less time for the priming on lower level nodes to summate and thereby increases the probability that the wrong node will become activated under the most-primed-wins principle (see MacKay, 1982, 1987). However, this speed–accuracy trade-off effect will be confined *within a system:* lower level units will exhibit greater errors than higher level units only *within the same system* because the timing nodes that determine activation rate emit faster pulse rates for lower level systems than for higher level systems (see above; MacKay, 1987).

The *discontinuity* in the distribution of naturally occurring speech errors across systems is attributable to practice and "connectivity" under the node structure theory. That is, word errors occur more frequently than syllable errors (see Garnham *et al.*, 1982) because lexical nodes have less prior practice than syllable nodes, and because lexical nodes enjoy greater connectivity: they are directly connected to a large number of sensory and conceptual systems that phonological nodes are not directly connected to (see MacKay, 1987, p. 38). These systems contribute additional sources of extraneous priming to lexical nodes, so that word errors are more likely than phonological errors.

AMBIGUITY AND SPEECH ERRORS

Effects of ambiguity on speech errors fall into two classes: direct effects and indirect effects. I argue below that these effects of ambiguity are attributable to three mechanisms that serve many other functions within the node structure theory: mental or perception–production nodes, the priming–activation relationship, and the most-primed-wins activation principle. These same three mechanisms are also required for explaining experimentally induced "Freudian" slips (see Motley & Baars, 1979) and the more general class of word substitutions that Meringer (1908) called "situational intrusions," which are attributable to priming arising from contextual factors within an ongoing conversational situation: objects just noticed, words just read or heard, the nature of the relationship between the speaker and the listener, and things recently thought of or weighing on one's mind.

Direct Top-Down Effects of Ambiguity on Speech Errors

Significantly more ambiguous than unambiguous fragments in MacKay (1966, 1969) prompted irrelevant (tangential) completions or evoked ungrammatical completions, spoonerisms, and word substitutions, and priming from the unseen meaning was directly responsible for these effects. Tangential completions were defined as ones that the subject agreed during the post-experimental interview had no logical connection with the original fragment. Example tangential completions are "Knowing that visiting relatives can be bothersome, I was confused" and "Knowing how little jockeys drove cars, I mumbled." Ungrammatical completions were defined as ones where the subject agreed during the postexperimental interview that the sentence would not be acceptable as grammatical English. Examples are "Knowing the minister's hope of marrying Anna was impractical, he *disbanded* the idea" and "Although the officers were convincing men, the *message* they gave *were* not." Other errors included spoonerisms, for example, "Having a ball with his case, Merry Pason, I mean Perry Mason ... " and word substitutions such as "After stopping arguing in the court, Wimbleton was perjured, I mean, disqualified." The unseen meaning in this last example must have primed extraneous nodes, including *perjured* (past participle), which became activated in error under the most-primed-wins principle when the (past participle) activating mechanism was applied.

Misreadings—as in "Although the idea of Hitler was awful" misread as "Although that idea of Hitler's was awful"—were attributable to ambiguity, but not directly. In this and all other misreadings of ambiguous fragments, the misreading disambiguated the fragment by eliminating the meaning that the subject claimed not to have seen when thinking up the completion. Here the conscious representation of the sentence overrode the primary stimulus for reading, that is bottom-up priming from the sentence itself.

Errors that Ambiguity Does Not Cause. I conclude this section with a note on errors that ambiguity does *not* cause (see also MacKay, 1987, p. 119): Ambiguity does not cause garden path errors in production resembling the garden path errors that occur in comprehension, where a listener perceives the wrong meaning of an ambiguous word—such as, say, *crane*—and mistakes the topic of conversation to be *bird cranes* rather than *machine cranes*. Production errors resembling garden path miscomprehensions have never been reported: Normal speakers never begin to discuss, say, *machine cranes* and then *inadvertently* end up discussing *bird cranes*.

Indirect Top-Down Effects of Ambiguity on Speech Errors

MacKay (1966) found that stuttering (segment repetition) occurred more frequently in ambiguous than in unambiguous fragments, and MacKay (1969) used an error induction technique to demonstrate that this finding must reflect an indirect rather than a direct effect of ambiguity on phonological errors. The phonological errors were induced experimentally by means of delayed and amplified auditory feedback (DAAF). When hearing DAAF from their own voice with a 0.2-second delay, speakers reliably generate large numbers of phonetic and phonological errors, including transpositions, prolongations, omissions, slurs, substitutions, and repetitions, or stutters (Fairbanks & Guttman, 1958).

As in MacKay (1966), the subjects in MacKay (1969) thought up a relevant completion for a sentence fragment but then produced their completed sentence aloud as quickly as possible *under DAAF*. The dependent variable was probability of repetition errors, and ambiguous sentences elicited significantly more repetitions than did ambiguous sentences, both wile the subject was reading the fragments and while the subject was producing the completions.

(Structural complexity and possible speed–accuracy trade-offs were controlled across ambiguous versus unambiguous sentences.)

These findings indicate that ambiguity at sentential levels can indirectly influence repetition errors involving phonological units, and this indirect top-down effect is readily explained under the node structure assumption that phonological nodes for perceiving and producing speech are identical. During perception, the unseen meaning of the ambiguous fragments automatically primes extraneous lexical nodes, which in turn prime extraneous phonological nodes, and during production, this extraneous top-down priming combines with extraneous bottom-up priming from the DAAF arriving at a just-activated phonological node (see MacKay, 1987, pp. 178–190). Ambiguity therefore increases repetition errors by increasing the likelihood that just-activated phonological nodes receive the greatest priming in their domain and become reactivated in error under the most-primed-wins principle.

As an interesting footnote, MacKay (1969) replicated all of the above findings *without DAAF* by having pathological stutterers complete the same sentence fragments in a separate experiment. However, recent theoretical analyses suggest that it is important to distinguish between "intrinsic" and "feedback-induced" stutterers (see MacKay, 1987, pp. 192–193) in future versions of this replication experiment. MacKay (1987, pp. 160–161) presented convincing evidence that "intrinsic stuttering" originates within the muscle movement system (unlike "feedback-induced" stuttering, which originates within the phonological system), and if both intrinsic and feedback-induced stutterers can be shown to exhibit an effect of ambiguity during sentence completion, then priming must spread to a much greater extent than MacKay (1987, p. 10) assumed, that is, all the way from sentential nodes representing the ambiguities to muscle movement nodes, where intrinsic stuttering originates.

As another interesting footnote, the basic mechanisms discussed above (priming, most-primed-wins activation, and mental or perception–production nodes) may also underlie errors that are induced experimentally via anticipatory bias techniques (where a cue signals that the subject must produce a pair of "target words," but unbeknownst to the subjects, the preceding word pairs have primed the spoonerized version of these words; see Baars, Motley, & MacKay, 1975); via word-order competition techniques (where a cue signals that the subjects must produce a pair of visually presented words in reverse order; see Baars & Motley, 1976); via phrase-order competition techniques (where a cue signals that the subjects must produce a pair of visually presented phrases in reverse order; see Baars, 1980); and via "tongue twister" or rapid iteration techniques (see, e.g., MacKay, 1971; as MacKay, 1982, pointed out, the term *tongue twister technique* is a misnomer: these techniques induce phonological errors rather than "neuromotor" errors, as Motley, Baars, & Camden, 1983, assumed).

Other Indirect Top-Down Effects on Speech Errors.   MacKay and Bowman (1969) reported another indirect top-down effect of semantics on speech errors induced experimentally by means of DAAF. The top-down effect resulted from practice at the sentential/semantic level: The subjects (highly proficient German–English bilinguals) practiced producing a sentence 12 times, each time at maximal rate with normal feedback, and then put on a pair of earphones and produced another, "transfer," sentence in their other language as rapidly as possible with a 0.2-second delay in DAAF. The transfer sentence had either an identical meaning to or a completely different meaning from the sentence practiced. For example, if the originally practiced sentence was "The wanderlust seized him as it once had his grandfather," then "Die Wanderlust packte ihn wie einst seinen Grossvater" is a transfer sentence with virtually identical meaning but, of course, radically different phonology from the original.

The results were dramatic: Significantly fewer DAAF errors were observed for transfer sentences with identical meaning than for those with different meaning. This finding indicates that practice at the sentential level (in one language) influences the probability of phonological errors (in the other language). Under the assumption that nodes representing the same sentential concepts are identical whatever the language, practice increased the linkage strength of sentential system nodes for producing the transfer sentences and thereby increased the transmission of priming to appropriate lower level phonological nodes, so as to reduce the probability of DAAF errors (see MacKay, 1982).

Ambiguity in General

Ambiguity is often defined as an *input* phenomenon (ambiguous stimulus patterns are open to two or more distinct interpretations), but this "surface definition" has always raised problems because ambiguous stimuli are not necessarily *psychologically* ambiguous (see MacKay, 1966, 1970). However, node structure mechanisms underlying the processing of ambiguity enable a *theoretical* definition that is much more general in nature and seems immune to this problem: Ambiguity occurs in the theory whenever two or more nodes in the same domain simultaneously receive comparable levels of priming (MacKay, 1987, pp. 138–139). Under this definition, ambiguity is a ubiquitous issue, applying to any node in any system, and represents the major cause of errors in all input and output domains. Indeed, MacKay (1987) viewed ambiguity as one of the main reasons for the evolution of the most-primed-wins principle and mental or perception–production nodes. Baars (1983, 1985) also saw the need for a "deep" or theoretical definition of ambiguity as a "choice point." However, output choice points in Baars (1985) correspond to different ways of saying something, another problematic "surface definition."

Node Commitment and Decommitment

Let us return now to the development of the node structure theory. The term *node commitment* refers to an extremely general process in which new or never previously activated nodes become activated. As we will see, node commitment is triggered automatically by "pertinent novelty," requires neither intention nor volition, provides the basis for consciousness, and explains the awareness puzzle.

Uncommitted Connections and the Commitment Threshold

Uncommitted connections are prestructured connections with such weak linkage strength that they pass on too little priming to enable a connected node to become activated when its triggering mechanism is applied. Nodes receiving nothing but uncommitted connections are uncommitted nodes, and all mental nodes begin this way. Each connects initially to thousands of other nodes, and during the lifetime of an individual, only a small fraction of these prestructured connections becomes committed or capable of transmitting enough priming to permit activation of the connected node. Node commitment therefore enables a select few out of an excess of weak but prestructured connections to become functional.

Commitment Threshold. The term *commitment threshold* refers to the minimum level of priming that a node must receive in order to become activated; below this minimum level, even multiplication by an activating mechanism cannot boost priming to the activation threshold. For example, let us say that a sequence node self-sustains its activation for a set period of 20 milliseconds and multiplies the priming of its connected nodes by a factor of 1.2 every millisecond. If the original degree of priming of the most primed content node in the domain exceeds commitment level, this multiplication factor suffices to cause activation within 20 milliseconds or less. However, if the original priming of the most primed content node falls below commitment level, the multiplied priming remains subthreshold, so that activation cannot occur. Note that many nodes are likely to have multiplied priming values that fall between resting level and commitment threshold (see Figure 4), so that sequence nodes have no way of directly activating a specific uncommitted node.

The Commitment Mechanism: Binding Nodes

Binding nodes provide a booster input that enables the extremely weak connections to an uncommitted node to become strong enough to transmit commitment levels of priming, so that the uncommitted node is transformed into a committed node that consistently codes a specific cognitive content. Like

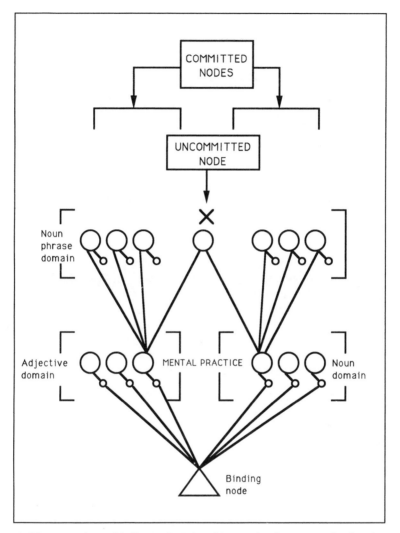

FIGURE 4. The noun phrase binding node (triangle) commits the uncommitted node *mental practice*(noun phrase), by inhibiting the inhibitory satellites (small circles) of parent nodes (larger circles) in the (adjective) and (noun) domains.

sequence nodes, binding nodes connect with a large number of content nodes, usually in two or more sequential domains, but unlike sequence nodes, binding nodes are relatively few in number, are *inhibitory* in nature, and act on the self-inhibition mechanism of content nodes. That is, binding nodes connect with the self-inhibitory "satellite," and not with the "parent" node itself, so that when a binding node becomes activated, it prevents self-inhibition in all the content nodes to which it is connected. This means that currently activated nodes will remain activated for a prolonged period of time because their self-inhibitory mechanism now fails to shut them off. In this way, a binding node transmits nonspecific input simultaneously to two or more domains of content nodes but alters the activity pattern only of specific "target nodes" (those nodes undergoing activation at the time) and selectively enhances convergent priming to a single uncommitted node that can then become activated under the most-primed-wins principle. If binding nodes directly boosted the activity of specific target nodes rather than indirectly inhibiting the self-inhibition mechanisms of many unspecified nodes, too many binding nodes would be needed, that is, as many binding nodes as there are pairs of content nodes.

Activating an uncommitted content node in this way increases the linkage strength of its bottom-up connections, thereby improving the asymptotic level and rate of priming via those connections. The commitment of top-down connections follows almost immediately, without further engagement or reactivation of the binding nodes. Specifically, once an uncommitted node becomes activated, it transmits first-order priming to all of its connected nodes, including the two lower level nodes that are still undergoing prolonged activation. Because a connection transmitting first-order priming to activated nodes constitutes the basic condition for a major increase in linkage strength, top-down connections become strengthened soon after their newly committed node becomes activated. With further activations, linkage strength increases further, until bottom-up and top-down priming exceeds commitment threshold. At this point, the connections have become committed so that activation can proceed automatically without calling for booster input from binding nodes.

Decommitment

A newly committed node with recently strengthened bottom-up and top-down connections represents a specific cognitive content, but relatively weakly. Minor increases in linkage strength resulting from one or even several activations of an uncommitted node are relatively fragile and can decay over a period of, say, hours. As a result, unless newly committed nodes undergo repeated activation, their connections can become decommitted or revert to uncommitted status. To permanently commit a node for a particular pertinent novelty, repeated engagement of a binding node may sometimes be necessary. By contrast, highly practiced nodes have relatively unfragile linkage strength that endures for many years.

PERTINENT NOVELTY AND ORIENTING REACTIONS

The term *pertinent novelty* refers to a coincidence of node activations (internally or externally triggered) that has never occurred in simultaneous combination before but calls up an established sequence node. For example, the phrase *pertinent novelty* constitutes an instance of pertinent novelty if the hearer "knows" that *pertinent* is an adjective, that *novelty* is a noun, and that an adjective followed by a noun constitutes a noun phrase, but he or she has never experienced this particular combination of adjective and noun before; that is, there exists no node committed to the content *pertinent novelty*(noun phrase).

When pertinent novelty occurs, the pertinent sequence node (NOUN PHRASE in the example above) will be activated but will fail to activate any of the nodes in its domain and will therefore fail to quench. It is this "failure to quench" that signals pertinent novelty and triggers the binding nodes: like content nodes, binding nodes receive input from a sequence node but have a much higher threshold and become activated only following prolonged input from a sequence node that has failed to quench. That is, novel inputs will activate a pertinent sequence node whose failure to quench will activate its connected binding node. As a result, the process of node commitment runs off automatically if the timing nodes for a system have been engaged.

Orienting Reactions: Side Effects of Pertinent Novelty

Besides calling up binding nodes, pertinent novelty triggers orienting reactions that include emotional components (e.g., surprise); autonomic components (e.g., increased skin conductance, cardiac deceleration, and pupil dilation); and behavioral components (e.g., inhibition of ongoing activity) (Neumann, 1987). As discussed below, instances of pertinent novelty such as speech errors often trigger these orienting reactions, but because errors often pass undetected (see below), they cannot be operationally identified with orienting reactions or other measures of surprise, contrary to Baars (1985). Note also that, unlike other theories (e.g., Baars, 1988), the node structure theory generates orienting responses without complicated mismatch mechanisms for comparing representations of an intention with representations of the resulting error.

Examples of Pertinent Novelty and Bottom-Up Binding

I will illustrate the bottom-up binding process first abstractly, and then concretely. Pertinent novelty occurs when an uncommitted node, X, receives conjoint first-order priming from two or more lower level nodes, $A, B, \ldots$, and calls up its sequence node. Because A and $B, \ldots$, normally become self-inhibited soon after activation, spatiotemporal summation of priming from A and $B, \ldots$, fails to reach X's commitment level without outside help. The outside help comes when X's sequence node fails to quench and activates its binding node: The binding node inhibits the relevant self-inhibitory satellites, causing prolonged activation of A and $B, \ldots$, which increases the time available for temporal summation at uncommitted node X and enables X to reach commitment threshold and become activated.

As a more concrete illustration of how binding nodes work, consider the child who knows the concepts *mental* and *practice* but encounters for the first time a pertinent novelty, the expression *mental practice*. That is, there exist the two already-committed parent nodes with inhibitory satellites shown in Figure 4: *mental*(adjective) and *practice*(noun). *Mental*(adjective) is connected to several nodes in the (noun phrase) domain, including committed nodes such as *mental arithmetic*(noun phrase) and uncommitted nodes such as X in Figure 4. The other committed node, *practice*(noun), is also connected to uncommitted node X as well as to perhaps several hundred other nodes, including, say, the committed node *basketball practice*(noun phrase).

Now, only uncommitted node X receives convergent (spatially and temporally summating) priming during the normal period that *mental*(adjective) and *practice*(noun) remain activated, but this convergent priming is too weak to enable activation of X when its triggering mechanism (NOUN PHRASE) is called up and applied. This constitutes an instance of pertinent novelty: NOUN PHRASE will continue its activation unquenched, causing activation of its binding node, NOUN PHRASE (underlined capitals denote binding nodes and square brackets denote the corresponding domain *of the binding node,* so that the domain of NOUN PHRASE is [noun phrase]). NOUN PHRASE now inhibits the self-inhibitory mechanisms for [noun phrase], the domain of inhibitory satellites for all potential noun phrase constituents, including (adjective) and (noun). Consequently, [noun phrase] nodes that are currently undergoing activation—namely, *mental*(adjective) and *practice*(noun)—fail to self-inhibit and so engage in prolonged activation. The resulting temporal and spatial summation provides uncommitted node X with the required boost up to commitment levels of priming, enabling NOUN PHRASE to activate X. Activation of X, in turn, increases the linkage strength of bottom-up connections to X, and enables X eventually to code the content *mental practice*(noun phrase) without engaging the binding node for introducing prolonged first-order bottom-up priming.

CONSCIOUSNESS, NODE COMMITMENT, AND CREATIVITY

The prolonged activation of content nodes that occurs during node commitment corresponds to consciousness under the node structure theory: we become conscious of a concept during the time when the node representing that concept is undergoing prolonged activation. This explains why we normally become conscious of what is new, rather than of what is old or highly familiar; neither priming nor self-inhibited activation of old or automatically activated connections is *per se* sufficient for consciousness: the self-inhibitory process normally shuts off activation after a set period and prevents awareness. It also explains why stimuli that are repeated or presented for prolonged periods drop out of awareness, as in habituation: repeated activation of a node results in satiation, which reduces the degree of priming and the probability of both activation and prolonged activation.

Awareness, Practice, and Level in the Hierarchy

As noted in discussing the practice puzzle, we normally become aware of the higher level aspects of a conversation, but not of the phonetics or phonology of pronunciation. Under the node structure theory, this correlation between consciousness and level of processing is related to the linkage strength of units in the hierarchy: consciousness is usually limited to higher level concepts because pertinent novelty triggers consciousness, and what is novel in sentences is generally not phonemes but higher level concepts (see also Sokolov, 1963). However, linkage strength and level in the hierarchy are not perfectly correlated. For example, adults occasionally learn new words, which approach automaticity at the phonological and lexical levels only after considerable practice. Moreover, concepts at levels much higher than the word can also achieve automaticity, given sufficient practice. Even very high level (supra-sentential) patterns of thought sometimes become so practiced as to be triggered unconsciously (see, e.g., MacKay & Konishi, 1980). Although consciousness *usually* begins at the lexical level, the many clear exceptions to this pattern are readily explained in the theory.

Awareness and Creativity in Language Production

Creativity requires the formation of new connections under the node structure theory, and connection formation invariably gives rise to awareness. However, the awareness puzzle, Part 1, provides what seems to be an exception: the context-sensitive adjustments for about-to-occur speech errors illustrate preprogrammed creativity that does not give rise to awareness. Speakers are unaware of choosing a new but appropriate plural ending after making an error such as *track cowz* instead of *cow tracks;* the original intention to pluralize may be conscious, but not the choice of the appropriate plural, /z/ rather than /s/, when the last segment of the error word is voiced rather than unvoiced. Paradoxical lack of awareness also occurs when speakers produce rule-governed aspects of never-previously-encountered words, for example, adding appropriate plural or verb agreement endings or aspirating unvoiced stops (/p, t, or k/) in word-initial but not in noninitial positions (see MacKay, 1982, for other examples).

Preprogrammed creativity is unconscious under the node structure theory because there exist highly practiced programs for introducing context-sensitive changes without forming new connections at the phonological or phonetic levels (see MacKay, 1982). For example, the program for pluralization consists of a content node in the sentential system that represents the concept *regular plural* and transmits priming to a phonological "archiphoneme" node that nonspecifically represents both s and z, transmitting priming to all of the feature nodes for /s/ and /z/ except those for voicing (i.e., + voice and – voice). Now, activating a word-final segment node that is *voiced,* as in *cow,* will automatically prime /z/ bottom up, and being most primed in its domain, /z/

will become activated, causing production of *cowz*. However, activating a word-final segment node that is unvoiced, as in *track*, will automatically prime /s/ bottom up, and being most primed, /s/ will become activated, giving *tracks*. As a result, producing regular plurals or any other highly practiced context-sensitive accommodation requires neither awareness nor the formation of new connections.

PERTINENT NOVELTY AND ERROR DETECTION

Error detection illustrates a special case of the relation between novelty, awareness, and node commitment in the node structure theory. Note first that errors invariably result in the production of units that are novel *at some level*. For example, *dump seat* misproduced as *sump deat* involves novel lexical units because *sump* and *deat* are nonwords in English. Similarly, *crawl space* misproduced as *crawl srace* involves novel phonological units because syllable-initial *sr* does not occur in English; *Fly the plane and buy the boat* misproduced as *Fly the boat and buy the plane* involves a novel propositional unit because boats do not fly. Similarly, *tool carts* misproduced as *cool tarts* in the intended sentence *They were moving tool carts down the assembly line* involves a novel propositional unit if the speaker lacks a committed node for *They were moving cool tarts down the assembly line*(proposition) (examples from Motley *et al.*, 1983).

Note also that the nodes activated in novel combination in speech errors invariably fall into familiar classes or domains, so that speech errors represent instances of pertinent novelty that can potentially trigger orienting reactions for signaling the occurrence of the error. However, different errors differ in how many connections separate the units produced in error from the new or uncommitted node that they prime, and this "distance" plays a critical role in error detection. Compare the effects of this distance for two phonological trans-position errors (above): *crawl srace* instead of *crawl space*, and *cool tarts* instead of *tool carts* in the intended sentence *They were moving tool carts down the assembly line*. In *crawl space*, no committed node represents *sr*(initial consonant group) for speakers of English, so that when *s*(initial stop) and *r*(initial liquid) are activated in error, first-order bottom-up convergent prim-ing is transmitted immediately (distance 0) to an uncommitted phonological node, thereby triggering binding nodes and orienting reactions, causing output to terminate), and *awareness* (prolonged activation) that enables error detec-tion. Indeed, this rapid detection sequence may explain why phonologically novel errors are so rare in overt speech (see Fromkin, 1971): These errors can be detected so rapidly that speakers can stop speaking and prevent their occurrence before they appear in the surface output (see Levelt, 1984; MacKay, 1988).

However, the theory predicts that error detection will be both less efficient and less likely when many intervening connections separate the uncommitted node from the phonological units produced in error. In the *cool tarts* error, for example, nodes higher in the hierarchy already exist for representing the segments *c*(initial consonant group) and *t*(initial consonant group), the syllables *cool*(stressed syllable) and *tarts*(stressed syllable), and the words *cool*(adjective) and *tarts*(noun). Even *cool tarts*(noun phrase) is likely to exist as an already-committed node, so that the possibility of orienting reactions and error detection at that level is precluded. However, the proposition node *They were moving cool tarts down the assembly line*(proposition) almost certainly does not exist as an already-committed node, so that activating *cool tarts*(noun phrase) in the context *move down the assembly line* could potentially trigger orienting reactions and awareness of the error. However, *cool tarts*(noun phrase) is unlikely to achieve greatest priming in its domain and become activated while the subject is producing the remainder of this sentence because of the number of connections separating *cool tarts*(noun phrase) from its source of first-order priming at the phonological level, so that such an error is likely to pass undetected. More generally, the node structure theory predicts that the probability of error detection will vary with the proximity of the units produced in error to the uncommitted node that they jointly prime. This proximity factor may also contribute to the fact that speakers fail to correct about 40% of all word substitution errors.

It is important to note that *correct* output cannot trigger a similar process for indicating that the output is, in fact, correct. Appropriate or intended-to-be-activated nodes transmit convergent priming to existing higher level nodes that have just been activated and have quenched their activating mechanism, and that therefore cannot trigger surprise, awareness, and detection that the output is, in fact, error-free (which may explain why determining that a response is correct is so difficult; see MacKay, 1987, p. 166). It is also important to note that other-produced errors cannot be detected in the same way as self-produced errors under the node structure theory. For a self-produced error (as in "How many animals of each kind did Moses, I mean, Noah bring on the ark?"), orienting reactions indicating that an error has taken place can be triggered soon after the activation of the wrong node, *Moses*(proper noun). However, there is no similar basis at this level for a listener to detect an *other-produced* error: listeners will be engaged in node commitment regardless of whether the input is correct ("How many animals of each kind did Noah bring on the ark?") or incorrect ("How many animals of each kind did Moses bring on the ark?"). (The reader is referred to MacKay, 1987, p. 166, for a detailed discussion of other differences between detecting self-produced and detecting other-produced errors, e.g., the fact that detecting other-produced errors depends on the size or level of the units involved, whereas detecting self-produced errors does not.)

Error Detection and the Flexibility of Awareness

As already noted, adults *normally* become aware only of higher level concepts (words and above) and *normally* remain unaware of the phonemes making up the words and phrases. However, speech errors can automatically trigger shifts in the level of awareness. Even subphonemic errors such as the slurring of a speech sound can enter consciousness, so that the speaker becomes aware of what sound was slurred, and perhaps even of the higher level (pragmatic) implications of the slur, for example, possible drunkenness and the inadvisability of driving a car (see MacKay, 1988). The reason is that even phonetic errors constitute pertinent novelty that can engage the mechanism for consciousness and connection formation for nodes currently undergoing activation at any level in the system. However, these lower level errors will enter awareness only when lower level systems are being activated, as must invariably occur during self-produced speech, but not necessarily during perception of other-produced speech (see MacKay, 1987, pp. 62–89).

Other Theories of Error Detection

The editor in editor theories (such as e.g., Baars *et al.*, 1975) is a mechanism that "listens to" self-produced internal or external feedback, compares this feedback with the intended output, identifies errors, and then computes corrections by using a duplicate copy of the information originally available to the motor system. As MacKay (1987, pp. 167–168) pointed out, editor theories encounter difficulties in explaining why errors occur at all, why errors sometimes pass unnoticed, why detecting correct responses takes more time than detecting incorrect responses (Rabbitt, Vyas, & Fearnley, 1972), and why detecting self-produced errors differs from detecting other-produced errors, or, more generally, how error detection relates to detection at large. MacKay (1973), Motley, Camden, and Baars (1982) and Motley *et al.* (1983) discussed additional difficulties facing editor theories. The node structure theory avoids all of these difficulties and can also account for the data that have been gathered in support of editor theories. The node structure theory also avoids the pitfalls of the "formulation hypothesis," until recently the main alternative to editor theories (see Motley, Baars, & Camden, 1983). Under the formulation hypothesis, "unacceptable" errors almost never get formulated, because the full range of units for expressing them does not exist. For example, nonword errors such as *bart doard* instead of *dart board* are rare because there are no lexical units representing *bart* and *doard*. As Motley *et al.* (1983) pointed out, the formulation hypothesis fails to explain why errors that are unacceptable at the pragmatic level (e.g, *cool tits* instead of *tool kits*) are so rare in studies of experimentally induced speech errors, why correct responses to these targets exhibit long latencies and increased skin conductance, and why increased skin conductance also accompanies near-miss errors of this sort (e.g., *cool kits* as well as *cool tits*). None of these phenomena present problems for the node structure theory.

AMBIGUITY AND AWARENESS

As MacKay (1988) pointed out, a tripartite distinction between priming, activation, and prolonged activation is needed to account for conscious and unconscious processing in language perception and production. This same tripartite distinction is also required to explain the automatic resolution of ambiguity, sequential awareness in the perception of sentential ambiguity, and semantic blending in the completion of ambiguous sentences.

Automatic Resolution of Ambiguity

The most-primed-wins principle resolves ambiguities on the basis of priming from any type of contextual source (including states of mind; Baars, 1988), and the fact that priming spreads rapidly and in parallel enables large amounts of heterogeneous information arriving either before or after an ambiguous word to quickly resolve ambiguities within 700 milliseconds (Swinney, 1979) or less (MacKay, 1970). Even without context, the most-primed-wins principle disambiguates words on the basis of conceptual frequency (linkage strength) (see MacKay, 1987, p. 135). Finally, the most-primed-wins mechanism explains why we almost invariably resolve ambiguity in an either-or way: we initially comprehend only one meaning of an ambiguous word or sentence (MacKay, 1966, 1970) because only the node receiving the greatest priming in a domain can become activated at any one time.

Sequential Awareness of Ambiguous Alternatives

Whereas both interpretations of ambiguous sentences are primed rapidly, unconsciously, and in parallel, prolonged activation and awareness of the two alternatives is slow and sequential under the node structure theory. When a subject is processing a lexically ambiguous sentence, both of its alternative readings receive unconscious processing (priming) at the same time, but only one alternative meaning at a time becomes conscious. When subjects are instructed to become aware of *both* meanings, as in MacKay and Bever (1967), awareness is sequential: they perceive one meaning after the other. Moreover, the second meaning is perceived relatively slowly: the MacKay and Bever (1967) subjects took a remarkably long time to become aware of both meanings of lexically ambiguous sentences (about 7.5 seconds on the average). The reason is that a nonautomatic process is required to boost the priming of nodes representing the second meaning so that these primed but not activated nodes can become activated under the most-primed-wins principle when the activating mechanism is applied again. More generally, the fact that consciousness requires prolonged activation in the node structure theory predicts that all conscious processing will be relatively slow.

Semantic Blending

The term *semantic blending* refers to an effect of unseen meanings on the completions of ambiguous fragments reported in MacKay (1966, 1969). Examples are *Discussing the problems with the mathematicians in Germany, Oppenheimer grew red in the face* (where the speaker interpreted the fragment to mean "mathematical problems" but not "mathematician problems") and *Claiming the work was done over on the roof, he asked them to do it again* (where the speaker claimed awareness of the meaning "the work was completed over there" but not "the work was redone"). Again, the unseen meaning must have contributed priming that helped determine which nodes for generating the completion received the most priming and became activated under the most-primed-wins principle. A similar semantic blending process may underlie the "atmosphere effects" reported in Motley and Baars (1979) and Motley, Camden, and Baars (1983).

Conclusions

Relations between priming, activation, and prolonged activation in the node structure theory provide a solution to the awareness puzzle: Priming and activation are unconscious, and contextual sources of priming enable preformed programs to become activated, so as to automatically introduce context-sensitive adjustments to an about-to-occur error. However, contextual sources of priming also represent the basic cause of errors, and by introducing such a contextual source of priming, ambiguity causes errors during sentence completion: nodes for both meanings of an ambiguity automatically become primed, even though only one becomes activated and triggers awareness, and priming from nodes representing the unseen meaning directly causes errors such as *After stopping arguing in the court, Wimbleton was perjured, I mean, disqualified,* and indirectly contributes to errors under DAAF.

Explaining the error detectability puzzle is only slightly more complicated: Awareness occurs at lower-than-normal levels following speech errors because errors constitute instances of pertinent novelty that can trigger the mechanisms for prolonged activation (consciousness) and connection formation at any level. However, other-produced errors are detected less often than self-produced errors because lower level errors can trigger prolonged activation (awareness) only when lover level systems are being activated, which invariably occurs when one is *producing* speech, but not necessarily when one is perceiving other-produced speech.

Finally, the node structure theory suggests some interesting reasons for the complexity of the practice puzzle. Four interacting factors in the theory contribute to the complex distribution of naturally occurring speech errors across different levels in an output hierarchy: (1) the fact that phonological nodes tend to have greater prior practice than lexical nodes (so that lexical nodes are more prone to error) but (2) are activated at a faster rate than lexical nodes, thereby becoming *more* prone to error (speed–accuracy trade-off across systems), (3) the fact that lexical nodes have greater connectivity or sources of extraneous priming (which tend to increase the probability of word errors relative to phonological errors); and (4) the fact that lower level nodes in a system are activated at faster rates than higher level nodes *within the same system,* so that they become more prone to error (speed–accuracy trade-off within a system).

ACKNOWLEDGMENTS

The author thanks B. Baars for helpful comments on an earlier version of this chapter. Aspects of this chapter were presented to the Conference on Action, Attention, and Automaticity, held at the Center for Interdisciplinary Research, University of Bielefeld, November 26–30, 1984.

REFERENCES

Anderson, J. R. (1983). *The architecture of cognition.* Cambridge: Harvard University Press.
Baars, B. J. (1980). On eliciting predictable speech errors in the laboratory. In V. A. Fromkin (Ed.), *Errors in linguistic performance: Slips of the tongue, ear, pen, and hand.* New York: Academic Press.
Baars, B. J. (1983). Conscious contents provide the nervous system with coherent global information. In R. J. Davidson, G. E. Scwartz, & D. Shapiro (Eds.), *Consciousness and self-regulation (Vol. 3).* New York: Plenum Press.
Baars, B. J. (1985). Can involuntary slips reveal one's state of mind?—With an addendum on the problem of assessing repression. In M. Toglia & T. M. Shlechter (Eds.), *New directions in cognitive science.* Norwood, NJ: Ablex.
Baars, B. J. (1988). *A cognitive theory of consciousness.* Cambridge: Cambridge University Press.
Baars, B. J., & Motley, M. T. (1976). Spoonerisms as sequencer conflicts: Evidence from artificially elicited speech errors. *American Journal of Psychology, 89,* 467–484.
Baars, B. J., Motley, M. T., & MacKay, D. G. (1975). Output editing for lexical status in artificially elicited slips of the tongue. *Journal of Verbal Learning and Verbal Behavior, 14,* 382–391.
Chomsky, N. (1957). *Syntactic structures.* The Hague: Mouton.
Dell, G. (1980). *Phonological and lexical encoding in speech production: An analysis of naturally occurring and experimentally elicited speech errors.* Unpublished doctoral dissertation, University of Toronto.
Dell, G. S. (1986). A spreading-activation theory of retrieval in sentence production. *Psychological Review, 93,* 283–321.
Eriksen, T. D., & Mattson, M. E. (1981). From words to meaning: A semantic illusion. *Journal of Verbal Learning and Verbal Behavior, 20,* 540–551.
Fairbanks, G., & Guttman, N. (1958). Effects of delayed auditory feedback upon articulation. *Journal of Speech and Hearing Research, 1,* 12–22.
Fromkin, V. A. (1971). The non-anomalous nature of anomalous utterances. *Language, 47,* 27–52.
Garnham, A., Shillcock, R. C., Brown, G. D. A., Mill, A. I. D., & Cutler, A. (1982). Slips of the tongue in the London-Lund corpus of spontaneous conversation. In A. Cutler (Ed.), *Slips of the tongue and language production* (pp. 251–263). Amsterdam: Mouton.
Garrett, M. F. (1980). The limits of accommodation: Arguments for independent processing levels in sentence production. In V. A. Fromkin (Ed.), *Errors in linguistic performance: Slips of the tongue, ear, pen, and hand.* New York: Academic Press.

Gazdar, G. (1981). Unbounded dependencies and coordinate structure. *Linguistic Inquiry, 12,* 155–184.

James, W. (1890). *The principles of psychology.* New York: Holt.

Lashley, K. S. (1951). The problem of serial order in behavior. In L. A. Jeffress (Ed.), *Cerebral mechanisms in behavior.* New York: Wiley.

Levelt, W. J. M. (1984). Spontaneous self-repairs in speech: Processes and representations. In M. P. R. Van den Broecke & A. Cohen (Eds.), *Proceedings of the Tenth International Congress of Phonetic Sciences* (pp. 105–111). Dordrecht: Foris.

MacKay, D. G. (1966). To end ambiguous sentences. *Perception and Psychophysics, 1,* 426–436.

MacKay, D. G. (1969). Effects of ambiguity on stuttering: Towards a theory of speech production at the semantic level. *Kybernetik, 5,* 195–208.

MacKay, D. G. (1970). Mental diplopia: Towards a model of speech perception at the semantic level. In G. D'Arcais & W. J. M. Levelt (Eds.), *Recent advances in psycholinguistics* (pp. 76–100). Amsterdam: North-Holland.

MacKay, D. G. (1971). Stress pre-entry in motor systems. *American Journal of Psychology, 84*(1), 35–51.

MacKay, D. G. (1972). The structure of words and syllables: Evidence from errors in speech. *Cognitive Psychology, 3,* 210–227.

MacKay, D. G. (1973). Complexity in output systems: Evidence from behavioral hybrids. *American Journal of Psychology, 86*(4), 785–806.

MacKay, D. G. (1974). Aspects of the syntax of behavior: Syllable structure and speech rate. *Quarterly Journal of Experimental Psychology, 26,* 642–657.

MacKay, D. G. (1978). Speech errors inside the syllable. In A. Bell & J. B. Hooper (Eds.), *Syllables and segments.* Amsterdam: North-Holland.

MacKay, D. G. (1979). Lexical insertion, inflection and derivation: creative processes in word production. *Journal of Psycholinguistic Research, 8*(5), 477–498.

MacKay, D. G. (1982). The problems of flexibility, fluency, and speed-accuracy trade-off in skilled behavior. *Psychological Review, 89,* 483–506.

MacKay, D. G. (1983). A theory of the representation and enactment of intentions with applications to the problems of creativity, motor equivalence, speech errors, and automaticity in skilled behavior. In R. Magill (Ed.), *Memory and control of action* (pp. 217–230). Amsterdam: North-Holland.

MacKay, D. G. (1985). A theory of the representation, organization, and timing of action with implications for sequencing disorders. In E. A. Roy (Ed.), *Neuropsychological studies of apraxia and related disorders* (pp. 267–308). Amsterdam: North-Holland.

MacKay, D. G. (1987). *The organization of perception and action: A theory for language and other cognitive skills.* New York: Springer.

MacKay, D. G. (1988). Theoretical and empirical relations between perception, action, and cognition. *Perception and Action Report #147,* Center for Interdisciplinary Research, University of Bielefeld, FRG. Also in O. Neumann & W. Prinz (Eds.), (1990), *Relationships between perception and action: Current approaches* (pp. 269–303). Berlin: Springer-Verlag.

MacKay, D. G., & Bever, T. G. (1967). In search of ambiguity. *Perception and Psychophysics, 2,* 193–200.

MacKay, D. G., & Bowman, R. W. (1969). On producing the meaning in sentences. *American Journal of Psychology, 82*(1), 23–39.

MacKay, D. G., & Konishi, T. (1980). Personification and the pronoun problem. In C. Kramarae (Ed.), *The voices and words of women and men.* London: Pergamon Press.

Marcel, A. J. (1983). Conscious and unconscious perception: Experiments on visual masking and word recognition. *Cognitive Psychology, 15,* 1197–1239.

McClelland, J. L., Rumelhart, D. E., & the PDP Research Group. (1986). *Parallel Distributed*

Processing. Explorations in the microstructure of cognition: Vol. 2. Psychological and biological models. Cambridge: MIT Press.

Meringer, R. (1908). *Aus dem Leben der Sprache.* Berlin: Behrs Verlag.

Motley, M. T., & Baars, B. J. (1979). Effects of cognitive set upon laboratory induced verbal (Freudian) slips. *Journal of Speech and Hearing Research, 22,* 421–432.

Motley, M. T., Camden, C., & Baars, B. J. (1982). Covert formulation and editing of anomalies in speech production: Evidence from experimentally elicited slips of the tongue. *Journal of Verbal Learning and Verbal Behavior, 21,* 578–594.

Motley, M. T., Baars, B. J., & Camden, C. T. (1983). Experimental verbal slip studies: A review and an editing model of language encoding. *Communication Monographs, 50,* 79–101.

Motley, M. T., Camden, C., & Baars, B. T. (1983). Polysemantic lexical access: Evidence from laboratory induced double-entendres. *Communication Monographs, 50,* 193–205.

Neumann, O. (1987). Beyond capacity: A functional view of attention. In H. Heuer & A. Sanders (Eds.), *Perspectives on perception and action* (pp. 361–394). Hillsdale, NJ: Erlbaum.

Rabbitt, P. M. A., Vyas, S. M., & Fearnley, S. (1975). Programming sequences of complex responses. In P. M. A. Rabbitt & S. Dormic (Eds.), *Attention and performance* (Vol. 5, pp. 395–317). London: Academic Press.

Reason, J. (1984). Lapses of attention in everyday life. In R. Parasuraman & D. R. Davies (Eds.), *Varieties of attention.* New York: Academic Press.

Shattuck-Hufnagel, S. (1983). Sublexical units and suprasegmental structure in speech production planning. In P. F. MacNeilage (Ed.), *The production of speech* (pp. 109–136). New York: Springer-Verlag.

Sokolov, Y. N. (1963). *Perception and the conditioned reflex.* New York: Macmillan.

Swinney, D. A. (1979). Lexical access during sentence comprehension: (Re)consideration of context effects. *Journal of Verbal Learning and Verbal Behavior, 18,* 645–659.

Treiman, R. (1983). The structure of spoken syllables: Evidence from novel word games. *Cognition, 15,* 49–74.

Wickelgren, W. (1979). *Cognitive psychology.* Englewood Cliffs, NJ: Prentice-Hall.

3

Cognitive Underspecification
Its Variety and Consequences[1]

James T. Reason

If cognitive science is to make a useful contribution to the safety and efficiency of future technological systems, it must be able to offer designers some workable generalizations regarding the information-handling characteristics of a system's human participants (see Card, Moran, & Newell, 1983). This chapter explores the generality of one such approximation:

When cognitive operations are underspecified, they tend to default to contextually appropriate, high-frequency responses.

Exactly what information is missing from a sufficient specification, or which controlling agency fails to provide it, varies with the nature of the cognitive activity being performed. The crucial point is that, notwithstanding these possible *varieties* of underspecification, their *consequences* are remarkably uniform: what emerge are perceptions, words, recollections, thoughts, and actions that recognizably belong to an individual's well-established repertoire for a given situation. Or to put it another way, the more often a cognitive routine achieves a successful outcome in relation to a particular context, the more likely it is to reappear in conditions of incomplete specification.

Frequency biasing gives predictable shape to human errors in a wide

JAMES T. REASON • Department of Psychology, University of Manchester, Manchester M13 9PL, United Kingdom.

[1]Professor Reason's ideas as presented in this chapter are developed in more detail in his recent work *Human Error* (1989).

Experimental Slips and Human Error: Exploring the Architecture of Volition, edited by Bernard J. Baars. Plenum Press, New York, 1992.

variety of activities and situations (see Norman, 1981; Rasmussen, 1982; Reason & Mycielska, 1982). The psychological literature is replete with terms for describing this pervasive error form: *conventionalization* (Bartlett, 1932), *sophisticated guessing* (Solomon & Postman, 1952), *fragment theory* (Neisser, 1967), *response bias* (Broadbent, 1967), *strong associate substitution* (Chapman & Chapman, 1973), *inert stereotype* (Luria, 1973), *banalization* (Timpanaro, 1976), *strong habit intrusions* (Reason, 1979), and *capture errors* (Norman, 1981). But irrespective of whether the consequences are erroneous, this tendency to "gamble" in favor of high-frequency alternatives when control "statements" are imprecise is generally an adaptive strategy for dealing with a world that contains a great deal of recurrence as well as a large measure of uncertainty.

There is a close similarity between the idea of *specification,* as expressed here, and the notion of *description,* as used by Norman and Bobrow (Bobrow & Norman, 1975; Norman & Bobrow, 1979) in relation to memory retrieval. In most essentials, the two concepts are identical. The only difference is that the present account focuses on frequency gambling and elevates this result of imprecise characterization to the status of a generalization. Although Norman and Bobrow restricted themselves to memory retrieval, the following comment could be taken as an invitation to pursue a more general enquiry: "The idea that the specification of information might vary along a dimension from vague to unique can be applied to a number of different aspects of human behavior" (Norman & Bobrow, 1979, p. 108).

SOME GENERAL ASSUMPTIONS REGARDING COGNITIVE CONTROL

In order to give an adequate account of underspecification, it is necessary to begin with some broad assumptions regarding the mechanism of cognitive control. Although no single agreed-upon model yet exists, the renewal of interest over the past decade in the cognitive psychology of everyday life, and especially in naturally occurring slips, lapses, and mistakes, has yielded a number of global theories that seek to describe, in very general terms, the processes involved both in the guidance of correct performance and in the production of relatively systematic error forms (see Baars, 1983; Norman, 1981; Norman & Shallice, 1980; Rasmussen, 1982; Reason, 1979, 1984a,b; Reason & Mycielska, 1982; Woods, 1984). Unlike the more restricted models derived from laboratory data, these broad-brush theories of action are complementary rather than competing accounts of cognitive executive processes. Because, in any case, the available data are not adequate to test between them, it is more useful to focus on their points of agreement than to pursue the more conventional path of evaluation.

Though idiosyncratic in its perspective and terminology, the following list attempts to signpost some of these areas of common ground.

1. The cognitive system is extremely good at modeling and internalizing the useful regularities of the past and then reapplying them whenever their

"calling conditions" are supplied by intentional activity or by the environment. The minutiae of mental life are governed by a vast community of specialized processors (schemata), each an "expert" on some recurrent aspect of the world, and each operating over brief time spans in response to very specific triggering conditions (activators). This schematic control mode can process familiar information rapidly, in parallel, and without conscious effort. There are no known limits either to the number of schemata that may be stored, or to the duration of their retention. By itself, however, this automatic mode is relatively ineffective in the face of change.

2. In contrast, the *attentional control mode*—closely identified with working memory and consciousness—is limited, sequential, slow, effortful, and difficult to sustain for more than brief periods. It can be thought of as a highly restricted workspace into which the products of parallel search processes (carried out by the schematic mode) are delivered, and within which powerful computational operators (subsumed under the general heading of *inference*) are brought to bear in a largely voluntary and conscious manner. These resource limitations confer the important benefit of selectivity because several high-level activities are potentially available to the conscious workspace at any one time.

3. Unlike the schematic mode, these higher levels of the control system are freed from the immediate constraints of time and place. Their main concerns are with setting goals, selecting the means to achieve them, monitoring progress toward these objectives, and detecting and recovering errors. The attentional mode is essential to dealing with novelty and to coping with the unexpected disruption of plans.

4. Cognitive processes receive their guidance from a complex interaction between the attentional and schematic modes. The former specifies the strategic direction and redirection of action (both internal and external), and the latter provides the fine-grained tactical control.

5. The term *schema(ta)* is used here to embrace all stored knowledge "packages," irrespective of their sphere of operation (i.e., perception, action, language, memory retrieval, thought, judgment, etc.). Schemata possess two closely related components: they embody generic or prototypical knowledge regarding specific aspects of the world, and they constitute a set of preprogrammed instructions for generating particular actions, or words, that are available to conscious awareness.

6. Schemata require a certain threshold level of activation to call them into operation. The various sources of this activation can be divided into two broad classes: specific and general activators (see Figure 1).

7. *Specific activators* bring a given schema into play at a particular time. Of these activators, intentional activity is clearly the most important. Plans constitute "descriptions" of intended actions. For adults, these descriptions usually comprise a set of brief jottings on the mental scratch pad (e.g., "Go to the post office and buy some stamps"). There is no need to fill in the "small print" of each detailed operation; these low-level control statements are already present within the constituent schemata. The more frequently a par-

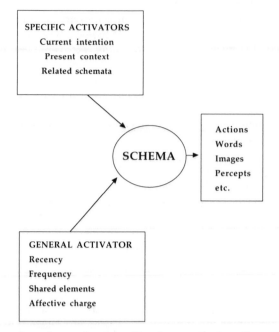

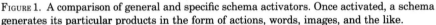

FIGURE 1. A comparison of general and specific schema activators. Once activated, a schema generates its particular products in the form of actions, words, images, and the like.

ticular set of actions is performed, the less detailed are the descriptions that need to be provided by the higher levels. But this steady devolution of control to schemata carries a penalty. To change an established routine of action or thought requires a positive intervention by the attentional control mode. The omission of this intervention in moments of preoccupation or distraction is the commonest cause of absentminded slips of action (Reason, 1979).

8. *General activators* provide background activation to schemata, irrespective of the current intentional state. Of these, frequency of prior use is probably the most influential. The more often a particular schema is put to work, the less it requires in the way of intentional activation. Quite often, contextual cuing is all that is needed to trigger it, particularly in very familiar environments. The issue of priming by active schemata possessing shared elements will be considered in detail at a later point.

THE VARIETIES OF UNDERSPECIFICATION

Correct performance in any sphere of cognitive activity is achieved by activating the right schemata in the right order at the right time. Cognitive control therefore hinges critically on the retrieval of these knowledge "packages" from long-term memory. Some of the necessary calling conditions are supplied by intentions (usually via prospective memory), others by environmental signals, and yet others by descriptions passed on by task-linked schemata (see Bobrow & Norman, 1975). Much of the time, these various calling conditions are sufficient to identify the appropriate schemata. Occasionally, however, these descriptions are incomplete or ambiguous. The usual consequence is that a number of partially matched schemata are activated. Because both a given set of effectors and the limited conscious workspace can respond to or accommodate only one schema at a time, some selection has to be made from among these partially matched "candidates." This selection is biased to favor high-frequency (HF) candidates.

These two search processes—(1) the matching of calling conditions (activators) to stored schema attributes and (2) frequency gambling—are assumed to operate in a parallel, distributed, and largely automatic fashion. They constitute the computational primitives of the schema retrieval system. In contrast, the conscious, inferential aspects of schema search function in a predominantly serial manner. Here, speed, effortlessness, and unlimited resources are sacrificed in order to achieve selectivity, intentional coherence, and a wide variety of powerful computational procedures. It is only the serial component of this dual architecture system that can override the default options selected by parallel processing. The conscious workspace can reject an HF candidate and reinstate the parallel search by generating a revised set of calling conditions.

As indicated earlier, different types of cognitive activity involve different kinds of underspecification. Some of the more obvious of these distinctions are summarized in Table 1. Excluded from this table, though relevant to the broader discussion, is any mention of the chronic underspecification brought about by brain damage or pathology (see Chapman & Chapman, 1973; Luria, 1973; B. Milner, personal communication, 1986).

WHAT IS MEANT BY "CONTEXTUALLY APPROPRIATE"?

Specifications Are Context-Dependent

As Bobrow and Norman (1975) made clear, descriptions are *context-dependent:* "We suggest that descriptions are normally formed to be unambiguous within the context in which they were first used. That is, a description defines a memory schema relative to a context" (p. 133).

Even the most ill-formed or high-flown intention must boil down to a selection of ways and means if it is to be considered at all seriously. Sooner or later, the planner must move down the abstraction hierarchy (Rasmussen, 1982) from a vague statement of some desired future state to a detailed review of possible resources and situations. And as soon as that occurs, the intentional activity becomes context-dependent. When a context is identified, the range of possible schema candidates is greatly restricted. This is indicated in Figure 2 by the contextual frame. Whenever the individual moves from one physical

TABLE 1
Types of Cognitive Underspecification

Domain	Type of underspecification	Consequences
Perception	Attenuated, ambiguous, or incomplete sensory data.	False recognition of contextually HF[a] object or event.
Action	Absence of positive attentional involvement at branch point in an action sequence that is required to deviate from habitual practice.	Unintended action taking the form of a contextually typical HF routine.
Memory	When automatic retrieval of known item fails, a conscious search is conducted with very fragmentary retrieval cues.	Recurrent retrieval of wrong item, which shares features with target, and which is more frequent than target in the search context.
Category generation	Only the semantic category is specified, and subjects are required to output as many exemplars as they can in a given period.	Output order corresponds closely to frequency of item encounter. HF items are emitted first.
Semantic knowledge retrieval	Underspecification may arise from either incomplete calling conditions or incomplete domain knowledge, or both. These two possibilities are equivalent.	Elicitation of the most commonly encountered items within the semantic context of search.
Planning, problem solving, decision making, design	Underspecification is intrinsic in these activities. Sources: (1) uncertainty about the future; (2) inadequate knowledge of effects and side effects of planned actions; (3) resource limitations on serial processing; (4) "keyhole" view of the problem space as a whole; and (5) imperfect understanding of statistical and logical principles.	A strong tendency to "fight the last war," i.e., to apply proven, HF solutions to novel problems.

[a]HF = high frequency.

location to another, either in action or in thought, the schemata within the contextual frame change accordingly. Comparatively little in the way of additional specification is needed to retrieve the appropriate schemata once this frame has been established.

Each schema was originally acquired in relation to a particular context. That contextual information forms an intrinsic part of the schema's "knowledge package." Any subsequent encounter with that context will serve to raise

Schema candidates

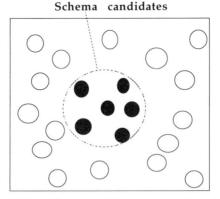

FIGURE 2. An illustration of how schema candidates are preselected according to either a physical or semantic contextual framework. Merely entering a context will cause a context-related schema to be activated. The black circles indicate schemata within the context that partially match the current calling conditions.

the schema's level of activation; thus, another way of looking at the idea of a contextual frame is as a cognate set of currently active schemata.

Though individual schemata are context-dependent, the cognitive system as a whole is not context-bound. As indicated earlier, one of the central properties of the attentional control mode is its power to transcend these immediate contextual constraints. But this demands processing resources that are not always available.

Contexts Are Semantic as well as Physical Locations

The idea of a semantic context is not new. The notion was clearly expressed by Hotopf (1980) in relation to his analysis of whole-word slips of the tongue:

> If the word we intend to speak is highly associated with another word that meets the contextual constraints operating within the utterance, then, given a certain time limit, that other word may be produced instead. The error word needs to be a word of high frequency or one whose threshold for production is lowered by other events occurring at the same time for it to have the necessary short latency in response. (p. 106)

Some recent studies (Reason, 1986), using phonological priming to manipulate "thresholds of production," provided strong evidence for the existence of semantic contextual constraints, at least in one rather specific verbal domain. As is well known to children, same-sound priming can be a very effective way of tricking people into producing what is immediately recognized as the wrong answer to a simple question. A well-known instance of these word games is the "oak–yolk" effect (see Kimble & Perlmuter, 1970):

Q. What do we call the tree that grows from acorns?
A. Oak.
Q. What do we call a funny story?
A. Joke.
Q. What sound does a frog make?
A. Croak.
Q. Who is Pepsi's major competitor?
A. Coke.
Q. What is another word for cape?
A. Cloak.
Q. What do you call the white of an egg?
A. Yolk *(sic!)*.

The first study investigated the effects of varying the number of "oak–yolk" primes on the naming of the white of an egg. A total of 80 undergraduate subjects were used, divided into four groups of 20. Each subject was questioned individually, and no testing session lasted more than about three minutes. To establish a baseline, one group was simply asked the key question: "What do you call the white of an egg?" (zero primes). The remaining groups received either one, three, or five "oak–yolk" primes (selected randomly from the set of primes listed above) before being asked to name the white of an egg. The subjects were instructed to respond as quickly as possible, with the first word that came to mind, and they were told that single-word answers were needed throughout. Only the responses to the key question were recorded, and their relative proportions are shown in Figure 3.

These results confirmed the potency of the "oak–yolk" priming effect and showed that erroneous "yolk" answers increased with the number of prior rhyme primes. The frequency of primes, as well as the presence of common phonological elements, clearly played an important part in determining the likelihood of a "yolk" response. This is in general agreement with the schema-activating assumptions shown in Figure 1.

A question of special interest was: Can phonological priming spread into other "egg subdomains"? Figure 4 shows the relevant egg subdomains.

In a further study, involving three groups of 20 students, the subjects received either three, five, or seven "shell" primes and were asked the same key question ("What do you call the white of an egg?"). These primes consisted of a series of simple questions eliciting monosyllabic answers rhyming with "shell" (e.g., "What rings in a belfry and on a bicycle?" and "From what did people once draw water?" and "The Swiss folk hero that shot an apple off his son's head was called William ... ?").

The most important finding was that only 2 of the 60 subjects produced a "shell" response to the key question (see Figure 5). The results are consistent to the cooked-egg subdomain (as directed by the semantics of the key question). Within that contextual frame, the "bell–shell" priming appears to have activated the other two monosyllabic and readily available responses: "white" and "yolk." The "don't know" responses were probably made by people who realized

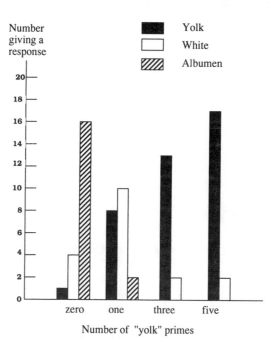

FIGURE 3. Naming the white of an egg: Incremental "oak-yolk" priming. These data show the effect of increasing the numbers of prior "oak-rhyming" primes on the likelihood of responding with "yolk" when asked, "What is the white of an egg?"

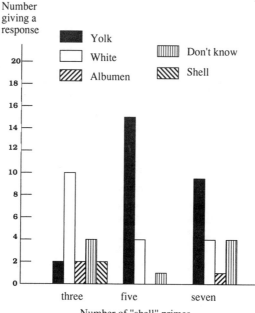

FIGURE 4. Naming the white of an egg: Incremental "bell-shell" priming. These data show that "bell-rhyming" primes, even in fairly large numbers, hardly ever elicit a "shell" response to the question "What is the white of an egg?"

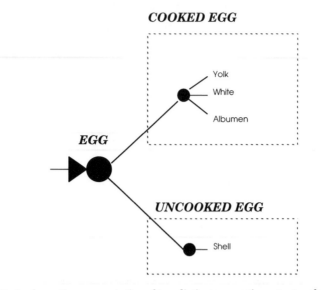

FIGURE 5. A schematic representation of two distinct semantic contexts relating to the parts of an egg: cooked and uncooked.

that there was a technical term for the white of an egg, but who either did not know it or could not then retrieve it.

A symmetrical way of testing the relative impermeability of the contextual frame was to prime "yolk" and to direct the semantics of the key question not to the white of an egg, but to the outside of an egg. In the fourth study, two groups of 10 students were used. One group was simply asked the question "What do you call the outside of an egg?" The other group was asked the same question after first receiving five "oak–yolk" primes. The results were very clear-cut. All the subjects in both groups produced the correct "shell" answer.

Taken as a whole, the results of these three studies provided a clear demonstration of (1) the incremental potency of phonological or "shared-element" priming within the appropriate semantic context and (2) the relative absence of any spillover of these priming effects from one contextual frame to another. This finding suggests that, although prior priming may initially activate all words in the mental lexicon sharing the same phonetic and structural characteristics, these effects are "delivered" to only a very specific semantic context by the final key question. This finding is also borne out by the absence of any interference from one priming question to the nest: each addressed a different semantic context, and none had any high-frequency competitors sharing common elements.

Preliminary results from a similar children's word game (Q. How do you pronounce the letters S-H-O-P? A. Shop. Q. What do you do at a green light? A. Stop) indicate that erroneous antonymic reversals are readily induced by only one phonological prime. This finding is consistent with the high incidence of antonymic reversals in naturally occurring slips of the tongue (Freud, 1901/1966; Hotopf, 1980; Meringer, 1908), and suggests that the boundaries imposed by different semantic categories are likely to differ in their permeability to priming effects. The word-game paradigm offers a promising way of mapping out these various semantic boundaries, particularly when it is enhanced by latency data lacking in the present studies.

DEMONSTRATIONS OF FREQUENCY GAMBLING

The purpose of this section is to present sufficient evidence to demonstrate the pervasiveness of frequency gambling in varied conditions of cognitive underspecification. The emphasis here is on the responses, rather than on the eliciting conditions.

Word Identification

The large literature dealing with the recognition of words presented for very brief durations or in noise has been discussed elsewhere (see Broadbent, 1967; Catlin, 1969; Howes & Solomon, 1951; Nakatani, 1973; Neisser, 1967; Newbigging, 1961; Pollack, Rubinstein, & Decker, 1960; Savin, 1963; Solomon & Postman, 1952; Spence, 1963). A number of theories have been advanced to explain the *word-frequency effect,* that is, the repeated finding that common words are more readily recognized than infrequent ones when presentation is rapid or attenuated. For our present purposes, Newbigging (1961) provided a useful summary statement:

> when a word is presented at a short duration, only a few letters or a fragment of the word are seen by the subject. This fragment may be common to a number of words, and if the subject is instructed to guess the word presented he will respond with the word of the greatest frequency of occurrence (response strength) which incorporates the fragment. (p. 125; see also Neisser's discussion of fragment theory, 1967, pp. 115–118)

An important corollary to this view is that seen fragments of low-frequency words are liable to be erroneously perceived as high-frequency words sharing the same features. Both phenomena are in keeping with the cognitive underspecification generalization.

The Recall of Verbal List Items

The word-frequency effect also appears in the recall of word lists. Commonly occurring words tend to have a higher probability of recall than less frequent words. Likewise, HF words are more common as intrusions when the subject is attempting to recall a previously presented list. (See Gregg, 1976, for an excellent review of this and the related "frequency paradox" literature.)

Slips of Action

Diary studies of naturally occurring slips of action (see Reason, 1984a,b,c; Reason & Mycielska, 1972) reveal that they are most likely to occur during the performance of highly automatized tasks in very familiar surroundings, while one is experiencing some form of attentional "capture" (preoccupation or distraction). A large proportion of these slips (40% in one study) took the form of well-organized action sequences that were judged by their makers to belong to some other task or activity, not then intended. These "other activities" were rated as being recently and frequently executed, and as sharing similar location, movements, and objects with the intended actions. In summary, the largest single category of action slips was strong habit intrusion, possessing structural or contextual elements in common with the planned actions.

Recurrent Intrusions in Blocked Memory Searches

Freud (1901/1966) noted that, when we are laboriously searching memory for a known name or word whose retrieval is temporarily blocked (the target), other items, "although immediately recognized as false, nevertheless obtrude themselves with great tenacity" (p. 15). In a recent diary study, Reason and Lucas (1984) investigated the hypothesis that these recurrent intruders in tip-of-the-tongue states (TOTs) are analogous to the strong habit intrusions observed in action slips.

Sixteen volunteers kept "extended" diaries of their resolved TOT states over a period of four weeks. The study yielded 40 resolved TOTs. Twenty-eight of these (70%) involved the presence of recurrent intruders—recognizably wrong names or words that continued to block access to the target during deliberate search periods.

These recurrent intruders were judged by the diarists as being more frequently and recently used than both the related targets and the nonrecurrent intermediate solutions. The diarists also rated recurrent intermediates as being more closely associated with the target than other intermediates generated during that particular TOT state. In 50% of the TOT states with recurrent intruders, the blocking word or name was ranked higher than the target for frequency and recency in the context of the search. In 77% of the blocked TOTs, the recurrent blocker was ranked higher than the target on either frequency or recency, or both. Comparisons of these recurrent intruders with the eventually retrieved target revealed that they shared common phonological, contextual, and semantic features.

The data are consistent with the view that recurrent intruders emerge in TOT states when the initial fragmentary retrieval cues are sufficient to locate the context of the sought-for item, but not sufficient to provide a unique specification for it. Recurrent intruders appear to be high-frequency names or word within this context.

Category Generation

In continuous recall tasks, the only specification offered to subjects is the name of a semantic category. They are then asked to generate as many category exemplars as possible (usually within a set time period) without repetition.

Beginning with Bousfield and Barclay (1950), several investigators have found substantial correlations between the dominance of a particular item (the number of times a given exemplar is generated by a group of individuals) and its average position in the output order. The most popular exemplars appear earliest. In the case of Bousfield and Barclay's categories, these correlations ranged between >97 and >88. In a later study involving 56 semantic categories, Battig and Montague (1969) obtained dominance/output order correlations (for the Maryland sample, $N = 270$) ranging between .252 and .857 down to a frequency of five or more types. When these correlations are averaged by means of Fisher's z transformations, the mean dominance–order correlation is .64. When the same correlations are computed for only the 20 most dominant types in each category, this mean value rises to .76. Such findings are in keeping with the prediction of the spew hypotheses (Underwood & Schulz, 1960), of Zipf's law (Zipf, 1945, 1949), and of Hull's habit strength postulate (see Bousfield & Barclay, 1950).

The dominance of a particular exemplar within a semantic context (e.g., *dog* within the category "four-footed animals") reflects its "salience-in-the-world" in that particular subculture. This, in turn, is likely to correspond to its frequency of encounter by the subculture as a whole. The dominance orders of categories whose types are subject to the influences of fashion or location vary according to time and place. Thus, when American college students of a generation ago were asked to produce exemplars of "a type of dance," the first eight types in the dominance order were waltz, frug, twist, fox-trot, cha-cha, monkey, and jerk (Battig & Montague, 1969). It is doubtful whether many, or even any, of these types would appear high in a contemporary listing. The dominance orders of other categories (e.g., precious stones, units of time, relatives, and metals), being universals, are extremely stable across groups within the same broad culture.

In a category generation study by Reason (1984c), the relationship between output order and frequency of encounter was assessed directly, rather than via dominance assumptions. Different groups of undergraduates were each asked to produce up to 20 exemplars of nine categories, varying in their degree of search specification. The data were collected in individual interviews, lasting about 30 minutes. After they had generated their items, the subjects were asked to make metacognitive ratings, on 1–7 scales, of the following features of each exemplar (fed back to them in random order): recency of encounter (REC), frequency of encounter (FOE), feeling of knowing about the item (FOK), strength of affect (AFF), and effort required to elicit the item (EFF).

The product–moment correlations between the output order and the average ratings for each group are shown in Table 2, and these clearly demonstrate that items produced early in the output sequence are judged to be more recent, more frequent, more known about, and more affectively charged than those produced later. These data provide strong support for the assertion that deliberately underspecified memory search causes the most activated schema to be called to mind first. Although these correlations do not provide unambiguous evidence for the primacy of frequency, it is not unreasonable to assume that factors like recency, knowledge, and affective tone are heavily dependent on the number of times a particular item has been encountered in the past (see also Matlin, Stang, Gawron, Steedman, & Derby, 1979).

There was also a moderate to good correspondence between the number of occurrences of an item in a subject group (dominance) and its mean serial position. These rank-order correlations are shown in Table 3. They confirm earlier findings (Battig & Montague, 1969; Bousfield & Barclay, 1950), and indicate that items that come early in the output order not only receive high metacognitive ratings but are also the most popular exemplars.

The close relationship between dominance and output order raises the question of whether the subjects made their metacognitive ratings simply on the basis of general impressions of an item's "salience-in-the-world." In order to investigate this possibility, it was necessary to use a category with zero dominance, that is, one in which each item produced by a member of the group was unique to that individual. A class of 76 first-year undergraduates, then in their second week of university, were asked to write down the names of 10

TABLE 2
Product–Moment Correlations with Output Order[a]

Category	N	REC	FOE	FOK	AFF	EFF
1. Cities of the world	(20)	−.69	−.75	−.79	−.75	+
2. Cities beginning with B	(20)	−.59	−.47	−.40	−.25	+
3. Most populous cities	(20)	−.82	−.85	−.81	−.69	+
4. Famous people, living or dead	(11)	−.44	−.67	−.52	−.45	+
5. Political figures	(10)	−.79	−.69	−.78	−.60	+
6. Best actors/actresses	(10)	−.48	−.69	−.55	−.56	+
7. Any supermarket items	(20)	−.74	−.81	−.63	−.58	+
8. Fruit and vegetables	(20)	−.64	−.57	−.50	+.13	+
9. Tinned foods	(20)	−.90	−.84	−.79	+.71	+
Average coefficients (via z transformations)			−.71	−.73	−.66	−

[a]Negative correlations indicate that the highest mean ratings were associated with the earliest items in the output order.

TABLE 3
Rank-Order Correlations between Item Dominance and
Mean Serial Position in the Output Order

Categories of freedom[a]	Spearman's rho	Degrees of freedom
1. Cities of the world	−.79	7
2. Cities beginning with *B*	−.89	7
3. Most populous cities	−.56	8
4. Famous people, living or dead	−1.0	1
5. Political figures	−.68	5
6. Best actors/actresses	−.60	2
7. Any supermarket items	−.52	5
8. Fruit and vegetables	−.64	5
9. Tinned foods	−.42	9

[a]To be included in this analysis, an item had to be given by five or more people.

people whom they had known before coming to Manchester, and who were not currently present in the group. Then, they rated each person (on 1–7 scales) for (1) frequency of prior encounter and (2) degree of liking. The group mean intercorrelations between serial position and the frequency and liking ratings were all better than .95. This finding indicated that people are capable of making metacognitive salience rating without resort to some common cultural referent, and it provided some indirect validation of the frequency and other judgments obtained in the earlier study.

"Educated" and "Ignorant" Guessing in Impoverished Knowledge Domains

A cognitive activity in which it is possible to vary both the specificity of the calling conditions and the adequacy of the stored schemata is that of answering general knowledge questions. Given some approximate idea of how much (or how little) information a group of individuals has about a particular knowledge domain, and providing the questions are posed in a way that encourages guessing, the answers obtained tend to be highly predictable. For example, when a group of British undergraduates were asked to identify the source of the quotation "The lamps are going out all over Europe; we shall not see them lit again in our lifetime" (answer: Sir Edward Grey, British Foreign Secretary, at dusk on August 3, 1914), over 80% of them confidently attributed it to Winston Churchill. Nevill Chamberlain and Franklin D. Roosevelt also received a few mentions. None identified the correct source (Reason, Horrocks, & Bailey, 1986).

Aside from the fact that Sir Edward Grey is now an obscure figure, it is not difficult to see why this eerily familiar quotation was so consistently misattributed. The topic and style of the quote point to a statesman. The language is English English. And the sense locates it as being said on the eve or during the early days of world war. For contemporary psychology undergraduates, with limited historical backgrounds, this probably means World War II (i.e., the remote past), and within the category "English-speaking statement of the 1939–1940 era," Winston Churchill is undoubtedly a megastar. In short, the context of the quotation identifies a very limited number of "candidates" (largely because of ignorance), among whom references to one in particular, Churchill, have been encountered very frequently indeed by this particular subject group.

Clearly, frequency gambling is not the only strategy involved in retrieving knowledge items, even from relatively impoverished domains. The results of a memory search will also depend on identifying and matching the appropriate calling conditions. Inferential activities, in which conscious problem solving is applied to search-relevant knowledge, play a major part in knowledge retrieval when the answer to a particular question is not matched automatically.

Some evidence that other search mechanisms can moderate frequency gambling was obtained when 126 psychology students were asked to identify the source of the quotation "The buck stops here." Sixty-three percent of the subjects correctly identified the source as an American president, and these attributions were compared with the dominance gradient (probability of recall of U.S. presidents in five minutes) obtained from the same group of undergraduates on an earlier occasion. These comparisons are displayed in Figure 6. Mean frequency-of-encounter ratings (FOE) for each president were also obtained from the same subjects. They were given a list of 39 U.S. Presidents in random order and were asked to rate FOE on a 1–7 scale, where 1 = hardly encountered at all, and 7 = encountered very frequently indeed. "Encounter," in this context, was by any means: reading about, hearing about, thinking about, media contact, and so on. The correlation between the mean FOE ratings and p(recall) was .93 (21 df).

The data revealed a substantial degree of frequency gambling: the first five Presidents on the dominance gradient received 80% of the attributions. But frequency gambling alone would have produced a pattern of attributions that mirrored the dominance gradient exactly. This was not the case. The modal attribution was Richard Nixon: fourth in rank for both p(recall) and FOE. Subsequent questioning indicated that the inferential sequence went something like this: "The word *buck* suggests American. It has to be a famous American—probably a president. What presidents do I know? Reagan? Doesn't fit somehow. Kennedy? No. Carter? I don't think so. Nixon? Yes, it could have been Nixon. He was mixed up in some shady deals." Interestingly, many subjects equated *buck* with *dollar* rather than *responsibility*. It seems that some of them interpreted the quotation as meaning that the speaker took bribes or a "piece of the action." No matter how curious their reasoning, the fact that they reasoned at all shows that there was more involved in the attribution process than frequency gambling alone.

The more people know about a particular topic, the less likely it is that

probability

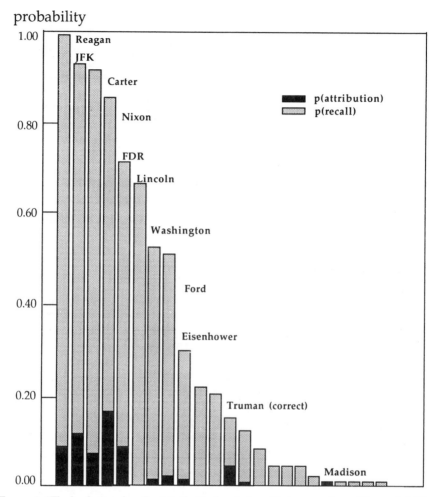

FIGURE 6. "The buck stops here": p(attribution) and p(recall). A comparison of the probability of recall of American presidents by British undergraduates with the probability of their attributing the source of the quotation "The buck stops here." The labeled bars identify presidents for whom attribution data was collected. It is suggested that the displayed attributions show a subtle interaction of frequency and similarity biases.

their answers will reveal the influence of frequency gambling. This notion was tested for the U.S. president domain by means of multiple-choice quotation questions. A questionnaire was administered to 95 psychology undergraduates (Reason *et al.*, 1986). The first part involved a recognition test in which the subjects were required to identify the names of 39 presidents among 78 eminent American contemporaries. The recognition score (corrected for false positives) was taken as a rough indication of domain knowledge. The second part contained four presidential quotations (chosen to promote guessing rather than direct identification), and for each one, the subjects were required to make an attribution from among eight presidents (one of whom was the true source). Each of the presidential choices had a frequency score, obtained from the mean FOE ratings described earlier. Two scores were derived for each subject: a knowledge score (from the recognition test) and a frequency-gambling score (obtained by summing the frequency values of their presidential selections). The correlation between these two scores was $-.348$ (93 df; $p <$ .001). The hypothesis was thus supported, even though the average recognition score (mean = 9.88; range 3–30) lay well toward the "ignorant" end of any notional expertise dimension.

The Francis and Kucera (1982) frequency counts for presidential names correlated well with (1) FOE ratings; (2) p(recall) and p(recognition) for British students; and (3) p(recall) for American undergraduates (Roediger & Crowder, 1976). Only 23 presidents were used in this analysis; those sharing the same name (Harrison, Adams, Johnson, etc.), were excluded.

STRESS AND UNDERSPECIFICATION

A common reaction to many types of stress is the tendency to restrict attention to a limited number of previously reliable and frequently consulted sources of information (Davis, 1945; Hockey & Hamilton, 1970; Hockey, 1973). On the output side, there is an increased routinization of performance; that is, stressed behavior is characterized by the overuse of the more automatic parts of the response repertoire for a given situation.

Another way of expressing these effects is to say that stressors induce cognitive underspecification. The precise nature of this underspecification varies from situation to situation, but its origins appear to lie in the reduced flexibility of the resource-limited attentional control mode. As a result, the selection of both inputs and responses is largely governed by contextually appropriate, high-frequency schemata.

CONCLUDING REMARKS

Various categories of evidence have been assembled to support the generalization that human cognition is biased to select contextually appropriate, high-frequency responses in conditions of underspecification. There is little new in this assertion (see Thorndike, 1911). What is perhaps more unusual is that the evidence has been drawn from a wide range of cognitive activities.

Howell (1973) offered two reasons why the general significance of frequency in cognition has been largely unappreciated. The first is that the majority of investigators most interested in frequency have preferred not to deal in cognitive concepts. The second is that "frequency has become tied to the particular vehicle by which it is conveyed (e.g., words, numbers, lights, etc.) and the particular paradigm in which it occurs (e.g., paired-associate learning, decision-making, information transmission)" (p. 44).

The revival of the schema concept in the mid-1970s created a theoretical climate in which it is now possible to regard frequency in a less paradigm-bound fashion. Common to the schema concept, in all its many contemporary guises (scripts, frames, personae, etc.), is the notion of high-level knowledge structures that contain informational "slots" or variables. Each slot will accept information only of a particular kind. When external sources fail to provide data to fill them, they take on "default assignments," where these are likely to be the most frequent (or stereotypical) instances in that context.

Inevitably, frequency is intimately bound up with many other processing and representational factors, of which "connectedness" is probably the most significant. How can we be sure that it is frequency and not connectedness that determines these default assignments? The short answer is that we probably can never be certain, and that it probably does not matter. Frequency and connectedness are inextricably linked. The more often a particular object or event is encountered, the more opportunity it has to form episodic and semantic linkages with other items. Just as all roads lead to Rome, so all—or nearly all—associative connections within a given context are likely to lead to the most frequently used schema. Such a view is implicit in recent computer models of parallel distributed processing (see McClelland & Rumelhart, 1985; Norman, 1985). But irrespective of whether it is frequency logging or connectional weighting that is the more fundamental factor, the functional consequences are likely to be the same.

In recent years, strong cases have been made for the largely automatic encoding of event frequency (Hasher & Zacks, 1983), and for its privileged analogue representation of memory (Hintzman, Nozawa, & Irmscher, 1982). These observations prompt the question: If frequency information is so special, what is it good for? This chapter has attempted to provide one very general answer. It has also attempted to show that systematic error forms are rooted in those things at which human cognition excels. But useful properties tend to get overexploited; as Crocker (1981) neatly put it, "Like all gamblers, cognitive gamblers sometimes lose."

References

Baars, B. J. (1983). Conscious contents provide the nervous system with coherent global information. In R. Davidson, G. Schwartz, & D. Shapiro (Eds.), *Consciousness and self-regulation* (Vol. 3). New York: Plenum Press.

Bartlett, F. J. (1932). *Remembering*. Cambridge: Cambridge University Press.

Battig, W. F., & Montague, W. E. (1969). Category norms for verbal items in 56 categories: A replication and extension of the Connecticut category norms. *Journal of Experimental Psychology Monograph, 80*, 1–46.

Bobrow, D. G., & Norman, D. A. (1975). Some principles of memory schemata. In D. Bobrow & A. Collins (Eds.), *Representation and understanding: Studies in cognitive science*, New York: Academic Press.

Bousfield, W. A., & Barclay, W. D. (1950). The relationship between order and frequency of occurrence of restricted associative responses. *Journal of Experimental Psychology, 40*, 643–647.

Broadbent, D. E. (1967). Word-frequency effect and response bias. *Psychological Review, 74*, 1–15.

Card, S. K., Moran, T. P., & Newell, A. (1983). *The psychology of human-computer interaction.* Hillsdale, NJ: Erlbaum.

Catlin, J. (1969). On the word-frequency effect. *Psychological Review, 76*, 504–506.

Chapman, L. J., & Chapman, J. P. (1973). *Disordered thought in schizophrenia.* Englewood Cliffs, NJ: Prentice-Hall.

Davis, R. (1945). *Pilot error.* London: Her Majesty's Stationery Office.

Francis, W. N., & Kucera, H. (1982). *Frequency analysis of English usage.* Boston: Houghton Mifflin.

Freud, S. (1901/1966). *The psychopathology of everyday life* (A. Tyson, Trans.). London: Benn.

Gregg, V. (1976). Word frequency, recognition and recall. In J. Brown (Ed.), *Recall and recognition.* London: Wiley.

Hockey, G. R. J. (1973). Changes in information selection patterns in multisource monitoring as a function of induced arousal shifts. *Journal of Experimental Psychology, 101*, 35–42.

Hockey, G. R. J., & Hamilton, P. (1970). Arousal and information selection in short-term memory. *Nature, 226*, 866–867.

Hotopf, W. H. N. (1980). Semantic similarity as a factor in whole-word slips of the tongue. In V. Fromkin (Ed.), *Errors in linguistic performance.* London: Academic Press.

Howell, W. C. (1973). Representation of frequency in memory. *Psychological Bulletin, 80*, 44–53.

Howes, D. H., & Solomon, R. L. (1951). Visual duration threshold as a function of word probability. *Journal of Experimental Psychology, 41*, 401–410.

Kimble, G. A., & Perlmuter, L. C. (1970). The problem of volition. *Psychological Review, 77*, 361–383.

Luria, A. R. (1973). *The working brain: An introduction to neuropsychology.* Harmondsworth, England: Penguin Books.

Masher, L., & Zacks, R. T. (1986). Automatic processing of fundamental information: The case for frequency of occurrence. *American Psychologist, 39*, 1372–1388.

Matlin, M. W., Stang, D. J., Gawron, V. J., Steedman, A., & Derby, P. L. (1979). Evaluative meaning as a determinant of spew position. *Journal of General Psychology, 100*, 3–11.

McClelland, J. L., & Rumelhart, D. E. (1985). Distributed memory and the representation of general and specific information. *Journal of Experimental Psychology: General, 114*, 159–188.

Meringer, R. (1908). *Aus dem Leben der Sprache: Versprechen, Kindersprache, Nachahmungstrieb.* Berlin: Behrs Verlag.

Mintzman, D. L., Nozawa, G., & Irmscher, M. (1982). Frequency as a nonpropositional attribute of memory. *Journal of Verbal Learning and Verbal Behavior, 109*, 98–117.

Nakatani, L. H. (1973). On the evaluation of models for the word-frequency effect. *Psychological Review, 80*, 195–202.

Neisser, U. (1967). *Cognitive psychology.* New York: Appleton-Century-Crofts.

Newbigging, P. L. (1961). The perceptual redintegration of frequent and infrequent words. *Canadian Journal of Psychology, 15*, 123–132.

Norman, D. A. (1981). Categorization of action slips. *Psychological Review, 88*, 1–15.

Norman, D. A. (1985). New views of information processing: Implications for intelligent decision support systems. In E. Hollnage, G. Mancini, & D. Woods (Eds.), *Intelligent decision aids in process environments.* San Miniato, Italy: NATO Advanced Study Institute.

Norman, D. A., & Bobrow, D. G. (1979). Descriptions: An intermediate stage in memory retrieval. *Cognitive Psychology, 11*, 107–123.

Norman, D. A., & Shallice, T. (1980). *Attention to action: Willed and automatic control of behavior.* CHIP Document No. 99, Center for Human Information Processing, University of California—San Diego, La Jolla.

Pollack, I., Rubinstein, H., & Decker, L. (1960). Analysis of incorrect responses to an unknown message set. *Journal of the Acoustical Society of America, 32,* 454–457.

Rasmussen, J. (1982). Human errors: A taxonomy for describing human malfunction in industrial installations. *Journal of Occupational Accidents, 4,* 311–335.

Reason, J. T. (1979). Actions not as planned: The price of automatization. In G. Underwood & R. Stevens (Eds.), *Aspects of consciousness: Vol. 1. Psychological issues.* London: Wiley.

Reason, J. T. (1984a). Absent-mindedness and cognitive control. In J. Harris & P. Morris (Eds.). *Everyday memory, actions and absent-mindedness.* London: Academic Press.

Reason, J. T. (1984b). Lapses of attention. In R. Parasuraman & D. Davies (Eds.), *Varieties of attention.* New York: Academic Press.

Reason, J. T. (1984c). *Order of output in category generation.* Paper given to the Cognitive Section, British Psychological Society, Oxford.

Reason, J. T. (1986). *Naming the white of an egg: Evidence for semantic constraints upon phonological priming.* Unpublished report.

Reason, J. T., & Lucas, D. (1984). Using cognitive diaries to investigate naturally occurring memory blocks. In J. Harris & P. Morris (Eds.), *Everyday memory, actions and absent-mindedness.* London: Academic Press.

Reason, J. T., & Mycielska, K. (1982). *Absent-minded? The psychology of mental lapses and everyday errors.* Englewood Cliffs, NJ: Prentice-Hall.

Reason, J. T., Horrocks, B., & Bailey, S. (1986). *Multiple search processes in knowledge, retrieval: Similarity-matching frequency-gambling and inference.* Unpublished report.

Roediger, H. L., & Crowder, R. G. (1976). A serial position effect in the recall of United States Presidents. *Bulletin of the Psychonomic Society, 8,* 275–278.

Savin, H. B. (1963). Word frequency effect and errors in the perception of speech. *Journal of the Acoustical Society of America, 35,* 200–206.

Solomon, R. L., & Postman, L. (1952). Frequency of usage as a determinant of recognition thresholds for words. *Journal of Experimental Psychology, 43,* 195–201.

Spence, J. T. (1963). Contribution of response bias to recognition thresholds. *Journal of Abnormal and Social Psychology, 66,* 339–344.

Thorndike, E. L. (1911). *Animal intelligence.* New York: Macmillan.

Timpanaro, S. (1976). *The Freudian slip.* London: New Left Press.

Underwood, B. J., & Schulz, R. W. (1960). *Meaningfulness and verbal learning.* Philadelphia: Lippincott.

Woods, D. D. (1984). Some results on operator performance in emergency events. *Institute of Chemical Engineers Symposium Series No. 90,* 13–21.

Zipf, G. K. (1945). The meaning-frequency relationships of words. *Journal of General Psychology, 33,* 251–256.

Zipf, G. K. (1949). *Human behavior and the principle of least effort.* Cambridge, MA: Addison-Wesley.

4

A New Ideomotor Theory of Voluntary Control[1]

Bernard J. Baars

INTRODUCTION: IS THERE A PROBLEM OF VOLITION?

A century ago, psychology was defined as the study of three core topics: *conation* (i.e., volition or will), *cognition,* and *emotion* (Hilgard, 1980). But since the advent of behaviorism and logical positivism, the first of these topics—the question of *volition,* or *will*—has been almost entirely neglected. *Cognition* and, to some extent, *emotion* have been revived by the "cognitive revolution in psychology," which has made it possible to approach these topics as inferential constructs that can be used with scientific rigor if they are properly operationalized (Baars, 1986; see Ekman, 1984). But until very recently, no systematic attempt has been made to approach volition with modern theoretical and empirical tools (Baars, 1988; Kimble & Perlmutter, 1970). Still, this missing element is being increasingly recognized. George A. Miller, one of the foremost leaders in the cognitive shift in psychology, has called volition one of the few

[1]This chapter can be read in conjunction with my book *A Cognitive Theory of Consciousness* (1988), which develops in greater detail many of the points made here (see especially Chapters 7–9).

BERNARD J. BAARS • The Wright Institute, 2728 Durant Avenue, Berkeley, California 94704.

Experimental Slips and Human Error: Exploring the Architecture of Volition, edited by Bernard J. Baars. Plenum Press, New York, 1992.

"constitutive topics" of psychology—one of those central questions that define its natural domain:

> [Volition] keeps coming back to me as a critically important thing. I think 'will' is terribly important. . . . As I used to say to my students, I can foul up any of your experiments by an act of will. Now why doesn't that make 'will' more important than the stuff *you're* studying? (in Baars, 1986, p. 221)

A number of empirical observations raise the question of volition very directly. Consider the deceptively simple example explored in Chapter 1: the case of a person *making* a slip and then *repeating* it deliberately. The observable *behavior* is the same in both cases. But the reported experience differs enormously. Not only is the slip inconsistent with some levels of its governing intention, but it is likely to occasion surprise or embarrassment, whereas its repetition does not. The slip, we believe, *would have been avoided* if possible, if only the speaker had taken more time, paid more attention, been less distracted, or adopted any other strategy to maintain better control. But of course, the voluntary repetition of the slip would not have been avoided. The slip is also likely to be *disavowed* by the speaker, as soon as it is recognized: it might be spontaneously corrected and attributed to some causal agency other than the speaker's own intentions. No current theory attempts to explain such differences, but they must be explained by any full-fledged theory of action control (see the Preface and Chapter 1).

Volition as a topic lost popularity during the behavioristic era because it was widely believed that normal, goal-directed action could be reduced to simpler conditioned stimulus–response (S-R) connections (Baars, 1986; Hilgard & Marquis, 1940; Pavlov, 1904). However, S-R reduction cannot explain the major psychological difference between making and repeating a slip, because the *observable behavior* is the same in both cases; behaviorally, the two cases appear to be equally complex. One cannot then account for the difference by claiming that the involuntary slip is somehow a "simpler" reduction of its voluntary version.

In fact, there are numerous pairs of matching actions that make exactly the same point. The upper half of Table 1 shows pairs of actions that are behaviorally identical; but of each pair, one is *counter*voluntary (that is, it actively mismatches the intention), whereas its match is voluntary. A slip and its voluntary repetition are good examples of this distinction. In contradistinction, the lower half of the table shows paired contrasts between *non*voluntary events (those that are automatic but *consistent with the intention*) and voluntary ones. A good example here is a skill like typing *before* it has become habitual and the same skill *afterward*. A complete theory of voluntary control must explain the nature of voluntary, nonvoluntary, and countervoluntary actions. Such a theory is highly constrained by the paired contrasts shown in Table 1.

Commonsense psychology assumes a close connection between volition and consciousness; indeed, the terms *voluntary control* and *conscious control* are often used interchangeably. If someone commits murder "with malice

TABLE 1
Contrasts between Matched Voluntary and Involuntary Actions

	Involuntary actions	Voluntary actions
Countervoluntary actions: (Unwanted)	Slips of speech and action	Purposeful imitations of slips
	Voluntarily resisted automatisms (e.g., unwanted habits)	Voluntarily permitted automatisms
	Pathological symptoms: out-of-control actions, images, inner speech, or emotions	Purposeful imitation of these symptoms
Nonvoluntary automatisms: (Wanted, but not controlled in detail)	Automatic components of normal actions	The same components before automaticity due to practice
	Reflexes	Purposeful imitation of reflexes
	Autonomic functions	The same functions under temporary biofeedback control
	Automatic aspects of memory encoding (Hasher & Zacks, 1979)	Effortful aspects of memory encoding
	Spontaneous emotional facial expressions (Ekman, 1984)	"Social" expressions

aforethought"—that is, with conscious access to, and consideration of, the planned act and its consequences—Western law treats the crime differently than if the act was committed involuntarily, without conscious forethought or control. In murder trials, this distinction may mean the difference between life and death. This crucial legal point is based, of course, on commonsense psychology. But what does it mean scientifically? Can we provide a scientific account that makes sense of the popular distinction between voluntary and involuntary action? And is the perceived similarity between "voluntary control" and "conscious control" also meaningful?

GLOBAL WORKSPACE THEORY AND VOLUNTARY CONTROL

Over the past 10 years I have developed a theoretical approach to conscious experience that also suggests a plausible role for volition. It is proposed that conscious experience reflects the operation of a "global workspace" in the nervous system, a central information exchange that is used by multiple specialized processors to communicate with each other (Baars, 1983, 1988). Similar proposals have been made by Shallice (1978), Norman and Shallice (1980), Reason (1983), Bower and Cohen (1982), and McClelland (1986, Chapter 16).

A great deal of evidence exists for this kind of nervous system architecture, both psychological and neurophysiological. For instance, many areas of the cortex are locally specialized and unconscious, though these specialized areas may cooperate in any complex task, like language comprehension or spatial analysis (Geschwind, 1979; Luria, 1980). Several neuroscientists have suggested that such local cortical areas act as "distributed modules," that is, specialized processors that are extremely efficient in their particular tasks (e.g., Arbib, 1980; Grossberg, 1982; Mountcastle, 1970). Cortical activity *by itself* appears to be unconscious (e.g., Libet, 1978, 1985). One can, for example, remove very large amounts of cortex without affecting the state of consciousness.[2]

Cognitive science models also suggest that a collection of distributed specialized processors is very useful for handling routine tasks. However, this kind of distributed system does not provide much *flexibility* in the face of *new* conditions—and yet, the human nervous system is extraordinarily flexible and plastic (e.g., Luria, 1980). A number of artificial intelligence models have therefore added a "global workspace" to distributed systems—a memory whose contents are broadcast globally to all the specialized processors (e.g., Hayes-Roth, 1984; Reddy & Newell, 1974). Such a workspace permits specialized processors to cooperate with each other, so that together they can solve problems that cannot be handled by any single processor working alone. This system architecture seems to facilitate adaptive responses to new conditions. It also has a family resemblance to well-known psychological ideas about short-term memory and "working memory" (Baddeley, 1976). However, it is clear that these types of rehearsable memory are only partly conscious: at any one moment, working memory contains mostly *un*conscious items, which can be readily retrieved and thereby made conscious. Further, working memory is not conceived of as an information exchange between unconscious specialized processors. Hence, working memory and the conscious global workspace are related but different constructs.

Baars (1983, 1987, 1988) has presented a "contrastive analysis," comparing well-established conscious and unconscious phenomena that are functionally similar, and shows that these paired phenomena can all be explained on the assumption that a global workspace is associated with conscious events, whereas matching unconscious events are carried out by specialized distributed processors. Conscious representations seem to require at least three necessary properties[3]: They are *broadcast globally* throughout the system of distributed specialists; they are *internally consistent;* and they are *informative,* in the sense that they trigger adaptation from an "audience" consisting of other specialized processors. Numerous sources of evidence and testable pre-

---

[2]Neurophysiologically, waking consciousness is associated with a narrow vertical series of reticular structures, beginning in the brain stem, flowing up toward certain nuclei of the thalamus, and hence projecting upward very diffusely to the cortex (see Baars, 1988).

[3]In the expanded version of the theory, the number of necessary conditions for conscious experience rises to six (Baars, 1988). However, for this discussion, the three mentioned here are sufficient.

dictions based on this architecture are presented in *A Cognitive Theory of Consciousness* (Baars, 1988).

We have noted that "voluntary control" and "conscious control" are often used as near synonyms. Global Workspace (GW) theory invites a natural interpretation of the relationship between conscious access and voluntary control. In particular, it suggests that conscious images may serve as *rough-and-ready goals* for highly sophisticated effector systems, which are "distributed"; that is, they control muscle systems in a way that leaves room for considerable local autonomy, so that they are sensitive to their local contexts (see Figure 1 of this chapter and Figure 1 in Chapter 1). Conscious images of a planned action (especially novel, significant, or conflicting aspects of the action) are broadcast by the global workspace to these specialized effector systems, much as the commands of an army general may be broadcast to the troops. Local details are left up to the local effector mechanisms, just as in telling an army to move toward a certain objective, a commanding general would not want to tell the soldiers which foot to put forward first (see Greene, 1972). In sum, global considerations are handled by the global workspace, and local issues are left to the specialized effector systems.

Figure 1 shows the three basic elements of GW theory, matched with roughly equivalent terms that are widely used. The first construct is the global workspace itself, which corresponds *very roughly* to concepts like short-term memory, working memory, consciousness and attention, and the limited-capacity system. The second theoretical construct is the unconscious specialized processor, which corresponds to the "parallel distributed processors" as used by Rumelhart, McClelland, and the PDP group (1986), or to the notion of a local "module" as used by Mountcastle (1978), Fodor (1983), and others, or to the idea of an automatism, as used by LaBerge (1980) and Shiffrin and Schneider (1977). Notice that different perceptual specialists can compete with each other for access to the global workspace. For instance, an auditory click and a simultaneous visual flash in different spatial locations will compete with each other for access to consciousness (Blumenthal, 1977).

The third and final element in GW theory is called a *goal hierarchy,* which is conceived of as an unconscious goal structure that *makes use* of the global workspace in order to recruit and control subgoals and effector systems.[4] When a given goal hierarchy can control access to the global data base (see Figure 1), it is called a *Dominant Goal Hierarchy* (see also Figure 1 in Chapter 1). Goal hierarchies correspond to "preparatory set," "activated action schemata," and the kind of "set" involved in the tip-of-the-tongue (TOT) phenomenon. These are seen as complex and multileveled data structures that are not qualitatively conscious (just as the tip-of-the-tongue state does not have conscious perceptual qualities) but that *can* compete for access to the global workspace and thereby control the entire voluntary control system (see Baars, 1988, Chapter

---

[4]In *A Cognitive Theory of Consciousness* (1988), I describe other structures that can dominate the global workspace, called *contexts,* but in this chapter the notion of *goal hierarchies* will suffice.

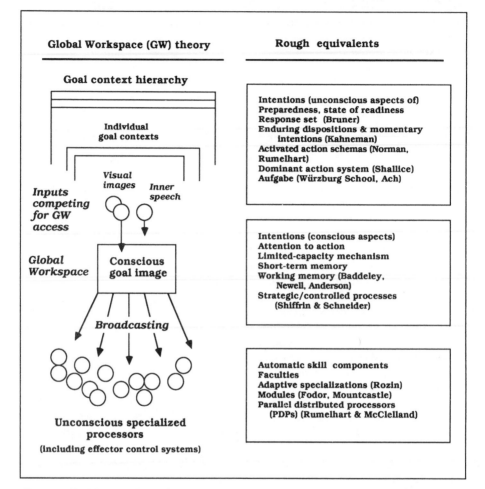

FIGURE 1. Rough equivalences between the basic concepts of Global Workspace (GW) theory and other widespread terms. Notice that GW theory has only three main constructs: the global workspace, unconscious specialized processors, and goals contexts. Each one has a graphic symbol associated with it so that the theory can be expressed in intuitively obvious diagrams.

6). For instance, when someone is busy searching for a certain word, the goal of doing so—the word that is sought—is not qualitatively conscious. However, this nonqualitative state of mind does occupy the limited-capacity system, to the extent that one cannot be searching for two wholly different words at the same time; nor can one be searching in the TOT mode and also be conscious at the same time of an unrelated stream of perceptual information (see Figure 1, in Chapter 1, showing a linguistic goal hierarchy with many unconscious levels of control).

The most important point about the global workspace perspective, for our current purpose, is that it views consciousness as the premier mechanism for creating novel *access* between otherwise dissociated mechanisms. In a sense, consciousness is the "publicity organ of the nervous system." For example, to establish a novel relationship between a largely unconscious goal system and the effectors that are supposed to carry out the goal, one is required to *publicize* the new goal via the global workspace, so as to recruit, integrate, and control the effectors that can work to reach the goal. Thus, consciousness is not merely a way of representing the perceptual world, and it certainly is not just a by-product of neural functioning, as the philosophy of epiphenomenalism would have it. Rather, it is the primary organ by which humans adapt to novelty—and that includes, of course, novel aspects of motor control.

The notion that consciousness serves as the major integration mechanism of the nervous system has many important implications. We will sketch some here and develop them in greater detail below:

First, this notion explains why competition between different goal systems is important and occurs rather frequently. In Chapter 1, we argued that perhaps the most common cause of slips is competition between different plans for access to the limited-capacity system (see also Chapter 6). However, we did not provide a detailed rationale for *why* it might be important for different plans to compete for the limited-capacity system. Why is such competition sufficiently *functional* to justify the cost of many otherwise preventable errors? Global Workspace theory provides an answer: For a goal system to gain control of any novel voluntary activity, it *must* first gain access to the global workspace, in order to recruit the subgoals and effector systems that can carry out the goal[5] (see Figures 1–3 and Figure 1 in Chapter 1). Thus, access to the global workspace *provides the ability to recruit and control* new sets of distributed effectors and subgoal systems (see Figure 2).

Competition for GW access can also create erroneous plans by fusion between two competing, correct plans, as shown by numerous techniques for eliciting laboratory slips (Figure 2; see Chapter 6). GW theory therefore explains the empirical evidence for competition between alternative plans, and as noted above, it also gives an important reason for plans to compete; The winning plan, after all, can recruit and control the voluntary musculature as well as voluntary mental activities, like recall, control of imagery, inner speech, and rehearsal.

Notice that competition between alternative plans also takes up limited capacity. The Competing-Plans Hypothesis of Chapter 1 maintains that most slips require two simultaneous events: a fusion between alternative plans *and* a momentary overload of the limited-capacity system. Plan competition for the global workspace supplies both of these necessary conditions.

---

[5]Of course, these goals must be mutually consistent; otherwise, they would begin to compete *against* each other for access to the limited-capacity system, according to the ideomotor theory. One function of conscious error detection is presumably to detect and repair such between-goal conflicts.

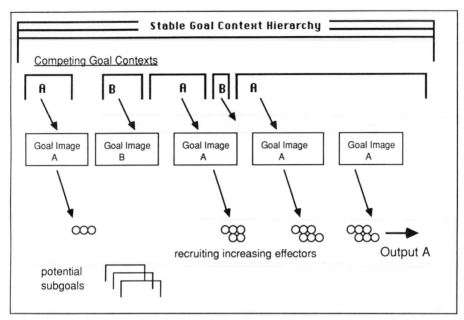

FIGURE 2. Access to the global workspace (GW) provides the ability to recruit and control new sets of distributed effectors and subgoal systems. Competition for GW access can also create erroneous plans by fusion between correct plans. James's ideomotor theory (1890/1983, p. 1130) suggests that conscious thoughts are inherently impulsive; if a conscious goal image is not carried out, it is because contrary images or intentions block it. This is consistent with the view in GW theory that conscious events are globally broadcast, so that they can recruit and trigger unconscious goal systems and effectors needed to carry out an action. In the figure, Goal Image A encounters brief competition from the countervailing image not-A but overcomes this opposition and executes Output A. An interesting feature of the GW model is that in principle many specialized processors can block execution of any conscious goal image. Evidence for such "universal editing" is described in the text.

Second, and particularly relevant to the question of slips, the GW architecture suggests the existence of one kind of "goal editing." In GW theory, the most stable, overarching, and enduring Dominant Goal Hierarchy can exclude unwanted goals that may try to gain access to the global workspace. That is, the enduring policies and goals of human beings—goals like survival and the search for social support—have such dominant control of the GW that they usually manage to exclude contrary conscious goal images (Figure 1 and 3, Figure 1 in Chapter 1). Thus in order for some novel goal system to gain access to the conscious/limited-capacity system, it must generally be consistent with the currently dominant goal hierarchy (as shown in Figure 1, Chapter 1). If we take the example of the Reverend Spooner, making his famous slip in announcing the hymn at the compulsory chapel service at Cambridge ("Kinquering Congs Their Titles Take"), we can safely guess that part of Spooner's normal dominant goal hierarchy would be to have the respect of his students and faculty; to show expected competence in speaking and acting; to display a dignified demeanor, especially in the religious context of chapel services during the 1930s, and the like. Thus, "Kinquering Congs" violates the normal goal hierarchy in several ways. Ordinarily, the system must be organized to catch and avoid such errors.

A simple everyday observation provides unmistakable evidence of *unconscious* editing of *conscious* targets. To illustrate this we need only to imagine some action that we *could* perform, even though it runs against all of our normal goals. We could imagine jumping off a bridge, slapping the face of a distinguished colleague, walking backward into a formal gathering, speaking in nonsense phrases at a scientific conference, violating a rule of syntax, and so on. In general, it appears that such conscious goal imagery (visual or auditory) can be edited and stopped from executing by multiple unconscious rule systems, including criteria that are never conscious. Thus, the subtle rules of phonology may serve to cancel a conscious plan to say something that violates English phonology. The same may be said of the unconscious but very powerful rules of syntax, semantics, pragmatics, conversational norms, articulatory and acoustic constraints, discourse rules, and many, many others (see Figure 1, Chapter 1). In all these cases, it is the *unconscious,* highly sophisticated, and overpracticed automatisms that appear to detect and halt the execution of a *conscious* goal image.

Anything that can interfere with limited-capacity processes should also hinder this kind of editing ability because whatever is conscious is vulnerable to editing by onlooking specialized processors. That is why the Competing-Plans Hypothesis of Chapter 1 suggests that slips involve at least a fleeting failure of editing, one that occurs during a momentary overload of the conscious/limited-capacity system due to plan competition. GW theory thus provides the necessary ingredients needed to explain a very large class of slips. It does so with great economy—indeed, without needing any additional constructs at all.

Third, the GW architecture can explain why a person who commits murder willfully, "with malice aforethought," is treated differently in our commonsense psychology from someone who caused an accidental death. The commonsense inference in this case is that, *if* the goal of committing murder was conscious, competing thoughts and intentions *must have arisen* in *most* people that would normally interfere with carrying out the conscious thought of committing murder. An acceptable member of our culture might experience competing conscious feelings of guilt or shame, entertain the thought of the consequent suffering to the victim and the survivors, or perhaps contemplate the probability of being caught and punished for the murder. If, in spite of such contrary thoughts, the person proceeds to kill "in cold blood"—that is, without inner resistance—we make a simple (and probably accurate) inference about the murderer: He or she lacks the internal controls we demand of each other in our culture. Lacking such control, this person may kill again. These commonsense inferences make good sense in the GW framework.

A number of other observations about voluntary control and its relationships with conscious experience can be handled by GW theory (see Baars 1988, Chapter 7, for details). But first, before attempting to define the nature of voluntary control in a general way, we will explore a modern version of William James's theory of voluntary control, which comes to very similar conclusions.

JAMES'S IDEOMOTOR HYPOTHESIS AND THE GLOBAL WORKSPACE THEORY

In his justly celebrated *Principles of Psychology* (1890/1983), William James suggested a connection between voluntary control and conscious experience that fits the framework sketched above remarkably well. His *ideomotor* theory proposed that voluntary actions are initiated by uncontested conscious goal images. These conscious images are viewed as inherently impulsive. Conscious goals, James suggested, tend to trigger action automatically, *unless* they encounter competition from other conscious thoughts or active intentions. Action and speech are, of course, determined in large part by *un*conscious goals and automatisms. Nevertheless, conscious ideas, for James, are the key to action, because they are needed to specify those components that are *novel, conflicted,* or especially *significant.* We need be conscious of only a few crucial aspects of an action, typically those that are not habitual or automatic. James called this the "ideomotor" theory of voluntary action because it is the conscious "ideas" that trigger the habitual, unconscious "motor activity" that carries out the ideas.

The Chevreul pendulum provides the classical demonstration of the powerful effects of ideomotor imagery. The subject simply holds a string with a small weight at the end, trying as hard as possible to keep it completely steady. (The reader is encouraged to try this: a paper clip and a rubber band will make an adequate pendulum.) Now, while continuously intending *not* to move the pendulum, one begins simply to *imagine* it swinging on a north–south axis, away from and toward oneself. Without any perceived effort, the pendulum will begin to swing north and south. Again, making every effort *not* to move it, the subject begins merely to imagine the pendulum swinging left and right, east and west. The pendulum soon begins to follow the subject's mental images, even though there is no noticeable effort or movement of the hand. This seems to many subjects a dramatic illustration of the idea that conscious images are more powerful than deliberate intentions.

It is not easy to adapt this classical demonstration to the rigors of modern investigation. But it is difficult to doubt that there are conscious events related to goals: people can report their own conscious thoughts and images about a planned action and can usually predict their intended actions *in the short run* quite accurately (Ericsson & Simon, 1980; Nisbett & Wilson, 1977; see Baars, 1988). We can consciously intend to close this book and do so. But do those conscious events actually trigger the action? The ideomotor theory needs more empirical support than just this. We will therefore examine the evidence for four subhypotheses of James's theory. Each hypothesis will be described in terms of our modern framework, the Global Workspace theory. Then, we will examine the empirical evidence for each hypothesis.

For James, the only conscious components of action are the following:

1. The "idea" or conscious goal image (that is, a mental image of the outcome of the action), which is impulsive; that is, it tends to trigger action automatically if it does not encounter interference.
2. Perhaps some other goal-image can serve to "edit"—to halt and modify—the original goal image by competing with it for access to consciousness.
3. The "fiat"—the "go signal" that can trigger a previously prepared action—is also conscious.
4. Sensory feedback from the action, which can serve to confirm or modify the goal image if necessary, is conscious.

We will now discuss the evidence for each of these four claims and its relationship to Global Workspace theory.

The Impulsive Nature of Conscious Goal Images

The first hypothesis is that conscious goal images tend to trigger action spontaneously, barring interference from other, competing goal images or intentions. This claim is easily interpreted in GW theory; after all, it is a primary assumption of a distributed architecture that the detailed intelligence of complex systems like language, perception, and action control is widely distributed among relatively opaque specialized processors. A global message is able to activate those processors, even though it is quintessentially simple. Thus, conscious goal images may provide the significant and novel parameters for an action, but detailed action control is left to specialized effector control systems.

We can cite four sources of evidence for this claim:

1. *Conscious priming increases the frequency of experimentally evoked slips of speech and action.* Some slip techniques use phonological priming— that is, conscious exposure to words that resemble the slip—to elicit spoonerisms. For example, the reader can ask someone to repeat the word *poke* about half a dozen times and then ask, "What do you call the white of an egg?" Most people will answer, "The yolk," even when they know better. They have evidently been primed by the conscious word *poke* to retrieve a similar-sounding word from memory (Kimble & Perlmutter, 1970; Reason, Chapter 3, this volume). This technique may work because it simulates the conscious goal images that normally shape the action to be taken.

In general, spoonerisms can be elicited by consciously priming the speaker with word pairs that resemble the predicted error (Chapter 6, this volume). Thus, the slip "barn door—darn bore" can be elicited by showing a subject a series of word pairs like *dart board, dark bowl,* and *dot bone.* Because the subjects do not know ahead of time which word pair they must say out loud, they must be prepared to say each one. This state of readiness apparently primes the system to make an error when the phoneme pattern is switched.

Once we have a technique that elicits involuntary verbalizations, we can ask whether *adding* a semantic prime to the phonological prime at a different level will increase the chances of the slip's occurring over the rate achieved by the phonological prime alone. For example, if we presented the semantically related conscious words *terrible error* in addition to phonological priming words, would that presentation increase the chances of the spoonerism *bad goof?* Motley and Baars (1976) showed that it does indeed. Further, if people are presented with a social situation such as the presence of an attractive member of the opposite sex, slips related to the situation are made much more often (see Motley & Baars, 1979). In all these cases, a semantic prime coming just before an opportunity to make a related slip sharply increases the chances of making the slip. This finding suggests that conscious events can help recruit actions that are consistent with the conscious events. (See Chapter 12, this volume, for a more complete discussion.)

2. *Mental practice improves performance.* Some evidence of the influence of conscious goals comes from the experimental literature on mental practice, showing that consciously imaging an action can sometimes improve performance as much as actual physical practice (Drowatsky, 1975). Conscious imaging of goals is used extensively in clinical practice and to improve athletic performance (Singer, 1984). There is no doubt that conscious images of goals can have a powerful influence on effective action. We also know that there is a momentary increase in mental work load immediately before the onset of an action (Keele, 1973), a fact that is consistent with the idea that there is at least a momentary conscious goal before action. Conversely, Libet (1985) has presented arguments that we may become conscious of some actions only *after* the brain events that immediately trigger them. But this cannot be true in every case; surely, there are a great many times when people are conscious of what they are about to do seconds or hours before they do it, as shown by the fact that they can accurately discuss and predict their actions beforehand. The reader may make a conscious and reportable decision right now to turn the page and may then actually do so. This is hardly surprising, but any theory that cannot handle this elementary fact is incomplete.

3. *Loss of conscious access leads to loss of voluntary control.* Further, we know that the opposite case also holds: Loss of conscious access to an action can lead to a loss of control. Reason's analysis (1984a,b) of spontaneous errors and accidents shows that many errors occur because of absentmindedness; further, these errors show a relationship between automaticity (which implies loss of conscious access to the details of action) and loss of control (also see Reason, this volume). Langer and Imber (1979) also showed that automatization due to practice in a simple symbol-coding task leads to a loss of the ability to evaluate one's own performance on the task. The more practice the subjects gained, the

more they lost the ability to report the number of steps in the task; further, they were more likely to accept an *incorrect* assessment of their own performance than less well-practiced subjects. The authors argued that overlearning leads to automaticity, which can *reduce* the knowledge a subject has about how the task is performed. Under these circumstances, subjects should be more vulnerable to negative attributions regarding their own performance because they can no longer evaluate the evidence by themselves. Automatization implies that goal images become less and less consciously available, and therefore, the actions themselves become less and less accessible and modifiable.

4. *Executive ignorance: We are not aware of the details of action.* Try wiggling a finger. Where are the muscles located that control the finger? Most people believe that they are located in the hand; but in fact, they are in the forearm, as one can tell simply by feeling the muscles contracting in the forearm while moving the fingers.[6] Or consider, what is the difference between pronouncing /ba/ and /pa/? Most people simply do not know. Only in the last 20 years has research shown that the difference is a minute lag between the opening of the lips and the beginning of vocal cord vibration (Liberman, Cooper, Shankweiler & Studdert-Kennedy, 1967). Or ask a skilled typist to tell where the *p* is located on the keyboard—without actually performing a typing movement, mentally or physically. Most highly practiced typists will not be able to do this.

These examples can be multiplied indefinitely. We simply have no conscious, reportable access to the details of well-practiced actions.

A Possible Counterargument.   Notice that conscious images that appear to precede and initiate an action may be quite simple, variable, and even superficially irrelevant to the action itself. The act of walking to the kitchen may be triggered by many different goal images. One can image a tempting peanut-butter-and-jelly sandwich or leftovers from last night's dinner; one can remember that the stove needs cleaning or imagine the odor of cooking gas. We need not call up any of these images in great detail. A fragment of a related image will do quite nicely to trigger a habitual action. Just as in language there are often dozens of ways of saying the same thing, in action control many different conscious events can trigger the same action. In an ideomotor conception of action control, a conscious cue may be interpreted by many different context-sensitive systems. We do not need a detailed conscious plan or command, as the action is carried out by specialists that know more about local conditions than we do consciously. Various unconscious specialists keep continuous track of our posture, balance, and relationship to gravity; they trigger

---

[6]I want to thank Donald A. Norman for calling my attention to the finger-wiggling example of executive ignorance.

salivation and digestive enzymes to prepare for eating; they make it possible to remember the route to the kitchen; and so on.

This point has important implications for research. We must not fall into the trap of looking for *the* goal image for walking, or talking, or for any other action that appears to be the same in different circumstances. This is what misled introspectionists like Titchener and Külpe, who were astonished to find the great range of variation in mental imagery in different observers. Our modern ideomotor theory indicates that many different goal images can serve to recruit and initiate any given action. Imagining a tuna sandwich while lost in the desert must not trigger an automatic "walk to the kitchen," but it can stimulate new efforts to find food and water. Thus, goal images may vary tremendously in different situations and subjects and may yet be quite effective in controlling normal voluntary action.

We can conclude this section on the Jamesian claim about the "impulsive nature" of a conscious goal with some satisfaction that the claim makes sense, both empirically and in terms of Global Workspace theory. Now we can examine the second proposition of the ideomotor theory.

Competition between Goals

Some potentially conscious event may serve to "edit"—to halt and perhaps modify—the original goal image by competing with it for access to consciousness.

Like the previous point, this one has a straightforward interpretation in GW theory. If global broadcasting is required to trigger automatic systems able to carry out the goal, then competing against the original goal image is one way to stop the action, and perhaps to allow other "repair" systems to modify and correct it. However, GW theory goes beyond James's original conception in suggesting that the competing goal images themselves may be controlled by complex goal contexts. Thus, the conscious play between competing images may reflect underlying goal systems that are using the conscious images to gain control over the global workspace. The following two points flow from these considerations:

1. *Automatic editing of conscious targets:* Conscious goals seem to be inspected and edited by multiple, simultaneous, unconscious criteria. One function of competing goal contexts may be to "edit" the first goal image, to improve and correct it, to eliminate conflicts with existing goals, and the like. We have already pointed this out in Chapter 1 and will discuss it further in Chapter 11. Here, we merely note that the editing of conscious images by unconscious systems may operate through competition for access to the conscious global workspace.

2. *Default execution: In the absence of corrective conscious events, unconscious effector systems tend to carry out a conscious goal automatically, "by*

default." How do we know that conscious goals tend to be executed, in the absence of contrary conscious or intentional events? One source of evidence comes from demonstrations of automaticity (e.g., LaBerge, 1980; Shiffrin & Schneider, 1977): try looking at a word without reading it, for example. Once we allow ourselves to become conscious of a printed word, it appears that automatic complex systems that scan, identify, and interpret the word are triggered. There are many other well-known examples, such as the Stroop effect (the inability to stop reading a word when it is presented quickly), and the case of rapid memory scanning in the Sternber (1966) memory search task, which is difficult or impossible to stop even when the correct item is found. All such tasks are characterized by *conscious* triggering conditions that initiate *unconscious,* automatic, and complex subsystems that are not under detailed voluntary control.

Again, we can consider spontaneous absentminded errors, such as those collected by Reason (1983, 1984a,b, 1992). Reason reported that strong habit intrusions occur in the course of normal actions when the actor is absent-minded or distracted, and hence unable to pay attention, that is, to be conscious of the relevant aspect of the action. These cases argue for default execution. It seems that prepared action executes even when it should not, if contrary conscious events do not block the faulty action. Indeed, the failure to block a faulty goal image can have catastrophic consequences. Reason (1983) analyzed a number of airplane disasters and road accidents, concluding that many may be caused by the intrusion of automatic processes in combination with a low level of conscious monitoring.

A child of 6 knows how to keep such errors from happening: You must *pay attention* to what you're doing. That is, you must be conscious of the novel circumstances and goals. When we pay attention, erroneous default executions do not occur, presumably because "editing" systems send competing goal images to the global workspace. However, it seems likely that default execution is used in executing correct actions most of the time. We do indeed seem to carry out conscious goals automatically, unless contrary images and intentions block them before execution.

The Action Fiat: The "Go Signal" that Can Trigger a Prepared Action

In James's view, people must be conscious of the moment of execution of an action, at least if it is not routine or habitually predictable. In rhythmic, repetitive actions, conscious control of timing may not be needed, but it is indispensable when the moment of action onset is unpredictable.

In Global Workspace theory, we can interpret this view to suggest a two-stage conception of action control. In the first stage, a goal image may prime unconscious effectors in a "feedforward" manner; once prepared, the action is triggered by another conscious event, perhaps one that is controlled by a specialized timing system. Alternatively, one can think of the "action fiat" as an inhibitory system that competes against a conscious "go signal" until it is time to execute, when inhibition is released. What evidence exists for such ideas?

1. *We can suspend the execution of almost any prepared action until the right moment.* We can prepare an action and suspend it until some conscious go signal is given, as at the start of a foot race. Even the timing of an internal go signal can be conscious; witness the fact that people can often tell us at will that they will execute a voluntary action at some arbitrarily chosen point in time. In that sense, people clearly can have conscious access to, and control of, an action fiat.

2. *Many voluntary actions have two distinct stages.* A division between a preparation and an execution phase seems to exist in many discrete actions, even when execution is not artificially delayed. Many actions have these two phases quite naturally. For example, in the elegant and precise movements of the cat, whose neurophysiology of action control has been worked out in considerable detail, there seems to be a natural division between the preparation and the execution of a movement. As Greene (1972) wrote:

> When a cat turns its head to look at a mouse, the angles of tilting of its head and flexion and torsion of its neck will tune spinal motor centers in such a way that its brain has only to command "Jump!" and the jump will be in the right direction. . . . The tilt and neck flexion combine additively to determine the degrees of extension of the fore and hind limbs appropriate to each act of climbing up or down, jumping onto a platform, standing on an incline, or peering into a mousehole; the neck torsion regulates the relative extensions of left and right legs when preparing to jump to the side. These postures must be set as the act begins: for if they were entirely dependent upon corrective feedback, the cat would have stumbled or missed the platform before the feedback could work. A few of these reflex patterns of feedforward are adequate for the approximate regulation of all feline postures and movements required in normal environments for a cat. (p. 308)

Some evidence for the concept of an action fiat is therefore available, though more research is needed to test this hypothesis. Again, the Jamesian theory fits both the evidence and our modern information-processing framework.

The Fourth Conscious Component: Conscious Sensory Feedback from the Action

In human beings, with our long period of helpless dependency in childhood, essentially all usable actions must be learned. That is to say, in humans all actions start with approximations that are less than perfect. Conscious feedback in such a species has enormous importance because it allows many systems to work cooperatively to halt, modify, and correct imperfect actions. This is of course precisely the functional significance of a global workspace architecture, in which many highly complex and effective specialists have access to the same globally distributed focal information. Sensory feedback from an action can serve to confirm or modify the goal image if necessary, or to recruit and shape new effector coalitions able to come closer to the goal. Thus, learning an action—from the babbling of a toddler to the long-term goals of an athlete or a musician—always requires conscious, sensory access to the action and its consequences.

In this connection, it is worth noting some of the extraordinary results found with biofeedback training. Note that biofeedback training *always,* without exception, consists of *conscious* feedback from a system—either a single neuron or a population of neurons—that normally provides little or no conscious feedback. Yet, with this single condition, essentially any set of neurons or effectors in the body can come under discrete and delicate voluntary control (Buchwald, 1974). Basmajian (1979) has shown, for example, that if one provides an auditory click by means of loudspeaker whenever a certain spinal motor unit fires (among the many millions of motor units controlled by the spinal cord), given a half hour of practice, a subject can learn to play drum rolls on the single motor unit! (This occurs while the adjacent motor unit activity is typically suppressed.) The most obvious interpretation from our theoretical perspective is that local "effector controllers" separate themselves from the mass of unconscious receiving specialists and are able to correlate their activity with the globally broadcast message provided by the conscious auditory click. As usual, the local specialist handles the details, and the conscious involvement is essentially blind to its local effects, except, of course, by way of the conscious feedback signal. The global feedback signal therefore seems to serve to correct and control the timing of the specialized subsystem.

In summary, the global workspace framework can incorporate the basics of James's ideomotor theory of voluntary control quite naturally, indeed, without adding any new theoretical costs at all. And we have previously seen how phenomena like editing, the Competing-Plans Hypothesis of Chapters 1 and 6, and everyday ideas about responsibility for one's actions make a good deal of sense in the global workspace framework. The empirical evidence for the four conscious elements claimed by the ideomotor theory—the conscious goal image, any competing images or intentions, the action fiat, and sensory action feedback—seems at least moderately strong. More testing is required, of course, but we can see noticeable progress.

Next, we develop a view of the cause of slips that is consistent both with the Competing-Plans Hypothesis of Chapter 1 and with the Global Workspace theory.

SLIPS IN THE NEW IDEOMOTOR THEORY

Chapter 1 suggests that many slips originate in fusions between otherwise correct plans that are competing with each other, combined with a momentary occlusion of the limited-capacity system, and specifically of the ability of that system to edit and prevent overt errors. In this chapter, we have seen why alternative action plans must compete for access to the conscious/limited-capacity system because that competition would allow a dominant goal image to recruit, activate, and trigger the specialized unconscious effector systems that control the details of action. Further, we have seen that the same system allows for a certain kind of editing, which could prevent a covert erroneous plan from being carried out. Thus, if alternative plans are competing for access to the global workspace or its neural equivalent, they could satisfy *both* conditions for slips: the competing plans may fuse, if they can, and the fused plan would not be edited and stopped from execution in time because the limited-capacity system is occluded by the ongoing competition.

Figure 3 shows a graphic version of this train of events. If conscious goal images tend to be carried out by default when there are no competing elements, and if editing systems need time to compete effectively against faulty goal images, there must be a "horse race" between the time it takes to execute the initial faulty goal image and the time that the editing systems require to interfere with the error. In the case of slips, the editing systems lose the horse race because execution time is faster than editing time. The faulty action is executed before the editorial systems have a chance to compete against the goal image of the faulty action.

The diagram shows competition between two plans, one for saying the phrase "competing plans" and the other for the synonymous "plans that compete." This competition leads to a fused "spoonerized" plan: "completing pans." This is a lexical error, and a lexical control system detects the error and attempts to interrupt its execution. There follows a horse race between the erroneous goal image A and an error message B that attempts to block A, but too late to prevent its execution.

There is one obvious example where such a horse race may happen: the case of automaticity due to practice. For example, it is generally impossible to stop reading a word once we become aware of the printed stimulus. In general, a well-learned, automatic action can be carried out more quickly, and with less conscious involvement, than the editing systems that attempt to catch up to the conscious component of the error.

There is good evidence that practiced mental images fade from consciousness or become very fleeting, and that highly practiced, predictable actions become more efficient and less conscious as well. A series of studies by Pani (1982) on the automatization of mental images show the first pattern. Pani showed that conscious access to the visual images used in solving a visual matching problem drops with practice in a highly predictable way. In terms of our model, we can suppose that images become globally available for shorter and shorter periods of time, until finally they are globally available so briefly that they can no longer be reported, even though they continue to trigger highly prepared effector systems. Presumably, highly prepared processors can react very quickly, whereas the nonautomatic act of reporting goal images may take more time. Alternatively, it is possible that goal images are simply lost from the global workspace, that they are not even fleetingly available. (In the

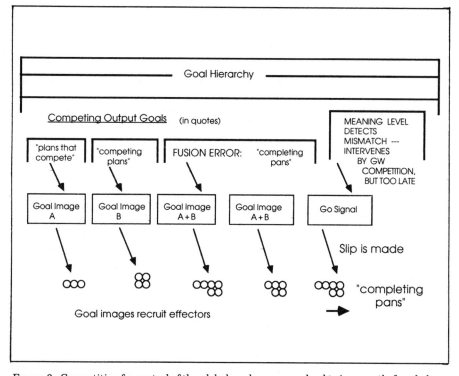

FIGURE 3. Competition for control of the global workspace may lead to incorrectly fused plans which may in turn lead to overt slips, if the appropriate control level detects the error too late. The dominant goal hierarchy corresponds to the ongoing long-term goals and policies of a person. Thus errors and non-dominant goals may violate the dominant goal hierarchy. If conscious goal images tend to be carried out by default when there are no competing conscious elements, and if editing systems need time to compete effectively against faulty goal images, there may be a "horse-race" between the execution of the faulty goal image and the time it takes the editing system to block the error. In the case of slips, the editing systems lose the race because the execution time is faster than the editing time. The faulty action is executed before the editorial systems have a chance to compete against its goal image. (See also Chapter 1, Figure 1.)

remainder of this discussion, I will assume that the first case is true, that, with practice, goal images are still broadcast globally, but more and more fleetingly. Naturally, this hypothesis must be tested; see the section below, "Some Testable Predictions.")

If goal images become more and more briefly available with practice, the important findings by Langer and Imber (1979), mentioned above, begin to make sense. The reader may recall that these authors found that more highly practiced subjects in a coding task lost track of the details of the task and were more willing than less practiced subjects to accept an incorrect assessment of their own performance. This is exactly what we would expect, given the assumption above that the goal image becomes less and less available with practice. Automatic, highly prepared effector systems can continue to carry out the task (because they become more well prepared and efficient with practice and therefore need less of a goal image to be triggered). But asking subjects to do something novel, such as evaluating their own performance, should become more difficult, because the global goal image on which the evaluation can operate is available only fleetingly.

Thus, the goal image controlling the "countervoluntary" act may be available long enough to trigger a prepared action, but not long enough to be vulnerable to interference from the editing systems.

THE MEANINGS OF "VOLUNTARY CONTROL"

We can now attempt some generalizations about the nature of voluntary control, the question with which we began this chapter. What is the meaning of *voluntary control?* Or in terms of observable events, what is the difference between a slip and its voluntary repetition? What if the Reverend Spooner just repeated his own spoonerisms voluntarily?

Based on all the foregoing ideas, we can suggest three complementary ways of looking at voluntary control. First, voluntary acts always involve a complex set of automatisms that are organized by a goal structure that is itself also largely unconscious, but that operates in the service of a consciously available goal (Figure 1, Chapter 1). Second, a voluntary act is always consistent with one's dominant, long-lasting goals, or what we have called the *Dominant Goal Hierarchy*. Third, a voluntary act is one whose novel, highly significant, or conflictual components have been anticipated, edited out, and eliminated. We take each point in its turn:

1. *A voluntary act may be viewed as a group of automatisms, organized by a goal structure that is operating in the service of a consciously available goal.* This perspective has been largely developed in Chapter 1 (see Figure 1 in Chapter 1). That chapter concludes that slips can be viewed as "automatisms that are liberated from their guiding goal hierarchy." Conversely, normal voluntary action can be viewed as a set of automatisms that are successfully guided by a goal hierarchy. Within this complex and largely unconscious goal hierarchy, there are conscious components, especially having to do with novel aspects of the planned action. The conscious goal of doing something is generally reportable and clearly serves to recruit a goal structure and the specific automatisms needed to organize and control the details of the planned action. This is an attractive definition, in part because it corresponds well to the commonsense use of the term *voluntary action*. However, it does not specify the terribly important role of the currently dominant goal hierarchy that exists before the conscious goal, and that, indeed, is involved in generating the conscious goal. The next view of voluntary control makes this point.

2. *Voluntary acts are consistent with one's dominant goal hierarchy.* We have previously advanced the notion that any single act or utterance is guided,

not by a single goal, but by a large hierarchy of goals, all of which must be satisfied for the action to be acceptable. Thus, in Chapter 1, Figure 1, only a part of the linguistic goal hierarchy for a single spoken sentence is shown, including articulatory, phonemic, morphemic, lexical, syntactic, and semantic criteria, all of which must be satisfied for the sentence to be normal.

In addition to the linguistic goal structure, there are a host of nonlinguistic goals. Humans may speak to gain attention, respect, and affection from other people, or merely to indicate membership in a certain social group; to complain, command, or encourage others to obtain some goal; to question, gossip, investigate, or reveal; to distract listeners; and so on. Perhaps, several of these goals are pursued with the same action. Even if the hierarchies of these goals are not entirely conscious when they guide an action, a *failure* to meet any one of the guiding goals can generally be detected consciously, so that unconscious information-processing resources can be recruited to repair the error.

Persistent failure to detect and repair admitted errors is often treated as a sign of pathology, ranging from stuttering to aphasias or schizophrenic speech. A person who continually speaks out loud to no one in particular may be suspected of psychotic behavior (which may be considered behavior that appears to persistently violate normally shared human goals). Without such shared and recognizable goals, or the means to carry them out, it is essentially impossible to take part in a normal social group.

We have previously considered the case of the Reverend A. W. Spooner, making one of the famous slips that has been attributed to him, for example, "our queer old Dean" for "our dear old Queen" (Chapter 1). If he actually made such a slip, it would have violated the pragmatic and semantic levels of control, but not the syntactic, lexical, phonemic, or articulatory goal of normal English. Now let us suppose that Spooner simply repeated his slip voluntarily, as exactly as possible, so that it was said again by the same speaker, in the same tone of voice, at the same speaking rate, and so on. What is the difference between the slip and its voluntary repetition? Surely, there is no basic physical difference, nor any real linguistic difference. The main difference is psychological.

In the first case, the speaker fails to execute his intention. If he becomes conscious of his error, he will experience surprise at his own utterance and will show the whole panoply of physiological reactions that make up the orienting response. He may be embarrassed and apologetic. Having first failed to carry out his intention, he may try again. If he makes involuntary errors so often that he can no longer function effectively, he will certainly lose his position, is likely to be examined for neurological problems, and so on. None of these consequences follow from doing physically identical imitations of the slips, if they are voluntary. However, such physically identical voluntary imitations must conform to the entire dominant goal hierarchy; for example, one may repeat such a slip to correct or disavow it, or to amuse one's audience, or for any other reason that is consistent with the dominant goal hierarchy. Thus, from this point of view, a voluntary action is guided by *all* the currently dominant goals.[5]

The single exception to these observations is the case of a novice who is just beginning to learn an action that is consistent with the goal hierarchy, such as a young child or, for that matter, an aphasic who is learning to regain normal speech. Such a person may have the goal of speaking normally and yet may not be able to do so; he or she may nevertheless be understood by others as acting in the service of an understandable goal hierarchy.

There is a third way of defining voluntary control. We can look at it in terms of those action components that are novel, conflictual, or especially significant, and that therefore tend to be conscious before execution. These conscious components give a different perspective on the question.

3. *Voluntary acts are characterized by preparatory editing of conscious elements, typically those that are novel, conflictual, or especially significant.* As described above, one use of the GW architecture is to have multiple unconscious systems inspect a single conscious goal, and to compete against it if it is inadequate. That is to say, the architecture allows multiple unconscious criterion systems to *monitor, edit,* and *repair* a conscious goal or plan. This kind of "many-to-one" editing fits the evidence about what happens when errors become conscious (see Chapter 11, this volume).

If there is indeed such "universal" editing of conscious goal components, we can make the inference that all of the conscious aspects of any voluntary action *must have been tacitly edited* for consistency with the currently dominant goal hierarchy before execution. Again, take the example of premeditated murder. If a normal, rational person has thought for weeks about committing murder and proceeds to do so, we immediately make the inference that *contrary thoughts must have been entertained and rejected:* the murderer must have anticipated the chances of being caught, the likely disapproval of others, and perhaps the suffering of the victim and his or her family. That is to say, for any conscious impulse to action that was considered for some time, we immediately infer that competing alternatives must have been evaluated, especially if the action has heavy potential costs. If the action was taken in spite of these "editing" thoughts, we make inferences about the value system of the murderer, or perhaps about mitigating circumstances such as self-defense. The important point for us here is the idea that conscious impulses are presumed to have been edited before action (assuming that there was enough time and freedom from distraction to edit them).

It is, of course, the novel and conflictual features that require the integrative capacities of a global workspace. They are exactly the features that are likely to need editing, and that are therefore apt to become conscious. A

[5]Of course, these goals must be mutually consistent; otherwise, they would begin to compete *against* each other for access to the limited-capacity system, according to the ideomotor theory. One function of conscious error detection is presumably to detect and repair such between-goal conflicts.

major claim in this chapter is that *voluntary action is, in its essence, action whose conscious components have been edited to an acceptable level before being carried out.* In contrast, countervoluntary actions such as slips are *editing failures,* actions that would have been edited and changed had there been an opportunity to do so before execution.

But what about the components of normal action that are already proficient because of practice? Can we claim that they have been edited? The answer, over the longer run, turns out to be yes. The conclusion that follows from this discussion is that even skilled, automatic components of action *must have been conscious at some time in the past, when they were first shaped.* They therefore must have been implicitly or explicitly edited at that time, so as to be make consistent with the then-dominant goal hierarchy. The overall conclusion is therefore that *voluntary action can be defined as action all of whose components have been edited, over one's lifetime, in terms of consistency with one's dominant goal hierarchy, and for effectiveness in achieving its goals.* This definition complements the previous claim that voluntary action is definable as action that is consistent with the dominant goal hierarchy, and it adds a historical dimension to that claim.

SOME TESTABLE PREDICTIONS

One way to test the ideomotor theory is to use experimentally elicited slips as actions to be triggered by ideomotor goal images. A slip such as "darn bore—barn door" may increase in frequency above the base rate if one shows a rapid picture of a farm immediately before the slip. We know this is true for relatively long exposures of words related to the slip (Motley & Baars, 1979), but it may occur even if the exposure is so fast that it cannot be reported accurately, much like the classic Sperling grid.

A further refinement might be to evoke an *internally generated* conscious image immediately before the action. Here, we may be able to study the effects of the automatization of the goal image. Highly automatized actions such as those studied by Shiffrin and Schneider (1977) should be executed even with fleeting goal images (see Pani, 1982). But novel actions require longer-lasting goal images; hence, forcing someone to perform a novel or conflictual action at the same speed as automatic actions should lead to a breakdown of voluntary control.

Finally, one might induce a cue-dependent mental image by means of posthypnotic suggestion, with amnesia for the suggestion. A highly hypnotizable subject may be told to feel an itch on his or her forehead when the experimenter clears his throat; one would expect the subject to scratch the hallucinatory itch, even though the subject has not been told to scratch, merely to itch. But of course, this should generalize to images and actions other than itching and scratching. If the subject is sitting, he may be told to imagine (on cue) how the room looks from the viewpoint of someone who is standing up. If the ideomotor theory is correct, the subject should tend to stand up spontaneously. But as there has been no suggestion to stand up, this tendency cannot be attributed directly to hypnosis.

Similarly, one could induce competition against certain goal images and study the ways in which the inhibition of a planned action can be lifted. In social situations, there is a set of prohibitions against inappropriate actions, which may be induced by means of experimentally evoked slip techniques. If we evoked an aggressive slip directed to the experimenter, such as "yam doo—damn you," and created a distraction immediately after the onset of the slip, would the inhibitory restraints be lifted? If subjects were given a posthypnotic suggestion to feel an itch on cue, but to be embarrassed to scratch the itch, would the inhibition be lifted by distraction? All these techniques are potentially informative about the ideomotor hypothesis.

SUMMARY AND CONCLUSIONS

We began this chapter by noting that the problem of volition has been largely neglected since the beginning of the behavioristic era, about 1913. It is easy to show, however, that volition is indeed a real and fundamental question in psychology, simply by comparing very similar action pairs, when one member of the pair is perceived and reported to be *in*voluntary, and the physically identical member is voluntary (Table 1). Involuntary actions have clear psychological consequences, such as surprise, disavowal of control or responsibility, and attempts to anticipate and repair the slip. There is no current theory of action and speech that can explain the difference between a slip and its voluntary repetition, a psychologically fundamental difference. Thus, the problem of volition is very real indeed.

Global Workspace theory suggests an interpretation of the commonsense connection between voluntary control and conscious access. The conscious components of a planned action may be broadcast widely to a distributed system of specialized processors, including the effector and subgoal systems needed to carry out the action. Further, the limited-capacity system associated with consciousness seems to be dominated by a goal hierarchy that controls the action. That is, there are a set of implicit but very active goals that compete against any contrary goals that may seek access to the global workspace. Finally, conscious components appear to be "edited," monitored, and repaired by multiple unconscious systems, a configuration that is likewise easily viewed in terms of Global Workspace theory.

The application of GW theory to the problem of voluntary action was anticipated in William James's ideomotor theory a century ago. James suggested that conscious goal images are impulsive—that they tend to be carried out automatically, unless there is a contrary conscious or intentional interference with the conscious goal in the limited-capacity "space." This claim makes perfect sense in terms of GW theory. We can also easily accommodate other features of James's theory, including the possibility of competition between alternative goals, the notion that the action fiat (the immediate command to act) must be consciously available, and the notion that, for successful action control, one needs conscious feedback from the action.

The GW interpretation of James's ideomotor theory allows us to understand the nature of slips as involuntary acts. Most slips are probably induced by competition between alternative goals or subgoals, which need to gain access to the conscious/limited-capacity system in order to recruit and command the distributed systems that control the actual effectors. If this competition is not resolved in time, a fused and incorrect plan can gain control over the global workspace and can trigger an action. Normally, such incorrect goal images are edited and repaired before action, by means of unconscious specialists that receive information from the global workspace, and that can, in return, compete for access to it in order to block execution. However, if the conscious/limited-capacity system is itself momentarily overloaded, such automatic editing can be blocked, and the slips allowed to escape voluntary control. The same plan competition that may create the flawed conscious goal image in the first place may also block access by the editing systems to the global workspace long enough for the error to be made overtly.

We can therefore assign three mutually consistent meanings to the notion of voluntary control. First, voluntary actions consist of a group of automatisms' being executed in the service of a consciously available goal. This is easy to operationalize simply by asking people whether their action is consistent with their own knowledge of the conscious components of the intention. This view of volition corresponds closely to common sense.

A second, somewhat broader, perspective indicates that voluntary actions are consistent, not just with a single goal, but with an entire hierarchy of goals that currently dominate the global workspace (see Chapter 1, Figure 1). Those goals are not themselves qualitatively conscious in the sense that they are perceptual or imaginable. Nevertheless, someone in a tip-of-the-tongue (TOT) state cannot entertain thoughts or intentions that are inconsistent with the goal hierarchy that defines the TOT state, a finding indicating that non-qualitative systems may dominate access to the conscious/limited-capacity system.

A third definition of voluntary control focuses on the issue of the editing of unwanted aspects of the action. In some sense, all the available degrees of freedom in a normal, learned action have at some time in the past been conscious. Because conscious goal images are made available, in GW theory, to all sorts of unconscious distributed systems, including goal systems, they can be monitored, edited, and repaired by such unconscious automatisms. This statement implies that all aspects of a current voluntary action were edited, at some time in the past, by reference to one's overall hierarchy of goals. Thus, either voluntary control can be defined in terms of its consistency with the dominant goal hierarchy, or, it can be defined in terms of all the aspects of the action that were *at one time* consciously decided on. The commonsense association between voluntary control and conscious access thus makes perfect sense in this theoretical framework.

We concluded with some suggestions for the empirical testing of these theoretical claims. Altogether, there is a surprisingly good fit between our intuitive notions of voluntary control, James's ideomotor theory, and our modern information-processing architecture, the Global Workspace theory. Many more implications and predictions from this framework are explored in Baars (1988), and the interested reader is referred to that source for further details.

REFERENCES

Arbib, M. A. (1980). Perceptual structures and distributed motor control. In V. B. Brooks (Ed.), *Handbook of physiology* (Vol. 3). Bethesda, MD: American Physiological Association.

Baars, B. J. (1983). Conscious contents provide the nervous system with coherent, global information. In R. Davidson, G. Schwartz, & D. Shapiro (Eds.), *Consciousness and self-regulation* (Vol. 3, pp. 47–76). New York: Plenum Press.

Baars, B. J. (1986). *The cognitive revolution in psychology.* New York: Guilford Press.

Baars, B. J. (1987). What is conscious in the control of action? A modern ideomotor theory of voluntary control. In D. Gorfein & R. R. Hoffman (Eds.), *Learning and memory: The Ebbinghaus Centennial Symposium,* Hillsdale, NJ: Erlbaum.

Baars, B. J. (1988). *A cognitive theory of consciousness.* New York: Cambridge University Press.

Baddeley, A. D. (1976). *The psychology of memory.* New York: Basic Books.

Basmajian, J. V. (1979). *Biofeedback: Principles and practice for the clinician.* Baltimore, MD: Williams & Wilkins.

Blumenthal, A. L. (1977). *The process of cognition.* Englewood Cliffs, NJ: Prentice-Hall.

Bower, G. H., & Cohen, P. R. (1982). Emotional influences in memory and thinking: Data and theory. In M. S. Clark & T. S. Fiske (Eds.), *Affect and cognition* (pp. 291–331). Hillsdale, NJ: Erlbaum.

Buchwald, J. S. (1974). Operant conditioning of brain activity—An overview. In M. M. Chase (Ed.), *Operant conditioning of brain activity.* Los Angeles: University of California Press.

Drowatsky, J. N. (1975). *Motor learning: Principles and practice.* Minneapolis, MN: Burgess Press.

Ekman, P. (1984). Expression and the nature of emotion. In K. R. Scherer & P. Ekman (Eds.), *Approaches to emotion.* Hillsdale, NJ: Erlbaum.

Ericsson, K. A, & Simon, H. A. (1980). Verbal reports as data. *Psychological Review, 87,* 215–251.

Fodor, J. A. (1983). *The modularity of mind: An essay on faculty psychology.* Cambridge: MIT Press.

Geschwind, N. (1979). Specializations of the human brain. *Scientific American, 241*(3), 180–201.

Greene, P. H. (1972). Problems of organization of motor systems. *Journal of Theoretical Biology, 4,* 308–338.

Grossberg, S. (1982). *Studies of mind and brain.* Boston: Reidel.

Hayes-Roth, B. (1984). A blackboard model of control. *Artificial Intelligence, 16,* 1–84.

Hilgard, E. R. (1980). The trilogy of mind: Cognition, affection, and conation. *Journal of the History of the Behavioral Sciences, 16*(2), 107–117.

Hilgard, E. R., & Marquis, D. G. (1940). *Conditioning and learning.* New York: Appleton-Century-Crofts.

James, W. (1890/1983). *The principles of psychology.* New York: Holt. (Reprint, Cambridge: Harvard University Press.)

Keele, S. W. (1973). *Attention and human performance.* Pacific Palisades, CA: Goodyear.

Kimble, G. A., & Perlmutter, D. (1970). The problem of volition. *Psychological Review, 77*(5), 361–384.

LaBerge, D. (1980). Unitization and automaticity in perception. In J. H. Flowers (Ed.), *1980 Nebraska Symposium on Motivation* (pp. 53–71). Lincoln: University of Nebraska Press.

Langer, E. J., & Imber, L. G. (1979). When practice makes imperfect: Debilitating effects of overlearning. *Journal of Personality and Social Psychology, 37*(11), 2014–2024.

Liberman, A. M., Cooper, F., Shankweiler, D., & Studdert-Kennedy, M. (1967). Perception of the speech code. *Psychological Review, 74,* 431–459.

Libet, B. (1978). Neuronal vs. subjective timing for a conscious sensory experience. In P. A. Buser & P. Rougeul-Buser (Eds.), *Cerebral correlates of conscious experience* (pp. 69–82), INSERM Symposium No. 6. Amsterdam: North-Holland/Elsevier.

Libet, G. (1985). Unconscious cerebral initiative and the role of conscious will in voluntary action. *Behavioral and Brain Sciences, 8,* 529–566.

Luria, A. R. (1980). *Higher cortical functions in man* (2nd ed.) New York: Basic Books. (Russian language edition, 1969.)

McClelland, J. L. (1986). A programmable blackboard. In D. E. Rumelhart, J. L. McClelland, & the PDP Group, *Parallel distributed processing: Explorations in the microstructure of cognition: Vol. 1. Foundations.* Cambridge: MIT/Bradford Press.

Motley, M. T., & Baars, B. J. (1976). Semantic bias effects on the outcomes of verbal slips. *Cognition, 4,* 177–187.

Motley, M. T., & Baars, B. J. (1979). Effects of cognitive set upon laboratory-induced verbal (Freudian) slips. *Journal of Speech and Hearing Research, 22,* 421–432.

Mountcastle, V. B. (1978). An organizing principle for cerebral function: The unit model and the distributed system. In G. M. Edelman & V. B. Mountcastle (Eds.), *The mindful brain.* Cambridge: MIT Press.

Nisbett, R. E., & Wilson, T. D. (1977). Telling more than we can know: Verbal reports on mental processes. *Psychological Review, 86*(3), 215–255.

Norman, P. A., & Shallice, T. (1980). *Attention and action: Willed and automatic control of behavior.* Report, Center for Human Information Processing, University of California, San Diego, La Jolla.

Pani, J. R. (1982). *A functionalist approach to mental imagery.* Paper presented to the Psychonomic Society, Baltimore.

Pavlov, I. P. (1926). *Conditioned reflexes.* Oxford: Oxford University Press.

Reason, J. T. (1979). Actions not as planned: The price of automatization. In G. Underwood & R. Stevens (Eds.), *Aspects of consciousness: Vol. 1. Psychological issues* (pp. 67–89). London: Academic Press.

Reason, J. T. (1982, June). Learning from absent-minded mistakes. *SSRC Newsletter, 46,* 19–26.

Reason, J. T. (1983). Absent-mindedness and cognitive control. In J. Harris & P. Morris (Eds.), *Everyday memory, actions and absentmindedness* (pp. 113–132) New York: Academic Press.

Reason, J. T. (1984a). Lapses of attention in everyday life. In R. Parasuraman & D. R. Davies (Eds.), *Varieties of attention* (pp. 515–549). New York: Academic Press.

Reason, J. T. (1984b). Little slips and big disasters. *Interdisciplinary Science Reviews, 9*(2), 11–19.

Reason, J. T. (1992). *Human error.* Cambridge: Cambridge University Press.

Reddy, R., & Newell, A. (1974). Knowledge and its representation in a speech understanding system. In L. W. Gregg (Ed.), *Knowledge and cognition,* Potomac, MD: Erlbaum.

Rumelhart, D. E., McClelland, T. L., & the PDP Group (1986). *Parallel distributed processing: Explorations in the microstructure of cognition: Vol. 1. Foundation.* Cambridge, MA: MIT/Bradford.

Shallice, T. (1978). The dominant action system: An information-processing approach to consciousness. In K. S. Pope & J. L. Singer (Eds.), *The stream of consciousness: Scientific investigation into the flow of experience.* New York: Plenum Press.

Shiffrin, R. M., & Schneider, W. (1977). Controlled and automatic human information processing: 2. Perceptual learning, automatic attending, and a general theory. *Psychological Review, 84,* 127–190.

Singer, J. L. (1984). The private personality. *Personality and Social Psychology Bulletin, 10*(1), 1–29.

5

Opportunistic Planning and Freudian Slips

Lawrence Birnbaum and Gregg Collins

Freud's study of the psychology of errors (see, e.g., Freud, 1935), including notably slips of the tongue, led him to the conclusion that many such errors are not merely the result of random malfunctions in mental processing, but rather are meaningful psychological acts. That is, they are intentional actions in every sense of the word, reflecting and indeed carrying out the goals, whether conscious or not, of the person who commits them. In particular, Freud argued, such errors stem from attempts to carry out suppressed intentions, intentions that have been formed but then in some sense withdrawn because they conflict with other, more powerful intentions.

For example, in the simplest case, a person may decide to say something but then change his or her mind and decide to say something else instead. Nevertheless, the original intention somehow intrudes itself in his or her utterance. Freud (1935) discussed the example "Dann aber sind Tatsachen zum Vorschwein gekommen" ("and then certain facts were revealed/disgusting"), in which *Vorschwein* is a conflation of *Vorschein* ("revealed") and *Schweinereien* ("disgusting"). The speaker related that he had originally intended to say that the facts were disgusting but controlled himself and decided to say something milder instead. In spite of this decision, however, the suppressed intention apparently exerted an influence on his speech.

Examples of this sort show that goals, once formed, can influence subsequent behavior despite intervening decisions to suppress them. Viewed from

LAWRENCE BIRNBAUM and GREGG COLLINS • The Institute for the Learning Sciences, Northwestern University, Evanston, Illinois 60201.

Experimental Slips and Human Error: Exploring the Architecture of Volition, edited by Bernard J. Baars. Plenum Press, New York, 1992.

an information-processing perspective, however, there are two radically distinct models of how this influence might be exerted. On one account, no further processing of the goal is undertaken after its suppression, and the influence is simply a residue of the processing that took place before that suppression. In the above example, for instance, it may simply be that the prior contemplation of the goal to say the precise word *Schweinereien* activated that word in memory, and that this residual activation had an effect on the process of choosing what words to say, thus causing the slip. On this account, although the slip does in some sense reflect the suppressed goal, it is not really an attempt to carry out the goal.

However, more complex examples show that this sort of residue explanation is not, in general, adequate. Consider Freud's example of the toast "Gentlemen, I call on you to hiccough to the health of our chief," in which the word *aufzustossen* ("hiccough") has been substituted for the word *anzustossen* ("drink"). In his explanation, Freud argued that this slip was a manifestation of an unconscious goal on the part of the speaker to ridicule or insult his superior, suppressed by the social and political duty to do him honor. However, notice that, in this case, in contrast with the simpler example above, one cannot reasonably expect that the speaker's intention to ridicule his superior gave rise originally to a plan involving the use of the word *hiccough*. That word can have been chosen only in the course of attempting to retrieve the consciously intended word *drink,* to which it bears a close similarity in German. Yet, if we accept Freud's analysis of the example, the word *hiccough* was selected because it achieved the speaker's goal to ridicule his superior. Thus, we are forced to conclude that this goal was still active during the attempt to retrieve the word *drink* even though it was suppressed before that attempt.

The mere fact that suppressed goals are able to affect the overt behavior of planners is enough to justify the assertion that they are active. However, the sense of activity implied by examples like the above transcends this ability alone. There is no way that a planner could have reasonably anticipated that the goal of ridiculing or insulting its superior would be satisfied by uttering the word *hiccough*. If for no other reason, this is because there are hundreds of *a priori* more plausible words and phrases that can be used to insult or ridicule someone. However, if the planner was not looking for this opportunity in particular, then it must have been looking for any opportunity in general. In this case, recognizing the opportunity involved realizing that the substitution of the word *aufzustossen* ("hiccough") for the word *anzustossen* ("drink") would, within the context of the toast, result in a ridiculous and insulting utterance. Because the effect of the substitution depends on the context, considerable inference is needed to determine whether it would, indeed, serve to carry out the goal of insulting the superior. Thus, the planner must have expended considerable cognitive resources in checking potential opportunities from the time of the goal's formation to the time that this particular opportunity in fact arose.

But why would a planner expend such resources on a goal that it had already determined not to pursue? In fact, there is no coherent way to view the planner as a whole as the agent behind the expenditure of cognitive resources in the pursuit of suppressed goals. What examples like the above seem to indicate, therefore, is that the goals themselves are active congnitive agents, capable of commanding the cognitive resources needed to recognize opportunities to satisfy themselves, and the behavioral resources needed to take advantage of those opportunities. In a very real sense, such goals must be actively observing the mental processing being carried out for other goals, not only inspecting features of that processing, but also drawing inferences about how those features might be useful in their own satisfaction. They are not merely, for example, data structures in some monolithic planning system, which could be trivially suppressed simply by being erased or marked as inactive. They must be actively suppressed, and such suppression may in fact, fail.

We now come to the central question of this chapter: Is the conception of goals and goal processing needed to explain Freudian slips functionally justifiable, or does it merely reflect an accidental attribute of human psychology?

Fundamental to the above explanation of Freudian slips is the ability to recognize and seize opportunities. In Birnbaum (1986), it is argued that this ability is a fundamental element of intelligent planning in general (see also Hayes-Roth and Hayes-Roth, 1979). To take a simple example, suppose you go to the store to buy something. If, while you are at the store, you notice on sale an item that you want, you may then decide to purchase the item, even though you did not originally go to the store in order to satisfy that intention. The point here is that it is not, in general, possible to foresee all the situations in which an unsatisfied goal may be satisfiable. Intelligent behavior requires the ability to recognize and seize such unforeseen opportunities to satisfy goals.

As we saw in the case of Freudian slips, recognizing opportunities may entail significant inference. This is particularly true if we consider people's ability to seize novel opportunities. It is easy enough to suppose that some features of situations would point directly to goals that they satisfy. For example, it is arguable that, indexed under the feature "money," we have the goal of possessing money. Thus, it isn't hard to see how the opportunity implicit in seeing some money on the street would be recognized.

On the other hand, suppose a person goes to a hardware store and sees a gadget that she or he did not previously know existed, for example, a router. People seem perfectly capable, at least sometimes, of constructing the inferential chain necessary to recognize how such a novel opportunity might facilitate the achievement of a goal that they could not, ahead of time, have known that it would facilitate. For example, someone who had the goal of possessing bookshelves would seem perfectly capable of realizing that a router would be useful in building them. This seems plausible even if she or he had not intended to build the bookcases but had intended to buy them. In that case, the person probably would not have given much thought to how they might be built. But once the person understands what a router does, she or he may realize that it can be used to cut channels in the side boards of the bookcase, into which horizontal boards can be fitted as shelves.

Although the need for this kind of opportunistic processing provides us with a functional justification for the ability of a goal to recognize the means of its own accomplishment when they unexpectedly present themselves, it remains to be explained why goals that have for good reason been suppressed should be able to overcome their suppression when opportunities for their achievement arise. That is, why should an intentional system lack the means to deny such a suppressed goal access to the mechanisms for producing real behavior?

Surprisingly, it turns out that opportunistic processing even offers a functional justification for this seemingly unproductive characteristic of an intentional system. Consider first what it means for a goal to be "suppressed." A goal would need to be suppressed if it were found to be in conflict with another goal in the system. There are two ways that a goal conflict could arise: either because the goals themselves are inherently mutually exclusive, or because some rather more contingent problem arises in attempts to plan for both of them. That is, it might be that two goals are found to be in conflict based on the planner's judgment of the resources and options available under the circumstances in which the goals are being weighed. (See Wilensky, 1983, for an analysis of the considerations involved in making such judgments.) For example, the goal of insulting one's boss is presumably suppressed because it conflicts with more important social and political goals. However, the conflict between these goals is situation-dependent. It is perfectly possible, although unlikely, that there may be some future situation in which insulting the boss and achieving one's political ends would be compatible.

Once a goal conflict is recognized, a planner must decide to suppress one goal and pursue the other based on an assessment of which course of action is most reasonable in the light of current or expected future circumstances. However, it is quite possible that, in fact, future circumstances will be different than originally foreseen. Thus, an opportunistic planner must be able to override previous decisions about which of its goals to pursue. Decisions made when one is formulating the plans currently being pursued should not be immutable.

Consider the following example. Suppose a person is out in the forest and is both hungry and thirsty. Given his knowledge about food sources and water sources, and given whatever other pragmatic considerations pertain in the circumstances, he decides that these two goals conflict, and that he will suppress the thirst goal while he pursues the aim of satisfying his hunger. While pursuing his plan to obtain food, however, he comes upon a stream that he hadn't previously known about. This is precisely the kind of situation in which we would expect—or, indeed, demand—an opportunistic response, regardless of any previous decision to suppress the thirst goal.

The implication here is that the decision to suppress a goal is really just a decision to forgo pursuing that goal for the time being, and that, in an opportunistic processor, no goal is ever really "suppressed." Viewed in this light, the fact pointed to by Freudian slips, that goals that have putatively been suppressed can still take advantage of opportunities for their own achievement, can not only be understood but can be seen to be a desirable and possibly necessary aspect of a planner.

What still remains unexplained, however, is why opportunities would be acted on even when further reflection by the planner would presumably reaffirm the decision to suppress them, as is undoubtedly the case with Freudian slips. It would seem somewhat counterproductive not to demand that the planner be allowed to reconsider the reasons why a goal was suppressed, in light of the sudden appearance of an opportunity to achieve the goal. We might expect, for example, that despite the opportunity to insult or ridicule one's boss, this opportunity would not be taken because it would still be impolitic to do so. We might, in fact, assume that this is often what happens. In the case of the hungry and thirsty person, for example, it would make sense for that person, on finding the stream, to reconsider why he thought there was a conflict between those goals.

There will not always be time for this reconsideration, however. The fortuitous presence of a rock or a stick, for example, noticed in the course of a struggle with an animal, is an opportunity that, to be helpful, would have to be seized virtually without thought. Thus, we might expect that when there is severe time pressure in deciding whether to pursue an opportunity or not, action can be taken without due consideration by the planning mechanism as a whole. Lexical selection, although lacking the life-or-death implication of struggles with predators, is nevertheless a process that must occur in split seconds to produce smooth vocalizations. We might, therefore, view Freudian slips as an unfortunate but unpreventable side effect of the need for this kind of opportunistic short cut to behavior.

In conclusion, we have argued that, in order to accept Freud's intentional explanations for slips of the tongue, we must postulate that goals are active mental agents, commanding the cognitive resources needed to recognize opportunities to satisfy themselves, and capable of acting on such opportunities even when suppressed or unconscious. We have further shown that such a conception of goals can be functionally justified on the grounds that it fulfills the requirements of opportunistic processing. In particular, we have seen that the ability of such goals to manifest themselves even after their "suppression" is not merely a flaw in human beings, but a necessary attribute of an adequate opportunistic processor. Thus, it seems that the kind of intentional machinery needed to support opportunistic planning would quite naturally exhibit Freudian slips.

REFERENCES

Birnbaum, L. (1986). Integrated processing in planning and understanding (Research report no. 489). New Haven, CT: Yale University, Department of Computer Science.

Freud, S. (1935). *A general introduction to psychoanalysis* (J. Riviere, trans.). New York: Liveright.

Hayes-Roth, B., and Hayes-Roth, F. (1979). A cognitive model of planning. *Cognitive Science, 3*, pp. 275–310.

Wilensky, R. (1983). *Planning and understanding.* Reading, MA: Addison-Wesley.

III

METHODS FOR INDUCING PREDICTABLE SLIPS IN SPEECH AND ACTION

This section is focused on methodology. Chapters 6, 7, and 9 present new methods for eliciting slips of various kinds in the laboratory. Chapter 6 demonstrates a dozen techniques, all involving competition between output plans. These competition techniques yield a great variety of slips. Plan competition can be specifically related to the theoretical approaches developed previously in Chapters 1 and 4. Chapter 7 reports on some specific methods for inducing slips of (nonverbal) action, and in Chapter 9, we show that a class of sentential slips that has been claimed to provide evidence for Chomskian transformational errors can, in fact, be induced by competition between paraphrastic sentence plans. Finally, in Chapter 8, Joseph Stemberger shows that experimentally induced spoonerisms are quite similar phonetically to spontaneous spoonerisms.

6

A Dozen Competing-Plans Techniques for Inducing Predictable Slips in Speech and Action

Bernard J. Baars

INTRODUCTION

Psychologists have studied the inner workings of input processes like sensation, perception, and comprehension in great detail and with considerable success. Mediating processes like memory and thinking have also come under close scrutiny. But until recently, the mechanisms underlying *action* have been comparatively neglected. One of the main reasons for this neglect was apparently already known to Wilhelm Wundt (1862/1961): "It must be admitted that it is primarily the sensory side of psychic life which accords the widest prospect for experimental investigation" (p. 72). In perception and memory studies, the problem of *experimental control* is clearly solvable: one needs only to control the stimulus conditions. But it is much more difficult to manipulate the preconditions of spontaneous thought and action.

BERNARD J. BAARS · The Wright Institute, 2728 Durant Avenue, Berkeley, California 94704.

Experimental Slips and Human Error: Exploring the Architecture of Volition, edited by Bernard J. Baars. Plenum Press, New York, 1992.

In this chapter, we describe a family of techniques for eliciting predictable slips of speech and action, most of them developed over the last 15 years. These slips can apparently be induced at all levels in speech and action, from abstract plan representation to actual control of the muscular effectors; further, they are demonstrably involuntary; and they can be designed to meet (or violate) a host of preselected criteria. The family of elicitable slips includes spoonerisms, blends, word exchanges in sentences, syllable exchanges between words, and reversals of subject and object in a sentence, as well as nonverbal slips of typing, gestures, and object manipulation. All of the elicitation techniques appear to work by creating *competition* between alternative output plans (see Chapter 1). This fact has many implications, but methodologically it implies that the set of techniques is expandable, so that new slip inductions may be designed to test specific hypotheses (e.g., Chen & Baars, Chapter 9, this volume; Dell & Repka, Chapter 10, this volume; Baars & Mattson, 1981, and Chapter 11, this volume). In addition to plan competition, all of the techniques discussed here involve some time pressure, and the plan conflict is also likely to load the central limited-capacity system, at least momentarily. Thus, all induction methods fit the Competing-Plans Hypothesis discussed in Chapters 1 and 4.

Once we gain experimental control over lifelike slips in speech and action, a number of hypotheses become testable. A prominent example is the Freudian slip hypothesis, which has been the subject of widespread speculation since Freud's first book on the topic (1901/1938). Until recently, Freud's hypothesis was as untestable as it was famous, because any given spontaneous slip can be explained in many different ways. Having experimental control over the occurrence of slips puts us in a much better position to test the Freudian hypothesis (see Chapter 12). Later in this chapter, we will briefly discuss these substantive applications and implications of the slip induction techniques. Last, we will consider whether experimentally induced slips are "ecologically valid," that is, whether they are sufficiently lifelike to bridge the gap between laboratory findings and the real world.

COMPETING-PLANS TECHNIQUES

Table 1 gives an overview of the slip techniques, which will be described one by one.

A number of researchers have attempted to replicate spontaneous slips in the laboratory. McKay (1971) attempted to simulate the conditions leading to spontaneous spoonerisms by having people repeat a syllable string in which only one syllable was to be stressed and reported that the stressed syllable tended to preenter in the sequence. MacKay and Soderberg (1971a,b) reported experimentally induced finger slips analogous to linguistic blends. Finally, errors of various kinds have been evoked as a by-product of other tasks (e.g., McKay, 1976).

TABLE 1
Competing Plans Tasks that Elicit Slips in Speech and Action

A. Tongue twisters: Phonological–motoric competition
   1. Overt tongue twisters (e.g., MacKay, 1971)
   2. Tongue twisters in inner speech (Dell, 1980; Dell & Repka, Chapter 10, this volume)
   3. Phonological fusion task (Laver, 1980)
B. Phonological bias techniques
   4. For spoonerisms (Baars & Motley, 1974; Motley & Baars, 1974)
   5. For word retrieval errors (Kimble & Perlmutter, 1970; Reason, Chapter 3, this volume)
C. Ordinal conflict techniques
   6. Spoonerisms (Baars & Mattson, 1976)
   7. Syllable switches (Baars & Mattson, & Cruickshank)
   8. Word exchanges between phrases in a sentence (Baars, 1977)
      a. Socially inappropriate
      b. Semantically anomalous
      c. Transformational errors (Chen & Baars, Chapter 9, this volume)
   9. Question-answering technique (Baars & Mattson, 1981)
   10. Typing errors (Mattson & Baars, 1985)
   11. "Simon Says" task (Mattson & Baars,)
   12. Table-setting task (Mattson & Baars, 1987)
D. Techniques that use competition between alternative words in memory
   13. Word blends (Baars, 1977) (See also B.5 above)
E. Techniques that use competition by deliberate transforms
   14. Irregular vs. regular verb competition (MacKay, 1976)
   15. Active–passive competition (Baars, 1977)

A. Tongue Twisters: Phonological–Motoric Competition

1. Overt Tongue Twisters. Tongue twisters have long been known to induce predictable errors. MacKay (1971) noted that they are characterized by successions of similar phonemes, which often pose some difficulty in pronunciation: one effective trick is to have alternating consonants that differ in only one feature in identical syllabic positions, such as "The Leith police dismisseth us." All the /th/'s can exchange with /s/'s, because they are all in the final syllabic consonant position. The fact that the two consonants differ only in one feature seems to be critical in ensuring a high rate of dysfluencies and errors.

The rapid alternation of phonemes differing in only one distinctive feature can easily be interpreted from a competing-plans perspective. Tongue twisters appear to involve competition for output under time pressure between two minimally different phonemes. Thus, at first glance, tongue twisters seem to satisfy at least two of the conditions for the competing-plans techniques: competition, time pressure, and perhaps momentary overloading of the limited-capacity system due to the speed of the task.

There has been a tendency at times to dismiss tongue twisters as merely motoric confusions. If by *motoric* one means "simple" or "merely physical," that view is clearly wrong. After all, we know well that phonemes are complex *classes* of physical events, not single events. Liberman, Cooper, Shankweiler, and Studdert-Kennedy (1967) pointed out, for example, that in different vowel contexts, different consonants are shaped differently, both acoustically and motorically. If the /b/ or "bad goof" migrates to the position of the /g/, the resulting error is shaped differently spectrographically and articulatorily. Thus, even in discussing phoneme exchanges, we are already addressing a fairly high level of abstraction.

In addition to tongue twisters, sheer speeded speaking can apparently induce errors (Cohen, 1973; MacKay, 1982; Nooteboom, 1969). Errors induced by a high speaking rate are not specifically predictable, however, unlike the other competing-plans tasks discussed in this chapter. In addition, it is difficult to know exactly what causes these errors because the exact items are rarely given in experimental reports. Thus, there may be a "tongue-twister component" in a speeded speaking task if similar phonemes alternate, or if they are difficult to pronounce. Further, speeded tasks are likely to overload the limited-capacity system, a factor that is also likely to contribute to errors (Chapter 1).

2. Tongue Twisters in Inner Speech. Dell (1980) and Dell and Repka (Chapter 10, this volume) have shown that tongue twisters in inner speech resemble those produced overtly. This finding—which is one of the few things we know about the very important modality of inner speech—also emphasizes the nonphysical nature of tongue twisters. After all, if tongue twisters were only physical events, they would not occur in inner speech, unaccompanied by any effector movements.

3. Phonological Fusion Task. Laver (1980) reported a procedure in which competition is induced between the vowels in /pUp/ (as in "poop") and /pip/ (as in "peep") by repeating these syllables in rapid alternation. Laver's monolingual English speakers sometimes produced the fused vowel /püp/—a vowel that does not exist in standard English, and that most English speakers cannot produce voluntarily (that is, the vowel /ü/ as in French *mur*, or in German *für*). This vowel is located precisely between /U/ and /i/ in the linguistic vowel circle. This may be taken as further evidence that tongue twisters involve phonemic output processes, which go beyond merely "low-level" motoric processes.

B. Phonemic Bias Techniques

4. Phonemically Induced Spoonerisms. Probably the best-known technique for eliciting slips is the phonemic biasing method for producing spontaneous spoonerisms (Baars & Motley, 1974; Motley & Baars, 1974). It works as follows. Subjects are shown a series of word pairs displayed for a duration of 1–2 seconds by means of a memory drum or a computer terminal.[1]

The instructions are as follows:

> This is an experiment to test your immediate memory for word pairs. Please
> 1. Pay careful attention to each word pair as it appears, so that you can recall it immediately afterward; and
> 2. When you see the cue RESPOND, say the preceding word pair out loud, as quickly as you can.

The reader is encouraged to try the task in Table 2 by cutting a small horizontal slit in a card and moving it down each column, exposing only one word pair at a time. (Table 2 does not contain a short practice list, filler items, and "false alarm" response cues, which were, of course, used in the experimental task to break up any predictable patterns.)

This simple task tends to create a readiness to say *each* word pair as it appears, so that the subject can say it rapidly afterward, if the response cue appears. The phonemic priming items resemble the desired slip as much as possible. (Notice that the biasing material resembles the slip not just in its initial phonemes, even though those are the phonemes that must exchange to create the spoonerisms.) This task reliably elicits a reasonable slip rate— perhaps 10–20% of trials—depending on many factors, including the exposure and interexposure interval, the verbal facility of the subjects, the kinds of linguistic materials used, and whether the slips are consistent with or violate any linguistic or social expectations (Chapter 11). Further, the degree of priming, the presence of a concurrent limited-capacity loading task (Chapter 1), and the like are apt to influence the error rate.

Table 2 can also be used to illustrate the ordinal conflict task for spoonerisms (Baars & MacKay, 1978; Baars & Motley, 1976). The reader needs only to use the same card with a horizontal slit, simply *reversing the order* of the last word pair that appeared, just before RESPOND. Imagine, for example, that the response cue is REVERSE instead of RESPOND. Now, even in the absence of phonemic priming, spoonerisms will be elicited at a reasonable rate. The same ordinal conflict effect also works to produce syllable exchanges, word exchanges in sentences, and action spoonerisms (see below).

5. Phonemically Induced Word Retrieval Slips. Phonemic bias can also trigger errors in word retrieval. The most famous example of this is the "poke-poke-poke" technique (Kimble & Perlmutter, 1970; Reason, Chapter 3, this volume). In this case, one merely asks the subject to repeat "poke, poke, poke" a number of times (about seven seems adequate) and then asks the subject to answer the question, "What do you call the white of an egg?" Re-

---

[1]Informal observation suggests that the rather loud, regular relay click of the memory drum may serve to pace the subjects's speech, thereby increasing the slip rate. This can be simulated on a microcomputer by a brief 0.1-second tone, sounded simultaneously with each change in the display.

TABLE 2
Demonstrating the Phonemic Bias and Ordinal Conflict
Techniques for Eliciting Spoonerisms

bill deal	rack seal	sane foam
bark dog	read sale	sell phone
bang doll	real sick	seal fog
darn bore	soul rock	seem fine
		RESPOND
give book	take ball	
go back	tall box	cell roll
get boot	bail toss	same row
bad goof	RESPOND	sane rope
RESPOND		rafe sode
	gait bosh	RESPOND
ball doze	can't bowl	
bash door	cat boast	kid lot
bean deck	cad bossed	kicks log
bell dark	bet gashed	guess lock
darn bore	RESPOND	liss kong
		RESPOND
RESPOND	RESPOND	
		fail sun
RESPOND	key door	
	keen dog	ladle food
ripe log	deep cot	lake faint
real long	RESPOND	fate lame
long rice		RESPOND
RESPOND	cot bed	
	code bit	toe dead
big dutch	cod bait	code bit
bang doll	bought cat	tome dive
bill deal	RESPOND	doan tef
bark dog		RESPOND
dart board		
RESPOND		

markably, the wrong answer (the yolk) is obtained almost 100% of the time, if the subjects answer quickly enough. For those who are genuinely unfamiliar with the right answer (the egg white, or albumen), this is of course not a real slip because it does not violate their intention to say what they believe to be the right word; but those who do know the answer also make the error remarkably often. This technique will trigger slips at a higher rate than any other method discovered so far, so that it may be an optimal tool for exploring some aspects of the speech system (viz. Chapter 12).

"Priming" or "biasing" is of course a familiar tool for cognitive psychologists. It generally involves the conscious presentation of some stimulus that is closely related to the event to be tested (Baars, 1988). Priming works not just phonemically, but probably at every level of psycholinguistic control. For example, if one elicits a certain spoonerism such as "darn bore—barn door" at a reasonable rate, one can add semantic primes (such as "farm gate"), which will significantly increase the rate of errors like "barn door" (Motley & Baars, 1976). Thus, different sources of priming or activation seem to be additive, providing they are all compatible with the same slip.

C. Ordinal Conflict Techniques

It is not clear that phonemic priming is likely to trigger errors in spontaneous speech. Baars and Motley (1976) argued that it is not, and that spoonerisms that can be evoked phonemically in the laboratory may be due to higher level problems in spontaneous speech. Specifically, order competition between two different lexical orders may serve to confuse the order of phonemes; thus, competition at one level may *propagate* to the next lower level to create a spoonerism. If that is so, then order competition between two words may cause phoneme exchanges (spoonerisms).

6. Spoonerisms. As predicted by the above argument, phonemic priming is not the only way to elicit spoonerisms. Baars and Motley (1976) showed that creating order competition within word pairs does indeed generate phoneme exchanges, as predicted. The reader may demonstrate this effect with the materials given in Table 2, using the second (REVERSE) method. Order competition can generate many other kinds of slips, as the following sections indicate.

7. Syllable Exchanges. Baars, Mattson, and Cruickshank (1985) showed that syllables can switch between two multisyllabic words if uncertainty is created about the order of the words. Notice that the target word pairs have parallel stress patterns and receptive syllabic and phonemic contexts— thus, "horrible miracle—*mir*able *hor*ricle," (Table 3). Pacing may need to be rather rapid in this demonstration.

8. Word Exchanges between Phrases in a Compound Sentence. Baars (1977) and Baars and MacKay (1978) have shown that this Ordinal Conflict Effect applies to phrases in a sentence as well, as demonstrated in Table 4. The two phrases are syntactically parallel, but the syntactic structure of the phrases can vary quite a bit. (In the examples below, the phrases themselves are in brackets [], and the switching words are underlined.) Thus:

1. [The infant's height is *good*] but [his weight is *moderate*].
2. He [*fixed* his trousers] and [*dropped* his watch].
3. The woman [worked *incessantly*] while the nun [waited *patiently*].
4. The housewife [*bought* the cat food] and [*obtained* the detergent].
5. The picky gourmet [*covered* his dinner] and [*threw up* his hands].

TABLE 3

Eliciting Syllabic Spoonerisms with the Ordinal Conflict Effect

recapturing discovery	discreditable pedestrian
REPEAT	REPEAT
distressing reflection	horrible miracle
REPEAT	REPEAT
recurrent dependence	interfering homophone
REPEAT	REVERSE
magnanimous regretfulness	interrupted undertaking
REPEAT	REPEAT
reporters discussants	underhanded takeover
REVERSE	REPEAT
guilty switches	intervening centuries
REPEAT	REPEAT
nullified syllable	cancerous mystery
REVERSE	REPEAT
orderly cardinal	dignified monastery
REVERSE	REVERSE

Evidently, the syntax can vary quite a bit, as long as some parallelism is maintained. Notice that nouns may switch in these sentences as well as verbs, adjectives, or adverbs. Indeed, in many of the slips obtained, it is difficult to be sure which elements have actually moved—assuming that the sentence frame has remained stable, so that we can talk about "movement" at all with respect to some stable string of words.

Some fairly complex syntactic and semantic accommodation seems to occur. In Sentence 5, the particle *up* tends to travel with its verb *throw,* whereas the other verbs move without any prepositions. If we were to present in Sentence 1 the adjectival phrases *good* and *only moderate, only* is likely to move along with *moderate* rather than produce the somewhat anomalous slip "The infant's height is *only good.*"

Once we can manipulate the content of a sentence, it is fairly easy to create sentential slips that meet or violate normal expectations. Thus, we can create slips that are:

1. Socially appropriate or inappropriate (Baars, 1977).
2. Semantically normal or anomalous (Baars, 1977).
3. Putative "transformational errors" (Chen & Baars, Chapter 9, this volume).
4. Sentences that are false as opposed to true (Baars & Mattson, 1981).
5. Slips that express emotional conflict (Baars, Chapter 12, this volume).

Examples 4 and 5 above also make an interesting contrast: 4 is essentially a switch in synonyms and therefore is not a semantic error at all. It is entirely correct at all purely linguistic levels, except possibly for stylistic preferences between the formal *obtained* and the less formal and more specific *bought.* In contrast, 5 involves a major change in meaning: "The gourmet *threw up* his

TABLE 4

Eliciting Word Exchanges between the Phrases of a Sentence by
Means of the Ordinal Conflict Effect[a]

The woman [heard the melody] and [remembered the story].
REPEAT
The mother [tossed the ball] and [cuddled the baby].
REPEAT
The girl [caught the train] and [saw the show].
REVERSE
The maid [took the apple] and [ate the cake].
REPEAT
The watchman [ripped the letter] and [sent the signal].
REVERSE
He [dropped a watch] and [fixed his trousers].
REVERSE
She [touched her nose] and [picked a flower].
REVERSE
He [left his seat] and [kissed the girl].
REPEAT
My wife will [buy a puppy] and [nurse the baby].
REPEAT
We will [improve the cancer problem] and [intensify the research].
REVERSE
The housewife [helped the maids] and [stripped the beds].
REPEAT
The gourmet [smelled his food] and [ordered his bill].
REVERSE
He [scratched his chin] and [rubbed his nose].
REPEAT
She [covered the cheese] and [served the cake].
REVERSE

---

[a]Phrases to be reversed in order are shown in brackets [ ].

dinner and *covered* his hands." Experimental materials can be designed in which all factors except one are kept constant in the two comparison conditions, so that very good experimental control is maintained. As noted before, sentential slips can be designed to meet or violate a large number of semantic and pragmatic criteria, thereby allowing us to confront the speech production system with a real problem: Does it manage to avoid making the error overtly? In general, the answer seems to be that it does, most of the time, though not always (Baars, 1977; Baars & MacKay, 1978; Baars & Mattson, 1981). Possible mechanisms for maintaining this kind of output control are examined in Mattson and Baars (Chapter 11, this volume), and the Freudian slip issue is discussed in Baars, Cohen, Bower and Berry (Chapter 12, this volume).

9. Question-Answering Technique. How can uncertainty about the order of two phrases occur naturally? From the beginning of this research program, we have been concerned with the issue of naturalness. Above, we argued that phonemic priming may not happen naturally but may be caused by order conflicts at the lexical level. Ordinal conflict seems much more natural because the fundamental task of speech production is to string words in the proper order, in one of many optional ways.

One case where conflict may happen naturally is the following. Suppose we are answering a question relating two clauses, and we wish to answer using the same vocabulary—perhaps because it is in short-term memory and therefore readily available. These conditions are satisfied by the task illustrated in Table 5. Notice that a subject in this task frequently has to choose between the order of the two clauses, as well as opposite adjectives like *above* and *below*. Baars and Mattson (1981) showed that this task does indeed lead to a variety of errors, including exchanges of words between the clauses. This must be one of quite a large number of cases in which the speech production system is faced with a reordering of known lexical units. The job of choosing a particular order among several possibilities may be quite a productive source of linguistic errors.

We can generalize the Ordinal Conflict Effect to other slips, including nonverbal actions. The need to order components is not limited to speech; it is part of any action that is extended over time. Thus, we have found that we can elicit typing errors using the ordinal conflict effect, as well as errors in the

TABLE 5

The Ordinal Conflict Effect Induced by
Answering a Question[a]

1. Does the wet fall come before the cold winter?
2. Are the green hills below the snowy mountains?
3. Is the blue sky below the gray sea?
4. Is chilly Norway south of sandy Egypt?
5. Do you drink your soup before you start dessert?
6. Can you die happily before living peacefully?
7. Is chilly Norway north of sandy Egypt?
8. Are the leafy tree branches below the intricate roots?
9. Are the green hills above the lush mountains?
10. Can you die quickly after living vigorously?
11. Is our friend Canada north of our neighbor Mexico?
12. Is a fast car smaller than a racing bicycle?
13. Can you eat a light lunch after a big dinner?
14. Does the wet fall come after the cold winter?

[a]Subjects are required to answer *with the same words* used in the question. "No" answers therefore always involve phrase reversals. Thus, the correct answer for Question 3 is "No, the gray sea is *below* the blue sky." Several types of slips are possible, including a false answer using a correct preposition, and a switch of adjectives or nouns between the phrases. A complete list of instructions, questions, and sample slips is given in Baars and Mattson (1981).

so-called "Simon Says" task, and in a table-setting task (Mattson, 1987; Mattson & Baars, 1985).

10. Typing Errors. Although the relationship between hands and finger strokes is not the same as the relationship between words and phonemes, creating order competition between two hand orders (right-left vs. left-right) also tended to trigger simple finger-stroke errors. However, complete exchanges of finger strokes between the two hands were rare. (See also MacKay & Soderberg, 1971b.)

11. "Simon Says" Task. This task is named after the children's game in which the leader calls out "Simon says do this!" followed by some action. One tends to become so primed to the act of following the leader, that when the leader simply calls out, "Do this!" the followers have a tendency to move, even though the crucial words "Simon says" have been omitted. We have used an analogous follow-the-leader task, in which the subjects imitate a videotaped action, followed by a cue that signals the subject to copy the action either in order or in reverse order.

12. Table-Setting Task. Mattson (1987) chose the task of setting a table as a socially well-defined action and induced errors by means of order competition. As expected, components of the task were executed out of order or even exchanged, in much the way phonemes are exchanged to create spoonerisms. (See Mattson & Baars, Chapter 11, this volume.)

D. Creating Competition in Deliberate Memory Retrieval

13. Word Blends. It has been known for many years that word blends often seem to fuse two equally likely synonyms. It is easy to evoke such blends in the laboratory. For example, Baars (1977) gave subjects a list of similar-sounding synonym pairs to remember and instructed them to say one synonym whenever the other was presented. Thus, whenever *ghastly* appeared, the subject was to say *grizzly,* and vice versa. Table 6 provides a number of synonym pairs to memorize (Column 1) followed by individual words that serve as cues for their synonymous associates (Column 2). With reasonable pacing, the second column will evoke some blends between the paired synonyms.

E. Creating Competition by Deliberate Transforms

14. Irregular versus Regular Verb Competition. In a study on the speed of regular versus irregular past-tense formation, MacKay (1976) obtained such incorrect past tenses in a task in which the subjects were given the

TABLE 6
Eliciting Blends between Two Related Words

Paired associates to memorize	Task: given one associate, quickly say the other
ghastly—grizzly	muggy
	grizzly
shout—yell	scary
	hugged
scary—screaming	touch
	plucked
good—fine	yell
	small
slick—slippery	buy
	shady
muggy—sweaty	shout
	good
stop—halt	wish
	sweaty
kissed—hugged	picked
	get
checked—fixed	need
	feel
feel—touch	screaming
	checked
picked—plucked	fine
	ghastly
low—small	stop
	need
buy—get	cool
	picked
need—wish	slick
	low
cool—shady	slippery

present-tense forms and were asked to provide the past tenses as rapidly as possible.

15. Active–Passive Competition. It is easy to show subjects the relationship between active and passive versions of the same sentence. If they are asked to make active versus passive transformations as quickly as possible, would we find blends or more complex combinations of the two sentences? Baars (1977) showed that some of these errors are indeed induced.

In sum, these are the fourteen slip induction techniques, all understandable in the framework of competing plans, that are now available to psycholinguists for further exploring speech and action control.

Common Principles of the Slip Induction Techniques

A few major principles underlie all the slip induction techniques developed so far:

1. *Competition between alternative speech plans.* Competition can be induced by means of a misleading preparatory set, by asking people to reverse unexpectedly the order of two units, by creating competition in memory retrieval, or by asking people to rapidly transform difficult input voluntarily.

2. *Time pressure.* In addition to competition, all of our slip techniques demand a quick response from the subjects. We suspect that the time pressure keeps subjects from "sorting out" the competing plans and from editing out some anomalies.

3. *Momentary overloading of limited capacity.* As we argued in Chapter 1, any task in which different goals or plans are contending for access to the conscious/limited-capacity system is likely to overload this system at least momentarily. This is indeed likely to happen even if the task is not particularly designed to overload limited capacity. Overloading of the conscious/limited-capacity system may block effective monitoring, editing, and repair during a critical phase in the production of speech or action (Baars, 1988). In this chapter, we focus primarily on a more easily observable level: the application of the competing-plans techniques in the induction of a great variety of slips (Baars, 1980). It is important, however, to keep in mind that several other factors may be operating at the same time.

Substantive Implications of the Techniques

What can we learn from the techniques themselves about the control of speech and action? First of all, they support the idea that competition between different speech plans may be a general source of problems in planning and control. One continuing theme is that many—perhaps all—slips seem to emerge from choice points in the control of speech and action. Indeed, a principled argument can be made that competition between alternative plans is to an output system what ambiguity is to input: it defines a choice point between alternative paths in the flow of processing. Such choice points are obviously of critical importance in any comprehensive theory of action (see Freud, 1901/1938; MacKay, 1987; Norman, 1981).

Competition between alternative plans probably occurs naturally in spontaneous speech (see Chapter 1). We have pointed out that there are often many ways to express a thought or to carry out any single purpose. This implies that, starting from an abstract intention to say or do something, the system must make choices between alternative ways of realizing the abstract plan. This need to choose between alternatives can be a source of competition between speech plans, and one can easily imagine other sources as well. To give some idea of the generality of this problem, consider some points made by Greene (1972):

A person can perform the same action in many different ways; for example, he can write with his arm held high or low or loaded with a weight, or even with a pencil held in his teeth, and although his muscles move differently in each, the same handwriting always results. An infinity of motions can lead to a single result. . . . Surely [the] brain does not store . . . all the possible configurations of all his hand muscles. . . . The nervous system avoids this storage through a style of motor control whereby subsystems having many degrees of freedom are governed by a central control system having a few degrees of freedom. . . . The highest control center selects an appropriate combination that almost fits what it wants to do, and transformations at lower levels shape these combinations into a better approximation of the desired action. (p. 304)

It appears, therefore, that choice points are often desirable in control systems—and that they can also lead to real difficulties.

It is very clear that most details of speech articulation are not normally under voluntary control. Indeed, one of the dramatic facts about speaking is how much of it is left to unconscious mechanisms: we are not aware of the syntactic rules we use, of the details of lexical search, or of the detailed movements of the mouth. Moreover, movements of the articulatory organs—the tongue, lips, jaw, glottis, velum, and vocal cords—have enormous variability and flexibility. We can speak in an understandable way even if some of those articulators are obstructed by large wads of chewing gum, head colds, or laryngitis. Thus, it makes sense to suppose that many details of speech are controlled by subsystems that are not under immediate voluntary control. The fact that highly rule-governed, involuntary errors are made overtly at all suggests that subsystems occasionally escape from executive control (see Table 1 in Chapter 1).

We can draw further substantive implications. For example, the success of the priming technique for inducing slips supports the idea that action systems are prepared before execution by mean of "feedforward" from an abstract action plan (e.g., Gel'fand, Gurfinkel, Fomin, & Tsetlin, 1971; Greene, 1972; Norman, 1981). There are a number of functional arguments in favor of this position. The idea of preparatory feedforward is made even more plausible by the empirical effectiveness of phonetic and semantic *priming* in inducing slips. In terms of the ideomotor theory developed in Chapter 4, such priming may correspond to conscious goals or goal fragments, which are believed in that theory to recruit the unconscious subgoals and effectors that carry out the ultimate action.

Finally, the Ordinal Conflict Effect (OCE) has interesting implications for a comprehensive theory of action. Here, we find that an order conflict at the level of words shows up as an error in phoneme and syllable sequencing, that an order conflict of phrases shows up in word sequencing, and that in a typing task, an order conflict of hands shows up as a slip in finger sequencing. Conflicts of order between higher level units seem to cause a switch of subordinate units. The OCE may in fact be a general property of the organization of serial action. It clearly involves an interaction between different levels of control.

One could imagine a number of scenarios to explain this interaction. One scenario was proposed by Baars and Motley (1976), who suggested that sometimes a speaker may want to insert a word into a planned sentence after the sentence has already been partly executed. This desire may create a conflict of order between two words in the sentence, which may lead to the activation of initial phonemes out of order. For instance, in the case of a slip such as "bad good—gad boof," the speaker may have started to say, "I really made a goof," and decided to insert the adjective *bad* after beginning to say the word *goof.* Thus the initial phoneme /g/ of *goof* might already be activated when one inserts the initial phoneme /b/ of *bad.* The highest activations are then /g/ and /b/; however, phoneme sequencing constraints rule out a combination such as /gb/, and syntactic constraints prohibit /goof bad/, leaving the system with only one viable plan, "gad boof." This is only one possible scenario; others can be devised rather easily. Further work needs to be done to test different explanations of this apparently quite general effect.

Using Experimental Slips to Study the Control of Speech and Action

In consequence of these new techniques, we have been able to test a set of substantive hypotheses about speech production, some of which were previously resistant to experimental investigation. These include the problem of anticipatory control of errors in speech planning, the issue of "Freudian slips," and some aspects of the organization of serial action (Baars, 1977; Baars, Motley, & MacKay, 1975; Motley & Baars, 1976; Motley, Baars, & Camden, 1979). We have also begun to focus with one of these techniques on the issue of intentionality in the control of speech and action (Baars & Mattson, 1981; Mattson, 1987).

Specifically;

1. The effect of multiple levels of priming. For example, a slip like "barn door" is increased in frequency with a preceding semantic prime like "farm gate."
2. Studying the interaction between "units" and "integration mechanisms" in speech and action (see Chapter 1).
3. Error-minimizing mechanisms, such as anticipatory editing of speech plans prior to articulation (see Chapter 11).
4. The question of Freudian slips (see Chapter 12).
5. Limited-capacity overload and the Competing-Plans Hypothesis (see Chapter 1).

Are Induced Slips "Artificial"?

Are our experimentally induced slips like those observed outside of the laboratory? Any experimental technique is useful if it gives insight into normal conditions; for this purpose, it is not always necessary to reproduce the exact phenomena found in nature. For example, there are extensive research literature on reaction time, on subliminal perception, and on lexical decision tasks, even without a guarantee that such tasks are naturalistically important. Presumably, then, if the slip induction techniques yield insight into the mysteries of speech and action production, their naturalistic status would be of secondary importance. Scientific yield is the major criterion for judging any experimental task. Nevertheless, it is still useful to clarify the relationships between the experimental and naturalistic slips, because a great literature has emerged on the latter phenomena.

Naturalness of Induced Slips

Do induced slips resemble spontaneous slips? Because we are speaking of a *family* of slip techniques, the answer is not a simple yes or no. In general it would seem that, *to the extent we can plausibly simulate the triggering conditions of natural slips* in the laboratory, and *to the extent that we find similar error patterns in consequence,* we can claim a successful simulation of natural slips. We now have a growing body of evidence that some of the causal conditions of real-world slips can be closely simulated in the laboratory (see Dell, 1980; Stemberger, Chapter 8, this volume).

Controversy over the naturalness of experimental slips has emerged in one case so far. Baars *et al.* (1975) found that experimentally elicited lexical spoonerisms are made several times more often than matched spoonerisms that are nonlexical. This result has been replicated directly (Dell, 1980). However, there has been some disagreement over whether the lexical-slip-rate advantage exists in spontaneous slips. Fromkin (1980) found that, in the UCLA corpus of speech errors, nonsense slips occurred about 60% of the time compared to 40% lexical slips and suggested that the results of Baars *et al.* (1975) therefore do not apply to spontaneous speech. Unfortunately, she did not suggest a null hypothesis with which to compare this observed rate of lexical slips, so that the logic of her argument raises difficulties. No one would claim that there are simply *more* lexical than nonsense spoonerisms; most of the time, creating spoonerisms between neighboring words is going to create nonsense. The argument is rather that one observes more lexical slips than would be expected *by chance.* MacKay (1970) and others have pointed to the necessity of comparing observed rates of naturalistic slips with some plausible null hypothesis before any firm conclusion can be drawn. And indeed, an informal analysis of the published UCLA corpus comparing lexical with nonsense errors suggests that lexical errors occur much more often than would be expected by chance.

Garrett (1975) calculated such a null hypothesis based on random phoneme exchanges in a *Playboy* interview and found, on this basis, that slips in the MIT corpus do not show a lexical preference. However, Dell (1980) took the more conservative approach of finding his null hypothesis *in the error corpus itself,* and he found that, indeed, there is now reliable evidence for a lexical bias in spontaneous slips. This result has now been replicated several times (see Stemberger, Chapter 8, this volume).

It is also worth pointing out that numerous effects analogous to the results of Baars *et al.* (1975) have been found, as discussed in Chapter 11: with spoonerisms, syntactically correct slips are made several times as often as nonsyntactic ones (Motley, Baars, & Camden, 1981); further, socially acceptable spoonerisms are made more often than taboo spoonerisms (Motley, Baars, & Camden, 1979); and in the case of word exchange slips, we have found similar effects with semantically normal versus anomalous slips, true versus false slips, pronounceable versus hard-to-pronounce slips, socially acceptable versus unacceptable slips, and so on. Again, it is difficult to believe that this highly consistent pattern of results—replicated with different techniques in several laboratories over a period of years, with more than a thousand subjects—has no reflection in nature.

On more general considerations, it would be very surprising indeed if there were *no* lexical preference in slips, given the major lexical bias that has traditionally been found in studies of lexical versus nonsense items in memory and perception (e.g., Miller, 1956; Rumelhart & McClelland, 1982). Indeed, it is difficult to find any evidence for the *similarity* of lexical and nonsense materials, and most psycholinguistic theories of the lexicon aim to take account of such a very general and reliable fact.

It would be senseless to claim that all experimental slip techniques replicate natural conditions *under all circumstances*. Surely, the speech control system has many operating modes; for example, from merely shadowing or reading speech, to the careful and purposeful crafting of an entirely new sentence. Thus, slips in such different conditions, if they are to be simulated in the laboratory, must reflect the different conditions. Hence, the idea that all experimental slips replicate all natural conditions is not even desirable. Further, in some sense, Garrett (1975) must be correct in believing that experimental spoonerisms differ from spontaneous ones; the question is whether this difference is *essential* or *incidental* to the hypothesis being tested. If one experimental technique is not appropriate for testing some particular hypothesis, one could develop another technique, using the flexible and powerful principles outlined here. For example, the question-answering technique used by Baars and Mattson (1981) was motivated in part by an effort to find a natural example in which conversational interactions would produce competition of the order of two phrases in a compound sentence (see Table 5).

Too often in the past, psychologists have embarked on experiments that had no noticeable connection with real life. The solution, however, is not to give up experiments. In the case of slips, experimental work gives us an opportunity to elicit very predictable and meaningful slips that we could never observe naturalistically. Spontaneous slips are far too rare and too variable to let us test the Freudian hypothesis naturalistically. The solution, then, is to do experiments that sample the real world, not crudely but in its essence. And the only way to define the essence of a real phenomenon is to use appropriate theory. Thus, theory, experiment, and ecological validity compose a triad of interacting values, mutually supportive if we approach them properly. If one or two of the members of this triad are missing, our research will ultimately be sterile. But if we can respect natural phenomena, perform careful experiments, and develop imaginative theory, we stand a better chance today than ever before of gaining scientific insight into the human condition.

There is always a trade-off between the pros and cons of experimental and naturalistic work. We should be very much aware of the richness of naturalistic data, and of their usefulness. Equally, psycholinguists working with naturalistic slip corpora should be aware of the advantages of experimental techniques for testing causal hypotheses about the control of speech and action. What is needed is a close marriage between the two methodologies, so that each one can make up for the limitations of the other.

We believe there is good reason to think that experimental slip techniques represent the essentials of some situations that produce spontaneous slips. Although some arguments have been made to the contrary, these arguments appear to be based on shaky evidence. Following are some reasons for holding this position:

1. *Experimental slips closely resemble spontaneous ones.* On the surface at least, it is difficult to tell the difference between a spoonerism elicited in the laboratory and one made spontaneously. We have induced spoonerisms more frequently than any other slip, and particularly spoonerisms that involve initial consonant switches between two single-syllable words or nonsense syllables. Since 1973, we have run thousands of subjects in spoonerisms tasks, and in general, the slips we obtain conform to the descriptions given in naturalistic corpora (MacKay, 1981). A spoonerism in the laboratory, like those found in the real world, always turns out to be a "phonetically possible noise" (Wells, 1951). Further, with the word-reordering technique described above we do not experimentally control the particular phoneme that will switch, and in this case, initial consonants always switch with other initial consonants, final consonants with other final consonants, and vowels, of course, switch only with other vowels, just as they do in nature. The subjects are often surprised at their own slips, just as they are in real life, so that in the laboratory we can measure significant changes in the galvanic skin response (GSR) for slips, but not for correct responses (Motley, Baars, & Camden, 1979). Furthermore, people will often correct themselves if they have the opportunity to do so (Baars & Mattson, 1981).

All this is different from spoonerisms that are made deliberately. One can explain to naive subjects what a spoonerism is and ask them to produce spoonerisms voluntarily, on demand—this is a critical test in many ways—and it shows clearly that deliberate spoonerisms are not sensitive to many of the subtle rules of English to which unnatural and experimentally induced spoonerisms conform. For example, we have asked people to create spoonerisms from a word pair like "Freudian slip." Many subjects say, "Sreudian flip," which violates phonological rules because the initial /sr/ is not permissible in English. This impermissible sequence of phonemes is never found in spontaneous slips (Fromkin, 1973), nor have we observed it in experimentally induced slips. And of course, deliberate slips are not surprising to the speaker, nor are they self-corrected.

It may seem curious that deliberate "slips" are more likely to violate the rules of English than unintentional slips, but on reflection, it will be clear that this result is really quite general. It is only when we think *consciously* about doing some skilled act that we are likely to lose the smooth, subtle, automatic control that characterizes normal, proficient action.

2. *The conditions that give rise to experimental slips have plausible counterparts in ordinary speech and action.* There are more reasons to think that experimental slips reflect important aspects of spontaneous speech and action. We have pointed out that competition between alternative plans may be common in ordinary speech and action, and that biasing techniques simulate the kind of preparatory feedforward of action subsystems that many researchers have postulated. The very effectiveness of our slip induction techniques suggests that we are manipulating properties of the system that are powerful enough to be an important part of normal control. Indeed, it would be strange if some strong pattern of experimental results were entirely unrelated to the identical pattern in nature.

3. *Because there is an expandable family of techniques, one can develop the most natural possible analogue of any spontaneous type of slip one wishes to study.* We have done this at several points. After developing the phonetic biasing technique for spoonerisms, we felt that phonetic bias was unlikely to be the proximate cause of spoonerisms; it seemed more natural to think that phonetic bias itself was triggered by higher level processes. This line of thinking led us to suppose that order conflicts at the lexical level might create phonetic bias toward the wrong initial phoneme, and that this incorrect choice might be resolved by creating a complete spoonerism (Baars & Motley, 1976). More recently, we have felt that the phrase-reordering technique for inducing word exchange slips was somewhat unnatural and hence evolved a question-answering technique that elicits the identical slip, but under a set of conditions that simulate natural speech more closely. No doubt much more could be done along the line of marrying the laboratory work to the real world.

Summary and Conclusions

We have described in this chapter a research program aimed (1) at developing experimental control over high-level, predictable, and demonstrably unintentional speech and action; (2) at exploring the substantive implications of the techniques themselves; and (3) at using the resulting techniques to investigate substantive questions about speech production.

The first part of this research program has been quite effective, so that, if anything, we are now faced with an embarrassment of riches. There are so many new techniques for eliciting different kinds of slips that we have been able to investigate only a few in depth.

Second, slip induction techniques themselves have substantive implications for understanding speech and action control. The effectiveness of priming techniques may be due to the fact that, in normal voluntary action, conscious goal images may recruit and trigger unconscious effectors that control the action in all its details. The success of the Ordinal Conflict Effect in triggering spoonerisms, syllable exchanges, word exchanges, and slips of action suggests that competition between different goals and plans for the limited-capacity component of the nervous system may be quite common in spontaneous speech and action.

Third, we briefly listed ways in which slip induction techniques have been used to investigate new, and often otherwise untestable, questions (e.g., Chapters 11 and 12). And finally, we considered the criticism that induced slips may be artificial. Thus far, there is more evidence for convergence than for the divergence of induced and spontaneous slips. Further, there are numerous laboratory techniques in psychology that do not have an immediate and obvious parallel in the natural world, but that are believed to be scientifically very informative. Naturalness in induced slips is often desirable, however, and we can often use the competing-plans strategy to make the slip induction technique as lifelike as possible.

REFERENCES

Baars, B. J. (1977). *The planning of speech: Is there semantic editing prior to speech articulation?* Doctoral dissertation, University of California at Los Angeles Department of Psychology.

Baars, B. J. (1980). On eliciting predictable speech errors in the laboratory. In V. A. Fromkin (Ed.), *Errors in linguistic performance: Slips of the tongue, ear, pen, and hand.* New York: Academic Press.

Baars, B. J. (1988). *A cognitive theory of consciousness.* New York: Cambridge University Press.

Baars, B. J., & MacKay, D. G. (1978). Experimentally eliciting phonetic and sentential speech errors: Methods, implications, and work in progress. *Language in Society, 7,* 105–109.

Baars, B. J., & Mattson, M. E. (1981). Consciousness and intention: A framework and some evidence. *Cognition and Brain Theory, 4*(3), 247–263.

Baars, B. J., & Motley, M. T. (1974, Fall). Spoonerisms: Experimental elicitation of human speech errors. *Catalog of Selected Documents in Psychology, 3,* 28–47.

Baars, B. J., & Motley, M. T. (1976). Spoonerisms as sequencer conflicts: Evidence from artificially elicited errors. *American Journal of Psychology, 89,* 467–484.

Baars, B. J., Motley, M. T., & MacKay, D. G. (1975). Output editing for lexical status in artificially elicited slips of the tongue. *Journal of Verbal Learning and Verbal Behavior, 14,* 382–391.

Baars, B. J., Mattson, M. E., & Cruickshank, G. (1985). *The induction of syllable exchanges.* Unpublished manuscript, Department of Psychology, State University of New York, Stony Brook.

Cohen, A. (1980). Correcting of speech errors in a shadowing task. In V. A. Fromkin (Ed.), *Errors in linguistic performance,* (pp. 157–163). New York: Academic Press.

Dell, G. S. (1980). *Phonological and lexical encoding in speech production: An analysis of naturally occurring and experimentally elicited speech errors.* Unpublished doctoral dissertation, University of Toronto.

Freud, S. (1901/1938). *Psychopathology of everyday life.* In A. A. Brill (Ed.), *The basic writings of Sigmund Freud.* New York: Random House.

Fromkin, V. A. (Ed.). (1973). *Speech errors as linguistic evidence.* The Hague: Mouton.

Fromkin, V. A. (Ed.). (1980). *Errors in linguistic performance: Slips of the tongue, ear, pen, and hand.* New York: Academic Press.

Gel'fand, I. M., Gurfinkel, V. S., Fomin, S. V., & Tsetlin, M. L. (1971). *Models of structural-functional organization of certain biological systems.* Cambridge: MIT Press.

Greene, P. H. (1972). Problems in the organization of motor systems. *Journal of Theoretical Biology, 3,* 303–338.

Kimble, G. A., & Perlmutter, D. (1970). The problem of volition. *Psychological Review, 77*(5), 361–384.

Laver, J. (1980). Neurolinguistic control of speech production. In V. A. Fromkin (Ed.), *Errors in linguistic performance.* New York: Academic Press.

Liberman, A. M., Cooper, F., Shankweiler, D., & Studdert-Kennedy, M. (1967). Perception of the speech code. *Psychological Review, 74,* 431–459.

MacKay, D. G. (1970). Spoonerisms: The structure of errors in the serial order of speech. *Neuropsychologia, 8,* 323–350.

MacKay, D. G. (1971). Stress pre-entry in motor systems. *American Journal of Psychology, 84*(1), 21–43.

MacKay, D. G. (1972). The structure of words and syllables: Evidence from errors in speech. *Cognitive Psychology, 3,* 210–227.

MacKay, D. G. (1973). Complexity in output systems: Evidence from behavioral hybrids. *American Journal of Psychology, 86,* 785–806.

MacKay, D. G. (1976). On the retrieval and lexical structure of verbs. *Journal of Verbal Learning and Verbal Behavior, 15,* 169–182.

MacKay, D. G. (1981). Speech errors: Retrospect and prospect. In V. A. Fromkin (Ed.), *Errors in linguistic performance* (pp. 319–332). New York: Academic Press.

MacKay, D. G. (1982). The problems of flexibility, fluency, and speed-accuracy trade-off in skilled behavior. *Psychological Review, 89*(5), 483–506.

MacKay, D. G. (1987). *The organization of perception and action.* New York: Springer.

MacKay, D. G., & Soderberg, G. A. (1971a). Homologous intrusions: An analogue of linguistic blends. *Perceptual and Motor Skills, 32,* 645–646.

MacKay, D. G., & Soderberg, G. A. (1971b). Stuttering in rapidly produced patterns of finger movement. Unpublished manuscript, University of California at Los Angeles, Department of Psychology.

Mattson, M. E. (1987). *Sources of competing activation in action errors.* Doctoral dissertation, State University of New York, Stony Brook.

Mattson, M. E., & Baars, B. J. (1985). *Competition in activation networks: A test using laboratory-induced action blends and spoonerisms.*

Motley, M. T., & Baars, B. J. (1976). Semantic bias effects on the outcomes of verbal slips. *Cognition, 4,* 177–187.

Motley, M. T., & Baars, B. J. (1979). Effects of cognitive set upon laboratory-induced verbal (Freudian) slips. *Journal of Speech and Hearing Research, 22,* 421–432.

Motley, M. T., Baars, B. J., & Camden, C. T. (1979). Personality and situational influences upon verbal slips. *Human Communication Research, 5,* 195–202.

Motley, M. T., Baars, B. J., & Camden, C. T. (1981). Syntactic criteria in prearticulatory editing: Evidence from laboratory-induced slips of the tongue. *Journal of Psycholinguistic Research, 10*(5), 503–522.

Nooteboom, S. G. (1969). The tongue slips into patterns. In A. G. Sciarone, A. J. van Essen,

& A. A. van Raad (Eds.), *Nomen Society, Leyden studies in linguistics and phonetics* (pp. 114–132). The Hague: Mouton.

Norman, D. A. (1981). Categorization of action slips. *Psychological Review, 88,* 1–15.

Reason, J. T. (1982, June). Learning from absent-minded mistakes. *SSRC Newsletter, 46,* 18–26.

Reason, J. T. (1983). Absent-mindedness and cognitive control. In J. Harris & P. Morris (Eds.), *Everyday memory, actions and absentmindedness* (pp. 113–132). New York: Academic Press.

Reason, J. T. (1984a). Lapses of attention in everyday life. In R. Parasuraman & D. R. Davies (Eds.), *Varieties of attention* (pp. 515–549). New York: Academic Press.

Reason, J. T. (1984b). Little slips and big disasters. *Interdisciplinary Science Reviews, 9*(2), 3–15.

Reason, J. T. (1992). *Human error.* Cambridge: Cambridge University Press.

Shallice, T. (1978). The dominant action system: An information-processing approach to consciousness. In K. S. Pope & J. L. Singer (Eds.), *The stream of consciousness: Scientific investigation into the flow of experience.* New York: Plenum Press.

Stemberger, J. P. (1982). The nature of segments in the lexicon: Evidence from speech errors. *Lingua, 56,* 235–259.

Wells, R. (1951). Predicting slips of the tongue. In. V. A. Fromkin (Ed.), (1973). *Speech errors as linguistic evidence.* The Hague: Mouton.

Wundt, W. (1863/1961). Contributions to the theory of sensory perception. Translated from *Beiträge zur Theorie der Sinneswahrnemung.* Leipzig: C. F. Winter, 1863. Translation reprinted in T. Shipley (Ed.), *Classics in psychology.* New York: Philosophical Library.

7

Laboratory Induction of Nonspeech Action Errors

Mark E. Mattson and Bernard J. Baars

INTRODUCTION

There is a continuum of views on the uniqueness of language as a cognitive function, ranging from the linguist's view that language involves a special-purpose "mental organ," to the behaviorist's view that the same principles shape all behavior. Clearly, there are both similarities and differences between speech production and other actions, such as typing, manipulating objects, and driving a car. An intermediate view is that different action systems have unique, domain-specific constraints, but all action systems are influenced by certain general processing constraints.

One piece of evidence that is relevant to the question of general processing constraints on action systems is the fact that similar types of errors occur across a wide range of different types of action. For example, a common type of speech error is the spoonerism, named for an Oxford don noted for errors such as:

1. You have wasted the whole term. →
   You have *t*asted the whole *w*orm.

MARK E. MATTSON • Social Sciences Division LL 916, Fordham University, New York, New York 10023. BERNARD J. BAARS • The Wright Institute, 2728 Durant Avenue, Berkeley, California 94704.

Experimental Slips and Human Error: Exploring the Architecture of Volition, edited by Bernard J. Baars. Plenum Press, New York, 1992.

A spoonerism typically involves an exchange of phonemes between two separate words, so that the phonemes seem to leap-frog over the intervening segments. Analogous action errors have been reported by Reason (1979). For example:

2. "I unwrapped a sweet, put the paper in my mouth, and threw the sweet into the waste bucket."

3. "When I leave for work in the morning I am in the habit of throwing two dog biscuits to my pet corgi and then putting on my earrings at the hall mirror. One morning I threw the earrings to the dog and found myself trying to attach a dog biscuit to my ear." (p. 72)

In these examples, the objects involved in two actions seem to have been exchanged, just as the phonemes are exchanged in speech spoonerisms. Such errors are not just a source of amusement. The fact that they occur in such physiologically different action systems raises the question of whether the similarity between speech spoonerisms and action spoonerisms is superficial or is instead due to a fundamental similarity in the organization of all action systems. This chapter presents two studies that show that speech, typing, object-manipulation, and gesture errors can all be induced by the same method. These findings, then, are supportive of the claim that the apparent similarity between errors in different action systems is due to a common cause, rather than simply coincidental.

The organization of this chapter is as follows: First, some background on nonspeech errors and on the method for inducing errors is presented. Then, the two studies are detailed. In Experiment 1, expert typists made typing errors, and in Experiment 2, students made gesture errors and errors in manipulating objects. Finally, some general conclusions about action error are discussed.

NONSPEECH ACTION ERRORS AND ERROR INDUCTION

Typing

The study of typing errors as clues to understanding this behavior does not have as long a history as the study of speech errors; nevertheless, there are some landmarks to consider (see Cooper, 1983b, for a history of typing and a review of research findings). Lessenberry (1928) collected 60,000 substitution errors made by typists at all levels of skill and organized them into a confusion matrix. Davis (1935, as cited in Munhall & Ostry, 1983) compiled a similar matrix for the Dvorak simplified keyboard (both matrices are reprinted in Munhall & Ostry, 1983). In his classic paper on the problem of serial order in behavior, Karl Lashley (1951/1961) argued that both typing and speech errors provide evidence that action plans that are executed in sequence are simultaneously active. Lashley's evidence was anecdotal in nature, and as a result

MacNeilage (1964) was prompted to collect the errors made by five under-graduate touch typists in typing lab reports from rough drafts. MacNeilage developed a classification of the 623 errors he observed and proposed a hier-archically organized, three-stage model of typing. Shaffer and Hardwick (1968, 1969) looked at the influence of the expertise of the typist and the type of material (prose to random letters) on typing errors and typing speed, and Shaffer (1975, 1976) developed a two-stage theory of typing based on addi-tional data.

Recent theoretical and empirical work on typing may be found in the volume edited by Cooper (1983a). The terminology for keystroke sequences and typing errors from Gentner, Grudin, Larochelle, Norman, and Rumelhart (1983) is worth briefly reviewing and has been adopted in the description of Experiment 1. The mapping between fingers and keys is specified by the [H, F, P] triple, where H stands for hand, F for finger, and P for position on the keyboard. Substitution errors can be described by indicating which part(s) of the triple deviate from the correct response. For example, if f is typed instead of r, the error can be described as {H, F, Px] because the hand and finger used to type f and r are the same, but the position (home row versus top row) is incorrect. These errors, known as *column errors,* made up 15% of the substitu-tion errors observed by Lessenberry (1928, as reported in Grudin, 1983). The most frequently observed substitution error (43%) was the row error, as in a substitution of f for d. These errors may be [H, Fx, P], where the finger is incorrectly specified, or [H, F, Px], where the position is incorrectly specified. Homologous/mirror-image errors are cases where only the hand is incorrect, indicated as [Hx, F, P]; these accounted for 10% of Lessenberry's substitution errors. Sequences of keystrokes can be described by the number of hands or fingers required to type them. For example, *art* is a 1H sequence because it is typed with the left hand only, and it is a 2F sequence because it involves only the little finger and the index finger.

There are three types of errors that involve an apparent movement of one or more keystrokes to another serial position. Transpositions are cases in which the order of two sequentially adjacent keystrokes is switched, as in *hte* for *the.* The frequency of transposition errors is so great that some text-editing programs have a function that switches adjacent keystrokes to correct for these errors. Interchanges are errors in which keystrokes that are not serially adjacent are exchanged, as in *ehtm* for *them.* Note the similarity of transpo-sitions and interchange errors to the spoonerisms in speech and object man-ipulation described earlier. The third type of serial ordering error is the migra-tion, in which a keystroke either anticipates (*tpar* for *part*) or is late for (*artp* for *part*) its scheduled appearance.

The other error classes identified by Gentner *et al.* (1983) are omissions, in which one or more keystrokes are left out (*te* for *the*); insertions, in which an additional keystroke whose origin is not the immediate context is added to the sequence (*autol* for *auto*); doubling errors, in which the wrong keystroke is doubled (*aad* for *add*); and alternation errors, in which a planned alternation goes awry (*threr* for *there*).

Other Language-Based Actions

Errors have also been observed in other language-based actions. For example, Hotopf (1980) collected several samples of speech and writing errors for comparison. He found both similarities (i.e., the span ahead in syllables for speech and writing were similar) and differences (i.e., interchanges were observed in speech but were very rare in writing). Comparisons of different action modalities will be covered in the final section of this chapter. Newkirk, Klima, Pedersen, and Bellugi (1980) analyzed slips of the hand made by signers of American Sign Language. Among other errors, signers transpose the features of signs, producing errors that Newkirk *et al.* called "metatheses," which are analogous to spoonerisms and interchanges.

Non-Language-Based Actions

The work of Fitts and Jones (1947/1961) was a major landmark in the study of nonspeech action errors. They collected reports of 460 errors made by U.S. Air Force pilots in operating plane controls. The airplane cockpit made an excellent natural laboratory for the study of errors, with the practical consequence of design improvement recommendations. Shaffer (1981) approached skilled piano playing by studying the timing and duration of key depression, as well as the (relatively few) errors that occurred. Some examples from Reason's collection of action errors (1979; see also Reason & Mycielska, 1982) were presented in the introduction. Reason and his colleagues used both diaries and questionnaires to look at naturally occurring action errors. Norman (1981) based his categorization of action errors on some of the published corpora and his own collection. Dubrovsky (1986, 1987) used action errors to infer a set of eight functional stages in a simple action and also analyzed the costs of errors in terms of social exchange theory. Thus, there are a number of examples of naturalistic approaches to action errors. A complementary approach is to bring such errors into the laboratory.

Error Induction Method: The Ordinal Conflict Effect

Baars (1980a) reviewed several methods for inducing subjects to make speech errors that typically involve an interchange of some speech units. The method used in both experiments, which is called the *ordinal conflict effect* (OCE), is based on the observation that, when people are uncertain about the order of two actions, they tend to exchange components of the actions. Applications of the OCE to induce errors are summarized in Table 1. Baars and Motley (1976) presented subjects with pairs of words, each of which was followed by an arrow that pointed to the left or to the right. If the arrow pointed to the right and they heard a buzzer, their task was to say the preceding words in the order they appeared. If the arrow pointed to the left and they heard a buzzer, the

TABLE 1

Applications of the Ordinal Conflict Effect

Source	Stimuli	Task	Target → *Error*
Baars & Motley, 1976	Word pairs on memory drum, followed by → or ←.	Say word pairs followed by buzz out loud in the order indicated by the arrow.	"darn bore → *barn door*"
Baars, 1977	Two-phrase sentences, some followed by cue word "REVERSE."	Reverse order of the phrases and say cued sentence out loud.	"The girl caught the train and saw the show. → The girl *saw* the train and *caught* the show."
Mattson, Baars, & Motley, 1985	Two-phrase sentences followed by either "REPEAT" or "REVERSE."	Say each sentence out loud with phrase order determined by cue word.	Same as above.
Mattson, Stravitz, Baars, & Cruickshank, 1991	Pairs of three syllable words followed by either "REPEAT" or "REVERSE."	Say each word pair out loud in order based on cue word.	"involvement deposit → *in*post *de*volvement"
Experiment 1	Pairs of nonsense words followed by either "REPEAT" or "REVERSE."	Type each word pair in order based on cue word.	"arxe okpu → arxe *a*kpu"
Experiment 2	Videotape of pairs of actions like waving hands and nodding head followed by 1 or 2 beeps.	Mimic actions in order based on number of beeps (i.e., 1 beep "REPEAT," 2 beeps "REVERSE."	Nod "yes" then wave hand side to side →nod "no" then wave hand side to side.

subjects had to say the words in the opposite order. For example, if the subject saw "darn bore," followed by an arrow pointing left, she or he had to say "bore darn." This task frequently led to Spoonerisms like:

4. darn bore → *barn d*oor

Variants of this method have been shown to induce word exchanges between the phrases of sentences (see Table 1, Baars, 1977; Mattson, Baars, & Motley, 1985; see also Baars & Mattson, 1981) and syllable and morpheme exchanges between multisyllabic words (see Table 1; Mattson, Stravitz, Baars, & Cruickshank, 1991). Thus, interchanges of three different levels of speech units have been induced through the OCE. If similar errors can be induced in nonspeech actions by means of the OCE, then a general causal factor in action error will have been identified: ordering conflict. Experiment 1 extended the OCE to typing, and Experiment 2 extended it to gestures and object manipulation.

EXPERIMENT 1: INDUCTION OF TYPING ERRORS

This experiment has several motivations. The generality of the OCE is tested by extending it from speech to typing. Further, use of the OCE makes it possible to see whether expert typists make homologous errors more often than other types of 2H substitutions. Finally, the other typing errors that occur in the context of the experiment are examined.

Homology

MacNeilage (1964) observed what he termed "contralateral errors." These are cases in which the correct keystroke is replaced by the keystroke typed with the same finger on the same row of the keyboard, but with the other hand. A total of 11 contralateral errors, or roughly 2% of 623, were observed by MacNeilage.

An experiment performed by MacKay and Soderberg (1971) used a tapping task in order to examine the type of errors observed under more constrained laboratory conditions. The subjects had to tap with both hands at the same time on two sets of four telegraph keys. All of the subjects had experience with typing or playing a musical instrument, yet none of them were able to tap the sequences 20 times in a row without error. One very frequent type of error was a homologous intrusion, in which "an erroneous finger tapped in synchrony with an anatomically homologous finger of the opposite hand" (MacKay & Soderberg, 1971, p. 645). These errors were less likely to occur on the hand that the subject was attending to and also were less frequently observed on the dominant hand. In a second experiment, they were shown to be more likely to occur on stressed key taps than on unstressed control key taps. MacKay and Soderberg drew a parallel between these tapping intrusions and linguistic blends in speech. They claimed that both are cases in which simultaneously planned actions intrude on one another.

Rumelhart and Norman (1982) reported some typing errors from a 90,000-word text typed by Rumelhart from dictation. They observed homologous errors: a keystroke is replaced by a keystroke typed with the same finger on the other hand, in the mirror-image position with respect to the keyboard, that is [Hx, F, P]. Grudin (1983) reported that homologous errors were quite frequent in Lessenberry's corpus (1928). Rumelhart and Norman suggested that the reason was that Lessenberry's corpus was collected from typists of all skill levels, and that expert typists would not make this type of error. So Grudin (1983) compared the likelihood of homologous errors by expert typists and beginning typists and found that, although beginners made more homologous errors, experts still made some. One purpose of Experiment 1 is to compare the likelihood of homologous errors with other types of 2H substitutions made by expert typists.

It is necessary to differentiate between two different conceptions of homology. The term *homologous/mirror-image* is reserved here for errors in which the error keystroke involves the same finger and position as the correct keystroke: [Hx, F, P]. *Homologous* alone is to refer to cases in which the hand is incorrect, the finger is the same, and the position is not specified: [Hx, F, P?]. For example, the homologous/mirror-image substitute for *P* is *Q*, and homologous substitutes for *P* are *Q*, *A*, and *Z*.

Homologous/mirror-image errors were observed in typing by Lessenberry (1928), Davis (1935), MacNeilage (1964), Rumelhart and Norman (1982), Grudin (1983), and Munhall and Ostry (1983). MacKay and Soderberg (1971) found homologous intrusions in their tapping task. They claimed that these errors occurred because activating a finger on one hand leads to priming of the homologous finger on the other hand. One possible neuroanatomical basis for this priming is the connections between symmetrical parts of the motor cortex. According to Luria (1973), the anterior zones of the corpus callosum connect symmetrical portions of the motor and premotor cortex. Marteniuk and MacKenzie (1980) cited evidence that both cortical and subcortical connections are involved in coordinated two-arm actions. So there are some naturalistic data and a possible physiological mechanism on the side of homology and a theory-based claim that experts do not make such errors. Experiment 1 involved inducing typing errors and observing the resultant 2H substitution errors. If Rumelhart and Norman were correct, homologous 2H substitutions should be no more likely than other varieties of 2H substitutions.

Inasmuch as homologous errors are thought to involve a switch in the hand assigned to a keystroke, in order to create homologous errors we want to create competition between the two hands. To do this, pronounceable nonsense words were designed so that each word was typed with a single hand. In the terminology of Gentner *et al.* (1983), these nonsense words were 1H sequences. Then right-hand words were paired with left-hand words and competition was created via the OCE. For example, the word *ASER* is typed with the use of all of the fingers of the left hand, and *PLIN* is typed with the fingers of the right hand. The subjects were presented with word pairs like "ASER PLIN," followed by either a "REPEAT" or "REVERSE" cue. If they saw the cue "REPEAT," they had to type "ASER PLIN." If they saw the cue "REVERSE," they had to type "PLIN ASER." In the case of speech, this procedure often leads to phoneme switches between the words; in this experiment, we expected to see keystroke switches between the words. If expert typists are susceptible to homologous errors, more of the 2H substitutions should involve homologous fingers than any of the other possible 2H substitutions.

We also expected that switches between the words would be more likely to occur between keystrokes in the same serial position in the two words. Thus, to test this hypothesis and (perhaps) to increase the sensitivity of the test of homology, the stimuli were set up so that homologous fingers were in the same serial position in the word pairs. This is the case with "ASER PLIN"; the *A* and the *P* are both typed with the little finger, the *S* and the *L* with the ring finger, and so on. To avoid confounding the effect of homology and the effect of serial position, word pairs with nonhomologous fingers in the same serial position were also set up. An example of such a word pair is *ASER JILP*. In this word pair, parallel fingers are in the same serial position. Parallel fingers are fingers on the same side of the hands—just the opposite of homology. For example, *A* is typed with the left-most finger of the right hand. To the extent that serial position is important, we should see more homologous errors on homologous stimuli, more parallel errors on parallel stimuli, and so on.

Finally, all of the other errors that were observed can be examined in the light of the information on naturally occurring errors reviewed in the section above on nonspeech action errors. The major categories were:

1. Transpositions of adjacent keystrokes.
2. Omission of keystroke(s).
3. Insertion of keystroke(s).
4. Substitution of one keystroke for another.

Homologous errors, other 2H substitutions and 1H substitutions make up the category of substitution errors. Because the most general formulation of the competing-plans hypothesis does not predict the exact form of the errors produced by competition, it is not clear what effect this manipulation should have on the frequency of each of these categories, except that we expected to see 2H substitutions. The number of errors of all categories should be greater in the experimental situation than in a corresponding amount of natural typing because of the competition induced by the OCE.

Method

Subjects. The subjects were secretaries and clerks from the State University of New York at Stony Brook. Although they varied somewhat in their typing skills, all of the subjects had to type on a daily basis. They were unaware that the purpose of the task was to elicit errors, and they received five dollars for their participation. All of the subjects were women.

Apparatus. A Cromemco Z-2 microcomputer was used to control the presentation of the stimuli and to record the subjects' responses. The subjects typed on a Televideo 920C terminal interfaced with the microcomputer.

Stimuli. On each trial, the subjects saw two pronounceable four-keystroke nonsense words, followed by the cue word (either "REPEAT" or "REVERSE"). Each nonsense word could be typed with a single hand (1H), with no repeated fingers (4F), and each pair was made up of a right-hand and a left-hand word. There are 24 possible orderings of four fingers without replacement; nonsense words were designed for all possible orderings for both hands, yielding a total of 48 nonsense words. Table 2 shows the nonsense words used. Because of the constraints of the standard keyboard arrangement, certain letters appeared more frequently than others. The letter *P* appears in every right-hand word because it is the only letter typed with the right little finger.

Each index finger can be used to type six letters, but only five appear in the nonsense words (*B* and *M* were inadvertently excluded). In order to make the words pronounceable, it was necessary to reuse the vowels often, especially the left-hand vowels (*A* and *E*).

Left- and right-hand nonsense words were paired in three ways, as shown in Table 3. Homologous pairs had the homologous finger in the same serial position in both nonsense words: [Hx, F, P?]. For example, in "ASER PLIN" the *A* is typed with the little finger on the left hand, and the *P* (in the same serial position) is typed with the little finger on the right hand. Parallel pairs, on the other hand, had parallel fingers in the same serial position: in "ASER JILP," the *A* is typed with the little finger and the *J* with the index finger, and so on. As it happens, there is only one right-hand nonsense word that is entirely homologous with respect to a given left-hand nonsense word. This is also the case for the parallel pairs. This is not the case for the remaining group, called the *nonhomologous-nonparallel pairing* (NHNP pairing). One of the four possible NHNP pairings was chosen. The serial order relations between fingers for these stimuli can be seen in Table 3. Keep in mind that these pairs were set up so that homologous and parallel fingers did not occur in the same serial position. An example of one of these pairs was "ASER OPHI."

There were 24 pairs for each class of stimuli (homologous, parallel, and NHNP), yielding 72 items. Every pair was presented twice, once with a "RE-PEAT" cue and once with a "REVERSE" cue. Two lists of 144 pairs were made up by randomly assigning one ordering of each pair (e.g., a right-hand word followed by a left-hand word with a "REPEAT" cue) to List 1 and the other (left followed by right with "REPEAT" cue) to List 2. The other word order was assigned to the same list with the "REVERSE" cue, so that a particular ordering of the stimulus words appeared only once in each list. Odd-numbered subjects received List 1 and even-numbered subjects received List 2. Each subject received a different randomized presentation order.

Each trial started with a blank screen, followed by an arrow (→) that indicated where the stimulus pair was to appear. The arrow appeared at the beginning of the 11th line of the 24-line screen for 2 seconds. Then, the screen

TABLE 2
Nonsense Word Stimuli for Experiment 1

Left-hand words				Right-hand words			
ASER	SQER	DAWT	FASE	OPHI	PONK	NOPI	KLUP
ASFE	SARE	CARX	VAEX	OPIJ	PLIN	JOIP	KOPU
ZEWT	SEAF	ESAF	GWAC	OUPI	PULI	UPIL	IPLU
AERS	SERA	EWRA	TWEZ	LUIP	PYKO	UPOK	IPUO
ARXE	STAD	DRAS	TEAX	OKPU	PILU	JILP	KULP
ATES	STEZ	EFSA	FESA	LINP	PIJO	HIPO	KUPO

TABLE 3

Examples of Stimulus Word Pairs for Experiment 1

Type of stimulus	Homologous		Parallel		Nonhomologous-nonparallel	
example	ASER	PLIN	ASER	JILP	ASER	OPHI
hand	left	right	left	right	left	right
finge r[a]	l-r-m-i	l-r-m-i	l-r-m-i	i-m-r-l	l-r-m-i	r-l-i-m

[a] l = little finger; r = ring finger; m = middle finger; i = index finger.

was blanked again and the stimulus pair was presented, starting in the fifth column of the 11th line. The presentation number appeared in the upper-left-hand corner of the screen. The stimulus pair and the presentation number lasted for 4 seconds, the screen was blanked once again, and the cue word (either "REPEAT" or "REVERSE") was presented. The cue appeared on Line 11 starting in Column 14. The cue word remained on the screen until the subject completed her response (signaled by pressing "RETURN") or until 5 seconds had elapsed. If the subject did not complete her response within 5 seconds a beep sounded, signaling the end of the trial. The screen was blank during the intertrial interval. The mean intertrial time after trials in which the subjects made an error was 0.76 seconds and for correct trials was 0.43 seconds. The difference between these was the time necessary to preserve the error. The disk drives of the microcomputer made a click each time the disk was accessed. Each trial was preceded by one click as the stimulus pair was read into memory. Error trials were succeeded by an additional click as the error was stored on the disk. Note that both the time difference and the number of clicks may have acted as feedback about the accuracy of the response. No explicit feedback was given.

Procedure. The subjects were seated in front of the terminal. The following instructions appeared on the screen and were read out loud by the experimenter:

> The first thing we would like to do is make sure you are comfortable with the terminal keyboard. Following these instructions, a paragraph will appear on this screen. When you have read the paragraph, press "RETURN." There will be a beep, and you should begin to type the paragraph just as you see it. When you complete each line, press "RETURN" just as you would on a regular type-writer. Be as accurate as you can, but do not try to correct your mistakes. It isn't necessary to double-space as the machine will take care of that.

The subject was asked if she had any questions, then an 87-word paragraph from a fantasy novel (Tolkien, 1965) was presented on the screen. This paragraph was double-spaced, and it scrolled upward as the subjects typed it. After this task was completed, the instructions for the experimental task were presented on the terminal and read out loud by the experimenter:

> Thank you for your participation in this experiment on how the fingers and hands are organized in typing. Your task will be to type pairs of nonsense words (such as "ASEF PIOJ") that will appear on this screen. First an arrow will appear, indicating where the two words will appear. Then the screen will blank out and the words will appear. They will last for a few seconds; then, the screen will go blank again. When you see the word "REPEAT," please type the words just as you saw them. What you type will not appear on the screen, but the computer will record your response. Please try the example following these instructions.

An example of a "REPEAT" cue item was presented, followed by further instructions:

> Some of the word pairs will be followed by a different word, "REVERSE." If you see the word "REVERSE," you should type the word pair in the reverse order. For example, if you saw:
>
> ASEF PIOJ
>
> and the cue word was "REVERSE," you would type:
>
> PIOJ ASEF
>
> Please try the example following these instructions.

After the example of a "REVERSE" cue item, the final set of instructions was presented:

> Please use standard fingering for the words. As you have probably heard, there is a tone that tells you that your time is up. If you haven't typed the words and pressed "RETURN" within a short interval, this tone will sound and the next trial will begin. Following these instructions are some practice trials. The purpose of the practice trials is to ensure that you are comfortable with the procedure. Therefore, feel free to comment or ask questions during the practice. The practice will start as soon as you press "RETURN."

The practice list consisted of eight pairs of nonwords, half with "REPEAT" cues and half with "REVERSE" cues. The practice nonwords could be typed with a single hand, but they differed from the experimental stimuli in that they had repeated fingers. The practice list was repeated until the subject demonstrated an understanding of the task by getting items with both cues correct and indicating that she was comfortable with the task and ready to go on. After the experimental task, the subject was debriefed and paid for participation. On trials in which subjects made an error, the correct response, the error, and the time in milliseconds from the cue presentation to the end of the response (when the subject pressed "RETURN") were recorded. Because of a programming error, the times for the correct responses on specific stimuli were not available. The times were recorded in the same (random) sequence in which the stimuli were presented, so that it was impossible to match the times for correct items with specific stimuli.

Results

Homology. A total of 218 2H substitutions were observed, out of 2,125 errors observed overall. The frequency of these errors for each subject can be seen in Table 4. The 2H substitutions were defined as errors in which a keystroke in the stimulus pair was replaced in the subject's response by a keystroke typed with the other hand. Some examples of this type of error are:

5. ARXE OKPU→ ARXE *A*KPU

6. OUPI CARX → OUPI *K*ARX

7. VAEX KOPU → VAEX KOP*E*

8. SQER OPIJ → SEQR OP*ES* (also a transposition of *Q* and *E)*

9. SQER KULP → SQ*U*A *G*ULP (also a 1H substitution of *A* for *R)*

There were seven cases of 2H interchanges, which are analogous to spoonerisms:

10. VAEX PULI → VULI PAET

11. JOIP CARX → JOIX CARP

12. HIPO EFSA → HIFO EPSA

13. STEZ LUIP → STEP LUIZ

14. JOIP CARX → JOIX CRP (also an omission of *A)*

15. PLIN FESA → FILN PESA (also a transposition of *I* and *L)*

16. OPIJ ASFE → OSFE ASIJ (also an incorrect reversal and a 2H substitution of *S* for *P*—a triple!)

For the purposes of the present analysis, each of these 2H interchanges was counted as two separate 2H substitutions. The 2H substitutions form a corpus for examination of the role of homology. In Table 5 these errors are broken down by the type of stimulus item (homologous, parallel, or NHNP) and the relationship between the finger used to type the letter in the stimulus and the finger used to type the letter replacing it. Of all errors, 3% were homologous 2H substitutions. For the moment, let us focus our attention on the totals for the three kinds of errors that had the benefit of the same finger in the same serial position in both words: the homologous, parallel, and NHNP errors. A marginally significant difference was found between these three frequencies ($\chi^2 = 1.65$, $df = 2$, $p < .1$). NHNP 2H substitutions were the most frequent (78), followed by homologous (64), then parallel (53).

How likely were mirror-image errors? There were 36 homologous/mirror-image 2H substitutions, which made up 56.3% of the homologous 2H substitutions, compared to 25 (32.1%) NHNP/mirror-image and 7 (13.2%) parallel/mirror-image substitutions. Chance would be about 33%, as there are three rows on the keyboard.

The Effect of Serial Position. The chance probability of replacing a finger with one in the same serial position in the other nonsense word is 1 out of 4, or 25%. The observed frequency of such substitutions was 99 out the 218 2H substitutions, which is 45.4%. Two other results are relevant to the serial position effect.

If the subjects were likely to replace a keystroke with a keystroke typed by the finger in the same serial position in the other nonsense word, one would expect that few errors would occur if the fingers were never in the same serial position. This was the case for the NHNP-control errors. Each of the three stimulus types involved pairing a finger on one hand with a finger on the other. Only three of the possible four pairings were used as stimuli. The fourth pairing was the NHNP-control pairing. Table 6 gives the classification of each right-hand-finger–left-hand-finger pairing into homologous, parallel, NHNP and control. If we compare the frequencies of these four error types we find a highly significant deviation from the expected frequencies ($\chi^2 = 30.04$, $df = 3$, $p < .001$). As is obvious from Table 5, NHNP-control errors were far less likely than the errors associated with the stimulus types.

The relationship between stimulus type and error type was assessed by performing a chi-square on the frequencies of the stimulus by error matrix. This, too, was found to be significant ($\chi^2 = 26.98$, $df = 6$, $p = .001$). As can be seen in Table 5, the subjects were most likely to make homologous errors on the homologous stimuli, parallel errors on the parallel stimuli, and NHNP errors on these stimuli. The contingency coefficient, which measures the strength of this relationship, was 0.33.

Overall Error Classification. Table 4 presents the frequencies of the various types of errors made by each subject. The total number of errors observed was 2,125. The number of correct responses is given as well as the number of incorrect responses. Note that these columns always add up to more than the total number of trials (144) because on some trials the subjects made more than one error. Of a total of 144 trials, the subjects got an average of 88.2 completely correct. An average of 85 errors per subject was observed.

The 1H substitutions were defined as errors in which a keystroke was replaced by another keystroke typed with the same hand, except for those errors that involved the exchange of adjacent keystrokes. For example:

17. HIPO TEAX → HIP*I* TEAX

18. ZEWT PILU → SEWT PIL*Q*

TABLE 4
Frequency of Different Types of Errors Observed in Experiment 1[a]

S#	Corr. Resp.	Substitution		Doubling	Transpose	Omit	Incomplete	Insertions		No. Rev.	Inc. Rev.	MC	Unc.	All
		2H	1H					1H	2H					
1	126	1	10	1	2	0	2	3	0	2	0	2	0	23
2	122	6	6	0	1	3	1	4	1	0	0	1	0	23
3	46	15	19	3	17	21	27	6	0	4	0	19	6	137
4	114	2	12	0	5	3	8	2	0	0	1	2	1	35
5	82	4	13	2	15	26	13	12	1	2	0	3	9	101
6	108	2	11	4	16	1	6	4	1	1	0	0	2	48
7	42	10	26	5	27	22	27	11	6	12	0	10	13	169
8	0	5	62	0	6	21	143	6	0	7	3	16	8	277
9	105	3	18	1	14	2	2	4	0	1	0	1	1	47
10	55	29	41	4	26	15	19	11	8	0	1	16	9	179
11	67	18	12	4	9	2	32	15	7	1	1	8	5	114
12	108	4	12	2	11	3	6	1	1	2	0	3	1	46
13	101	3	12	1	8	3	19	3	0	0	0	2	2	53
14	74	8	22	3	16	26	5	4	0	0	0	3	1	88
15	72	7	29	3	27	7	6	5	1	2	0	13	9	109

16	117	11	11	4	5	1	4	2	0	0	0	1	0	39
17	110	4	2	0	10	5	14	1	1	0	0	4	3	44
18	72	12	21	5	20	3	22	6	8	2	0	4	3	106
19	123	0	2	3	3	0	0	16	0	0	0	1	1	26
20	98	8	22	1	10	11	9	4	1	1	0	2	5	74
21	114	1	17	8	0	3	3	3	1	0	3	0	1	40
22	90	9	34	5	11	4	5	3	4	0	0	5	3	83
23	114	8	7	1	15	3	0	2	2	0	0	2	1	41
24	89	16	18	6	16	7	7	2	0	1	0	1	2	76
25	58	32	37	4	21	8	24	2	1	2	1	10	5	147
sum		218	476	70	311	200	404	132	44	40	10	129	91	2125
% of all errors		10.3	22.4	3.3	14.6	9.4	19.0	6.2	2.1	1.9	0.5	6.1	4.3	

[a]Key to abbreviations: Corr. Resp. = completely correct responses; No. Rev. = failure to reverse word order; Inc. Rev. = incorrectly reversed "REPEAT"-cued pair; MC = multiple classification; Unc. = unclassifiable.

TABLE 5

Frequency of 2H Substitutions for Each Stimulus Type in Experiment 1

Stimulus type	Error type			
	Homologous	Parallel	Nonhomologous-nonparallel	Control
Homologous	29	10	16	8
Parallel	17	27	19	5
Nonhomologous-nonparallel	18	16	43	10
Total	64	53	78	23

All cases in which the "space" was replaced were counted as 1H substitutions. Out of the 476 1H substitutions observed, 30 1H interchanges were each counted twice. These errors are similar to transposition errors except they do not involve serially adjacent keystrokes. For example:

19. KOPU SERA → K*UPO* SERA

20. UPIL ESAF → UPIL E*FAS*

A doubling error was defined as the same keystroke repeated twice. Note that this definition differs from that of Gentner *et al.* (1983) in that there is no reason for activating the proposed doubling schema, because there were no doubled letters in the stimuli. It is possible that these doubling errors were misstrokes or cases in which the key was held down too long and the letter was repeated by the terminal (Grudin, personal communication, 1983). Of the 70 doubling errors observed, 31 resembled insertions, although they were counted only as doubling errors:

TABLE 6

Classification of 2H Substitutions by Finger and Hand for Experiment 1

		Left hand			
		Little	Ring	Middle	Index
	Little	HOM	NHNP	NHNP-C	PAR
Right	Ring	NHNP	HOM	PAR	NHNP-C
Hand	Middle	NHNP-C	PAR	HOM	NHNP
	Index	PAR	NHNP-C	NHNP	HOM

[a]Key: HOM = homologous; PAR = parallel; NHNP = nonhomologous-nonparallel; NHNP-C = nonhomologous-nonparallel control.

21. PYKO FASE → PYK*OO* FASE

Of the doubling errors, 31 resembled 1H substitutions and were counted in both of these categories:

22. ESAF LINP → E*AA*F LINP

The remaining 8 doubling errors were either multiple-category or unclassifiable errors. Another commonly observed error was a transposition of adjacent keystrokes:

23. EWRA UPOK → *WE*RA UPOK

All of the transposition errors were within one hand, because of the nature of the stimuli. Omissions were said to occur when any keystroke(s) was deleted, except the end of the response:

24. OUPI ZEWT → OPI ZEWT

Cases in which the last keystroke(s) was missing were categorized as incomplete:

25. SQER PONK → SQER PON

26. CARX IPUO → CARX I

Subject 8 failed to complete 143 of the 144 items, accounting by herself for more than one third of all of the incomplete responses observed. The single response that was complete was not correct, so this subject made all errors. The 1H insertions were defined as strings in which the inserted keystroke, typed with the same hand as the rest of the nonword, was not doubled:

27. OPIJ ASFE → OPI*N*J ASFE

It is tempting to characterize some of these 1H insertions as cases of self-correction (Baars & Mattson, 1981; Shaffer & Hardwick, 1969):

28. OPHI ASER → *P*OPHI ASER

Forty-four 2H insertions were also observed. They were defined as strings in which the keystroke inserted was typed with the other hand:

29. KOPU SERA → *D*KOPU SERA

30. ATES LINP → ATES *A*LIP (also omission of *N)*

These insertions are also interesting from the point of view of between-hand competition. No reversal errors were cases in which the response was the same as the stimulus on "REVERSE"-cued items:

31. NOPI GWAC → GWAC NOPI

The least frequent of the classified errors were the incorrect reversals. These 10 errors were the opposite of no-reversal errors. A "REPEAT"-cued item was erroneously reversed:

32. VAEX UPIL → UPIL VAEX

Some errors suggested more than one interpretation. These were identified as multiple-classification errors. Because of the similarity of some of the stimulus words, sometimes transposition errors could not be distinguished from cases in which the subjects typed the wrong stimulus word:

33. VAEX PULI → VAEX UPIL

Some errors looked like successive transpositions but could also be seen as a combination of insertion and omission:

34. SEAF KLUP → SEAF KUPL

The final category of errors was the unclassifiable group. Examples of this group:

35. PIJO GWAC → PIJO GWESS

36. OUPI ZEWT → PUIOASER

37. EFSA OPIJ → PILJA REVE

38. OPHI ASER → PHI ERASER (also an omission of *O*)

39. HIPO TEAX → HIPO HIPO

40. LUIP STEZ → TR (also an incomplete)

A total of 129 multiple-category and 91 unclassifiable errors was observed.

Subject 24 had her right hand shifted one key to the right for the first 43 items, as in the following example:

41. VAEX PULI → VAEX [P;O

Rather than consider these 1H substitutions, we translated each right-hand response one key to the left. In the example above, for instance, the bracket was translated to a *P,* the *P* to an *O,* the semicolon to *L,* and the *O* to *I.* The translated response was then classified by the type of error in the usual way, in this case a 1H substitution of *U* by *O.* If the translated response was completely correct it was not considered an error.

Time-outs. Table 7 presents the number of time-outs for each subject. A time-out occurred whenever a subject did not press "RETURN" within 5 seconds of the cue presentation. Subject 5 never pressed "RETURN"; hence, all of her responses were time-outs. The mean number of time-outs per subject was 4.8 for trials on which the response was correct, and 16 for error trials. With Subject 5 eliminated, the mean for the other 24 subjects was 1.5 time-outs for correct responses and 14.1 time-outs for error trials. A time-out on a correct trial meant that the subject did everything correctly except press "RETURN." Many of the time-outs on error trials were incomplete responses.

Latency to Carriage Return. On trials that were not time-outs, the amount of time between the cue presentation and "RETURN" was recorded. Table 7 presents the mean and standard deviation of the latency for non-time-out trials for each subject in milliseconds. The mean latency across all subjects for correct trials was 3,409 milliseconds, and for error trials was 3,844 milliseconds. Note that Subject 5 could not be included in this analysis because all of her response were time-outs.

Discussion

Effectiveness of the OCE. As predicted, the subjects made 2H substitutions and interchanges. There were a total of 218 2H substitutions out of 2,125 errors, or 10.3%, and only 7 2H interchanges (0.3%). Thus, the OCE can cause typing errors as well as speech errors.

Homology. Although homologous 2H substitutions were observed, they were not the most likely 2H substitutions. More NHNP errors occurred, a result consistent with the Rumelhart and Norman (1982) suggestion that expert typists do not make homologous errors. It is conceivable that expert typists have learned to suppress these errors, the result being the marginally significant difference between the homologous, parallel, and NHNP errors observed in this study. On the other hand, 56.3% of the homologous 2H substitutions were homologous/mirror-image errors, when chance is around one third. Mirror-image errors made up a smaller percentage of NHNP errors, and especially few parallel errors involved the same row. This finding suggests that anatomical homology plus mirror-image movement is more critical than pure homology in causing errors.

These findings, along with Grudin's naturalistic data (1983), suggest that the representation of keystrokes in typing involves a modifiable representation

TABLE 7

Number of Time-Outs and Latencies for Each Subject in Experiment 1

Subject number	Nonerrors			Errors		
	Number of time-outs	Mean latency ms	SD latency ms	Number of time-outs	Mean latency ms	SD latency ms
1	1	3,210	518	2	3,722	481
2	0	2,880	379	1	3,535	569
3	1	3,460	379	22	3,972	681
4	1	3,591	493	8	3,845	441
5	82	—	—	62	—	—
6	1	3,360	613	7	3,790	716
7	0	3,696	489	11	4,013	574
8	0	—	—	50	3,754	646
9	1	3,408	577	1	3,670	555
10	0	3,145	472	15	3,589	681
11	0	3,803	548	39	4,145	711
12	1	3,622	540	8	3,846	804
13	3	3,926	514	21	4,393	473
14	1	3,631	364	2	3,781	458
15	0	3,106	518	14	3,749	694
16	8	4,077	480	11	4,375	513
17	4	3,758	501	18	4,172	518
18	5	3,658	540	29	4,220	531
19	0	3,016	401	1	3,747	455
20	3	3,586	544	25	3,955	591
21	1	3,445	561	4	3,994	520
22	1	3,019	495	5	3,593	544
23	0	2,866	420	1	3,650	702
24	1	2,882	565	4	3,293	786
25	4	3,855	499	40	4,205	540
Mean	4.8	3,409	621	16.0	3,844	660

of homology, as nonexperts make many homologous errors in typing, and experts make relatively few. Because experts make more homologous/mirror-image errors than other homologous errors, Rumelhart and Norman's model (1982) ought to be modified to include a representation of mirror-image homology (see Grudin, 1981).

Serial Position. The effect of serial position was as follows: 2H substitutions were more likely to involve a finger in the same serial position than in any of the other positions in the other nonsense word. Although the chance probability of involving the same serial position was 25%, the observed probability was 45.4%, or almost half the 2H substitutions. This finding was also supported by two other findings. First, very few NHNP-control 2H substitutions occurred. Recall that these had no stimulus pairs associated with them;

hence, these fingers were never in the same serial position in the two words. Second, in each stimulus pairing, the most frequent error was the error associated with that pairing; that is, the substitutions involved fingers in the same serial position in the other word.

The serial position effect suggests that the nonsense words typed in this experiment were being prepared for execution simultaneously. It also suggests that the nonsense words share a positional representation that makes such confusions possible. This reasoning is similar to that used in explaining homologous errors: A particular type of error suggests the existence of a representation that permits such an error. The effect of serial position suggests that future experiments with this task should take advantage of the high competition between the same serial positions in the two words.

The Rumelhart and Norman model has no positional representation, and its ordering mechanisms (inhibition and triggering conditions) do not predict our results. In their model, an activated word sends activation to its component key-press schemata. Each key-press schema inhibits the key presses following it. If the two words were both equally activated (maximal competition), the two most highly activated schemata would be the two initial key presses. It is easy to see how an initial key press might replace another initial key press, but the prediction for subsequent key presses is less clear. Given that one of these initial schemata is selected and output, the next most highly activated schemata would be the remaining initial key press and the two second key press schemata. Because the unused initial key press schema was never inhibited, it should be the next chosen for output. Thus, we might find the two words interleaved with one another in the case of maximal competition:

42. *very* late → *vleartye*

In the case where one word is more highly activated than the other, the key press in the second, less highly activated, word that is most likely to show up in the first word is the initial key press as, of the keypress schemata in the second word, this one receives the least inhibition. So there is no apparent mechanism for the serial position effect observed in our experiment. It should be noted that Rumelhart and Norman stated that their model was not meant to explain performance on nonsense words. It might be argued that nonsense words involve an entirely different parsing system. Shaffer and Hardwick (1968, 1969) showed that nonsense words were typed slower and with more errors than random words and prose.

Other Errors Observed.   Overall, our subjects made errors on 39% of the trials. This is obviously far more errors than one is likely to see outside the laboratory, especially as our subjects had to type on a daily basis as part of their jobs. Like the serial position effect, the large number of errors, too, may also partially be a consequence of using nonsense words as stimuli. All of the major types of errors observed in naturalistic situations were made by our subjects, including omissions, insertions, transpositions, substitutions, and doubling errors.

The observation of doubling errors is somewhat curious, as there were no doubled letters in the stimuli. The naturalistic data make it seem as if these errors usually occur in words involving doubled letters. A doubling scheme à la Rumelhart and Norman should have had a very low activation during this task as a result of never being deliberately activated. Perhaps, sometimes, schemata that have already fired "forget" to deactivate themselves. This is how Rumelhart and Norman's doubling schema works; after firing, the key-press schema checks to see if the doubling schema is activated. If it is, the key-press schema deactivates the doubling schema and maintains its own activation. If schemata sometimes do not deactivate after firing, this would explain how doubling errors could occur when the doubling schema was presumably not activated. Another possibility is that the subjects occasionally maintained contact with the key long enough to activate the automatic repeat feature of this particular terminal. However, more than just two repetitions should have been observed occasionally if this was the principle reason for doubling, and this was not the case.

The large number of errors in the typing task suggests that the OCE leads to quite a substantial effect that is not specific to a particular type of error. Thus, it may be that the relatively large number of 2H substitutions were caused by this nonspecific effect, rather than specific activation of action subunits (in this case, key presses). Experiment 2 tested this hypothesis.

EXPERIMENT 2: INDUCTION OF GESTURE AND OBJECT MANIPULATION ERRORS

The purpose of this experiment was twofold: first, to extend the OCE to the domain of object manipulation and gestures, and second, to test the competing-plans hypothesis (Baars, 1980b). Previous studies have demonstrated that the OCE causes errors in speech and typing, two language-based action modalities. Experiment 2 extended the OCE to non-language-based actions, like waving the hands, nodding the head, and moving small objects around. If the action spoonerisms observed by Reason (1979) can be induced in the laboratory, then this would strongly support the claim that errors in different action modalities are similar because of their underlying causes. Specifically, this experiment would suggest that this underlying mechanism is not tied to language production alone.

The competing-plans hypothesis (Baars, 1980b) states that errors occur when (1) there is competition between alternative action plans, and (2) the time permitted for a response is limited. Thus, it predicts that the error rate will vary directly with the amount of competition and inversely with the time permitted to respond. What is competing in the OCE? By requiring subjects to

produce either ordering of the two actions on cue, competition is created between a plan that specifies the order "Action 1, then Action 2" and an alternative plan for "Action 2, then Action 1."

The subjects observed pairs of actions like:

43. Put the pen in the cup; then put the candy in the ashtray.

In the experimental conditions, the subjects repeated the actions just as they
saw them on half the trials and reversed them on the other trials. The prediction was that this task would induce competition and, as a result, lead to
errors, particularly action spoonerisms. These action spoonerisms should
involve interchanges of elements of the two actions. In the control conditions,
the subjects either repeated all the items or reversed all the items. Because
there was less uncertainty about the ordering of the actions in the control
conditions, there should be less competition and hence, fewer errors. Because
it is more common to perform actions in the sequence in which they are
presented than in the reverse order, the subjects should make more errors in
the all-"REVERSE" control condition than in the all-"REPEAT" condition. The
question of whether the OCE has a specific effect in increasing the likelihood
of action spoonerisms relative to the total number of errors was also examined.

Method

Subjects. The subjects were undergraduates enrolled in an introductory
psychology class. They were not aware that the purpose of the experiment was
to induce errors, and they received extra credit for their participation. Of 53
subjects, 36 were female and 17 were male. There were 14 subjects in one
experimental condition and 13 in each of the other three conditions.

Apparatus. The apparatus included two Sony AV 3400 videocorders.
One videocorder was hooked up to a JVC videomonitor (Model 6201) black-
and-white TV monitor and was used to present the stimulus tape. This monitor, which had a 12-inch/diagonal screen, was approximately 3 feet from the
subject's chair on a cart that was 3 feet high. The other videocorder was
connected to a Sony AV 3400 video camera and was used to record the subject's
responses.

The objects used in the second part of the experiment were laid out on a
16" x 28" x 27" table that could be placed in front of the subject. These objects
were a pen, a 12-inch ruler, a coffee cup, a pair of glasses with one red filter and
one blue filter (used to view 3-D movies), an ashtray, a pair of dice, a rubber
band, a Tootsie pop (the candy), some sheets of lined yellow legal-sized paper,
a piece of the same paper rolled into a ball, a cassette, a pack of matches, a

screwdriver, a tea bag, a spoon, and a roll of tape. The initial arrangement of these objects was constant across subjects and was indicated on a paper template that covered the top surface of the table. In addition, a waste basket was placed to the left of the subject's chair.

Stimulus Tape. The stimulus tape was a recording of the second author performing a series of pairs of actions. In the first part of the experiment, the actions were gestures like smiling broadly, wiggling the fingers, groaning, and clapping the hands. Verbal descriptions of all of the actions are given in Table 8. There were 30 trials in the first part, and after the 30th trial, the word "INTERMISSION" appeared on the screen. The actions in the second part involved manipulating the objects on a small table; the actions are listed in Table 8. There were 20 trials in the second part.

Each trial began with a low warning beep, then another low beep after a 2-second interval. At the second low beep, the model executed the first action. A third low beep 2 seconds later signaled the end of Action 1 and the beginning of Action 2 as performed by the model. Then one or two louder, different-sounding beeps came, 2 seconds after the third low beep. These beeps were the subject's cue. The model was motionless during the 4 seconds the subject had to respond. A fourth and fifth low beep at 2-second intervals gave the subjects feedback about the time permitted to mimic the two actions. All of the beeps were part of the soundtrack of the videotape. The quality of the videotape was less than ideal, but the subjects were able to mimic most of the actions with no difficulty. Trials that were extremely difficult to see are indicated in Table 8.

Procedure. On arrival, the subject was greeted and the experimenter introduced himself. The subject was asked what hand he or she used to write with, and this, as well as the sex of the subject, was noted on the response sheet. The subject was seated, and the following instructions were read by the experimenter:

> Your task is to copy the actions performed by the model on this TV screen. In each trial, you will hear a series of low beeps and see the model do two actions, such as waving his hands and then saying, "Oh." Next, you will hear one or two loud beeps.

The next section of the instructions depended on the condition the subject was in:

> *Experimental Group 1:* If you hear one beep, you should immediately perform the two actions in the same order in which the model did them: you would wave your hands, then say, "Oh." If you hear two beeps, you should immediately perform the two actions in the opposite order. To continue with the example, you would first say, "Oh," then wave your hands.
>
> *Experimental Group 2:* If you hear two beeps, you should immediately perform the two actions in the same order in which the model did them: you would wave your hands, then say "Oh." If you hear one beep, you should im-

TABLE 8
Verbal Descriptions of Stimulus Actions for Experiment 2

Part 1: Gestures

Action 1	Action 2	# Cue beeps
1. Stick out tongue.	Smile.	1
2. Open eyes wide.	Wiggle fingers on both hands.	1
3. Put left thumb in mouth.	Put right pinky in right ear.	2
4. Groan out loud.	Giggle softly.	1
5. Wave both hands left to right.	Raise eyebrows.	2
6. Rock body left to right.	Nod head up and down yes.	2
7. Hit feet together twice loudly.	Softly clap three times.	2
8. Shake head left and right no.	Flap hands up and down.	1
9. Softly pat head four times.	Clap hands loudly two times.	2
10. Pat legs two times.	Scratch left shoulder with right arm.	2
11. Close eyes.	Open mouth.	1
12. Scratch nose.	Pinch right ear with right arm.	2^a
13. Flap right hand.	Scratch right forearm.	1
14. Point right with right forefinger.	Stretch arms in front.	1
15. Give a right-turn signal.	Raise left leg.	2^a
16. Open and close right hand three times.	Open mouth wide.	1
17. Wrap arms around torso.	Stretch legs out.	1
18. Touch nose with right hand.	Turn head left.	1
19. Clap softly four times.	Shout "Bang."	2
20. Rub left ear with right hand.	Tap left leg with left hand four times.	2
21. Move right leg side to side.	Shake head "yes."	1
22. Point to the left with left arm.	Look right.	2
23. Spread arms.	Say "Ouch."	1
24. Move elbows back and forth two times.	Shrug left shoulder three times.	2
25. Wiggle left foot.	Flap right hand four times.	2
26. Open mouth.	Say "Eeee."	1
27. Lift right leg.	Raise left arm up and down.	2
28. Move head in circle.	Move arm up and down two times.	1
29. Say "whap" softly.	Bang left leg with left arm loudly.	2
30. Tap left leg three times with left hand.	Tap left foot on floor twice.	1

Part 2: Object manipulation

Action 1 Action 2	# Cue beeps
1. Draw circle on paper with right hand. Throw ball of paper into garbage (left hand).	2
2. Put matches in ashtray with right hand. Put cassette where paper ball was with right hand.	2

(continued)

TABLE 8 (*continued*)

Action 1 Action 2	# Cue beeps
3. Put on glasses and take off. Pretend to use screwdriver (take with left hand and switch to right).	1
4. Tea bag in cup (left hand). Spoon to mouth (right hand).	2
5. Tap pen on table with right hand. Wave ruler with left hand.	1
6. Candy in cup with right hand. Tea bag to mouth with left hand.	1
7. Piece of tape on paper. Put rubber band in ashtray with right hand.	1
8. Throw clean paper in garbage with left hand. Pretend to write on cassette with right hand.	2
9. Screwdriver in cup with left hand. Move ruler to left with right hand.	2
10. Put on and take off glasses. Throw cassette in garbage with right hand.	1
11. Take screwdriver out of cup with left hand. Put ruler in cup with left hand.	2
12. Roll dice with right hand. Put spoon to mouth with left hand.	1
13. Move tape to ball-of-paper place with right hand. Candy to mouth and back to cup with left hand.	1
14. Empty cup with left hand. Put dice in ashtray with right hand.	1
15. Take tape and look through the hole (right hand). Push glasses forward with both hands.	2
16. Empty ashtray with right hand. Put cup to lips with left hand.	1
17. Pick up matches with right hand. Pick up candy with right hand (hold both).	2
18. Put matches in cup with right hand. Put candy to left ear with right hand (hold candy).	2
19. Pick up pen with right hand. Tap candy with right hand (keep objects).	1
20. Put candy in ashtray with right hand. Put pen in cup with right hand.	2

[a]Video display problem makes actions difficult to see.

mediately perform the two actions in the opposite order. To continue with the example, you would first say, "Oh," then wave your hands.

Control Group 1: These loud beeps are the signal for you to immediately perform the two actions in the same order in which the model did them: you would wave your hands, then say, "Oh."

Control Group 2: These loud beeps are the signal for you to immediately perform the two actions in the opposite order from the way the model did them: you would first say, "Oh," then wave your hands.

The rest of the instructions were identical for all conditions:

> Please use the same hand or leg that the model does. That is, when he uses his right hand, you should also use your right hand. Also, try your best to do the repeated actions the same number of times as the model. Remember that the idea is to copy the actions as accurately as possible.
>
> We will try some practice trials before going on to the experiment. If you have any questions, please ask during the practice. Questions will not be appropriate during the actual experiment.

There were five practice trials. The practice trials were repeated until the subject did four out of five practice items correctly and indicated that she or he was ready to go on. Any errors that the subject made were corrected verbally, and any procedural questions were answered. Next these instructions were read:

> Now we will start the experimental trials. If you cannot properly see the actions on the screen because of display problems, please say, "I couldn't see it," or something like that, and continue with the task.

Both videocorders were started, and the first part of the experiment began. The experimenter recorded the subject's errors on the response sheet. The response sheet consisted of verbal descriptions of the actions in the order in which the subject was supposed to perform them. At the end of the first part of the experiment, the subject had a short break while the experimenter paused the two videocorders, moved the table and waste basket into place, and adjusted the camera for a closer view of the subject. Then the instructions for the second part were read to the subject:

> In the second part of the experiment, the rules are the same, but instead of just moving parts of your body, you will be manipulating the objects on the table. Remember to try to do the actions just as the model does them, and please say, "I couldn't see it," if you miss an action. Any question?

If there were no questions, the two videocorders were started again. During the second part of the experiment, it was occasionally desirable for the experimenter to retrieve or rearrange objects that were out of place because of errors that the subject had made. At the end of the second part, the subject was debriefed and thanked for participating.

The response sheets were checked against the videotapes, and any discrepancies were corrected. In most cases, this checking was done by one of the research assistants who had not run the particular subject being checked.

Results

A total of 60 full action spoonerisms and 325 partial action spoonerisms were observed. A full spoonerism was a case in which elements of the two actions were interchanged. In a partial action spoonerism, an element moved from one action to the other, as in an anticipation, delay, or perseveration error. Here are some examples:

44. Part 1: Gestures—full left/right spoonerism:
point to left, look to right → point to right, look to left.
45. Part 2: Object manipulation—full object spoonerism:
put pen in cup, candy in ashtray → candy in cup, pen in ashtray.

46. Part 1: Gestures—partial direction spoonerism:
nod "no," wave hands up and down → nod "yes," wave hands up and down.

47. Part 2: Object manipulation—partial object spoonerism and omission:
tap the pen, wave the ruler → tap the ruler.

A total of 983 nonspoonerism errors was observed. The frequency of error types by condition in Experiment 2 is given in Table 9. When the expected frequencies were adjusted to reflect the number of subjects in each condition, significantly more action spoonerisms occurred in the experimental conditions than in the control conditions (χ^2 = 7.5, df = 1, p < .01), and more errors that were not action spoonerisms were made in the experimental conditions (χ^2 = 7.3, df = 1, p < .01). In addition, subjects in the all-"REPEAT" control condition made significantly fewer nonspoonerism errors than those in the all-"REVERSE" condition (χ^2 = 6.15, df = 1, p < .025), but the difference for spoonerisms was not significant (χ^2 = 0.22, df = 1, p > .25). Finally, more nonspoonerism errors were made in condition E2 (one beep "REVERSE") than in E1 (one beep "REPEAT") (χ^2 = 12.74, df = 1, p < .001), though there was no significant difference for action spoonerisms (χ^2 = 0.04, df = 1, p > .25).

TABLE 9
Frequency of Error Types by Condition for Experiment 2

Type of error	Total	E1	E2	E	C1	C2	C
Action spoonerisms							
Partial	325	93	87	180	72	73	145
Full	60	21	22	43	6	11	17
Omit	357	91	90	181	87	89	176
No reverse	105	23	31	54	—	51	51
Incorrect reversal	70	23	40	63	7	—	7
Incorrect							
Number	87	18	28	46	18	23	41
Object/action	220	35	72	107	59	54	113
Left/right	101	29	32	61	19	21	40
Ambiguous left/right	43	21	10	31	4	8	12
Total	1368	354	412	766	272	330	602

[a]Key: E = total for two experimental conditions; E1 = one beep "REPEAT," two beeps "REVERSE"; E2 = one beep "REVERSE," two beeps "REPEAT"; C = total control conditions; C1 = all "REPEAT"; C2 = all "REVERSE."

Table 10 shows the frequencies of the various types of action spoonerisms that were observed in Experiment 1. A left/right exchange was scored when the subject used the hand or leg that was involved in the other action, as in Item 44 above. Left/right spoonerisms were the most frequent, making up 67% of all action spoonerisms. A direction switch involved an exchange of the direction of movement relative to the body, other than left/right orientation, such as movement up and down (as in Item 46 above) or toward and away from the body. If the subject switched the number of times the actions were repeated, this was scored as a number-of-repetitions spoonerism:

48. Part 1: Gestures—full number of repetitions spoonerism:
    tap foot twice, hand on leg three times → tap foot three times, hand twice. Items 45 and 47 are examples of exchanges of the objects.

Finally, exchanges of the action were cases in which the objects were correct, but the actions carried out with them were exchanged, as in:

49. Part 2: Object manipulation—partial action spoonerism:
    look through tape, push away glasses → look through tape then glasses.

A total of 1,368 errors was observed, which translates into a probability of an error on a single trial of 51.6%. The number of errors of each type by subject is given in Table 11. The other error types that were observed included omission errors, in which one or both actions were not carried out (as in Item 47), and incorrect left/right, number, and object errors, in which the source of the incorrect element was not the other action:

50. Part 1: Gestures—incorrect left/right substitution:
    scratch right forearm, flap right hand → scratch left forearm, flap left hand.

TABLE 10
Frequency of Action Spoonerisms by Type for Experiment 2

Element exchanged	Total	Experimental		Control	
		Partial	Full	Partial	Full
Left/right	259	116	35	94	14
Direction	16	12	2	2	0
Number of repetitions	36	20	1	12	3
Object	48	19	4	25	0
Action	26	13	1	12	0
Total	385	180	43	145	17

TABLE 11

Frequency of Error Types by Subject for Experiment 2

Experimental Group 1: One beep = "REPEAT," two beeps = "REVERSE"

	Action spoonerisms			No	Incorrect	Incorrect			
S#	Partial	Full	Omit	reversal	reversal	L/R	#	Object	Total
1	11	1	5	0	0	2	0	3	22
2	7	1	2	2	1	2	1	1	17
3	5	0	10	6	0	7	0	2	30
4	13	1	3	5	20	4	2	3	51
5	1	0	2	0	0	0	1	1	5
6	4	1	5	0	0	3	1	0	14
25	8	0	5	0	0	3	1	4	21
30	8	8	4	1	0	8	2	2	33
33	2	0	11	2	0	2	1	2	20
37	5	1	10	1	0	3	0	3	23
41	10	3	4	2	1	3	3	5	31
45	4	3	8	1	1	3	3	2	25
49	5	1	9	2	0	2	1	3	23
52	10	1	13	1	0	8	2	4	39
Total	93	21	91	23	23	50	18	35	354

Experimental Group 2: One beep = "REVERSE," two beeps = "REPEAT"

	Action spoonerisms			No	Incorrect	Incorrect			
S#	Partial	Full	Omit	reversal	reversal	L/R	#	Object	Total
7	13	6	5	4	14	11	0	5	58
8	4	0	4	0	0	0	0	2	10
9	3	2	5	3	1	1	1	2	18
16	5	1	5	2	0	0	1	2	16
19	2	0	5	3	0	2	0	3	15
22	4	0	6	4	0	1	1	3	19
26	8	0	8	0	0	6	1	3	26
31	7	0	20	3	0	2	1	4	37
34	16	3	4	7	8	9	7	8	62
38	10	2	4	1	0	4	5	6	32
42	4	3	5	0	0	1	1	7	21
46	8	4	6	2	17	4	4	14	59
50	3	1	13	2	0	1	6	13	39
Total	87	22	90	31	40	42	28	72	412

Control Group 1: All "REPEAT"

	Action spoonerisms			No	Incorrect	Incorrect			
S#	Partial	Full	Omit	reversal	reversal	L/R	#	Object	Total
10	9	0	5	—	0	1	3	2	20
11	5	0	5	—	0	2	0	1	13
12	10	0	4	—	0	3	2	3	22
17	12	1	5	—	0	2	0	3	23
21	7	0	9	—	0	0	1	6	23
23	2	0	8	—	1	1	1	1	14
27	3	0	5	—	0	1	2	2	13
32	4	1	15	—	1	5	3	5	34
35	7	0	5	—	0	1	0	7	20
39	2	1	4	—	0	0	0	2	9
43	1	0	4	—	2	2	2	9	20[a]
47	5	1	8	—	2	4	0	14	34
51	5	2	10	—	1	1	4	4	27
Total	72	6	87	—	7	23	18	59	272

Control Group 2: All "REVERSE"

	Action spoonerisms			No	Incorrect	Incorrect			
S#	Partial	Full	Omit	reversal	reversal	L/R	#	Object	Total
13	6	0	11	3	—	1	1	6	28
14	8	2	7	3	—	3	4	1	28
15	3	0	6	1	—	1	2	1	14
18	7	0	6	4	—	2	1	2	22
20	3	0	6	3	—	2	0	2	16
24	5	0	4	9	—	3	1	4	26
28	9	2	3	4	—	2	2	3	25
29	3	3	6	1	—	2	1	7	23
36	5	0	7	3	—	0	2	6	23
40	7	2	7	9	—	5	2	7	39
44	6	0	12	4	—	4	2	6	34
48	1	2	4	2	—	1	0	3	13
53	10	0	10	5	—	3	5	6	39
Total	73	11	89	51	—	29	23	54	330

[a]incomplete: missing Part 2 trials 4 through 20 because not videotaped

51. Part 1: Gestures—incorrect number substitution:
    clap four times, shout "Bang" → clap three times, shout, "Bang."

52. Part 2: Object manipulation—incorrect object substitution:
    pick up matches then candy → pick up dice then candy.

No reversals were failures to reverse "REVERSE"-cued items, and incorrect reversals were cases in which a "REPEAT"-cued item was reversed. Note that there can be no failures to reverse in the all-"REPEAT" control condition, and no incorrect reversals in the all-"REVERSE" condition. The categories of incorrect left/right and ambiguous left/right in Table 9 are combined into incorrect left/right for Table 11. Ambiguous left/right errors were cases in which it was not clear whether the left/right confusion was a spoonerism or incorrect:

53. Part 1: Gestures—ambiguous left/right substitution:
    stretch both arms to front, point to right with right forefinger →
    stretch both arms to front, point to left with left forefinger.

This error is ambiguous in that both arms participated in the first action, yet both arms did not participate in the error. Because the arms from the first action did not switch, even though one (the left) may have been said to switch, errors like this could be classified as an incorrect substitution of one arm for the other, or a partial exchange of the left arm.

Discussion

Effectiveness of the OCE. As predicted, action spoonerisms were induced by the OCE task, just as verbal spoonerisms and typing errors had been induced in the other studies (Table 1). Because the same method can induce analogous errors in these different modalities, it can be argued that the underlying cause of many naturally occurring errors is the same; the similarity in the form of the errors is not coincidental. In addition, this experiment showed that OCE-induced spoonerisms are not unique to language-based action. Comparisons of the specific results across action modalities are covered in the section "General Conclusions about Action Errors."

Competition. The prediction that increased competition will lead to more errors was also supported, as the subjects made significantly more errors in general and action spoonerisms specifically in the experimental conditions than in the control conditions. Competition was created by means of the OCE, in which the subjects were uncertain about the ordering of the two actions and had limited time to respond. Both possible orderings were prepared or primed, thus producing "competing plans" (Baars, 1980b) for a single action sequence. As a result of the activation of these two plans, elements of either action that are highly activated at an inopportune time may be selected for execution. In the control conditions, there was no uncertainty about the correct ordering of the two actions, as it was the same on every trial. Thus, any "competing plan" that led to errors in the control condition had to have a source other than ordering uncertainty. The finding that competition increases the likelihood of error is consistent with the findings of Chen and Baars (Chapter 9, this volume), who used a different technique to vary competition in a verbal sentence-retrieval task.

Comparison within the experimental and control conditions suggests that spoonerisms and nonspoonerisms are differently affected by different types of competition. The difference between the experimental and the control conditions was due to uncertainty about ordering. Competition due to ordering uncertainty led to more spoonerisms and nonspoonerisms. Within the experimental condition, differences between conditions E1 and E2 are hypothesized to result from greater "compatibility" of one beep for "REPEAT" (E1) as opposed to one beep for "REVERSE" (E2). The E2 subjects made significantly more nonspoonerisms than did the E1 subjects, but although the subjects made a few more spoonerisms in E2 than in E1, the two conditions did not significantly differ on spoonerisms. Perhaps the subjects occasionally erred in deciding on the ordering because of incompatibility. If this was the case, then the subjects should have been more likely to reverse incorrectly or to fail to reverse the items in the E2 condition, a result that was in fact observed (no-reversal and incorrect-reversal errors made up 25 of the additional 63 nonspoonerism errors observed in E2). The additional confusion in E2 involved the decision to repeat or reverse, which occurred before the actions were ordered and thus did not enhance competition between the two orderings enough to produce significantly more spoonerisms than in the E1 condition. This hypothesis can account for part of the observed difference in the likelihood of nonspoonerisms and for the lack of difference on spoonerisms between E1 and E2.

The difference between the control conditions C1 (all-"REPEAT") and C2 (all-"REVERSE") in terms of error production is based on the fact that it is more habitual or common to carry out actions in the sequence in which they are presented than in the reverse order. In giving verbal or written instructions (such as recipes), for example, one generally "begins at the beginning" and gives the instructions in the sequence in which the actions ought to be carried out. The forward ordering provides a potential "competing plan" in the all-"REVERSE" (C2) condition, if the perceptual sequence can activate the action sequence, or if the subject considers carrying out the actions in the more usual, forward ordering. It is rather unlikely that subjects who were never asked to "REVERSE" the actions would spontaneously consider the reversed plan in the all-"REPEAT" (C1) condition. These claims are supported by the observation that there were 51 no-reversal errors in the all-"REVERSE" condition, and only 7 incorrect reversals in the all-"REPEAT" condition. Therefore, most of the 58-error difference between C1 and C2 was due to a failure to carry out the instruction to reorder the actions. The trouble is that if there were competing plans, why were there not more spoonerisms in the all-"REVERSE" condition? Though there were six more spoonerisms in the C2 condition, this result was not a significant difference, which could lead us to conclude that the competing plan was not sufficiently activated to produce a significant difference in spoonerisms. Another possible explanation for the difference in the frequency of errors is that reversing requires more attentional resources than repeating, so that the subjects had fewer resources to maintain a representation of the two actions. This explanation says that the difference in error rate was due to memory failure, and that competing plans were not implicated, so the spoonerisms would not be expected to differ in frequency between the two conditions.

Action Spoonerisms.   The most frequent type of action spoonerism was the left/right exchange, which accounted for two thirds of the action spoonerisms (see Table 10). Several factors may have contributed to the predominance of these errors. First, when the model used his right hand, the hand on the TV monitor was on the left side of the screen. Thus, there may have been competition between using the same hand (in this case, the right) and doing the action on the same side of the screen (on the left). Second, there were only two possible directions, so that cases in which the subject guessed at the hand had a 50-50 chance of being an error—and there were fewer possible incorrect or ambiguous left/right errors. With object, action, and number of repetitions, there was a greater chance of an incorrect substitution. Third, the subjects may have favored their preferred hand and may frequently have substituted it for the less dominant hand. This was certainly a factor in determining the direction of the switch; in the E2 condition, for example, in which all of the subjects were right-handed, 75 of the left/right errors were from left to right, 24 were from right to left, and 18 involved an interchange. Finally, the same anatomical connections between cortical motor areas in the two hemispheres that were given a role in the explanation of homology may lead to a high incidence of left/right action spoonerisms, through symmetrical priming.

The different types of elements that were observed to switch provide information on the units of the representation of these types of action. The action or operation, the object of that operation, the number of times it is repeated, and the effector all are candidates for action units. This theme will be expanded in the "General Conclusions" section.

Other Types of Errors.   The error probability per trial of 51.6% seems fairly high, though perhaps it is not surprising for a fast-paced, relatively novel task that was designed to create competition. As far as the other error types that were observed (see Tables 9 and 11) are concerned, the most frequent error type was incorrect substitutions, followed by spoonerisms, and then omissions. No reversals and incorrect reversals were much less likely than these other categories of error.

GENERAL CONCLUSIONS ABOUT ACTION ERRORS

In this section, an attempt is made to reach some general conclusions from the applications of the ordinal conflict effect, and to outline a theoretical account of action planning and action error.

The Representation of Action

Dell and Reich (1980; Dell, 1986), Norman (1981), Rumelhart and Norman (1982), MacKay (1982), and Reason and Mycielska (1982) have provided activation network or "connectionist" accounts of action errors. Network activation models of action and speech production can capture the essential similarities between these output systems that lead to similar kinds of errors. Networks for action and speech production are typically organized into a hierarchical set of levels, in which nodes within levels compete in terms of their activation values. The nodes represent the units of action, which are linked to one another in such a way as to implement cooperative and competitive relationships between the units.

Earlier in the chapter, the claim was made that action errors reveal what the units of action are. The argument for this claim is analogous to the argument from psycholinguistics (e.g., Fromkin, 1973; MacKay, 1970/1973) that spoonerisms and word interchanges offer evidence of the psychological reality of phonemes and words as units. Research involving the OCE and other error induction tasks has provided additional evidence of the psychological reality of phonemes, syllables, and words that is complementary to the naturalistic error data. These units are the nodes in activation network accounts of speech production (Dell, 1986; Dell & Reich, 1980; MacKay, 1982; Stemberger, 1982). The set of units of a particular type make up a level or stage of a hierarchical network, in which each high-level unit is connected to its components in the next (lower) level. In Dell (1986), for example, morpheme nodes are linked with the appropriate syllable nodes, which are in turn linked to phonemes and rimes, and phonemes are linked to articulatory features.

The obvious unit of action in typing is the keystroke, and Experiment 1 supports this unit, as well as its hierarchical decomposition into hand, finger and position components (as in the coding system of Gentner et al., 1983). Our data also support some kind of representation of homology and serial position. These effects are perhaps better represented by links than by units: the idea is that links between units allow activation to spread from one unit to another. The intended keystroke is activated; then activation spreads from that unit to all those connected to it. When the keystroke node for A becomes activated, for example, the appropriate hand, finger, and position nodes become active also, because of the links between the keystroke node and these components. If homologous keystroke nodes are connected via their common relation to a particular finger node, then the keystroke node homologous to the intended keystroke node will be activated, providing a competing plan. In terms of activation networks, then, a competing plan is an activated node at the same level as an intended node. The action system must select the most highly activated node at a given level for execution, and errors result when the competing node is more active than the intended node.

In Experiment 2, the errors suggest that the following are units of action: the direction of movement, the particular action, the object of the action, the number of times the action is repeated, and the effector (i.e., the right hand or leg vs. the left). These units do not fall into a natural hierarchy; rather, they seem to be more similar to features in speech and the [H, F, P] representation in typing, in which different components of the action must be simultaneously activated. One additional candidate for an action unit is the amplitude or power of the action: contrast a light tap with a loud clap. It was found to be too difficult to reliably assess errors involving this variable in Experiment 2, though it seems intuitively plausible that errors involving the amplitude of actions occur. This remains a question for future research.

If the network is the structural part of the action theory, activation is the processing mechanism. Each node has an activation value, which at any given instant, is a function of the node's relevance to current processing. The initiation of an action is assumed to be the result of a conscious intention, which leads to the activation of the highest levels of the intended plan. The intended plan consists of the set of activated nodes that specify the information necessary to go from the (underspecified) conscious intention to the actual movements of the body. Very often, if not all of the time, other nodes at the same levels as nodes from the intended plan are also active. How do these competing plans become active? Five sources of competing activation were considered by Mattson (1987); here, the focus is on the OCE.

As suggested earlier, the competition in the OCE is assumed to be between plans representing the two possible orderings of the actions. The general sequence is as follows: The subject observes two actions (words, etc.) and then prepares to carry them out. At the time of stimulus presentation, the subject does not know which order the two actions must be produced in. While the ordering uncertainty is in force, the subject may (1) entertain two conscious intentions, one corresponding to the repeat ordering and the other corresponding to the reverse ordering; or (2) activate the two actions equally and wait until the signal to select any ordering; or (3) guess at the ordering and consciously intend one of the two possible orderings. When the cue indicating the ordering is presented, the subject consciously intends only that ordering. If the subject entertains both orderings, then the cued plan becomes the sole intended plan, and the lingering activation from the other activated ordering provides a competing plan. If the subject does not activate an ordering, then there will be less time to activate the ordering, so that the ratio of signal (intended plan) to noise (all competing plans) will be reduced, and the probability of an error will be enhanced. Finally, if the subject guesses at the ordering and is correct, the response should be fast and relatively error-free because no change in the conscious intention is necessary; but if the subject guesses wrong, then the original conscious intention yields a competing plan. The OCE suggests that common structural and processing characteristics underlie spoonerisms and other errors across modalities, and that activation networks provide a natural way to represent these commonalities.

Situations analogous to the OCE experimental situations occur in everyday life. As one example, imagine you are boiling water for macaroni and waiting for the oven to heat up to put something else in it (two actions that can be performed in either order). Just as the oven is ready and the water boils, the doorbell rings (providing time pressure). Now you must quickly decide the ordering of "put macaroni in boiling water" and "put casserole in oven." Under these conditions, spoonerisms and other errors should be more likely than they are when there is no ordering uncertainty or time pressure.

Quantitative Comparison of OCE Studies

Now that the common theoretical base for different action modalities has been established, we turn our attention to a comparison across the various applications of the OCE that were introduced in the first section (Table 1). Table 12 is a comparison of the average probability of an error on a single trial across these studies. Not all of the categories of errors that were observed are included, only those that were common across modalities. The probability of any sort of error is quite a bit higher in the nonspeech modalities (Experiments 1 and 2) than in the speech experiments (Baars, 1977; Mattson *et al.*, 1985; Mattson *et al.*, 1991). A number of factors may have contributed to this difference. First, it may be that the subjects were at different positions on the speed–accuracy trade-off in the different experiments, even though the instructions typically emphasized speed and were quite similar across the studies. Second, the speech studies involved real words and sentences, whereas the nonspeech studies involved nonsense words (Experiment 1) and the imitation of actions that were not necessarily habitual (Experiment 2). A general finding from many studies of speech errors is that they tend to follow the rules of language, so that "bad" errors, which violate some rule of language, are less likely than "good" errors, which are consistent with the rules. The lexicality of the stimulus and the error affect the probability of spoonerisms: people are more likely to make spoonerisms that end up as words than spoonerisms that create nonsense, unless all of the stimuli are also nonsense (Baars, Motley, & MacKay, 1975). Baars (1977) showed that subjects typically avoid making errors that produce anomalous sentences, and Mattson *et al.* (1985) demonstrated that subjects avoid making errors that produce phrases that are awkward to pronounce. The results in Table 12 of these studies are summed across conditions (normal versus anomalous or awkward errors). Finally, there may be some fundamental difference between speech and nonspeech modalities that account for some of the difference, such as the difference in the amount of practice in speech and typing, for example.

The probability of a full spoonerism ranges from the "floor" (one full-syllable spoonerism, given in Table 1) to 9.4% per trial in Baars (1977), Experiment 3. Partial spoonerisms range from the floor of 0.1% in the repeat condition of Baars and Motley (1976) to 13.4% in the E2 condition of Experiment 2. In order to look at the relationship between full and partial spoonerisms without confounding from the overall probability of errors across studies, the ratio of full spoonerisms to partial spoonerisms for each study is also given in Table 12. The most obvious fact about the spoonerism ratio is that it is always less than 1, except in the four experiments of Baars (1977). Thus,

TABLE 12

Comparison of Results across Modalities: Probability of Error per Trial[a]

Source	All errors (%)	Full spoons (%)	Part spoons (%)	Spoon ratio	Omit incomplete (%)	No reversal (%)	Incorrect reversal (%)
Baars & Motley, 1976:	NA	0.6	2.2	.275	NA	7.9	3.5
Word pairs	Reverse	0.6	2.1	.263	NA	7.9	—
	Repeat	0.1	0.1	.5	NA	—	3.5
Baars, 1977: Expt. 1	23[b]	4.9	1.7	2.8	8.8	7.8	—
Sentences 2	23[b]	6.1	2.3[b]	2.5[b]	10[b]	4.6[b]	—
3	30[b]	9.4	4.7	2.0	7.2	8.7	
4	28	6.9	5.4	1.3	11.6	4.0	—
Mattson, Baars, & Motley, 1985: Sentences	30.4	3.3	4.9	.669	20.8	1.4	NA
Mattson, Stravitz, Baars, & Cruiok- shank, 1991: Word pairs	30.5	0.2	1.8	.103	15.5	1.5	0.9
	Syllable	0.0	1.4	.032			
	Phoneme	0.1	0.4	.375			
Experiment 1: Typing	59.0	0.2[c]	5.7[c]	.034[c]	16.8	1.1	0.3
Experiment 2: E1	50.6	3.0	13.3	.226	13.0	3.3	3.3
Gestures E2	63.4	3.4	13.4	.253	13.8	4.8	6.2
and object C1	41.8	0.9	11.2	.083	13.4	—	1.1
manipu- C2	50.8	1.7	11.2	.151	13.7	7.8	—
lation							

[a]NA = data not available; — = error can't occur.
[b]Averaged over small discrepancies between the text and tables in Baars (1977).
[c]2H interchanges only.

partials are almost always more frequent than full spoonerisms. The highest ratios were observed in the phrase-reversal tasks of Baars (1977; ranging from 1.3 to 2.8) and Mattson *et al.* (1985; 0.669). The other relatively high ratio was 0.5 for the repeat items in Baars and Motley (1976), but this is not especially reliable because only three errors contributed to the ratio. The rest of the spoonerism ratios range from 0.375 for phoneme spoonerisms in Mattson *et al.* (1991) down to 0.032 for syllable spoonerisms in the same study and 0.034 for Experiment 1.

For comparison purposes, the ratios from several naturalistic collections of errors were also computed. The London-Lund corpus of spontaneous conversation contains 2 Exchange errors and 31 Anticipations and Perseverations, for a ratio of 0.065 (Garnham, Shillcock, Brown, Mill, & Cutler, 1982). Another tape-recorded corpus (Deese, 1984) contained only 1 error that may have been an exchange and 14 anticipations and perseverations, for a ratio of 0.071. Hotopf (1980) tabulated several corpora of speech and writing errors. The ratios of transpositions to anticipations and perseverations in his tape-recorded conference sample of speech was 0.065, which is remarkably close to the ratios for the other two tape-recorded corpora, and on the low side compared with most of the ratios from OCE studies. Hotopf's tabulation of the errors from Meringer's corpus of speech errors (1908; Meringer & Mayer, 1895, as cited in Hotopf, 1980) yields an overall ratio of 0.273, with 0.526 for transpositions of words and 0.194 for syllable or phoneme transpositions. Meringer's corpus may have been more subject to collection biases than were the tape-recorded corpora, and this may be the cause of the larger ratio for his corpus. No full-word transpositions in writing were observed, only full-letter and full-syllable transpositions, yielding ratios ranging from 0.054 to 0.222 (0.129 overall).

What factors affect the spoonerism ratio? Competition seems to have an effect when the ratios from Experiment 2 are inspected (Table 12): the ratios were greater in the experimental conditions than in the control conditions. Greater competition may also explain why the ratios were higher for OCE speech studies than for the tape-recorded corpora, as the task probably induced more competition than is the norm in speech. Competition was also probably greater in the experiments of Baars (1977) than in that of Mattson *et al.* (1985) because, in the former experiments, all of the target sentences had to be reversed, and they were always preceded by noncued items that included both orderings of the phrases in the target sentence. On the other hand, the overall error rates in these two sets of studies do not have the expected relation: they are roughly equal.

Word transpositions seem to be unique in terms of producing a greater ratio of full transpositions to partials. Ratios greater than 0.5 were observed in Baars (1977), in Mattson *et al.* (1985), and in the ratio of lexical errors from Meringer. Why are the ratios for words typically greater than the ratios for phonemes, syllables, writing, keystrokes, and action elements? In order to answer this question, a theory of how full and partial spoonerisms are produced is required.

One possibility is that there are no full spoonerisms *per se,* only pairs of partial spoonerisms that happened to occur on consecutive actions. If this is the case, then the probability of a full spoonerism should always be less than that of a partial spoonerism, which is not the case in the data of Baars (1977). Further, if we represent the probability of a partial spoonerism as p (partial), then the probability of two errors occurring on the same item—p(full)—should be:

$$p(\text{full}) = p(\text{partial}) \ p(\text{partial})$$

Inspection of Table 12 argues against this simple formulation: p(full) is always greater than would be predicted.

Another possible explanation is based on activation network theory. Once a node is executed, it is necessary to reduce its activation to prevent its firing again immediately. In Dell and Reich's model (1980), phoneme nodes are set back to zero activation after being output. If two initial consonants are competing (e.g., /b/ and /d/ from "barn door"), and one wins out (/d/ wins, yielding "darn"), it is set back to zero, and the other node (/b/) is still active when the next chance for an initial consonant comes up (/b/, still active, yields "barn"). If a node is not reset much, there will be a greater chance that that node will appear again, producing more perseverations, as well as more anticipations in which the anticipated unit also appears in its correct (later) position. It may be that, after execution, words are reset to a lower value than are any of the other units, and a greater likelihood of a full spoonerism is thus produced. This would not be surprising, as open-class words are far less likely to be repeated in a sentence than are phonemes, letters, or keystrokes in words. As pointed out earlier, the representation of nonlanguage action has no unit that corresponds directly to the word. It is conceivable that the word and syntactic representations in language are the peculiar specializations of normal action systems that support the uniqueness of human language.

Table 12 also depicts omissions, which ranged in probability from 7.7% in Baars (1977), Experiment 3, to 20.8% in Mattson *et al.* (1985), no-reversal errors, which ranged from 1.1% in Experiment 1 on typing, to 8.7% in Baars (1977), Experiment 3 and incorrect reversals, which ranged from 0.3% in Experiment 1 to 6.2% in the E2 condition of Experiment 2.

Conclusions

On the theoretical level, the activation network approach has been shown to be useful in a wide variety of contexts. It can account for many of our current findings, as well as the results of earlier work on speech production. The idea of competition fits in naturally with activation within a level or an equivalence class. The idea of plans, both intended and competing, can also be interpreted in this framework. We believe that competition underlies many errors. As a result, if we observe that a certain kind of similarity leads to a particular error that our current model does not produce, we should look for a way to represent the similarity relation via either new connections or a common node. This is the power of this kind of representation.

We have shown that the OCE leads to errors in speech, typing, gestures, and object manipulation, and that these errors can be used to examine specific hypotheses in these domains. We advocate the wider use of the OCE and other error-producing methodologies to gain a greater understanding of action in general as well as specific action systems such as speech and typing.

ACKNOWLEDGMENTS

The research reported as Experiment 1 was submitted by the first author in partial fulfillment of the requirements for a master of arts degree in psychology at the State University of New York at Stony Brook, and some of the results were reported at the Second Annual Applied Experimental Psychology Conference at Adelphi University in 1983. The original impetus for the study came from our interactions in the skills seminar of the LNR Research Group at the University of California at San Diego. Experiment 2 was presented at the Eastern Psychological Association Conference in New York, April 1986.

The research was supported by NSF Grant No. BNS-7906024 and NIMH Grant No. 1R03MH3333401 to Bernard J. Baars. In addition, we were supported on Sloan Foundation funds during our sojourn at the University of California at San Diego. We gratefully acknowledge the comments of David Cross, Marcia Johnson, Michael Motley, Carl Camden, Jonathan Grudin, Jenn-Yeu Chen, and other members of our research group; the help of Joan Abunaw and Olga Jabbour in running Experiment 1; and the help of Serge Campeau, Larry Cardano, and Chris Esposito in running Experiment 2.

REFERENCES

Baars, B. J. (1977). The planning of speech: Is there semantic editing prior to speech articulation? *Dissertation Abstracts International, 38,* 5.

Baars, B. J. (1980a). On eliciting predictable speech errors in the laboratory. In V. Fromkin (Ed.), *Errors in linguistic performance: Slips of the tongue, ear, pen, and hand* (pp. 307–318). New York: Academic Press.

Baars, B. J. (1980b). The competing plans hypothesis: An heuristic viewpoint on the causes of errors in speech. In H. Dechert & M. Raupach (Eds.), *Temporal variables in speech: Studies in honor of Frieda Goldman-Eisler* (pp. 39–49). The Hague: Mouton.

Baars, B. J., & Mattson, M. E. (1981). Consciousness and intention: A framework and some evidence. *Cognition and Brain Theory, 4,* 247–263.

Baars, B. J., & Motley, M. T. (1976). Spoonerisms as sequencer conflicts: Evidence from artificially elicited errors. *American Journal of Psychology, 89,* 467–484.

Baars, B. J., Motley, M. T., & MacKay, D. G. (1975). Output editing for lexical status in artificially elicited slips of the tongue. *Journal of Verbal Learning and Verbal Behavior, 14,* 382–391.

Cooper, W. E. (Ed.). (1983a). *Cognitive aspects of skilled typewriting.* New York: Springer-Verlag.

Cooper, W. E. (1983b). Introduction. In W. E. Cooper (Ed.), *Cognitive aspects of skilled typewriting* (pp. 1–38). New York: Springer-Verlag.

Davis, D. W. (1935). *Journal of Business Education.* Reprinted in A. Dvorak, N. Merrick, W. Dealey, & G. Ford. (1936). *Typewriting behavior.* New York: American Book Company.

Deese, J. (1984). *Thought into speech: The psychology of a language.* Englewood Cliffs, NJ: Prentice-Hall.

Dell, G. S. (1986). A spreading-activation theory of retrieval in sentence production. *Psychological Review, 93,* 283–321.

Dell, G. S., & Reich, P. A. (1980). Toward a unified model of slips of the tongue. In V. Fromkin (Ed.), *Errors in linguistic performance* (pp. 273–286). New York: Academic Press.

Dubrovsky, V. (1986). A functional structure of human performance. In W. Karwowski (Ed.), *Trends in ergonomics / human factors III.* Amsterdam: North-Holland.

Dubrovsky, V. (1987). A functional structure of complex human performance. In S. Asfour (Ed.), *Trends in ergonomics / human factors IV.* Amsterdam: North-Holland.

Fitts, P. M., & Jones, R. E. (1947/1961). Analysis of factors contributing to 460 "pilot-error" experiences in operating aircraft controls. Reprinted in H. W. Sinaiko (Ed.), *Selected papers in the design and use of control systems* (pp. 332–358). New York: Dover.

Fromkin, V. A. (1973). Introduction. In V. Fromkin (Ed.), *Speech errors as linguistic evidence* (pp. 11–45). Amsterdam: North-Holland.

Garnham, A., Shillcock, R. C., Brown, G. D. A., Mill, A. I. D., & Cutler, A. (1982). Slips of the tongue in the London-Lund corpus of spontaneous conversation. In A. Cutler (Ed.), *Slips of the tongue and language production* (pp. 251–264). Berlin: Mouton. (Also appeared in *Linguistics, 19,* 805–817.)

Gentner, D. R., Grudin, J. T., Larochelle, S., Norman, D. A., & Rumelhart, D. E. (1983). A glossary of terms including a classification of typing errors. In W. E. Cooper (Ed.), *Cognitive aspects of skilled typewriting* (pp. 39–43). New York: Springer-Verlag.

Grudin, J. T. (1981). *The organization of serial order in typing.* Unpublished doctoral dissertation, University of California at San Diego.

Grudin, J. T. (1983). Error patterns in novice and skilled transcription typing. In W. E. Cooper (Ed.), *Cognitive aspects of skilled typewriting* (pp. 121–143). New York: Springer-Verlag.

Hotopf, N. (1980). Slips of the pen. In U. Frith (Ed.), *Cognitive processes in spelling* (pp. 287–307). London: Academic Press.

Lashley, K. S. (1951/1961). The problem of serial order in behavior. In L. A. Jeffress (Ed.), *Cerebral mechanisms in behavior.* New York: Wiley. (Reprinted in S. Saporta (Ed.), *Psycholinguistics: A book of readings,* pp. 180–198. New York: Holt, Rinehart & Winston.)

Lessenberry, D. D. (1928). *Analysis of errors.* Syracuse, NY: L. C. Smith & Corona Typewriters.

Luria, A. R. (1973). *The working brain: An introduction to neuropsychology.* New York: Basic Books.

MacKay, D. G. (1970/1973). Spoonerisms: The structure of errors in the serial order of speech. *Neuropsychologia, 8,* 323–350. (Reprinted in V. Fromkin (Ed.), *Speech errors as linguistic evidence,* pp. 164–194. The Hague: Mouton.)

MacKay, D. G. (1982). The problems of flexibility, fluency, and speed-accuracy trade-off in skilled behavior. *Psychological Review, 89,* 483–506.

MacKay, D. G., & Soderberg, G. A. (1971). Homologous intrusions: An analogue of linguistic blends. *Perceptual and Motor Skills, 32,* 645–646.

MacNeilage, P. F. (1964). Typing errors as clues to serial ordering mechanisms in language. *Language and Speech, 7*(3), 144–159.

Marteniuk, R. G., & MacKenzie, C. L. (1980). A preliminary theory of two-hand co-ordinated control. In G. Stelmach & J. Requin (Eds.), *Tutorials in motor behavior* (pp. 185–197). Amsterdam: North-Holland.

Mattson, M. E. (1987). *Sources of competing activation in action errors. Dissertation Abstracts International, 48,* 6.

Mattson, M. E., Baars, B. J., & Motley, M. T. (1985). *Wrapping up the case against purely top-down models of speech production: Evidence from induced slips of the tongue.* Paper presented at the meeting of the Eastern Psychological Association, Boston, March 24.

Mattson, M. E., Stravitz, A., Baars, B. J., & Cruickshank, G. (1991). *The psychological reality of syllables: Laboratory induction of exchange errors.* Paper presented at the meeting of the Eastern Psychological Association, New York, April 12.

Meringer, R. (1908). *Aus dem Leben der Sprache: Versprechen, Kindersprache, Nachahmungstrieb.* Berlin: Behrs Verlag.

Meringer, R., & Mayer, K. (1895). *Versprechen und Verlesen: Eine psychologisch-linguistische Studie.* Stuttgart: Goschensche Verlagsbuchhandlung.

Munhall, K. G., & Ostry, D. J. (1983). Mirror-image movements in typing. In W. E. Cooper (Ed.), *Cognitive aspects of skilled typewriting* (pp. 247–257). New York: Springer-Verlag.

Newkirk, D., Klima, E. S., Pedersen, C. C., & Bellugi, U. (1980). Linguistic evidence from slips of the hand. In V. Fromkin (Ed.), *Errors in linguistic performance* (pp. 165–197). New York: Academic Press.

Norman, D. A. (1981). Categorization of action slips. *Psychological Review, 88,* 1–15.

Reason, J. (1979). Actions not as planned: The price of automatization. In G. Underwood & R. Stevens (Eds.), *Aspects of consciousness: Vol. 1. Psychological issues* (pp. 67–89). London: Academic Press.

Reason, J., & Mycielska, K. (1982). *Absent-minded? The psychology of mental lapses and everyday errors.* Englewood Cliffs, NJ: Prentice-Hall.

Rumelhart, D. E., & Norman, D. A. (1982). Simulating a skilled typist: A study of skilled cognitive-motor performance. *Cognitive Science, 6,* 1–36.

Shaffer, L. H. (1975). Control processes in typing. *Quarterly Journal of Experimental Psychology, 27,* 419–432.

Shaffer, L. H. (1976). Intention and performance. *Psychological Review, 83,* 375–393.

Shaffer, L. H. (1981). Performances of Chopin, Bach, and Bartok: Studies in motor programming. *Cognitive Psychology, 13,* 326–376.

Shaffer, L. H., & Hardwick, J. (1968). Typing performance as a function of text. *Quarterly Journal of Experimental Psychology, 20,* 360–369.

Shaffer, L. H., & Hardwick, J. (1969). Errors and error detection in typing. *Quarterly Journal of Experimental Psychology, 21,* 209–213.

Stemberger, J. P. (1982). The nature of segments in the lexicon: Evidence from speech errors. *Lingua, 56,* 235–259.

Tolkien, J. R. R. (1965). *The return of the king.* New York: Ballantine Books.

8

The Reliability and Replicability of Naturalistic Speech Error Data

A Comparison with Experimentally Induced Errors

Joseph Paul Stemberger

Empirical disciplines have long distinguished between two types of evidence bearing on behavior: experimental evidence and naturalistic evidence. In behavioral biology, both types of evidence are routinely used. It is generally recognized that naturalistic evidence cannot be dispensed with, because there is no way to guarantee natural behavior in an experimental setting. An effort is always made, however, to control observation as carefully as is possible. Within cognitive psychology, naturalistic data are not well respected. They are used most extensively in social psychology and in studies of child language acquisition, where the spontaneous speech of a child may be recorded for later analysis. They are also used in at least one aspect of adult cognitive behavior: the study of errors of performance, with the greatest emphasis on language errors. These studies are generally not very well controlled. Because errors occur at such a low frequency, it is not feasible to record large chunks of naturally occurring speech and analyze them for errors. Researchers have

JOSEPH PAUL STEMBERGER • Department of Communication Disorders, University of Minnesota, Minneapolis, Minnesota 55455.

Experimental Slips and Human Error: Exploring the Architecture of Volition, edited by Bernard J. Baars. Plenum Press, New York, 1992.

used the less controlled method of listening for errors and then recording them (generally using pen and paper, but with tape recording in at least two cases). There are enough problems with this methodology so that many cognitive psychologists are skeptical of the results of any studies based on naturally occurring errors. It is my purpose here to review evidence showing that naturalistic speech-error data are reliable and replicable. It is possible to induce errors in experimental settings, and the results generally agree with naturalistic studies. I will argue that studies based on naturalistic speech-error data provide interesting early data that should be considered important, though they are best when used in combination with experimental data, where they contribute greatly to our knowledge.

There are a number of well-known drawbacks to the observational method that are applicable to the way that naturally occurring speech errors are collected (Cutler, 1981; MacKay, 1980; Stemberger, 1982a). The major problem is the existence of perceptual biases to notice certain types of errors and to miss other types. It has been shown that listeners are more sensitive to some aspects of phonological information than to others. For example, listeners are more accurate in detecting errors at the beginnings of words than later in the word (Cole, Jakimik, & Cooper, 1978). Every study of naturally occurring speech errors has found more errors on word-initial (and syllable-initial) phonemes than on word-final (and syllable-final) phonemes, but this asymmetry may be uninteresting for speech production because it may result from this known perceptual bias (Cutler, 1981). A second major problem is that the chance expectancy for different types of errors is unknown. Sophisticated estimates of chance must be made on the basis of frequency counts and so on, and no checks on the accuracy of these estimates are available. A third problem is that the error that the researcher perceived may not have been a speech error but may have been a slip of the ear made by the researcher's own perceptual system. A fourth problem is that a given type of error that is of great theoretical relevance may not be frequent enough in a corpus of speech errors to yield reliable results. The collection procedure yields errors at such a low rate that decades or centuries may be required to address some questions. Last, there is always some indeterminacy in the categorization of a given error. For example, does a (hypothetical) error like *mad mother* instead of *sad mother* involve a word error *(mad* for *sad)* or a sound error (the anticipation of the /m/ of *mother* to replace the /s/ of *sad*)? Such indeterminacy, if the researcher is not careful, may yield erroneous results if there is a systematic misclassification of errors.

With such problems in mind, many cognitive psychologists mistrust or even reject studies that make use of naturalistic speech-error data. I feel that this rejection is unjustified on the basis of present evidence. The reliability of naturalistic data can be tested empirically. One approach is to make use of experimental paradigms that induce speech errors in the laboratory. If the same results can be obtained under these controlled conditions, the naturalistic data are replicable and can be considered reliable and useful for constructing models of language production. Naturalistic error data may have their problems, but so do all experimental techniques. The problems associated with naturalistic error data may be worse problems than those associated with many experimental tasks, but replicability will show that those problems do not impair the usefulness of the data.

In this chapter, I compare naturalistic and experimental studies of speech errors and show that the same results have been obtained in most cases, with most cases of apparent differences being attributable to task differences. I discuss places where the naturalistic data might be considered unreliable. Note that it is not my intention to provide a general overview of the speech error literature. I will review only those issues that have been examined with the use of both types of data. This comparison has become possible only in the past few years, as experimental studies inspired by naturalistic studies have become more and more common. Only now is it possible to use the experimental studies as a measure of the reliability and replicability of naturalistic speech-error data.

Many researchers who use naturalistic speech-error data have expressed skepticism about the relevance of experimentally induced error data to models of language production (Fromkin, 1980a; Garrett, 1976). There are worries about the ecological validity of these tasks. A comparison of results using both sources of data also addresses this issue. Insofar as the same results are obtained with the use of both types of data, the experimental tasks are validated as reasonable facsimiles of natural language production and are thus relevant in the construction of models.

It may be helpful to the reader to briefly review the experimental techniques that have been used to induce speech errors. There are essentially five techniques that have been used:

1. The SLIPS technique, originally developed by Baars and Motley (Baars, Motley, & MacKay, 1975; Motley & Baars, 1975), uses phonological priming to induce phonological errors. The subject silently reads pairs of words, one after the other. Several bias pairs build up an expectation that Word 1 will begin with Phoneme A and that Word 2 will begin with Phoneme B. The order of the phonemes is reversed in the target pair that is produced aloud. Errors occur where the phonemes are produced in the primed order rather than in the target order.

2. Tongue twisters have been used by a number of researchers to induce phonological errors, with the subjects repeating words or nonwords.

3. Errors can be induced by having the subject reverse the order of two units (Baars, 1980). If the units are words, phonological errors result. If the units are phrases or clauses, word-ordering errors result.

4. Errors can be induced by means of cued recall. After subjects are taught two options, one option is used as a cue for the subject to produce the other option from memory. On some trials, the subjects blend the two options together, producing blends of words or sentences.

5. There is one technique for examining morphological errors (Bybee & Slobin, 1982; MacKay, 1976; Stemberger & MacWhinney, 1986a). Subjects are presented with one form of a word, either the base form or an inflected form,

and are required to produce a given inflected form. Errors occur when the subject produce the base form or ungrammatical forms like *eated*.

PHONOLOGICAL ERRORS

The largest number of studies of errors in language production, whether naturalistic or experimental, involve phonological errors, where one or more words are mispronounced. Most studies show comparable results with the use of both types of data, but opposite results have been obtained in a few instances, as have null results.

Points of Agreement

Lexical Bias

It has long been conjectured that phonological errors tend to create new words. All of the errors attributed to Dr. Spooner result in real words, for example, "queer old dean" for "dear old queen." Baars *et al.* (1975) and Dell (1985) have experimentally demonstrated that this is the case: phonological errors that yield a real word in experimental settings occur two or three times more often than phonological errors that yield nonwords. Fromkin (1971, 1980a) and Garrett (1976) have argued that there is no such bias in naturally occurring errors, but Garrett recognized that it is difficult to determine how many errors should look like real words by chance. Dell and Reich (1981) presented a reasonable procedure for estimating chance and showed that there is a lexical bias in the Toronto corpus of naturally occurring speech errors. Stemberger (1984a) used this procedure with his own corpus of naturally occurring errors and found a small but significant lexical bias. Qualitatively, both types of data yield the same results.

Effect of Shared Features

Naturally occurring speech errors show that phoneme similarity, in the form of the number of features that are shared by two interacting phonemes, is a powerful determiner of error rates. All other things being equal, there are more errors involving two phonemes that differ by a single feature (e.g., /p/ and /t/), fewer errors involving two phonemes that differ by two features (e.g., /p/ and /d/), and even fewer errors involving two phonemes that differ by three or more features (e.g., /p/ and /z/) (MacKay, 1970; Nooteboom, 1969; Shattuck-Hufnagel, 1979; Stemberger, 1982a,b). Levitt and Healy (1985) replicated these results experimentally with an auditorily presented tongue-twister task and a visually presented SLIPS task.

Differential Error Rates on Different Features

Researchers have found that speakers tend to make more naturally occurring errors involving certain features than others. MacKay (1970) and Shattuck-Hufnagel and Klatt (1979) have reported that there are more errors involving changes in place of articulation, fewer errors involving changes in voicing, and the least number of errors involving changes in nasality. Using a tongue twister task, Kupin (1982) found the same hierarchy of error rates.

Effect of Shared Phonemes

MacKay (1970) showed that naturally occurring spoonerisms occur significantly more often when the two words involved in the error have the same phoneme before or after the phoneme on which the error occurred (e.g., "mad back") than when the phonemes are different (e.g., "mad bake"). Using errors from the Toronto corpus, Dell (1984) showed further that the rate of errors on word-initial consonants increases when the two words involved have the same word-final consonant. There is also an interaction: the effect of shared phonemes is greater for exchange errors than for anticipations and perseverations. Dell replicated these findings experimentally with the SLIPS technique.

Feature Errors versus Whole-Segment Errors

Two types of phonological errors have been observed relating to phonemes. In whole-segment errors, two phonemes, such as /p/ and /d/, are misordered as units (such as the hypothetical *depestrian* for *pedestrian*). In feature errors, only one feature, such as voicing or place of articulation, is misordered, and an error is produced with /t/ and /b/, for example, as in *tebestrian* (Fromkin, 1971). Researchers have noted that feature errors are significantly less frequent than whole-segment errors (Shattuck-Hufnagel & Klatt, 1979; Stemberger, 1982a; Stemberger & Treiman, 1986). Using a tongue-twister task to induce phonological errors, Kupin (1982) also found this to be true in his data.

Effects of Stress

MacKay (1971) looked at exchange errors within one word (such as *Roletta* for *Loretta*) in relation to the stressed syllable. He found for naturally occurring errors that there were fewer errors involving two unstressed syllables than expected by chance and that there were more interactions of stressed and unstressed syllables than expected. He also found that phonemes in the stressed syllable were more likely to be anticipated than to be perseverated. Using a tongue-twister task, he found the same results experimentally.

Palatalization

Using the naturally occurring errors in the MIT and UCLA corpuses, Shattuck-Hufnagel and Klatt (1979) found a strong asymmetry between alveolar and palatal consonants in English errors. There were far more errors where an alveolar was replaced by a palatal than the reverse. This finding was most pronounced for /s/ versus /š/, less pronounced for /t/ versus /č/, and uncertain for /d/ versus /ǰ/ because of the small numbers. Stemberger (1991) reported that this asymmetry was also present in his corpus of errors. Using a SLIPS task with only consonant-vowel (CV) nonsense stimuli, Levitt and Healy (1985) found no asymmetry for contextual errors. Stemberger (1991), however, using real words, showed that the bias is present in the SLIPS task. The asymmetry was strong with /s/ versus /š/ and /t/ versus /č/, but weak for /d/ versus /ǰ/, which were also least effective in inducing errors.

Lexical Frequency

Using Stemberger's corpus of naturally occurring errors, Stemberger and MacWhinney (1986b) showed that phonological errors are less likely to occur in high-frequency words than in low-frequency words. Dell (1991) replicated this result experimentally with the SLIPS technique.

Phonemic Variability of Certain Segments

Certain segments show variation between two phonemes in naturally occurring errors (Davidsen-Nielsen, 1975; Stemberger, 1983b). There is variability in the stop after an /s/ in relation to the voiced-voiceless distinction, and in the stop-affricate distinction in the coronal stop before an /r/. For stops after /s/, both voiced (/b/, /d/, and /g/) and voiceless (/p/, /t/, and /k/) stops result when /s/ is lost (e.g., *spot* yields both *bot* and *pot*), and /s/ can be added to both voiced and voiceless stops to produce a perceived /sp/, /st/, or /sk/. For coronal stops before /r/, both stops (/t/, /d/) and affricates (/č/, /ǰ/) result when the /r/ disappears, and /r/ can be added to both stops (e.g., "red trape—red tape") and affricates (e.g., "cream treese—cream cheese") to produce a perceived /tr/ or /dr/. Davidsen-Nielsen (1975) reported similar results using a tongue-twister task in which the subjects repeated stimuli such as *gaspate* and *kaspate,* with occasional errors such as *skapate* and *skabate* occurring. Using the SLIPS technique, I have observed similar variability in errors (unreported data from Stemberger, 1990; Stemberger & Treiman, 1986), but I have not examined the issue systematically.

Allophonic Accommodation to Phonological Errors

It has been noted by several researchers that misordered segments tend to be given the proper allophonic form for that phoneme in its new environment (Fromkin, 1971; Stemberger, 1983b). Using a tongue-twister task, Shattuck-Hufnagel (1985) showed this to be true of experimentally induced errors as well.

Consonant Cluster Errors

Stemberger (1990; Stemberger & Treiman, 1986) examined many types of errors involving consonant clusters, using both his own corpus of naturally occurring errors and the SLIPS technique for inducing errors experimentally.[1] The first consonant of a consonant cluster such as /pl/ will be referred to as

---

[1]The published version of Stemberger (1990) contains only analyses of naturalistic speech error data. The SLIPS experiments reviewed here are as yet unpublished.

C1, and the second consonant of the cluster will be referred to as *C2.* Consonants that are not a part of a cluster (such as the /p/ of *pat*) will be referred to as *singletons.* The results reported here hold for both naturally occurring and experimentally induced errors.

Addition, Loss, and Shift Errors on C1 versus C2. Stemberger and Treiman (1986) found that a consonant can be added to another consonant to create a cluster (e.g., by adding /r/ to /p/), and that a consonant can be lost from a cluster to create a singleton. Shift errors also occur, in which a phoneme is lost from one word and added to the other, so that a sequence such as /pr ... p/ becomes the error sequence /p ... pr/. Stemberger and Treiman examined clusters that begin with /s/, such as /st/, and clusters that do not, such as /tr/. For all types of errors and both types of clusters, there are significantly more errors involving C2 than involving C1.

Loss of /s/ versus Other C1 Consonants. Stemberger and Treiman (1986) noted the following interaction: when C1 is lost from a cluster, it is significantly more likely to be /s/ than other phonemes.

Substitution Errors in Clusters. Stemberger and Treiman (1986) also examined errors in which speakers produce the right number of consonants in a cluster but mispronounce one of the consonants, producing a substitution error such as /pl/ instead of /pr/. The results are different depending on whether the source of the consonant is another cluster or a singleton consonant. When the source is another cluster (as in the sequence /pr ... kl/), more errors occur on C2 than on C1. However, when the source is a singleton (as in the sequences /pr ... l/ and /pr ... k/), errors are equally likely on C1 and C2.

Substitution versus Addition and Its Relation to C1 versus C2. Stemberger (1990) noted that two types of errors result when the source of a consonant is a singleton. The consonant can be added as C1 or as C2 (e.g., /p ... r/ becomes /pr ... r/ or /p ... pr/), or a substitution error can occur (e.g., /p ... r/ becomes /r ... r/ or /p ... p/). Stemberger showed that substitution errors are significantly more common than addition errors when the consonant would have to be added as C1, but addition is as common as or more common than substitution when the consonant would be added as C2.

Contextual Addition versus Simplification of C2. Stemberger and Treiman (1986) examined the rate of errors involving the loss of C2 from clusters or the addition of a consonant as C2 to create a cluster. The contextual addition of C2 is far more common than the contextual simplification of C2. Using a tongue-twister task, Kupin (1982) reported similar findings.

Effects of Context on Addition Errors. Stemberger (1990) examined the effect of context on addition errors. He found that addition of C2 is most likely when the resulting consonant cluster is identical to the cluster that is the source of the error (e.g., /pr ... pr/), is less likely when the resulting cluster is different from the cluster that is the source of the errors (e.g., /pr ... fr/), and is least likely when the source of the error is a singleton (e.g., /pr ... r/). An effect of shared context without any identical phonemes is also evident in errors where a schwa is added to break up word-initial consonant clusters.

This occurs only when another word nearby begins with the sequence /C ə C/, as in "caross Nevada" for "cross Nevada."

Contextual versus Noncontextual Errors

The phonological errors discussed so far are all *contextual* in nature; that is, there is something in the context that looks like the source of the error. In *noncontextual* errors, however, there is nothing in the context that obviously accounts for the error. Stemberger (1991) demonstrated for naturally occurring errors that contextual errors occur at a much greater rate than noncontextual errors, when chance is taken into account. Levitt and Healy (1985) replicated this finding experimentally, using a visually presented SLIPS task and an auditorily presented tongue-twister task.

Stemberger (1982b) showed that the same range of errors occur with contextual and noncontextual errors, but that they are statistically quite different. Levitt and Healy (1985) arrived at the same conclusion on the basis of a SLIPS experiment. Only one exact comparison is possible. Comparing the target and intruding phonemes, Stemberger found that naturally occurring noncontextual errors tended to involve more similar consonants (88% differing by only one feature) than did contextual errors involving the interaction of two words (70% differing by only one feature). Levitt and Healy (1985) reported the same trend for their SLIPS task.

Morphological Accommodation to Phonological Errors

Morphological processes are sensitive to the phonological form of words, so that the plural suffix -*s* is pronounced /ə z/ after sibilant consonants, /s/ after other voiceless sounds, and /z/ after other voiced sounds. When a phonological error occurs on the phoneme that conditions this allomorphic variation, the suffix generally "accommodates" to the error, taking on the form appropriate to the new phoneme (Fromkin, 1971; Garrett, 1980; Stemberger, 1983a,b). For example, the target word *touches,* pronounced with /ə z/, was pronounced as *tucks* in an error, with the pronunciation of -*s* as /s/, as is appropriate after /k/. Although such accommodation has never been shown experimentally for English, Stemberger and Lewis (1986) demonstrated that it occurs with reduplication in the participle form in the West African language Ewe. Their experiment combined the SLIPS technique with a task to produce the participle form of the first word in the pair. In response to stimuli such as "fa ho," for which the correct response was "fafa ho," the subjects occasionally produced errors such as "haha fo," with accommodation of the reduplicated prefix, and never produced errors such as *"faha fo" with no accommodation. Thus, similar results have been obtained with both types of data, though in different languages.

Effect of Phonological Markedness

Motley and Baars (1975) showed that there is no tendency for unmarked phonemes to substitute for marked phonemes in the SLIPS task. For example, /m/ is marked relative to /n/, but there are as many errors where /n/ → /m/ as where /m/ → /n/. Shattuck-Hufnagel and Klatt (1979) reached the same conclusions on the basis of naturally occurring errors from the MIT corpus.

Effects of Redundant Features on Error Rates

Stemberger (1986) reported that liquids and glides (/r/, /l/, /w/, and /y/), which are always voiced, are significantly more likely to be involved in substitution errors with voiced stops than with voiceless stops. This finding shows that voicing is specified for liquids and glides, so that they are more similar to other voiced segments, even though the voicing is redundant. He also reported that this was true in Stemberger and Treiman's Experiment 3 (1986) using the SLIPS technique.

Various Impressions about Naturalistic Error Data

Several factors have been suggested as influencing error rates in normal speech that have never been carefully demonstrated by means of naturalistic error data: Freudian slips, speaking rate, and alcohol intoxication. Using the SLIPS procedure, Motley and Baars (1979) demonstrated that Freudian slips occur in experimental settings. An increase in the error rate due to talking quickly has been demonstrated by MacKay (1971) and Kupin (1982) in tongue-twister tasks and by Dell (1985) using the SLIPS technique. Using a within-subject SLIPS task, Stemberger, Pisoni, and Hathaway (1985) demonstrated that there are significantly more phonological ordering errors when a subject is legally drunk than when he or she is sober.

Points of Disagreement

There are seven cases in which different results have been obtained with the use of naturally occurring and experimentally induced phonological errors. In examining these differences, we must keep in mind two questions: (1) Could the differences be attributed to sampling biases in the naturalistic error data? (2) Could the differences be attributed to task differences? I will argue that task differences may be responsible for all but one case, which involves null results with one source of errors. Because null results are always difficult to interpret, I will divide the points of disagreement into clear differences and null results. Interestingly, the only clear differences involve questions of magnitude; I know of no cases where opposite results have been obtained.

Invoking task differences is not simply a cop-out. It is generally possible to test the task-differences explanation experimentally, by altering some crucial aspect of the task. I have not followed up the cases discussed here, but there is no reason that they could not be followed up.

Clear Differences

Frequency of Exchanges and Shifts versus Anticipations and Perseverations

Studies of naturally occurring errors are united in reporting that completed exchanges and shifts are much less common than anticipations or perseverations, though incomplete errors are common (Nooteboom, 1969;

Shattuck-Hufnagel, 1979; Stemberger, 1982b). Completed exchanges and shifts account for 5%–15% of all errors in most corpora. Exchanges and shifts appear to be relatively more common in the SLIPS task. In Motley and Baars (1975), completed exchanges accounted for half the data. In Stemberger and Treiman's Experiment 1 (1986), shifts accounted for 29% of the data.

The difference can be attributed to task differences. It seems clear that the rate of exchanges and shifts versus anticipations and perseverations in SLIPS experiments has been high because exchanges and shifts have been primed for. They are not as common if anticipations are primed for. This effect of what is primed for is indicated by some *post hoc* between-experiment comparisons using the experiments of Stemberger and Treiman (1986) and Stemberger (1990). In an experiment priming for the addition of C2 in the first word only, shifts accounted for only 2.9% of summed addition and shift errors (n = 34). In an experiment priming for shifts, shifts made up 50.0% of the summed addition and shift errors of the same type (n = 40), a higher proportion of shifts than when priming for additions (χ^2 (1) = 20.02, p < 0.0001). In an experiment priming for contextual simplification in the first word, shifts made up only 25.5% of summed simplification and shift errors (n = 55). In an experiment priming for shifts, shifts made up 81.8% of the summed simplification and shift errors of the same type, a greater proportion of shifts than in priming for simplification (χ^2 (1) = 12.83, p < 0.0005). These comparisons suggest that the rate of shifts (and presumably exchanges) in the experiments is small unless shifts (and exchanges) are specifically primed. Thus, the experimental and naturalistic data are compatible.

Magnitude of the Lexical Bias Effect

A lexical bias has been observed in both experimentally induced and naturally occurring errors. However, there is a clear difference in the magnitude of the effect when the different sources of data are used. With the use of the SLIPS technique, errors that produce lexical items are two or three times more common than errors that do not (Baars *et al.*, 1975; Dell, 1985). Baars *et al.* reported a significant effect based on only 42 experimentally induced errors. However, studies of naturally occurring errors show a much smaller difference (Dell & Reich, 1981; Stemberger, 1984). Indeed, Stemberger found that the effect is not significant for any given error type (e.g., exchanges) and is significant only when a sample of more than 1,000 naturally occurring errors is used.

This difference cannot be attributed to a sampling bias in naturalistic data. Any bias is likely to be toward detecting more errors that look like real lexical items, as these can be detected as lexical/semantic errors as well as phonological errors. Moreover, researchers class errors as phonological rather than lexical if they can do so. Sampling bias would thus accentuate a lexical bias rather than weaken it.

Stemberger (1984) argued that the greater lexical bias in the experimental studies results from task differences and their interaction with the time course of language production. Dell (1985; Dell & Reich, 1980) suggested that the lexical bias results from feedback from the phoneme level to the word level. Incipient errors that activate words are more likely to occur because they are reinforced with activation from the word that they activate. Dell (1985) showed that the lexical bias is accentuated as a function of time; more time before the words are produced allows more time for lexical items to reinforce errors that resemble lexical items. Stemberger (1984) pointed out that feedback from the phoneme level to the lexical level begins earlier in the SLIPS task than in natural speech. When there is priming for a particular order of phonemes, feedback is actually present before the subject even begins to process the target word pair. This allows extra time for lexical reinforcement and should accentuate the lexical bias effect relative to normal speech. The difference in the magnitude of the effect in the two sources of errors can be attributed to task differences. This can be tested by looking at the low-level errors in the SLIPS task that are unprimed (less than 1% of trials, generally), to compare the magnitude of the effect with primed trials.

Non-English Segments
No naturally occurring errors have yet been reported in the literature where a nonnative segment is produced, though they have apparently been observed on occasion (Baars, personal communication). Using a tongue-twister task with stimuli such as "pep poop," Laver (1980), in contrast, has found that subjects do make errors involving non-English vowels, such as the short mid-front rounded vowel in [pöp] (as in French *peu* "a little"). The absence of non-English segments in naturally occurring errors might be due to a sampling bias, where the listeners are unable to detect non-English phonemes (Cutler, 1981). It might also be due to task differences. Because tongue twisters may involve some interference at a low motor level, they may have a greater tendency to yield results that are not well-formed motor outputs for English.

Null Results

Cases of null results are very difficult to interpret. It is unclear whether they really show a difference between the two sources of error data. It may be that, for whatever reason, the tasks are just not sensitive enough to detect a difference. Attempts to replicate, using both types of data, are clearly called for. Until such replications are attempted, the five cases of null reports reviewed here cannot be viewed as demonstrating differences between naturally occurring and experimentally induced errors.

Effects of Phoneme Frequency
Motley and Baars (1975) reported that low-frequency phonemes are more likely to be replaced with high-frequency phonemes than the reverse in errors obtained with the SLIPS technique. Shattuck-Hufnagel and Klatt (1979) maintained that this bias is not present in naturally occurring speech errors.

Thus, significant differences were found with experimentally induced errors versus null results for naturally occurring errors. I can find no likely sampling bias or task difference that would account for this difference. Note, however, that Levitt and Healy (1985), using a SLIPS task, found only a slight tendency for low-frequency phonemes to be replaced by high-frequency phonemes in contextual errors. (They did find a very strong frequency bias in noncontextual errors, but this finding has yet to be addressed in natural speech.) Thus, it is also possible to obtain only a weak frequency effect by means of the SLIPS technique, so that the naturalistic results do not stand out from the variability of the experimental results.

Error Rates and the Position of Consonants in the Syllable

Every study of naturally occurring phonological speech errors that has examined the issue has noted that, for errors involving the interaction of two words, there are far more errors (about four times as many) on syllable-initial consonants than on syllable-final consonants (Nooteboom, 1969; Shattuck-Hufnagel, 1979; Stemberger, 1982a,b). This difference could be attributed to sampling biases in naturalistic error data. On the basis of experimental demonstrations that listeners are better able to detect syllable-initial (especially word-initial) errors than errors later in the syllable and word, Cutler (1981) and Stemberger (1982a) have noted that the results obtained with naturally occurring errors might be attributed to a perceptual bias on the part of those collecting the errors. Congruent with this suggestion, in her early work with a tongue-twister task, Shattuck-Hufnagel (1980) found no significant differences in the rates of syllable-initial and syllable-final errors.

The differences could also be attributed to task differences, however. Shattuck-Hufnagel (1981) noted that the tongue-twister task differed from normal speech by using nonsense syllables and by using a sequence of syllables, essentially a list with no syntax. Shattuck-Hufnagel performed several variations on the task, using real word in a list, and using both real words and nonsense words embedded in a phrase with English closed-class lexical items to give the semblance of English syntax. She found that, when real words were used in a phrase environment, more than 80% of the errors involved syllable-initial consonants, as in normal speech. Thus, the greater error rate on syllable-initial consonants in naturally occurring errors can be experimentally replicated provided that the experiment uses environments that approximate those in normal speech.

Contextual Simplification versus Repetition Loss

There are two types of loss errors that result from context. In contextual simplification, a phoneme is lost because it does not appear in a nearby word. In repetition loss, a phoneme is lost because it *does* appear in a nearby word. Stemberger (1990) showed that contextual simplification is about three times more common than repetition loss in naturally occurring speech errors. In unreported data from Stemberger and Treiman's Experiment 3 (1986) using the SLIPS task, however, contextual simplification and repetition loss were equally common: a null result. Using a tongue-twister task. Kupin (1982) also found roughly equal rates of contextual simplification and repetition loss errors. I can think of no likely sampling bias that would lead to this result.

This difference may result from task differences. Repetition loss results from some difficulty in accessing a given phoneme that has been or is being accessed nearby as well. Presumably, multiple occurrences of that phoneme nearby should make it all the more difficult to access the phoneme. It is possible that the SLIPS technique, by repeating a phoneme in two or three earlier word pairs as well as placing it in the second word in target word pairs, may be differentially exacerbating the problem with repeated access of the same phoneme. Thus, repetition loss should be increased in the SLIPS task relative to contextual simplification. The null results found with the use of experimentally induced errors may be due to task differences.

Position in the Cluster and Addition versus Substitution Errors

When there is competition between the singleton consonants that can be combined into a cluster, both substitution and addition errors occur. There is an interaction with position in the syllable because substitutions are significantly more likely than additions if the consonant would have to be added as C1, but this is not true if the consonant can be added as C2. This interaction is different for naturally occurring and experimentally induced errors. In naturally occurring errors, additions are significantly more frequent than substitutions if the consonant can be added as C2 (Stemberger, 1990). However, in the SLIPS task, there is no significant difference between additions as C2 and substitutions (unreported data from Experiment 3, Stemberger & Treiman, 1986). Again, there is a difference in naturally occurring errors but null results in experimentally induced errors. I can think of no likely sampling bias that could account for this difference.

This difference may be due to task differences. Stemberger speculated in advance of doing the experiment that, because the experiment stimuli heavily primed for the existence of a singleton consonant in all words, this priming might increase the rate of substitution errors, which have a singleton, and might decrease the rate of addition errors, which result in a cluster. It is possible that lessening the degree of priming leading to a substitution error (by reducing the number of priming word pairs to one, for example) might lead to a greater rate of addition errors. It is thus possible to attribute the null results in the SLIPS technique to task differences.

MORPHOLOGICAL ERRORS

There have been a number of studies examining morphological, especially inflectional, errors in both naturally occurring and experimental settings. For the most part, the same results are obtained by the use of both sources of data. There is one case in which apparent differences have been obtained.

Points of Agreement

Regularly Inflected Forms: Similarity of the Base and Inflection

Speakers occasionally use the base form of the word instead of the target inflected form. These are known as *no-marking errors*. Stemberger (1983a,b) reported that, for regular verbs, no-marking errors in natural speech are significantly more frequent than expected by chance when the last phoneme of the base word resembles the phoneme of the inflection, for example, with regular past-tense forms that end in /t/ or /d/ (phonemes that resemble the *-ed* suffix) than with other regular forms. This finding has been replicated experimentally (Bybee & Slobin, 1982; Stemberger & MacWhinney, 1986a).

Effects of Lexical Frequency on Regular Past-Tense Forms

Stemberger and MacWhinney (1986b) showed that no-marking errors are more common on low-frequency verbs than on high-frequency verbs. The relative frequencies of errors on high-frequency and low-frequency verbs were comparable in the two types of errors.

Irregular Past-Tense Forms

There are four types of errors involving irregular past-tense forms. In addition to no-marking errors (e.g., *cling* instead of *clung*), there are full regularizations, in which the base form is used with *-ed* added (e.g., *clinged*), partial regularizations, in which the past-tense form is used with *-ed* added (e.g., *clunged*); and wrong-ablaut errors, where an irregular form is used with the wrong vowel (e.g., *clang*). No-marking and full-regularization errors are significantly more common than partial-regularization errors and wrong-ablaut errors in both naturally occurring and experimentally induced errors (MacKay, 1976; Stemberger, 1983a; unreported data from the experiments of Stemberger & MacWhinney, 1986a).

Irregular Verbs that End in /t/ or /d/

In both naturally occurring and experimentally induced errors, irregular verbs that end in /t/ or /d/ (e.g., *eat* and *find*) have the same rate of no-marking errors as other irregular verbs (Bybee & Slobin, 1982; Stemberger, 1983a; Stemberger & MacWhinney, 1986a).

Wrong-Ablaut Errors

In both naturally occurring and experimentally induced errors, wrong-ablaut errors occur more often on irregular verbs (e.g., *clang* for *clung*) than on regular verbs (e.g., *clumb* for *climbed*) (Stemberger, 1983a; unreported data from the experiments of Stemberger & MacWhinney, 1986a).

Overgeneralization of Derivational Patterns

Fromkin (1971) reported that derivational patterns can be overgeneralized in naturally occurring speech errors, with one derivational affix replacing another (e.g., *excludement* for *exclusion*). Cutler (1980) reported that such errors tend to eliminate changes of the base word, so that it appears unmodified as in *excludement*, whereas consonants and/or vowels are modified in the correct form. Stemberger (1982a) reports the existence of errors such as *transmitsion*, containing the /t/ of the base form, which is eliminated in the correct form *transmission*. In an experiment where the subjects produced the derived nominal of a verb on presentation of the base form, MacKay (1978) reported the same findings for experimentally induced errors.

Points of Disagreement

No-Marking versus Full-Regularization Errors

Stemberger (1983a) noted that there is no significant difference between no-marking and full-regularization errors in naturally occurring speech errors, though there are slightly more no-marking errors than full-regularization errors. Stemberger and MacWhinney (1986a) did not report these data for their experiments, but the data are available to us. In seven experiments, there was a nonsignificant trend toward more no-marking errors in two of the experiments, a nonsignificant trend toward more full-regularization errors in two of the experiments, and significantly more full-regularization errors in the remaining three experiments. Significant results have thus been obtained experimentally that contrast with the null results of the naturally occurring error data, but null results have also been obtained in other experiments.

LEXICAL AND SYNTACTIC ERRORS

Few comparisons are possible between naturally occurring and experimentally induced lexical and syntactic errors. At this point, we know only that qualitatively similar errors are obtainable:

1. Word blends often occur in natural speech, where two semantically related words are blended into a single form (e.g., *flaste* for *flavor* and *taste*) (Fromkin, 1971). Baars (1980) has shown that blends of two words can be induced experimentally by means of the cued-recall method of error induction.

2. Garrett (1980) reported that words in different clauses can exchange places, and that such errors almost invariably involve words of the same syntactic category (e.g., two nouns or two verbs). Baars (1980) obtained similar errors by having subjects reverse the order of two conjoined clauses.

3. Fay (1980, 1981) and Stemberger (1982c) have discussed syntactic errors in natural speech involving passivization, particle movement, sub-

ject–auxiliary inversion, and other syntactic phenomena. Using the cued-recall method of error induction, Chen and Baars (1985) have induced the same sorts of syntactic errors.

GENERAL DISCUSSION

I have examined all instances in which similar questions have been addressed with the use of both naturally occurring and experimentally induced speech errors. They are summarized in Tables 1–3. In most cases, the same results have been obtained with the use of both types of data. Of those cases where differences have been obtained, most involve null results with one source of data versus significant results with the other source of data (a difference that is very difficult to interpret). In the three cases where clearly different results have been obtained, the differences may be due to task differences. This is demonstrably the cause for one instance on the basis of different experiments and is arguable in the others. Most of the cases involving null results may also be due to task differences.

The results thus far have been remarkably convergent. There are no points where opposite results have been obtained, and the differences that have surfaced are not obviously due to defects of naturalistic error data. These results show empirically that the total rejection of studies based on naturally occurring speech errors is unwarranted. Any given study is likely to be replicable experimentally and should be taken seriously.

However, it is true that there are many drawbacks to naturally occurring speech-error data, including serious methodological flaws. The most serious problem is sampling bias, especially perceptual bias that makes one type of error more salient and detectable than another type of error. We have noted several places where the naturalistic and experimental error data differ that could be due to sampling bias: the rate of exchange and shift errors versus anticipations and perseverations, the strength of the lexical bias in phonological errors, error rate as a function of position in the syllable, whether non-English segments occur, and the effects of stress on error rates. One should be cautious about naturalistic speech-error data if there is an *a priori* reason to suspect that a perceptual bias might be present. This is also true of comparisons of very different types of errors that have very different constraints on detectability. A reader would rightfully be skeptical of an argument that crucially hinged on the relative rate of errors on consonants versus vowels, or on the greater rate of phonological errors versus lexical errors.

This chapter has shown, however, that naturalistic speech-error data are reasonably reliable and replicable despite these flaws. Nonetheless, we have no way of knowing whether these results will hold as more studies are done using and comparing both types of error data. I suggest that the safest path is to use both naturally occurring and experimentally induced errors. Such dual studies have the advantage of reinforcing conclusions. The experimental data show that the naturalistic data are replicable and rule out perceptual bias as the sole factor leading to a given result. The naturalistic data show that the experimental data are ecologically valid, that the results are not due to task-specific strategies, and that the experimental error-induction techniques constitute a reasonable facsimile of normal language processing. I would encourage more dual studies in the future. Papers in which only natu-

TABLE 1

Points of Agreement between Naturalistic and Experimental Studies
of Speech Errors: Phonological (1–16), Morphological (17–22),
and Lexical-Syntactic (23) Errors

Subject	Result
1. Lexical bias	Increased error rate if a real word results.
2. Shared features	Increases error rate.
3. Error rate of features	Differs for different features; more involving place than voicing, more involving voicing than nasality.
4. Shared context in word	Increases error rate.
5. Size of error	More involving whole segments than features.
6. Stress	More errors on stressed syllables.
7. Palatalization	Bias to replace alveolars with palatals.
8. Lexical frequency	Fewer phonological errors on high-frequency words.
9. Ambiguous segments	Interact with both segments that they are ambiguous with.
10. Allophonic accommodation	Present.
11. Consonant clusters	Various points of agreement.
12. Noncontextual errors	Less common than contextual errors; statistical differences from contextual.
13. Morphological accommodation	Present.
14. Phonological markedness	No effect.
15. Redundant features	Affect similarity of two segments, and hence the error rate.
16. Drunkenness Freudian slips Speaking rate	Affect error rate.
17. No-marking errors	Increased if inflection similar to the end of the base word.
18. Lexical frequency	Lower rate of no-marking errors on high-frequency inflected forms.
19. Irregular past tense	No-marking and full-regularization errors are more common than partial-regularization and wrong-ablaut errors.
20. Irregular verbs ending in /t/ or /d/	Same error rate as with other irregular verbs.
21. Wrong-ablaut errors	More common on irregular verbs than on regular verbs.
22. Derivational "regularizations"	Present.
23. Lexical and syntactic errors	Qualitatively similar errors occur.

TABLE 2
Clear Differences between Naturalistic and Experimental Studies
of Errors: All Phonological

Subject	Naturalistic result	Experimental result
1. Proportion of errors that are exchanges	Small	Large
2. Magnitude of lexical bias	Small	Large
3. Non-English segments	Don't occur	Occur

ralistic error data are presented, however, should be treated as serious, valid work, with results and conclusions that are to be replicated or explored by means of other research techniques, as all work in cognitive psychology is treated.

ACKNOWLEDGMENTS

This work was supported in part by NIH Training Grant NS-7134-06 to Indiana University, while I was a postdoctoral student in Dave Pisoni's lab. I would like to thank Steve Greenspan, for suggesting that this chapter be written in the first place, and Gary Dell, for extensive comments on an earlier version of this chapter.

TABLE 3
Differences between Naturalistic and Experimental Studies of Errors
Involving Null Results with One but Not the Other: Phonological (1–4)
and Morphological (5) Errors

Subject	Naturalistic result	Experimental result
1. Phoneme frequency	No effect	Fewer errors on high-frequency phonemes
2. Types of loss errors	More contextual-simplification than repetition-loss errors	Same rate on both types of errors
3. Addition versus substitution with two singleton targets	More addition than substitution errors	Same rate on both types of errors
4. Position of consonant	More errors on syllable-initial than on syllable-final consonants	Same error rate (some experiments)
5. No-marking versus full-regularization errors	Same rate on both types of errors	More full-regularization than no-marking errors (some experiments)

REFERENCES

Baars, B. J. (1980). On eliciting predictable speech errors in the laboratory. In V. A. Fromkin (Ed.), *Errors in linguistic performance: Slips of the tongue, ear, pen, and hand.* New York: Academic Press.

Baars, B. J. Motley, M. T., & MacKay, D. G. (1975). Output editing for lexical status from artificially elicited slips of the tongue. *Journal of Verbal Learning and Verbal Behavior, 14,* 382–391.

Bybee, J. L., & Slobin, D. I. (1982). Rules and schemas in the development and use of the English past tense. *Language, 58,* 265–289.

Chen, J.-Y., & Baars, B. J. (1985). *The competing plans hypothesis as an alternative explanation of some "transformational errors."* Presented at the meeting of the Eastern Psychological Association, Boston.

Cole, R. A., Jakimik, J., & Cooper, W. E. (1978). Perceptibility of phonetic features in fluent speech. *Journal of the Acoustical Society of America, 64,* 44–56.

Cutler, A. (1980). Productivity in word formation. *Papers from the 16th Regional Meeting of the Chicago Linguistic Society* (pp. 45–51). Chicago: Chicago Linguistic Society, University of Chicago.

Cutler, A. (1981). The reliability of speech error data. *Linguistics, 19,* 561–592.

Davidsen-Nielsen, N. (1975). A phonological analysis of English *sp, st, sk* with special reference to speech error evidence. *Journal of the International Phonetics Association, 5,* 3–25.

Dell, G. S. (1984). The representation of serial order in speech: Evidence from the repeated phoneme effect in speech errors. *Journal of Experimental Psychology: Learning, Memory, & Cognition, 10,* 222–233.

Dell, G. S. (1985). Positive feedback in hierarchical connectionist models: Applications to language production. *Cognitive Science, 9,* 3–23.

Dell, G. S. (1991). Effects of frequency and vocabulary type on phonological speech errors. *Language and Cognitive Processes, 9,* 313–349.

Dell, G. S., & Reich, P. A. (1980). Toward a unified theory of slips of the tongue. In V. A. Fromkin (Ed.), *Errors in linguistic performance: Slips of the tongue, ear, pen, and hand.* New York: Academic Press.

Dell, G. S., & Reich, P. A. (1981). Stages in sentence production: An analysis of speech error data. *Journal of Verbal Learning and Verbal Behavior, 20,* 611–629.

Fay, D. (1980). Transformational errors. In V. A. Fromkin (Ed.), *Errors in linguistic performance: Slips of the tongue, ear, pen, and hand.* New York: Academic Press.

Fay, D. (1981). Substitutions and splices: A study of sentence blends. *Linguistics, 19,* 717–749.

Fromkin, V. A. (1971). The non-anomalous nature of anomalous utterances. *Language, 47,* 27–52.

Fromkin, V. A. (1980). Introduction. In V. A. Fromkin (Ed.), *Errors in linguistic performance: Slips of the tongue, ear, pen, and hand.* New York: Academic Press.

Garrett, M. F. (1976). Syntactic processes in language production. In R. J. Wales & E. Walker (Eds.), *New approaches to language mechanisms* (pp. 231–256). Amsterdam: North-Holland.

Garrett, M. F. (1980). The limits of accommodation. In V. A. Fromkin (Ed.), *Errors in linguistic performance: Slips of the tongue, ear, pen, and hand.* New York: Academic Press.

Kupin, J. J. (1982). *Tongue twisters as a source of information about speech production.* Bloomington: Indiana University Linguistics Club.

Laver, J. (1980). Slips of the tongue as neuromuscular evidence for a model of speech production. In H. W. Dechert & M. Raupach (Eds.), *Temporal variables in speech* (pp. 21–26). The Hague: Mouton.

Levitt, A. G., & Healy, A. F. (1985). The roles of phoneme frequency, similarity, and availability in the experimental elicitation of speech errors. *Journal of Memory and Language, 24,* 717–733.

MacKay, D. G. (1970). Spoonerisms: The structure of errors in the serial order of speech. *Neuropsychologia, 8,* 323–350.

MacKay, D. G. (1971). Stress pre-entry in motor systems. *American Journal of Psychology, 1,* 35–51.

MacKay, D. G. (1976). On the retrieval and lexical structure of verbs. *Journal of Verbal Learning and Verbal Behavior, 15,* 169–182.

MacKay, D. G. (1978). Derivational rules and the internal lexicon. *Journal of Verbal Learning and Verbal Behavior, 17,* 61–71.

MacKay, D. G. (1980). Speech errors: Retrospect and prospect. In V. A. Fromkin (Ed.), *Errors in linguistic performance: Slips of the tongue, ear, pen, and hand.* New York: Academic Press.

Motley, M. T., & Baars, B. J. (1975). Encoding sensitivities to phonological markedness and transition probability: Evidence from spoonerisms. *Human Communication Research, 2,* 351–361.

Motley, M. T., & Baars, B. J. (1979). Effects of cognitive set upon laboratory induced verbal (Freudian) slips. *Journal of Speech and Hearing Research, 22,* 421–432.

Nooteboom, S. (1969). The tongue slips into patterns. *Leyden studies in linguistics and phonetics.* The Hague: Mouton.

Shattuck-Hufnagel, S. (1979). Speech errors as evidence for a serial ordering mechanism in sentence production. In W. E. Cooper & E. C. T. Walker (Eds.), *Sentence processing* (pp. 295–342). New York: Halsted Press.

Shattuck-Hufnagel, S. (1980). *The single phonemic error predominates as error unit.* Presented at the 100th meeting of the Acoustical Society of America, Los Angeles.

Shattuck-Hufnagel, S. (1981). *Position of errors in tongue twisters and spontaneous speech: Evidence for two processing mechanisms?* Presented at the 102nd meeting of the Acoustical Society of America, Miami.

Shattuck-Hufnagel, S. (1985). *Segmental speech errors occur earlier in utterance planning than certain phonetic processes.* Presented at the 109th meeting of the Acoustical Society of America, Austin.

Shattuck-Hufnagel, S., & Klatt, D. (1979). The limited use of distinctive features and markedness in speech production: Evidence from speech errors. *Journal of Verbal Learning and Verbal Behavior, 18,* 41–55.

Stemberger, J. P. (1982a). *The lexicon in a model of language production.* Doctoral dissertation, University of California—San Diego. New York: Garland Publishing, 1985.

Stemberger, J. P. (1982b). The nature of segments in the lexicon: Evidence from speech errors. *Lingua, 56,* 235–259.

Stemberger, J. P. (1982c). Syntactic errors in speech. *Journal of Psycholinguistic Research, 11,* 313–345.

Stemberger, J. P. (1983a). Inflectional malapropisms: Form-based errors in English morphology. *Linguistics, 21,* 573–602.

Stemberger, J. P. (1983b). *Speech errors and theoretical phonology: A review.* Bloomington: Indiana University Linguistics Club.

Stemberger, J. P. (1984). *Lexical bias in errors in language production: Interactive components, editors, and perceptual biases.* Unpublished manuscript: Carnegie-Mellon University.

Stemberger, J. P. (1986). *Lexical phonology and slips of the tongue.* Unpublished manuscript, University of Minnesota.

Stemberger, J. P. (1990). Wordshape errors in language production. *Cognition, 35,* 123–157.

Stemberger, J. P. (1991). Apparent anti-frequency effects in language production: The addition bias and phonological underspecification. *Journal of Memory and Language, 30,* 161–185.

Stemberger, J. P., & Lewis, M. (1986). Reduplication in Ewe: Morphological accommodation to phonological errors. *Phonology Yearbook, 3,* 151–160.

Stemberger, J. P., & MacWhinney, B. (1986a). Form-oriented errors in inflectional processing. *Cognitive Psychology, 18,* 329–354.

Stemberger, J. P., & MacWhinney, B. (1986b). Frequency and the lexical storage of regularly inflected forms. *Memory and Cognition, 14,* 17–26.

Stemberger, J. P., & Treiman, R. (1986). The internal structure of word-initial consonant clusters. *Journal of Memory and Language, 25,* 163–180.

Stemberger, J. P., Pisoni, D. B., & Hathaway, S. N. (1985). Effects of alcohol intoxication on phonological errors in normal speech. *Research on Speech Perception Progress Reports No. 11.* Bloomington: Speech Research Laboratory, Department of Psychology, Indiana University.

9

General and Specific Factors in "Transformational Errors"
An Experimental Study

Jenn-Yeu Chen and Bernard J. Baars

Recently, there has been a belief in psycholinguistics that Chomsky's competence model of language (1965) could be extended to account for linguistic performance. Evidence was obtained from a certain class of speech errors made by normal English speakers, such as "Why do you be an oaf sometimes?" Fay (1978, 1980a,b), in particular, has argued that such errors, termed "transformational errors" (TEs) by him, could be explained as a result of the malfunctioning of the transformational mechanism during speech production. His view will be challenged in this chapter, and an alternative explanation that emphasizes such performance factors as competition, time pressure, and mental work load will be discussed.

The discussions start with a brief description of Chomsky's transformational theory, followed by Fay's transformational hypothesis. Then, an extended version of the competing-plans hypothesis (Baars, 1980a) is proposed and tested experimentally as an alternative explanation of the TEs.

JENN-YEU CHEN • Department of Child Psychiatry, New York State Psychiatric Institute, New York, New York 10032.   **BERNARD J. BAARS** • The Wright Institute, 2728 Durant Avenue, Berkeley, California 94704.

Experimental Slips and Human Error: Exploring the Architecture of Volition, edited by Bernard J. Baars. Plenum Press, New York, 1992.

CHOMSKY'S TRANSFORMATIONAL THEORY

According to Chomsky (1957, 1965), every sentence in a language has two syntactic representations: one is the deep structure of the sentence, the other is the surface structure. The deep structure is the first product of the language generation device. It is commonly interpreted by some psychologists as the base of the meaning of a sentence. The surface structure, on the other hand, controls what the speaker actually says after words are inserted into the syntactic frame. The two structures are mediated by a set of rules called the transformational rules, which derive the surface structure of a sentence from its deep structure. Here are some examples of surface versus deep structures:

1. Why did you do this?
2. Why was this done?
3. Q you PAST do this WHY

Sentences 1 and 2 are two surface structures that have the same deep structure 3, where Q is a question marker, and *PAST* indicates the tense. It is the shared deep structure that enables a native speaker of English to know that Sentences 1 and 2 are paraphrases of each other. The derivational processes from Sentence 3 to 1 and from 3 to 2 are given below:

Derivations	Transformational rules
Q you PAST do this WHY	← Deep structure
WHY you PAST do this	← WH- fronting
WHY PAST you do this	← Subj–aux inversion
WHY do + PAST you do this	← Do support
↓ Why did you do this?	← Morphophonemics

Derivations	Transformational rules
Q you PAST do this WHY	← Deep structure
WHY you PAST do this	← WH- fronting
WHY this PAST be + en do by you	← Passive formation
WHY this PAST be + en do	← Agent deletion
WHY PAST be this en do	← Subj–aux inversion
WHY PAST be this do + en	← Affix hopping
↓ Why was this done?	← Morphophonemics

Fay's Transformational Hypothesis

Based on Chomsky's transformational theory described above, Fay (1978, 1980a,b) made an attempt to explain a class of speech errors, observed in adults as well as in children, by attributing the errors to the malfunctioning of the transformational mechanism in the course of speech production. Such errors, accordingly termed *transformational errors,* were said to be syntactic and different from other types of speech errors commonly discussed in the literature. An example of a transformational error looks like this: "Why do you be an oaf sometimes?" The utterance was said to have violated a transformational rule, which normally requires both the tense marker PRESENT and the verb BE to be moved together to the left of the subject YOU. The error was that only the tense marker had been preposed, with the verb left behind in its original place. This led to the unavoidable do-support, that is, the attachment of the auxiliary *do* for the tense marker and hence the erroneous utterance "Why do you be an oaf sometimes?" The correct and incorrect derivations are both given below for a comparison.

Correct derivations
Q you PRESENT be an oaf sometimes WHY   ← Deep structure
WHY you PRESENT be an oaf sometimes   ← WH- fronting
WHY PRESENT be you an oaf sometimes   ← Subj–aux inversion
WHY be + PRESENT you an oaf sometimes   ← Affix hopping
Why are you an oaf sometimes?   ← Morphophonemics

Incorrect derivations (the step marked with an asterisk is the one that has gone wrong)
Q you PRESENT be an oaf sometimes WHY   ← Deep structure
WHY you PRESENT be an oaf sometimes   ← WH- fronting
*WHY PRESENT you be an oaf sometimes   ← Subj–aux inversion
WHY do + PRESENT you be an oaf sometimes   ← Do support
Why do you be an oaf sometimes?   ← Morphophonemics

Fay cited some 40 errors collected in natural situations and explained them in terms of transformational breakdowns. He then used these as evidence to support the existence of transformational operations in language production.

A CRITIQUE OF THE TRANSFORMATIONAL HYPOTHESIS

Fay's transformational hypothesis, although intriguing and having some advantages over other approaches, is questionable on several grounds. One criticism (Maratsos & Kuczaj, 1978) concerns Fay's explanation of the auxiliary overmarkings observed in children's speech. Children, for example, are sometimes found to say sentences like "I didn't missed it," where the past tense marker appears twice, as in *did* and in *missed*. Fay argued that in order to generate a surface sentence like "I didn't miss it" from its deep structure, one had first to move the word *not* from its presentential position to a position between the subject and the auxiliary. Then, one needed to move the auxiliary, the tense marker *PAST*, to the left of *not* by making a copy of it in its new position and erasing the one in the old position. Children who say, "I didn't missed it" must have somehow forgotten to erase the tense marker in its old position so that the sentence becomes overtensed.

The problem with such an explanation is that it seems arbitrary that *not* is the word to be moved instead of other elements, and that it is placed between the subject and the auxiliary, rather than after the auxiliary. Suppose one allows for a different movement. A different error will then be predicted by the transformational hypothesis, and yet, such an error cannot be found in the world (e.g., "not I didn't miss it," or "I didn't I missed it"). The same problem also exists in Fay's explanations of adult's speech errors (cf. Stemberger, 1982).

In addition to the aforementioned criticism, there are several other problems with the transformational hypothesis that should be pointed out.

First, as in most naturalistic studies of speech errors (for a detailed critique see Baars & Motley, 1981), the contexts in which the explained errors occurred were not given. This renders an unambiguous interpretation of the errors difficult because the same kind of errors may have been caused by different factors (Norman, 1981; for a discussion of the importance of context, see Clark & Carlson, 1981). What is more, some of the perceived errors may not be errors to the speaker who made them because of the idiosyncratic differences existing among individuals' speech, and also because some marginal English constructions[1] may not be easily determined as errors or not unless one refers to the speaker's intention. Without context, no unique explanation of the errors is possible.

Second, Fay's arguments entail the same reality problem as Chomsky's transformational theory. The fundamental problem with the transformational theory is its difficulty of experimental test. Fay's attempt to defend the theory does not get around this problem. As a competence model, failing an experimental test may not be a very big problem because one can always argue that experiments usually deal with performance, which is not the major concern of the model. But the same does not hold for a performance theory, which was what Fay tried to achieve.

Third, the transformational hypothesis implies that errors are mistakes that do not represent the normal functioning of the production system. However, studies in speech errors in the past decade have seen a developing trend toward a new perspective on errors. That is, errors are no longer taken as something exceptional; rather as constituting an integral part of the regular functioning of the system. Models based on such a perspective are then *capable* of generating errors as well as normal responses (e.g., Dell & Reich, 1980; MacKay, 1982), and they may be more representative of the human production system than an error-free model.

In addition to the general problems discussed above, the transformational hypothesis also suffers a specific deficiency; namely, it is not explanatorily

---

[1]In a personal communication, Dr. Mark Aronoff kindly pointed out to the first author that there are some English sentences that would usually be considered ungrammatical yet could be acceptable in special contexts. For example, the sentence "Why do you be an oaf sometimes," discussed as an error by Fay, can be a possible English construction.

complete. The hypothesis describes how overt errors (erroneous sentences) result from the covert ones (transformational malfunctioning) but does not say anything about why covert errors occur. In other words, it is not clear why and in what circumstances transformational breakdowns happen. Again, although both Chomsky and Fay have been fuzzy in specifying what the performance factors are, Chomsky's vagueness in this respect is more justifiable and tolerable than Fay's, simply because one is sheltered by the competence assumption and the other is not. It seems that Fay has attempted to walk out of the shelter without being aware of the problems he might encounter.

ALTERNATIVE VIEWS OF THE SAME PHENOMENON

Stemberger's Arguments

As it is frequently hard to prove or disprove a transformational hypothesis (Stemberger, 1982), what one can do, presumably, is to look for an alternative explanation—and, hopefully, a simpler and more informative one—of the same phenomena. So, for example, Stemberger (1982) argued that the transformational errors discussed by Fay could be equally well explained by an interactive activation model of word finding that does not necessarily involve any transformational mechanism. In the model, alternative surface structures for a sentence to be said could be generated directly from the syntactic component. Just as words may be incorrectly accessed, a wrong surface syntactic structure for a sentence can be retrieved, too. For example, a speaker intending to say, "I wonder how she can tell," may pick out the structure for a direct question and say instead, "I wonder how can she tell." Sometimes, two alternative structures appear in the same sentence. For example, if the speaker tries to say "Do I have to put on my seatbelt?" but simultaneously activates another possible structure, "put my seatbelt on," it is conceivable that he might end up saying, "Do I have to put on my seatbelt on?"

Stemberger's idea is subject to two criticisms. First, like Fay's, it fails to address the question of why incorrect access of syntactic structures would ever happen. In other words, Stemberger also ignored the performance factors in his explanation of speech errors. Second, the idea suffers the same difficulty of experimental proof as Fay's. That is, there is no direct way by which one can show that there is a separate syntactic store, like the lexicon, that collects a set of surface syntactic structures, and that these structures are readily usable for making sentences. Furthermore, this idea necessarily presumes the existence of a finite set of surface phrase structures just as there exists a finite set of vocabulary. Although a finite vocabulary is an acceptable assumption, a finite set of surface structures is not. In fact, such an assumption has long been criticized by linguists as explanatorily inadequate, and it is exactly for this reason that Chomsky added a transformational component to his theory (cf. Chomsky, 1965; Voegelin, 1967).

THE COMPETING-PLANS HYPOTHESIS

The alternative explanation to be proposed and tested experimentally in this chapter is an extension of the Competing-Plans Hypothesis first forwarded by Baars (1980a). The extended Competing-Plans Hypothesis (ECPH) emphasizes three performance factors in its account of speech errors in general. These factors are competition, time pressure, and mental work load. In addition, the semantic and syntactic similarities among alternative speech plans are considered a major cause of the "transformational errors" specifically.

Competition

Competition exists whenever two or more plans suit the same goal (e.g., two ways of expressing the same idea in speech, cf. van Dijk, 1977). Baars (1980a) noted that, very often in normal speech production, multiple plans may be developed although only one is ultimately to be used. Sometimes, two correct plans of this kind will be forced into execution before one is clearly favored over the other. This, then, may cause a "fused" plan for production. When this plan fails to be edited in time, an error occurs. According to this observation, competition is high when alternative plans are equally favored, or activated (Collins & Loftus, 1975; Green, 1986). If one plan is clearly more favored than others, competition will be very low and no errors are expected to occur.

It is possible to manipulate the extent of competition experimentally by varying the probability of alternative speech plans. For example, given two sentences, if either one is equally likely to be the response on any trial, it is reasonable to assume that the two sentences will be maintained at about the same activation level, and competition between them should be high. On the other hand, if the presentation of one sentence always indicates that the other sentence will be the response, then the unpresented sentence might be kept at a higher activation level than the presented sentence, although the presented sentence might be active as well because of its recent appearance. Still a third possibility is that the presentation of a sentence always indicates that it itself is going to be the response. In this circumstance, it is doubtless that this very sentence will be kept active, and that the other one will be suppressed.

Manipulations like these would allow different predictions to be made about the frequencies of errors for various amounts of competition. Specifically, the higher the competition, the higher the frequency of errors.

Time Pressure

The way time pressure is related to speech errors may be understood in the context of competition. That is, increasing the time pressure tends to decrease the chance of resolving competition in time; hence, errors are more likely to occur. Either way, the prediction would invariably be that high time pressure leads to more errors, a consequence of speed–accuracy trade-offs.

In previous studies of experimentally induced slips, time pressure has been created by imposing a response deadline for the subjects (e.g., Dell, 1984; Dell & Reich, 1981). In the present experiment, the stimulus presentation time, instead of the response time, was varied to manipulate the degree of time pressure. This approach was chosen because the use of sentences as the stimuli made it necessary to adopt a longer presentation time than is required with the use of words. From our pilot work, we suspected that the subjects may have taken advantage of the relatively long stimulus presentation time to plan for their responses, so as to make our error-inducing procedure quite unsuccessful even with a response deadline imposed.

Mental Work Load

A widely accepted notion about human attention is that there is a limit on the available processing resources (Kahneman, 1973; Moray, 1979; Navon & Gopher, 1979). Carrying out more than one task at a time means that these tasks have to share the limited resources. When the work load is high and exceeds the total number of resources available, some tasks will suffer. The only condition in which multiple processes are not affected by the limited pool of resources occurs when some of the tasks have been automatized (Shiffrin, Dumais, & Schneider, 1981). Because speech production involves some conscious planning (at least, in the present experiment), it is not an entirely automatic process and should be limited by the available processing resources. Accordingly, increasing the mental work load by, for example, adding a concurrent memory task might reduce the efficiency of the speech task, the result of which would be the occurrence of more errors.

The effect, however, would depend on whether the summed work load of the two tasks exceeds the total capacity or not. The effect of the concurrent memory task on the performance of the speech task will show only if the summed work load exceeds the total capacity. In other words, an interaction effect should be observed between the two tasks.

METHOD

Subjects and Apparatus

Sixty undergraduate students in an introductory psychology course at the State University of New York at Stony Brook participated in this experiment to fulfill part of their course requirements. All subjects were native speakers of English.

A Cromemco Z-2 microcomputer and a TVI-920C televideo terminal were used to control the experimental procedure. A TEAC A-170S stereo cassette deck was used to record the subjects' responses, which were to be transcribed afterward.

Materials

Ten "transformational errors" were selected from Fay's article (1980a). For each error, two paraphrases were then reconstructed. (The error sentences and their competing paraphrases are listed in Table 1.) All the sentences were given to the subjects, after the experiment, for judgments of the acceptability of the error sentences and the semantic similarity of the paraphrases. A seven-point scale ranging from 0 to 6 was used. Overall, the error sentences were considered rather unacceptable (the mean judged acceptability was 1.63), and the paraphrases were judged to be relatively good paraphrases (the mean judged similarity was 4.11).

Design and Procedure

The experiment was a $3 \times 2 \times 2$ between-subject design, with competition, time pressure, and mental work load as the three factors, respectively. Competition was either small, medium, or great. Time pressure was low or high. Mental work load was heavy or light. The subjects were randomly assigned to one of the 12 conditions, five subjects to each condition.

The experiment was made up of 10 blocks of 20 trials, with each block designed to replicate one kind of "transformational error." Within a block, the subjects first memorized two paraphrases for 10 seconds, for example, "What could I have done with the check?" and "What have I done with the check?" (The error to be induced from these paraphrases was "What could have I done with the check?") Then, they were given a recall test to ensure correct memory of the sentences. After recall, half the subjects saw a random three-digit number, which they had to report later. The number was presented for 0.5 seconds and there was an additional 1 second for rehearsal before the stimulus sentence came on. The other half of the subjects skipped the number. Next, one of the sentences appeared for either 0.5 or 1.5 seconds, for example, "What could I have done with the check?" The stimulus sentence was followed by a response cue, which was either "REPEAT" or "REVERSE." The "REPEAT" cue instructed the subjects to repeat the stimulus sentence, whereas the "REVERSE" cue asked them to recall the other sentence that was the paraphrase of the stimulus sentence.

One third of the subjects received the "REPEAT" cue consistently throughout the experiment. Competition for these subjects was small. Another third of the subjects received the "REVERSE" cue consistently throughout the experiment. Competition for these subjects was medium. The remaining third of the

TABLE 1

Transformational Errors (TEs) and Their Rated Degree of Acceptability on a
Seven-Point (0–6) Scale (1st Rows); Competing Paraphrases (CPs) and Their
Rated Degree of Similarity on a Seven-Point (0–6) Scale (2nd Rows)

			Mean	*(SD)*
1.	TE:	What could have I done with the check?	1.49	(2.01)
	CP:	What have I done with the check?	4.38	(1.91)
		What could I have done with the check?		
2.	TE:	What it is that has to be welded?	1.16	(1.60)
	CP:	What is it that has to be welded?	4.78	(1.21)
		I wonder what it is that has to be welded.		
3.	TE:	Where do you suppose are they?	1.48	(1.86)
	CP:	Where are they, do you suppose?	5.56	(1.00
		Where do you suppose they are?		
4.	TE:	They didn't actually withdrew the needle.	1.22	(1.88)
	CP:	They almost withdrew the needle.	2.89	(1.89)
		They didn't actually withdraw the needle.		
5.	TE:	It probably went under the radiator and melt.	1.33	(1.79)
	CP:	It probably went under the radiator and melted.	2.65	(1.72)
		It did go under the radiator and melt.		
6.	TE:	He always know what's to say.	1.22	(1.75)
	CP:	He always knows what to say.	3.57	(1.79)
		He always knows what's right to say.		
7.	TE:	I wonder how can she tell.	2.41	(2.11)
	CP:	How can she tell, I wonder?	5.52	(0.88)
		I wonder how she can tell.		
8.	TE:	Can I turn off this?	2.41	(2.01)
	CP:	Can I turn off this light?	2.59	(2.14)
		Can I turn this off?		
9.	TE:	That's the way it used to be, didn't it?	2.43	(2.32)
	CP:	That's the way it used to be, wasn't it?	4.56	(1.38)
		It used to be that way, didn't it?		
10.	TE:	He tended to chose the easiest way.	1.19	(1.68)
	CP:	He tended to choose the easiest way.	4.60	(1.31)
		He usually chose the easiest way.		

subjects received either the "REPEAT" or the "REVERSE" cue randomly. Competition in this condition was great.

Immediately after responding to the sentence, the subjects who had previously seen a three-digit number had to recall the number. The total response time for all subjects was 2 seconds. There were 20 test trials within each block.

Scoring

Only complete correct responses were considered correct. All the others were classified as errors except for the misses. Three types of errors were separately examined:

1. *Exact replications of Fay's error examples,* although they did not have to be perfectly verbatim. As long as the error showed, the sentence was considered an exact replication. For example, one of the subjects said, "What it is *(pause)* what is it that has to be welded?" The expected error was "What it is that has to be welded?" Although the subject corrected himself immediately, the error part "what it is" had already been made; therefore, the response was taken as an instance of exact replication.

2. *Close replications of Fay's error examples.* Close replications were those errors that were syntactic but were not exactly the same as Fay's error examples. For instance, a sentence like "I wonder what *is it* that has to be welded" would be considered a close replication of the error "What *it is* that has to be welded?"

3. *General errors.* These were total errors, including the exact replications and the close replications.

Examples of each type of error are shown in Table 2.

RESULTS

Overall, the experiment successfully elicited 9 of the 10 "transformational errors" that we set out to replicate. The effects of the three performance factors were examined by a three-way analysis of variance. The data that were entered into the analyses were the total number of errors that each subject made

TABLE 2
Sentential Errors of Exact and Close Replications
as Sampled from 60 Subjects

Exact replications
  I wonder how can—she can tell.
  It probably went under the radiator and melt.
  What it is—what is it that has to be welded?

Close replications
  That's the way it was, didn't it?
  It did go under the radiator and melted.
  He always know what to say.
  He always knows what's to say.
  What I have done with the check?
  I wonder where are they?
  How she—can she tell, I wonder?
  I wonder what is it that has to be welded?
  What it was that has to be welded?
  What could hi have done with the check?
  What could I have I done with the check?
  It used to be that way, wasn't it?
  He usually choose the easiest way.

throughout the entire experiment; it was summed across the 10 blocks of 20 trials (a total of 200).

Main Effects

In terms of the general errors (n = 1,901, or 15.8%), the predictions for the competition and mental-work-load factors were confirmed. There was a significant main effect for the competition factor: $F(2, 48) = 22.473, p < .001$. Pairwise comparisons further showed that high competition caused more errors than medium competition: $F(1, 32) = 4.559, p < .05$, and medium competition caused more errors than low competition, $F(1, 32) = 21.125, p < .005$. In other words, the subjects who experienced greater competition tended to make more errors than those who experienced less competition.

Also, there was a significant main effect in the mental-work-load factor. Subjects whose attentional resources were divided between the sentence and the digit made more errors than subjects whose attentional resources were not divided: $F(1, 48) = 5.917, p < .02$.

However, there was no significant main effect for the time pressure factor, although the result appeared to be in the predicted direction.

For the exact replications (n = 215, or 1.8%), no main effects in all the three factors were found in spite of the tendency in the predicted directions. When close replications (n = 320, or 2.7%) were added to the exact replications, a significant main effect in the competition factor was found: $F(2, 48) = 3.205$, $MSe = 84.650, p < .05$. The other two factors revealed a trend in the predicted directions, but the effects were not significant.

Interaction Effects

There were no significant interaction effects of any kind except for one, the competition by time pressure interaction for the combined exact and close replications: $F(2, 48) = 3.446, MSe = 84.650, p < .05$.

Number of Errors for Each Paraphrase Pair

Errors in each of the 10 pairs of competing paraphrases were summed across the 20 trials and the 60 subjects. As seen in Table 3, they did not induce the same number of "transformational errors," and pairs 3, 6, and 8 the fewest.

Sentence–Digit Trade-Offs

In any single trial, a sentential response and a digital response could be either right or wrong; therefore, four response combinations were possible:

TABLE 3

The Number of Errors Induced by Each Paraphrase Pair as
Summed across 20 Trials and 60 Subjects

Paraphrase pairs	Exact replications	Close replications	General errors
1	29	5	109
2	18	2	230
3	0	1	183
4	22	15	160
5	31	72	258
6	2	93	202
7	34	22	133
8	4	0	110
9	64	93	363
10	11	25	153
Total	215	320	1901

right-right, wrong-wrong, right-wrong, and wrong-right. Notice that only the last two cases (hereafter, the *discordant* responses) indicated sentence–digit trade-offs. The first two (hereafter, the *concordant* responses) were just the opposite of the trade-off effects. In order to show whether trade-offs existed in the subjects' responses, and how the trade-offs varied with the amount of competition involved in different conditions, a two-way ANOVA was applied to the response type (concordant or discordant) against the competition factor (low, medium, or high). A main effect was found in the response type; that is, the number of the concordant responses was significantly greater than that of the discordant responses: $F(1, 27) = 47.726$, $MSe = 756.68$, $p < .01$. Analytical comparisons further showed that this was also true of the low- and medium-competition conditions—$F(1, 9) = 61.911$, $MSe = 683.556$, and $F(1, 9) = 19.751$, $MSe = 782.578$, respectively, $p < .01$—although not for the high-competition condition: $F < 1$.

More important, however, was the significant interaction effect found between the response type and the competition factor: $F(2, 27) = 38.178$, $MSe = 756.68$, $p < .01$. As the amount of competition increased from low to high, there was a steady increase in the discordant responses, but a steady decrease in the concordant responses. This result indicated that the sentence–digit trade-offs became more and more evident when the competition increased.

Another piece of information related to the sentence–digit trade-off effects came from the comparison of the both-correct (i.e., both the sentence and the digit) responses with the both-wrong responses. The both-correct responses were significantly greater than the both-wrong responses: $F(1, 27) = 45.57$, $MSe = 1240.852$, $p < .001$. Also, there was a significant interaction between the response type and the competition factor: $F(2, 27) = 18.523$, $MSe = 1240.852$, $p < .001$. As the amount of competition in the sentence task increased, the number of both-correct responses decreased, and the number of both-wrong responses increased.

Among the discordant responses (i.e., either the sentence or the digit was wrong), the sentence-wrong cases were significantly less frequent than the digit-wrong cases: $F(1, 27) = 137.77$, $MSe = 262.837$, $p < .001$.

DISCUSSION

Overall, the results seemed quite consistent with our predictions.

Competition Effect

With respect to the competition effect, the data showed that higher competition caused more sentential errors than lower competition. This finding held for both the general errors and the combined exact and close replications. The exact replications also displayed the same trend although they did not reach the .05 significant level. A floor effect may have been present that explains why this was the case. The error rate for this type of errors was very low (less than 2%) as compared to the 10%–30% error rate previously found in spoonerisms or word switches (Baars, 1981a). If the error rate is raised by a better technique, the predicted effects might then be seen.

Time Pressure Effect

For the time pressure factor, no significant effect was found on all types of errors. One possible explanation of the failure of this prediction is that we might have manipulated the wrong time period. Although previous work in inducing slips of the tongue had all manipulated the response time (Baars, 1980a), the current experiment paced the subjects by manipulating the stimulus presentation time. The reason is that, in the pilot study, we discovered that the subjects seemed to be planning for the answer once the stimulus was shown. By the time the response cue came up, the decision had perhaps already been made; what was left to do was just to say the answer. Therefore, we decided that, if we wanted to manipulate the time for processing the sentence and expected any effect from such a manipulation, it should be the stimulus presentation time that was to be varied.

That no effect was found with this manipulation suggests that perhaps it is still the response time that is more critical and that should have been manipulated. However, this possibility awaits further experimentation.

Mental-Work-Load Effect

The increase of mental work load led to more general errors, but the exact and close replications did not show the same effect in a significant way. Again, we suspect that a floor effect may have been the reason for such an outcome.

Sentence–Digit Trade-Offs

Although the overall concordant responses outnumbered the discordant responses, a significant interaction between the response type and the competition factor demonstrated that there were clear trade-offs between the sentence task and the digit task, and that the trade-offs increased as the difficulty of the sentence task increased because of the greater competition involved. Moreover, among the concordant responses, the both-correct responses decreased and the both-wrong responses increased as the sentence task became more and more difficult. These results have important bearings on the issue of mental work load.

Previous studies (e.g., Moray, 1979; Navon & Gopher, 1979) have shown than, when subjects are completely overloaded (i.e., when the demanded resources far exceed the supplied resources), they tend to fail both the primary and the secondary tasks (Navon and Gopher called this effect "concurrent cost"). On the other hand, if subjects are pretty much underloaded, they tend to succeed in both tasks (this effect is "concurrent benefit" in Navon and Gopher's term). Thus, trade-offs seem to be the outcome of subjective task preferences when the demand for processing resources is close to the supply.

Transformational Errors Revisited

In spite of the low error rate, this experiment successfully demonstrated that Fay's transformational errors are, to a large extent, replicable experimentally. Although the specific error mechanisms were still unclear, the general factors that had caused errors to occur seemed certain. It is safe to conclude at this point that performance factors such as competition, time pressure, and mental work load are responsible for the occurrence of errors in general, whereas more specific factors are needed to explain error types. Transformational breakdown may be one such specific factor, although others are possible as well.

One possibility that was suggested by the results of the experiment is that at least some transformational errors can be explained as systematic sentence blends due to the structural similarity of the competing paraphrases. Take Pair 9 as an illustrative example. The competing paraphrases were:

That's the way it used to be, wasn't it?
It used to be that way, didn't it?

Each sentence consists of a main clause and a tag question, arranged in the same order in both sentences. The major constituent boundary between the main clauses and the tag questions makes the tag questions especially vulnerable to mutual exchange. Thus, we observed the most errors in this case. The errors were either "That's the way it used to be, didn't it?" or "It used to be that way, wasn't it?" The presence of both types of errors in our experiment suggested that one of them (the first one), interpreted as a transformational error by Fay, might just be a sentence blend resulting from a switch of the tag questions in the competing paraphrases. Similar explanations could also be applied to Paris 2, 4, 5, 7, and 10.

The explanation of "transformational errors" as systematic sentence blends is partially supported by other studies of speech errors and by studies of bilingual code switching. Garrett (1980a,b) observed that elements that were exchanged in a sentence tended to belong to the same grammatical category. Thus, noun phrases tended to switch with noun phrases and verb phrases with verb phrases. The phenomenon of intentional bilingual code switching also suggests that sentences mix only at the corresponding constituents in the two languages (Sridhar & Sridhar, 1980).

Admittedly, not all "transformational errors" induced in the present experiment could be readily explained as sentence blends. The error mechanisms underlying Pairs 1, 6, and 8 were less obvious and did not seem to resemble those of the other pairs. For example, the way Pair 1 worked to induce the error "What could I have done with the check" might be via the ordinal conflict mechanism (Baars, 1980b). That is, the order of "have I" in one of the sentences might have biased the other toward the same order—consequently, the error "What could have I."

Summary and Conclusion

In summary, both general and specific factors are necessary for a complete account of speech errors. The general factors like competition, time pressure, and mental work load explain why errors should ever occur, and the specific factors like Fay's transformational mechanism, or like structural similarity between competing speech plans as proposed in the present study, predict the type of errors that may occur.

The results of the present experiment provide support for the importance of the general factors. Green (1986) expressed very similar ideas of explaining speech errors as well as bilingual speech. The three factors he proposed—control, activation, and resource—bear close resemblance to the performance factors we proposed here. On the other hand, our results do not allow us to disconfirm the transformational hypothesis as a specific factor in the occurrence of "transformational errors," although they do point to another possibility of how "transformational errors" may have occurred, that is, as a result of systematic sentence blends. Further research is necessary to look into the specific factors of speech errors.

REFERENCES

Baars, B. J. (1980a). The competing plans hypothesis: An heuristic viewpoint on the causes of errors in speech. In Hans W. Dechert & M. Raupach (Eds.), *Temporal variables in speech.* New York: Mouton.

Baars, B. J. (1980b). On eliciting predictable speech errors in the laboratory. In V. A. Fromkin (Ed.), *Errors in linguistic performance.* New York: Academic Press.

Baars, B. J., & Motley, M. T. (1981). *A sympathetic critique of naturalistic studies of slips of speech and action.* Unpublished manuscript.

Chomsky, N. (1957). *Syntactic structures.* The Hague: Mouton.

Chomsky, N. (1965). *Aspects of the theory of syntax.* Cambridge: MIT Press.

Clark, H. H., & Carlson, T. B. (1981). Context for comprehension. In J. Long & A. Baddeley (Eds.), *Attention and performance IX.* Hillsdale, NJ: Erlbaum.

Collins, A. M., & Loftus, E. F. (1975). A spreading-activation theory of semantic processing. *Psychological Review, 82,* 407–428.

Dell, G. S. (1984). Representation of serial order in speech: Evidence from the repeated phoneme effect in speech errors. *Journal of Experimental Psycholog: Learning, Memory and Cognition, 10(2),* 222–233.

Dell, G. S., & Reich, P. A. (1980). Toward a unified model of slips of the tongue. In V. A. Fromkin (Ed.), *Errors in linguistic performance.* New York: Academic Press.

Dell, G. S., & Reich, P. A. (1981). Stages in sentence production: An analysis of speech error data. *Journal of Verbal Learning and Verbal Behavior, 20(6),* 611–629.

Dijk, T. A. van (1977). *Text and context: Explorations in the semantics and pragmatics of discourse.* New York: Longman.

Fay, D. (1978). Transformations as mental operations: A reply to Kuczaj. *Journal of Child Language, 5(1),* 143–149.

Fay, D. (1980a). Transformational errors. In V. A. Fromkin (Ed.), *Errors in linguistic performance.* New York: Academic Press.

Fay, D. (1980b). Performing transformations. In R. A. Cole (Ed.), *Perception and production of fluent speech.* Hillsdale, NJ: Erlbaum.

Foss, D. J., & Fay, D. (1975). Linguistic theory and performance models. In D. Cohen & J. R. Wirth (Eds.), *Testing linguistic hypotheses.* New York: Wiley.

Garrett, M. F. (1980a). Levels of processing in sentence production. In B. Butterworth (Ed.), *Language production, Vol. 1: Speech and Talk.* New York: Academic Press.

Garrett, M. F. (1980b). The limits of accommodation: Arguments for independent processing levels in sentence production. In V. A. Fromkin (Ed.), *Errors in linguistic performance.* New York: Academic Press.

Green, D. W. (1986). Control, activation, and resource: A framework and a model for the control of speech in bilinguals. *Brain and Language, 27,* 210–223.

Kahneman, D. (1973). *Attention and effort.* Englewood Cliffs, NJ: Prentice-Hall.

MacKay, D. (1982). The problems of flexibility, fluency, and speed-accuracy: Trade-offs in skilled behavior. *Psychological Review, 89,* 483–506.

Maratsos, M., & Kuczaj, S. (1978). Against the transformationalist account: A simpler analysis of auxiliary overmarkings. *Journal of Child Language, 5,* 337–345.

Moray, R. E. (1979). *Mental workload: Its theory and measurement.* New York: Plenum Press.

Navon, D., & Gopher, D. (1979). On the economy of the human processing system. *Psychological Review, 86,* 214–255.

Norman, D. A. (1981). Categorization of action slips. *Psychological Review, 88,* 1–15.

Shiffrin, R. M., Dumais, S. T., & Schneider, W. (1981). Characteristics of automatism. In J. Long and A. Baddeley (Eds.), *Attention and performance IX.* Hillsdale, NJ: Erlbaum.

Sridhar, S. N., & Sridhar, K. K. (1980). The syntax and psycholinguistics of bilingual code mixing. *Canadian Journal of Psychology, 34,* 407–416.

Stemberger, J. P. (1982). Syntactic errors in speech. *Journal of Psycholinguistic Research, 11,* 313–345.

Voegelin, C. F. (Ed.). (1967). *Constituent structures* (2nd ed.). The Hague: Mouton.

IV

FINDINGS AND THEORY DERIVED FROM INDUCED SLIPS

This section is about the scientific uses of induced slips. In Chapter 10, Gary S. Dell and Renee S. Repka show a simple way to study inner speech by the induction of internal tongue twisters. Rather surprisingly, the pattern of inner slips resembles that of actually spoken slips, a result with strong implications for any model of speech production. It is worth noting that inner speech—which is surely one of the most important modalities of human conscious experience—has been remarkably neglected in contemporary psychology. One of the real contributions of the Dell and Repka chapter is simply to show that noteworthy results may be obtained from straightforward manipulations of inner speech.

In Chapter 11, Mattson and Baars tackle the very difficult problem of anticipatory editing in the production of speech. Because the inner plan and any editing operations on it are naturally inferential, this is a difficult phenomenon to demonstrate conclusively. In particular, it is difficult to separate the effect of two plausible ways of reducing the likelihood of inner errors being made overt—the notion of *editing of flawed speech plans* versus the idea that speech production *naturally favors correct plans*—so that the preponderance of correct utterances may be explained without an editing component. There is indeed evidence in favor of both of these error-minimizing mechanisms.

The perennially contentious issue of Freudian slips is explored by Baars, Cohen, Bower, and Berry in Chapter 12. Given the ability to induce almost any slip experimentally, one can begin to test the otherwise largely anecdotal evidence for Freudian slips. Although some positive evidence about the Freudian hypothesis emerges from this approach, real problems have emerged in our attempts to generalize and systematically replicate the phenomenon. We present two experiments in which inner conflict between opposing emotions is likely to exist, and we show that, at least so far, the rate of emotionally expressive slips does not respond sensitively to the existence of conflict as such. Thus, previously reported positive findings in favor of the Freudian slip hypothesis must be viewed with caution. These results do not conclusively disprove some version of the Freudian slip hypothesis, but they do point to very real difficulties in testing its reality.

10

Errors in Inner Speech

Gary S. Dell and Renee J. Repka

Many people have the feeling that they can hear a little voice inside their heads. This inner speech accompanies reading and writing and often co-occurs with activities that involve mental planning such as problem solving (Sokolov, 1972). Clearly, inner speech is ubiquitous in our mental lives, and so it is not surprising that it has played a large role in psychological theory. For example, it has been proposed that inner speech is a necessary accompaniment to thought and even that inner speech is to be identified with thought (Watson, 1919). Although these radical views of the relation between inner speech and thought are held by few, if any, psychologists today, there is, nonetheless, widespread assent that the voice in the head is important.

In this chapter, we investigate the properties of inner speech in a somewhat unusual way, by looking at the "tongue" slips that seem to occur in it. The first experiment compared inner slips that subjects reported "hearing" when imagining tongue twisters with the overt slips that a different group of subjects made when saying the same stimuli aloud. The second experiment extended this comparison to practice effects. The subjects either mentally or overtly practiced saying tongue twisters, and the effect of this practice on the frequency of slips in both inner and overt speech was assessed. By way of introduction to our experiments, we first provide some background on inner speech and then discuss the theory and data concerned with speech errors.

GARY S. DELL • Department of Psychology, University of Illinois at Champaign, Champaign, Illinois 61820.   RENEE J. REPKA • Department of Psychology, University of Rochester, Rochester, New York 14627.

Experimental Slips and Human Error: Exploring the Architecture of Volition, edited by Bernard J. Baars. Plenum Press, New York, 1992.

INNER SPEECH

Inner, or mental, speech is a form of verbal imagery in which the image has both an auditory component—you hear the words in your mind's ear—and an articulatory component—you imagine your articulators moving the way they would during overt speech. Although the main feature of inner speech is this phenomenology, it does have one observable component: electromyographic activity in the appropriate muscles is associated with mental rehearsal in general and with inner speech in particular (Jacobson, 1930; Sokolov, 1972).

Inner speech, under various names, is an important construct in cognitive theory. The short-term retention and rehearsal of verbal material is said to involve a code that is either identical to or has much in common with inner speech (Baddeley, Thomson, & Buchanan, 1975; Conrad, 1964; Ellis, 1980). The subvocalization hypothesis of reading is, in essence, the claim that silent reading is mediated by inner speech, and although a pure subvocalization view of reading has been discredited (see Foss & Hakes, 1978), more abstract phonological recoding and dual-code theories, in which visual input is transformed into sublexical phonological forms, are claims about processes that may be related to inner speech. There are similar proposals about the role of a phonological code in writing (e.g., Hotopf, 1980).

Most research on these topics has been content to show that certain tasks, such as memorization or reading, make use of a speechlike code. What has been studied much less often is the basic nature of inner speech, specifically its relation to overt speech. A few studies have compared the rates of inner and overt speech. Although one study (Landauer, 1962) suggests that the rates are similar, most researchers have found that inner speech can be "articulated" more rapidly than overt speech (Anderson, 1982; MacKay, 1981; Weber & Castleman, 1970). This difference can be interpreted in at least two ways. One possibility is that overt articulation dynamics are a rate-limiting factor in overt speech, so that in the absence of articulation, inner speech can be faster. A second interpretation is that inner speech is actually abbreviated in some way. One can imagine that unimportant words or grammatical affixes may be dropped in inner speech (e.g., Vygotsky, 1962) or that the phonological form of the words is incomplete. Anan'ev (cited in Sokolov, 1972) claimed that words in inner speech are characterized primarily by their initial consonants, the remainder of the word is not being clearly articulated in the image.

Some sort of phonological abbreviation would make sense in light of the sequential nature of spoken words. The initial segments of words are more easily retrieved (Brown & McNeill, 1966). and are more important in word recognition than final segments (Marslen-Wilson & Welsh, 1978). Thus, it is conceivable that inner speech emphasizes initial segments in some way.

Although the characterization of inner speech as phonologically abbreviated seems consistent with experience and can account for the faster rate of inner speech, it requires more direct support. In particular, we need some way to assess which parts of words are actually covertly articulated. One way would be to have the subjects imagine words whose initial and noninitial parts require separate muscle groups and then to obtain the relevant myographic recordings. A simpler way, the one adopted here, it to look at the slips of the tongue that seem to occur in inner speech. Hockett (1967) reported, "I have observed 'slips of the tongue' in my own inner flow [of speech] often caught and edited out before they could be mapped into overt speech by tongue and lips" (p. 927). Dell (1978) showed that, when subjects mentally recite tongue twisters, they report errors that are similar to those that occur when tongue twisters are said aloud. Such comparisons can be used to investigate hypotheses about the nature of inner speech. In particular, if the covert articulation of inner speech is abbreviated as described above, we might expect inner slips to show a greater tendency than overt slips to involve the initial parts of words. To make this prediction more precise, however, we first need to consider some of the theoretical issues in language and speech production and how the study of speech errors has addressed these issues.

SPEECH ERRORS AND THEORIES OF PRODUCTION

It has often been proposed that speech errors provide important, if not the most important, data for the study of production (e.g., Cutler, 1981; Fromkin, 1971; Garrett, 1975; MacKay, 1970). Most theories of production have been designed either to account solely for speech errors (e.g., Dell, 1986; Fay & Cutler, 1977; Garrett, 1975; Shattuck-Hufnagel, 1979; Stemberger, 1985) or rely heavily on such data (e.g., Bock, 1982; MacKay, 1982). All of these theories follow Lashley (1951) in assuming that speech errors occur during the construction of internal representations of an utterance that are assembled before articulation. Among these representations are some kind of syntactic representation whose basic units are lexical items, a phonological representation whose units are segments and possibly features, and a motor program.[1]

What are typically called slips of the tongue are usually associated with the construction of syntactic or phonological representations, and not with the assembly of a motor program. Slips involving the misordering or substitution of words (e.g., "writing a mother to my letter") are assigned to processes that associate lexical items as whole syntactic entities with slots in a syntactic frame (e.g., Fay & Cutler, 1977; Garrett, 1975). Errors in which segments, features, or clusters are misordered, deleted or added (e.g., "blue bug—blue blug") are assigned to processes that link phonological units with slots in phonological frames (e.g., Dell, 1986; Shattuck-Hufnagel, 1979; Stemberger, 1985). Thus, although speech errors are called slips of the *tongue,* they are seen to occur in the nonmotoric linguistic planning of utterances. Evidence for this claim comes from the observation that speech errors are under the control of

---

[1]It is not clear that the motor program can be assembled substantially before articulation. For evidence that it can, see Sternberg, Monsell, Knoll, and Wright (1978).

phonological rules; that is, errors almost never result in sound sequences that do not occur in the language being spoken (Fromkin, 1971; Wells, 1951). Thus, a speaker might say *blug* for *bug,* but never *lbug.*

MacKay (1982, 1987) has outlined a general theory of the production of sequences that addresses both speech errors and inner speech. The theory proposes that production involves the top-down left-to-right activation of nodes in a (primarily) hierarchical network. The nodes stand for either mental (e.g., linguistic) or physical (visual, auditory, or motoric) units. With respect to speech production, we need consider only linguistic and motor nodes.

Both the linguistic and motor nodes can be subdivided into *content* and *sequence* nodes. Linguistic content nodes represent actual items (words, phonemes, etc.), and linguistic sequence nodes code the rules that govern how linguistic content nodes can combine. As in standard linguistic theory, the sequence nodes represent *categories* of content items. For example, a sequence node for NP (noun phrase) might specify a sequence of the category Det (determiner) followed by the category N (noun). There is an analogous division between content and sequence among the motor nodes, but these nodes are not important here.

Within the linguistic nodes, both content and sequence nodes are organized into levels, specifically a syntactic level, whose content nodes represent specific words and phrases and whose sequence nodes represent syntactic rules, and a phonological level, whose content nodes represent specific syllables, syllabic constituents, phonemes, and features, and whose sequence nodes represent syllable structure rules (e.g., Syllable → Onset Rhyme). Figure 1 shows the hierarchy of syntactic and phonological content nodes for the noun phrase "thirty-seven silver thistles." (Feature nodes have been omitted for the sake of clarity.)

The links among the content nodes specify constituent relations (e.g., the syllable /sIl/ connects to the onset /s/ and the rhyme /Il/). Links among sequence nodes specify both constituent relations and order relations. The sequence node for *syllable* connects to the sequence nodes for *onset* and *rhyme,* and special inhibitory links between *onset* and *rhyme* ensure the activation of *onset* before *rhyme.* Each sequence node, as well, connects to all content nodes in its categorical "domain." So, for example, the sequence node for *onset* connects to content nodes for every onset that occurs, and the sequence node for *noun* connects to content nodes for all nouns.

The production of a sentence involves the spreading of activation from the highest level linguistic nodes to the lowest level motor nodes. The activation of a content node at the lowest motor level results in the movement of a muscle. The dynamics of the spreading activation process are complex, but in essence, it works this way: Sequence nodes are activated in a top-down/left-to-right fashion (as in a depth-first search that always takes left branches first). As it is activated, each sequence node then activates the most "primed" content node in its categorical domain. Priming, in the theory, can be thought of as preparation for activation. Thus, when the sequence node for *onset* is activated, it activates that onset with the greatest degree of priming. Content nodes are

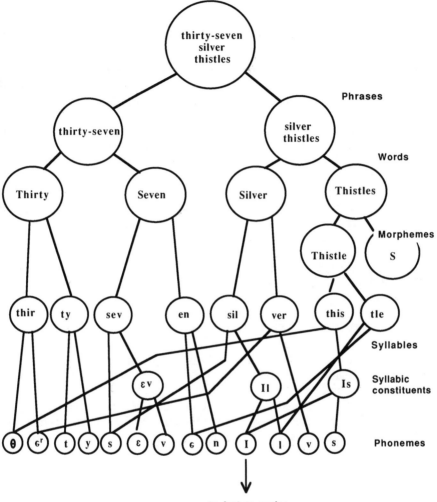

FIGURE 1. Linguistic content nodes for the phrase "thirty-seven silver thistles." Separate phoneme nodes are provided for pre- and postvocalic versions of each consonant following a suggestion of Dell (1986). Feature nodes have been omitted to simplify the figure.

primed when their parent content node is activated. Thus, the activation of the syllable /sIl/ would prime the onset /s/ and the rhyme /Il/, leaving these nodes in a position to be activated when the sequence nodes for *onset* and *rhyme* are activated. The end result is a proper sequence of activation of content nodes creating, ultimately, the proper sequence of behavior.

Dell (1980, 1985, 1986) and Stemberger (1982, 1985) have used similar models to give quantitative accounts of speech error distributions. Errors occurs when what MacKay would call a sequence node activates the wrong content node in its domain. Dell and Stemberger have shown how factors such as item similarity and familiarity can lead to the wrong node's being in a greater state of readiness than the correct one. In addition, they have provided good accounts of the variety of errors that occur at the lexical and phonological levels. A major difference between the approaches of Dell and Stemberger, on the one hand, and of MacKay, on the other, has to do with the levels at which sequence nodes select among the content nodes. According to MacKay, such selection takes place at every level in the hierarchy: phrase, word, morpheme, syllable, syllabic constituent, phoneme, and feature. Stemberger (1982) noted, however, that most speech errors involve either words or phonemes and the other levels much less often, and he suggested that the active rule-guided selection of content (in MacKay's terms, the activation of content nodes by sequence nodes) occurs only at the lexical and the phoneme levels. Dell (1986) showed by simulation that if phonological content selection takes place only at the phoneme level, the observed rates of syllable, syllabic constituent, phoneme, and feature errors can all be accounted for. Thus, it can be argued that, although the general framework of MacKay is correct, the actual interaction among content (linguistic items) and sequence (linguistic rules) may be more restricted than is proposed in the theory.

SLIPS OF THE TONGUE AND INNER SPEECH

Having provided background to both inner speech and speech errors, we are now in a position to consider what kinds of slips of the "tongue," if any, should occur in inner speech.

MacKay (1982) claimed that inner speech involves the activation only of linguistic nodes. Motor nodes are not activated but are instead primed by the activation of linguistic feature nodes, and this priming is responsible for electromyographic potentials. Given the assignment of speech errors to the linguistic levels in the theory and the claim that inner speech involves only the activation of those levels, one would expect to find inner slips and to find that these slips would be similar to overt slips. This expectation assumes, however, that the linguistic levels are fully activated. Earlier, we mentioned the possibility of some kind of abbreviation in this activity. Let us now consider some forms of abbreviation and what inner slip patterns they would be associated with. One possible abbreviation, which we call the *lexical opacity hypothesis,* is that only nodes at the word (or higher) level are activated in inner speech. In this view, hearing the words in inner speech with the mind's ear is the result of the activation of word nodes. Given that one of the primary functions of inner speech is the mental rehearsal of word sequences, this kind of abbreviation still allows for this function to be fulfilled.

If the lexical opacity hypothesis is correct, one would expect the following pattern of inner speech errors: First, there should be very few errors involving sublexical units (affixes, segments, clusters, etc.). If nodes at these levels are not activated, there can be no corresponding errors. Second, errors involving the movement or substitution of words could occur, but one would not expect phonological relatedness to affect the probability of any two words' interacting in an error. Such effects in overt word errors (e.g., "yoga—yoghurt") have, in the network models discussed earlier, been attributed to bottom-up feedback from phonological content nodes to word content nodes, making a similar, but incorrect, word more likely to be selected (Dell & Reich, 1981; Harley, 1984; Stemberger, 1985). However, if phonological nodes are not active in inner speech, there can be no such effect on inner slips.

Although the lexical opacity hypothesis is a logical possibility for inner speech in some situations, it has at least two empirical strikes against it. The first is the fact that appropriate neuromuscular activity accompanies inner speech, a finding that, at least within the confines of MacKay's theory, is totally incompatible with lexical opacity. The reason is that phonological nodes must be activated in order to prime the muscles. Second, it is well known that memory performance for subspan sequences is degraded when the items making up the sequence to be remembered are phonologically similar (e.g., Conrad, 1964). If inner speech is, in fact, the medium of representation in such tasks, the degradation due to phonological similarity is unexplained if no nodes "lower" than words are activated.

Thus, it appears that a pure lexical opacity view of inner speech will be unlikely to account for the data, and we will need to consider a less drastic form of abbreviation. As mentioned before, some discussions of inner speech suggest that not all components of words are phonologically encoded. This view is, in fact, quite consistent with MacKay's theory. Assume that, in inner speech, each word's lexical node and *some,* but not all, of its phonological nodes (syllables, syllabic constituents, phonemes, and features) become activated. If only some phonological nodes become active, these will tend to be nodes corresponding to the initial parts of words. The reason is to be found in the theory's mechanism for the storage of order in the linguistic sequence nodes. If Sequence Node A precedes Node B and both are immediate constituents of Sequence Node C, then B can never become activated until A has been activated, because when C is activated, it primes both A and B. However, because A precedes B, A inhibits B. The result is that priming builds up faster on A, causing it to become activated first, and leading to the selection of a content node in A's categorical domain. Once A and its corresponding content node have been activated, the theory assumes that A enters a period of self-inhibition, in effect, turning itself off and thus disinhibiting B and allowing B to be activated and to select its corresponding content node. Thus, if there are any activation failures, then either A and B, or B alone, will be left out. In other words, A cannot be eliminated without B's also being eliminated.

Consider what this means for the activation of phonological sequence nodes. If A and B are the initial and final syllables of a two-syllable word, and there is attenuation of processing in inner speech, the second syllable may never be activated. Similarly, at the next level in the hierarchy, the level dealing with syllabic constituents, we would expect to find that it is the rhyme portion of the syllable that is dropped, not the onset. In general, if there is incomplete activation of phonological nodes, it is the initial parts of words (the left branches in the phonological node hierarchies) that get through. This we will call the *partial-opacity hypothesis.*

If the partial-opacity hypothesis is correct, we expect to find two major differences between inner and overt speech errors. First, both phonological errors and whole-word errors involving phonologically related words should occur with a lower incidence in inner speech than in overt speech. When words are only partly represented phonologically, the interactions that result from phonological similarity will necessarily be fewer. Second, pure phonological errors in inner speech should be restricted largely to word-initial consonants, the onset portion of the first syllable. By *pure phonological error,* we mean a mispronunciation that creates either a nonword (e.g., "A bucket of blue *blug's* blood") or another word that is clearly the result of some phonological inter- action, such as "A bucket of blue bug's *bud."* Although *bud* is a word, it bears no semantic relation to any intended word. The error can be simply charac- terized as the deletion of /l/ from *blood.* These predicted differences between inner and overt slips can be contrasted with error phenomena that should not differ between them. Given the assumption of the partial-opacity hypothesis that the attenuation of activation is just phonological, then affix errors (e.g., shift of an affix, "black-backed bath brush—blacked-back bath brush") or se- mantically related word errors ("black-backed bath cloth") should be equally prevalent in inner and overt speech.

Thus, we have two contrasting views of abbreviation in inner speech, each associated with expectations about error patterns. To complete the picture, we mention a third hypothesis, the *full-specification hypothesis,* in which inner speech is associated with the full activation of all linguistic nodes. Here, we expect no differences between inner and overt slips because slips are regarded as a product of linguistic rather than motor processing.

Experiment 1 evaluated these hypotheses by comparing the inner slips that subjects report when mentally reciting tongue twisters with those that they report when reciting them aloud.

EXPERIMENT 1

Method

Subjects. Forty University of Rochester students from an introductory psychology class participated. All were native speakers of English.

Materials. The 20 phrases used are listed in Table 1. The first 13 phra- ses are tongue twisters; some are from traditional sources and others were constructed to follow tongue-twister patterns (see Kupin, 1979). Also included were five pseudo-tongue-twisters whose words bear clear similarity relations, but not the sort of relations leading to errors, and two non-tongue-twisters, phrases whose words bear no similarity relation. These latter two groups of phrases, especially the pseudo-tongue-twisters, were included to provide a weak test of the view that any reported inner slips are caused simply by subjects' acceding to the experiment's demand characteristics. If subjects report many inner slips on the pseudo-tongue-twisters—there should be very few overt slips to these stimuli—then one would be suspicious of the reported inner slips on the actual tongue twisters. Each phrase was printed on a single card with diacritical stress marks as shown in Table 1.

Procedure. Half the subjects (randomly determined) said the tongue twisters aloud and half imagined saying them. The instructions read to both groups of subjects are given below.

Overt Condition

Tongue twisters, as you may know, are short phrases that are difficult to say without making errors. In this experiment, you will be asked to say some phrases that may seem like tongue twisters in time with a metronome. Here's an example. *(A card is presented that contains the phrase "Lift the ládder, Léster.")* Each mark above the words means that you should try to coincide the

TABLE 1
Material Used in Experiment 1

Tongue twisters
Rúsh the wáshing, Rússell.
A sóldier's májor shoulder súrgery.
Lísten tó your lócal yókel yódel.
Bŕing back Bŕad's brand.
Gŕay géese gŕaze gŕacefully.
Thírty-séven sílver thístles.
A stewed sów's snout.
A búcket of blue bug's blood.
A próper cópper cóffee pot.
A black-bácked báth brúsh.
I think I've seen a single thong.
Bláckbéard's black béard.
Dáve dŕove the dúmptrúck.

Pseudo-tongue-twisters
My níce néw níghtshírt.
Séveral Símple Símons.
A péck of píckled péppers.
Móther mákes móst méals.
Bíll bínds bíg bóoks.

Non-tongue-twisters
Mány néw cándlestícks.
A tásty lémon cáke.

syllable of the word with a beat of the metronome. For each phrase, I will first read it slowly to you, indicating how you should time it with the metronome. Then, you should say it aloud, slowly using the same timing. Then, I will remove the card and speed up the metronome. You should then say the phrase four times in time with the metronome. Pause for four beats between repetitions. If you hear yourself make a mistake, *stop immediately* and report the mistake to me. Then, continue to the next repetition. For example, if you made a mistake on the third repetition, stop, report the error, and then go on to the fourth and final repetition. After these four repetitions, say the phrase one more time slowly. There will be one phrase for practice and an additional 20 phrases for you to do. I'll be taping the experiment so that I can record the errors that you make, if any. Any questions?

Inner Speech Condition

Imagine the word *ladder,* in particular the sound of the word. Can you hear it in your mind? Try it until you can. *(Subject reports being able to hear the word.)* Next, imagine the phrase "Lift the ladder, Lester." Try to hear the words as distinctly as possible. In this experiment, you will be asked to imagine some phrases that may seem like tongue twisters. Listen to the words as you imagine them, and report any errors that you hear. Try not to move your mouth or tongue as you imagine the phrases. You will be required to imagine each phrase in time with a metronome, like this. *(Card is presented to the subject that reads, "Lift the ládder, Léster.")* Each mark above the words means that you should try to coincide that syllable of the word with a beat of the metronome. For each phrase, I will first read it slowly to you, indicating how you should time it with the metronome. Then, you should say it aloud slowly, using the same timing. Then, I will remove the card and speed up the metronome. You should then *imagine* the phrase four times in time with the metronome. Pause for four beats between repetitions. If you detect an error *stop immediately,* and report it to me. Then, continue imagining the phrase beginning with the next repetition. *(The remainder of the instructions are identical to those in the corresponding section for the overt condition.)*

For both groups of subjects, the slow introductory repetition of phrases by the experimenter and then the subject was done at 0.8 stressed syllables per second. There were no errors at this rate. The rate for the four faster repetitions was 2.4 stressed syllables per second, a normal speaking rate. The 20 phrases were presented in random order.

Two aspects of the procedure should be noted. First, in both conditions, the subjects were repeating the phrases from memory (the card with the printed phrase had been removed). It turned out that the subjects had no trouble remembering the phrases; there was only one occasion on which a subject failed to repeat the phrase correctly in the slow overt repetition that concluded each trial. Second, in both conditions, the errors were detected and reported by the subject. Because this procedure is necessary in the inner speech condition it was required in the overt condition so that both conditions would reflect error-reporting biases. Of course, this does not mean that such biases are equal for the two conditions: we have no way to identify this bias in inner speech errors. We just felt that an imperfect control is better than none.

Results

As expected, both overt and inner slips were obtained, overt slips being reported more often (191) than inner slips (104). Nearly all of these errors were on the true tongue twisters for both inner speech (99 errors) and overt speech (187 errors). All subjects except two in the inner-speech condition reported errors, but only one subject reported more than 15. In the overt condition, all subjects except one reported errors, and three reported 15 or more errors.

Although there were clearly more overt than inner slips, there was very little difference in the variety of errors obtained. There were 67 distinct types of inner slips versus 72 types of overt slips. By a type, we mean a particular error, such as "blue bug—blue blug," as opposed to a token, a particular error event, such as subject three saying *blue blug* on the first repetition of the phrase. Of the 28 types that occurred with three or more tokens, 23 occurred as both inner and overt slips. Thus, despite the greater number of overt slip tokens, there was a great deal of overlap between inner and overt slips.

Table 2 presents a breakdown of inner and overt slips (both types and tokens) according to the size of the unit participating in the error. We should note that the lexical errors include any error in which a word or word stem is pronounced as another word in the phrase (e.g., "A bucket of blue bug's bug") or as a word from outside the phrase that is semantically related to one within the phrase (e.g., "A proper copper coffee pot—A proper copper coffee cup"). As mentioned earlier, an error such as "blue bug's bud" would be a phonological rather than lexical error. The table also provides a further breakdown of the

TABLE 2
Number of Tokens and Types of Inner and Overt Slips from Experiment 1

Unit size	Examples	Inner frequencies[a]	Overt frequencies[a]
Phoneme			
Initial consonant	"silver—thilver" "graze—gaze"	54 (32)	78 (27)
Medial consonant	"washing—wassing" "copper—coffer"	2 (1)	14 (7)
Final consonant	Brad's—Brack's" "blood—blug"	4 (4)	10 (7)
Vowel	"Russell—Roosell"	1 (1)	1 (1)
Syllable	"backed—backled"	2 (2)	0 (0)
Affix	"black—blacked" "mother—mothers"	6 (5)	7 (4)
Lexical	"soldier's—shoulder's" "yokel—local" "pot—cup"	35 (22)	81 (27)

[a]The number outside the parentheses is the number of error tokens obtained, and the number in parentheses is the number of types.

phoneme errors by type and location of the erroneous phoneme. Initial consonants were defined as those preceding the first vowel in a word, final consonants as those following the last vowel, and all others as medial consonants.

The relative percentages of the unit sizes are somewhat reminiscent of corresponding data from speech error collections in that single-phoneme and lexical errors predominate to a large extent. Also, initial consonant errors tend to predominate over other phoneme errors in speech error collections as they do here. The near absence of vowel errors in the data, however, is not typical. In our data, it undoubtedly reflects the fact that the stimulus phrases did not include tongue twisters that generate vowel errors (as happens when one says "toy boat" repeatedly). The table reveals principally that there is a strong reduction in the number of inner-slip tokens, but not types. The possible exceptions to this generalization are in the affix category, and in the positional distribution of consonant slips. (Here, we are ignoring the vowel and syllable categories as they have almost no errors.) With regard to the affix category, we can make a tentative claim that these errors are as prevalent in inner speech as in overt speech. Our claim is tentative because there are few errors in this category and because the range of affixes covered in the experiment was not extensive. Inner affix errors involved the regular possessive (three cases), the third-person singular present tense (two cases), and the regular past tense (one case).

In the distribution of consonant slips, there was a tendency for slips to be restricted to initial consonant positions to a greater extent in inner than in overt speech. For inner consonant errors, 90% of the tokens and 86.5% of the types involved consonants before the first vowel. In overt slips, these numbers were 76.5% and 65.9%, respectively, percentages that are marginally ($.05 < p < .10$) lower than their inner-speech counterparts. Because this difference is exactly the difference expected by the partial-opacity hypothesis, it is worth exploring.

Let us consider the possibility that the greater tendency to initial consonant errors in inner speech is simply due to an *error-detection bias* rather than an error-occurrence asymmetry. In this view, inner and overt speech generate slips of the same types with the same frequency. The process of detecting an error occurs by perceptual analysis of all available information, including, in the case of overt speech, auditory and kinesthetic feedback. For inner speech, the only available information is found in the verbal imagery (whatever that is) and perhaps in some minute kinesthetic feedback. If we further assume that this relative lack of information in inner speech makes it particularly difficult to "hear" anomalies that occur in noninitial parts of words, then the tendency for phonemic errors to be largely confined to initial positions is explained.

Although it is probably impossible to establish whether any differences between inner and overt errors are due to error occurrence or error detection, we feel that we can offer some arguments that the relative predominance of initial consonant errors in inner speech is not due to a detection bias of the sort described here.

Our first point concerns differences between lexical and phonemic errors. If the lexical errors are examined as if they were phonemic errors (e.g., if "local—yokel" is seen as an initial consonant substitution, and "brand—Brad" is seen as a final consonant deletion), we find no differences between inner and overt slips with regard to the distribution of consonant errors over positions (see Table 3). Here, there is no relative initialness effect for the inner slips. For inner slips, 49.1% of the tokens and 45.7% of the types are in the word's onset, compared with 51.8% and 43.5%, respectively, in the overt slips. This finding argues against a simple detection bias in which subjects are relatively unable to "hear" errors in noninitial positions in inner speech.

A similar point can be made about affix errors. The relevant affixes were all single phonemes (/s/, /z/, /t/, or /d/) occurring in word-final position. Yet these errors were reported about as often in inner and overt speech, again counter to the claim that anomalies in word-final position are hard to hear in inner speech. In general, the small word-position effect was restricted to the true phonological errors, errors in which segment-sized nonmorphological units were being manipulated.

Before we turn to a discussion of the results with respect to the hypotheses outlined in the introduction, there is one more asymmetry worth noting in the data. The large two-to-one advantage of overt slip tokens over inner slip tokens was not present on slips occurring on the first stress beat of the phrase (33 overt slip tokens, 30 inner slip tokens). This contrast is large and statistically significant for the other beat positions. For the second beat, there were 66 overt and 36 inner slips; for the last beat, 42 overt and 18 inner slips; and for the third (but not last) beat, 49 overt and 25 inner slips. Thus, we have another initialness effect, this time a phrase-initial effect. Like the word-initial effect for phonological slips, the phrase-initial effect is an instance of a relatively greater concentration of inner slips in initial positions.

Discussion

Probably the most important result of the experiment was the qualitative similarity of inner and overt slips. The same types of errors were obtained for

TABLE 3
Number of Consonant Error Types and Tokens as a Function
of Word Position for Lexical Errors Analyzed as if They Were
Phonemic Errors

	Consonant position		
	Initial	Medial	Final
Inner	26 (16)	19 (12)	8 (7)
Overt	72 (20)	48 (13)	19 (13)

the most part. There were, however, almost twice as many overt as inner slips, and there were tendencies for inner slips to occur relatively more often in the initial part of phrases and for inner phonological slips to occur in word onsets.

These results rule out the lexical opacity hypothesis, the hypothesis that inner speech involves the rehearsal of lexical, but not phonological, information, or, to use network activation terms, that it involves the activation of lexical but not phonological nodes. The presence of many phonological errors in word-initial positions shows that at least some phonological encoding processes occur in inner speech. The lexical slips in inner speech were also strongly phonologically motivated (e.g., "local—yokel"). In fact, only two inner lexical slips ("pot—cup" and "yodel—strudel") and two overt slips ("pot—cup" occurring twice) could be ascribed to nonphonological causes.

The two remaining hypotheses, also run into difficulty as complete accounts of the data. The full-specification hypothesis, in which all linguistic levels participate fully in inner speech, is contradicted by the finding that some kinds of inner slips in certain word and phrase positions were much less likely than the corresponding overt slips. To salvage this hypothesis, one would have to appeal to some form of detection bias. Such a bias would have to be sensitive to word and phrase position and linguistic level.

The partial-opacity hypothesis, in which some parts of the phonological level (primarily word onsets) are activated in addition to the lexical level, accounts for many features of the data, particularly the word-initial bias for inner phonological errors and the reduction in phonologically mediated lexical errors in inner speech. These latter slips should be less frequent because the lessened activity of the phonological level would reduce the interactions among the phonologically related words of the tongue twister. For example, the words *yokel* and *local* are confusing only if more than their initial consonants are activated. In fact, the only errors that should not be diminished in inner speech according to this hypothesis are semantically caused lexical errors and affix errors. Although there were very few errors in these categories (two semantic inner slips, two semantic overt slips, six affix inner slips and seven affix overt slips), there is, in support of the hypothesis, no evidence of an attenuation in inner speech.

The partial-opacity hypothesis as specified above cannot, however, account for the finding that inner slips were not reduced in the case of the first stress beat of a phrase. There seems to be a relatively full specification of the initial part of the phrase as revealed in the inner slips occurring there. Thus, we will have to consider a modification of this hypothesis.

Earlier we suggested that the word-initial effect might be expected from that aspect of MacKay's theory in which the activation of constituent-final nodes is contingent on that of constituent-initial nodes. Hence, if there are some nodes that do not become activated, these will tend to be constituent-final, or right-branching, nodes, the ones leading to noninitial parts of words. It turns out that this notion of contingent activation can explain both the word-initial and the phrase-initial effects in inner slips, and so, in the following discussion, we consider this explanation in detail.

Consider Figure 1 again, which presents the content nodes for the tongue twister "thirty-seven silver thistles," from the highest phrase node representing the entire phrase down to the phoneme level. Recall that each content node is activated by the activation of a particular sequence node, starting with a sequence node for the entire noun phrase. Thus, in the model, the successful activation of a given content node, j, depends on the activation of a set of *predecessor nodes,* nodes on which j's activation is contingent. This set includes both content and sequence nodes, and the number of them depends on the location of the node under consideration. The number of predecessor nodes, $N(j)$, turns out to be exactly

$$N(j) = 1 + 2l + 4r$$

where l and r are the number of left- and right-branching nodes, respectively, leading to j. Let us work through an example. To activate the content node for the syllable /ty/ in *thirty,* the following nodes must all be activated first: (1) the NP sequence node; (2) the content node for the entire phrase; (3) the sequence node corresponding to *thirty-seven* (syntactic category *quantifier*); (4) the actual constituent *thirty-seven;* (5) the sequence node corresponding to *thirty;* (6) the actual content node for *thirty;* (7) the sequence node for the initial syllable; (8) the syllable /θ ə^r/; and (9) the sequence node for a second syllable.[2] Thus, to activate /ty/, which is two left branches and one right branch from the top, we need to activate $1 + 2 \times 2 + 4 \times 1 = 9$ predecessors.

Now, let us assume that the difference between inner and overt speech is that, in overt speech, a given node always become activated if its predecessors do, whereas in inner speech, there is a small chance, p, that a node will fail to be activated in spite of its predecessors' being activated. There are several mechanisms by which this could happen in the theory (e.g., diminished priming and higher thresholds), but the exact mechanism is not of concern here. In any case, the result is that, in inner speech, the chance that a particular content node j will activate is $(1-p)^{N(j)}$.

Table 4 shows the probability that the phoneme content nodes in "thirty-seven silver thistles" will be activated if p is .05. There are several things worth noting about this calculation. One is that, even though p is small, its effects accumulate so that many of the phoneme nodes have a severely reduced chance of activation. However, the main point is that approximately the right sort of abbreviation results. The initial parts of words are retrieved more effectively than noninitial parts (the mean probability of activation for initial, medial, and final consonants is .56, .45, and .42, respectively), and in addition, the initial parts of the phrase have greater mean activation probabilities associated with their phonemes than the remainder of the phrase (.57, .48, .48, and .42 for the first through fourth words, respectively). One should note, as well, that the affix for the plural in *thistles* is stronger than the other phonemes in

---

[2]The reason that the content node for /θ ə^r/ must become activated is that it serves to deactivate the sequence node for the first syllable, which has been inhibiting the sequence node for the second syllable.

TABLE 4
Calculation of Activation Probabilities for Phonemes in
"Thirty-Seven Silver Thistles"

	θ	$\mathrm{ə^r}$	t	y	s	e	v	ə	n
N(j)	9	11	11	13	11	15	17	13	15
Activation probability (p = .05)	.63	.57	.57	.51	.57	.46	.42	.51	.46

	S	I	l	v	$\mathrm{ə^r}$	θ	I	s	ə	l	z
N(j)	11	15	17	13	15	15	19	21	17	19	13
Activation probability (p = .05)	.57	.46	.42	.52	.46	.46	.38	.34	.42	.38	.51

the word, despite its word- and phrase-final position. The reason is that grammatical affixes occupy a high position in the content node hierarchy, a position reflecting their status as morphemes. Finally, it should be noted that, although the probability of activating phoneme nodes is reduced, no node is expressly prohibited from becoming activated in this account of inner speech. As a result, there is no error type that is categorically impossible in inner speech. This result allows us to understand the finding that inner-speech errors were just about as diverse as overt errors as indexed by the number of types exhibited, in spite of the large differences in the actual number of error tokens.

Thus, we see that much of the pattern of abbreviation in inner speech can be explained by the hierarchical left-to-right nature of language. Lower level nodes and nodes that occur later in sequences depend on the activation of higher and earlier nodes. Hence, any attenuation in the processing prevents the activation of lower and later nodes.

In the next section of the chapter we apply this view of the relation between inner and overt speech to the question of practice, specifically to the effect of mentally or overtly practicing tongue twisters on error probability.

PRACTICE, MENTAL AND PHYSICAL

It is obvious to everyone that practice helps eliminate production errors. Consider what would be likely to happen if a speaker were to practice saying, "The sixth sick sheik's sixth sheep's sick" for 100 trials. For the first few trials, a correct rendition would be impossible—this is one of the hardest English tongue twisters were composed! However, by about the 30th trial, error-free performance would be the rule. An informal characterization of the learning process might be as follows. During the first one or two trials, there is difficulty remembering the phrase. It is close to memory span in length, and thus, many of the early errors would seem to the speaker to be due to uncertainty about exactly what the phrase is. Next would come a phase in which errors are common but are clearly production errors. The speaker would "know" the phrase but be unable to recite it at a normal speaking rate. Finally, there would be a period in which errors are rare, but practice would nonetheless bring about increasing speed, fluency, and automaticity. These three "stages" in practice are often proposed in the literature on skill acquisition (e.g., Fitts & Posner, 1967) and coincide with our own impressions when we actually performed this task.

Our concern here is primarily with the second stage, during which there are errors of production that are gradually reduced with practice. Within the framework of MacKay's theory, we propose two accounts of how practice reduces production errors. The first, which we call the *exercise hypothesis,* hearkens back to Thorndyke's law of exercise (1898). The basic idea is that errors occur because the connections among the content nodes are weak; that is, the priming delivered along these connections is less than it should be. Practice strengthens the connections and thus gradually eliminates errors.

In MacKay's theory, however, connection strength is a nonlinear function of practice. It has a maximum value, and its increase when below this maximum is a negatively accelerated function of practice. Frequently used connections, such as those between features, phonemes, syllables, and most words are assumed to be near maximum strength and so do not really benefit from practice. It is the higher level syntactic connections, those among phrasal content nodes and lexical content nodes, that are not often used and hence can benefit from practice (How often have you said the phrase "silver thistles"?). Thus, practicing a phrase changes the connection strengths among the syntactic content nodes, not the phonological ones.

One should also note that a set of weak connections is likely to have a greater variance in strength than a set of strong ones. All the members in a set of strong connections are near the maximum in strength, and hence, they have nearly the same strength. The strengths of weak connections can vary to a much greater extent. This large variance in the strength of weak connections, as well as their weakness *per se,* is what contributes to the errors in reciting unpracticed tongue twisters according to this hypothesis. This interpretation of MacKay's theory is similar to a claim made by Baars and Motley (1976), who argued that phonological slips can result from uncertainty in word order, which, in MacKay's theory, is coded in these higher level connections. The effect of practice is thus to bring all the weak high-level connections closer to maximum. With all the relevant connections near maximum strength, there is much less error variance in the activation process, and hence, errors are rare.

The second hypothesis regarding the effect of practice assigns a role to feedback in the learning process and therefore has its antecedents in Thorndyke's law of effect rather than in the law of exercise. This *feedback hypothesis* states that practice informs the system about the errors that it needs to prevent. When an error is detected, connection strengths are adjusted by some algorithm so as to decrease the likelihood of the error. If no error occurs, one could assume that all of the involved connections are strengthened or that nothing occurs. Recent work in learning has identified powerful algorithms for changing connection strengths in response to feedback (e.g., Hinton & Sejnowski, 1983; Rumelhart, Hinton, & Williams, 1986). For example, Rumelhart *et al.* showed how feedback delivered to a set of nodes can be used to adjust not only the connections leading directly to those nodes, but also connections leading to nodes leading to the informed nodes, and so on.

When a speaker makes a slip and detects it, the production system has very good feedback about what part of the network went wrong. For example, if one were to say "thirty-seven *thilver* thistles," the problem can be located in the relative degree of priming for the content nodes for initial /s/ and initial /θ/ (using the terms of MacKay's theory). Exactly what connections are changed in response to this identification depends on what learning rule is adopted and the assumptions about existing connections and their properties. If we stay within the confines of MacKay's theory, we would want to restrict modifications to the connections among the higher level content nodes. So, in this example, we might strengthen the link from *silver thistles* to *silver* and decrease the one from *silver thistles* to *thistles*. The result would be that the network would pay more "attention" to the word *silver* and relatively less to *thistles* and would perhaps keep the /θ/ from intruding into *silver*. Regardless of the specifics of the changes, however, the feedback hypothesis associates learning with the information provided by errors, and in this way, it differs markedly from the exercise hypothesis.

The feedback and exercise hypothesis lead to different predictions regarding the effectiveness of mentally practicing tongue twisters. Given that inner speech provides demonstrably different error feedback from overt speech, we would expect from the feedback hypothesis that mental practice would not be very effective in eliminating errors or, more specifically, that mental practice would not lead to immunity from error during overt recitation. This prediction obtains because we have solid evidence from the first experiment that subjects report only about half as many inner slips as overt slips. Thus, the feedback obtained during inner practice does not adequately inform the system about the difficulties it would experience during overt recitation. Note that this prediction does not depend on inner slips' being truly less frequent than overt ones; it holds even if they are simply harder to detect. In both cases, feedback is deficient.

The exercise hypothesis predicts that inner practice should be as effective as overt practice. Even if inner speech is abbreviated in the way that we outlined earlier, this abbreviation does not have a great deal of impact on the activation of the higher syntactic nodes, and it is the connections among these nodes that require exercise according to the exercise hypothesis.

In Experiment 2, we tested whether inner practice with tongue twisters facilitates their overt recitation. Specifically, we manipulated the type of practice (inner or overt), the amount of practice (0, 4, or 16 recitations) and the type of test (two overt recitations or two inner recitations).

EXPERIMENT 2

Method

Subjects. Seventy-two subjects participated, from the same population as in the first experiment.

Materials. Twelve phrases, including eleven tongue twisters and one pseudo-tongue-twister ("Lift the ladder, Lester") were selected from the phrases used in the first experiment. Each was printed on a card with stress marking as before.

Design. There were 12 distinct conditions created by crossing the three experimental factors of interest, practice type (two levels: inner and overt), amount of practice (three levels: 0, 4, and 16 trials), and test type (two levels: inner and overt). These were all manipulated in a within-subject fashion. Each subject was tested on all 12 phrases, each phrase associated with a single condition. The allocation of phrases to conditions was counterbalanced so that, across a group of 12 subjects, each phrase occurred in each condition. The testing of 72 subjects thus resulted in six replications of the design.

Procedure. Each subject was presented with the 12 phrases in random order. The experimenter read each phrase aloud in time with a metronome at 0.8 stressed syllables per second, and then the subject read it back at the same rate. After this, the card containing the phrase was turned over. On the back of the card were specified the type and amount of practice and the type of test for that phrase and subject. The experimenter increased the metronome rate to 2.4 stressed syllables per second, and the subject followed the instructions for practicing the phrase. Earlier, the subjects had been instructed on the nature of inner speech in a way similar to that in the first experiment. If the phrase was to be overtly practiced, the subject said the tongue twister aloud in time with the metronome for the designated number of recitations. The subject was instructed to pause for four beats between recitations. If the phrase was to be practiced via inner speech, the same procedure was followed except that the recitation was mental. For conditions in which zero practice trials were designated, the procedure moved directly into the test phase.

Following the designated practice, if any, the subjects were tested. They had to recite the phrase twice (with a four-beat pause as before) at 2.4 stressed syllables per second, either mentally, or overtly, as indicated on the back of the card. During the test recitations, the subjects were directed to report immediately any errors that they detected, as in the first experiment. Finally, following the test, the subjects slowly repeated each phrase aloud to make sure that it was remembered.

Each subject was given three practice trials before doing the 12 experimental phrases. The practice trials represented the conditions of mental practice with a mental test, mental practice with an overt test, and overt practice with a mental test.

Results

Inner and overt slips were obtained on all the tongue twisters, and none was obtained on the pseudo-tongue-twister. The number of errors occurring in the test phase as a function of conditions is presented in Table 5. As in the first experiment, inner slips (that is, errors reported during the mental test conditions) were much less frequent than overt slips (errors reported during the overt test conditions). To evaluate the effect of the type and amount of practice, separate analyses of variance were done for the inner and overt test conditions. These analyses used the error totals per condition per replication as the dependent variable.

For an overt test, overt practice led to fewer slips than inner practice: $F(1,5) = 9.15$; but more important, the type of practice interacted with the amount of practice: $F(2,10) = 4.52$. Overt practice successfully reduced overt errors: $F(2,10) = 10.99$; but inner practice did not: $F(2,10) < 1$.

In the inner test conditions, the pattern was different. Both inner and overt practice reduced errors to an equal extent: $F(2,10) = 11.67$. After 16 practice trials, inner slips were almost completely eliminated by either inner or overt practice.

Although this experiment yielded fewer errors than the previous one, it is possible to get additional data from it regarding the abbreviation of inner speech by looking at the inner and overt slips obtained in the test phase when

TABLE 5
Number of Errors Reported in the Test Phase
of Experiment 2

Condition	Amount of practice (trials)		
	0	4	16
Overt practice Overt test	33	20	9
Inner practice Overt test	28	33	31
Overt practice Inner test	9	9	1
Inner practice Inner test	12	6	2

there was no practice. The two principal findings from the first experiment were a tendency for inner slips to involve the initial beat of phrases and a (marginal) tendency for consonant inner slips to occur in word onsets. Both of these tendencies are present in the data of Experiment 2. For inner slips, 28.0% of the errors occurred on the phrase-initial beat, compared with only 13.8% of the overt slips. Initial consonant slips accounted for 83.3% of the tokens and 77.8% of the types of consonant slips in inner speech. For overt speech, initial consonant slips comprised 67.5% of the tokens and 64.0% of the types of consonant slips. Thus, the results of the second experiment provide additional support for the view that inner speech is relatively stronger in phrase- and word-initial positions.

Discussion

The results support the feedback hypothesis. Inner practice, which we argued provides inappropriate feedback for an overt test, did not aid performance on the overt test. In contrast, overt practice, which provides exactly the right feedback for the overt test, led to about a threefold reduction in errors in overt recitation. The exercise hypothesis cannot account the failure of inner practice. According to the exercise hypothesis, inner practice should have been effective because the practice "exercises" the weak connections among the phrasal and lexical nodes to the same extent as overt practice does.

The finding that inner practice is effective in reducing inner slips is also consistent with the feedback hypothesis. Feedback delivered by inner practice can be seen as appropriate *to the task of inner recitation*. Inner practice informs the system of the most likely inner slips, thus enabling it to learn effectively.

The finding that overt practice reduces inner slips can be explained by the feedback hypothesis only if an additional assumption is granted. This assumption is that the feedback obtained from overt slips is somehow appropriate for inner recitation. We think this is a reasonable assumption, given the first experiment's results. For every category of error, overt slips were more frequent than or as frequent as inner slips. In other words, there is no special kind of error that shows up preferentially in inner speech. Thus, the feedback from overt recitation is likely to be more than adequate to the task of informing the system about potential inner slips.

Although the feedback hypothesis can account for the observed pattern of transfer from practice to test conditions, there are limitations to the generality of this conclusion. Our finding that inner practice does not prevent overt errors is probably limited to the second stage of skill acquisition, the stage at which the phrase is memorized but there are still many production errors, rather than the first stage, where the phrase is still being memorized. Because all of our phrases were short enough to be memorized on first hearing, this first stage was not even investigated. It is possible that the inner practice of tongue twisters would be effective in reducing overt errors if the tongue twisters are long enough to be difficult to remember. In this case, inner practice would function as rehearsal does in serial learning, leading to better retention of the words and their order. Such a result would be consistent with our view of inner speech. Inner speech is hypothesized to be unabbreviated at the lexical, and higher, levels for the most part, and thus, the feedback at this level is informative for building up a representation of the phrase's word order. Where inner speech is assumed to be abbreviated, at the lower phonological levels, there is deficient feedback, but we claim that this feedback is not important for learning word order, only for learning about potential difficulties associated with the words' sounds.

A clear situation where inner practice does transfer to overt speech production was found by MacKay (1981). In this study, bilingual English–German speakers mentally or overtly practiced (non-tongue-twister) sentences in one language and then overtly recited translations of the practiced sentences in the other language and control sentences. Mental practice was as effective as overt practice in reducing the time to recite the translations. This result is consistent with our view of inner speech if we extend our claim that inner speech is not abbreviated at the higher linguistic levels to include the semantic level. Thus, inner practice should affect performance on semantically identical sentences to the same extent as overt practice.

Although our discussion has been limited to the mental practice of speech, we can speculate that our conclusions apply to mental practice in general. The claim is that mental practice can reduce errors in overt performance to the extent that the mental activity is not substantially abbreviated relative to overt activity *with respect to the error-generating mechanisms*. When this is the case, mental practice provides the right kind of feedback—feedback that informs the system about the kinds of errors that would happen in the overt activity. Research on mental practice has produced many contradictory results on its effectiveness (for reviews, see Drowatsky, 1975; MacKay, 1981; Richardson, 1965), but one general conclusion is that, for mental practice to be helpful, either the activity must be simple or the participant must have some familiarity with it. Whether these findings can be understood in our framework is a question that can be answered only by a determination of the components of each skill and the extent to which these components are abbreviated when the skill is performed covertly.

CONCLUSIONS

In this chapter we have investigated the nature of inner speech and found it to be closely related to overt speech. Our view, derived primarily from a model proposed by MacKay (1982), is that inner speech consists of a subset of the processes involved in overt speech, specifically that it consists of the activation of syntactic and some, but not all, phonological nodes in a hierarchical network. The pattern of abbreviation found in our first experiment can be accounted for by the model's assumption that each node's activation is contingent on the activation of a set of predecessor nodes and by an additional assumption that the difference between inner and overt speech is that, in inner speech, there is some small chance that each node will fail to activate, given the activation of its predecessors. As a result, nodes representing lower linguistic levels and nodes representing constituents later in a sequence will tend to be dropped more in inner than in overt speech.

We further showed that this abbreviated character of inner speech diminishes its effectiveness for practicing phonologically confusing phrases. Feedback regarding potential slips is seen to be deficient in inner speech relative to overt speech, and thus, inner practice does not help prevent slips in the overt repetition of such phrases.

When we say that inner speech is abbreviated in a particular way, we do not wish to claim that it is necessarily abbreviated in this way. We simply found this to be true in our experiments. Undoubtedly, people have some flexibility in how complete their inner speech is. It may be quite abstract, with very little phonological information present, or it could be fully specified at the linguistic levels. However, we expect that full linguistic specification will probably trigger a great deal of motor activity as well—a kind of soundless whispering. Ensuring the full activation of all linguistic nodes will strongly prime motor nodes, and because of random factors, some will activate.

Just how complete inner speech is very likely depends on its function and the conditions under which it is produced. For example, slow articulation rates probably contribute to a fuller specification. In MacKay's theory, priming takes time to accumulate, and so the extra time associated with a slow rate could overcome the hypothesized attenuation of activity in inner speech. Similarly, if inner speech is being used to retain a list of words for recall, it may be more abbreviated than if one is rehearsing, say, the recitation of a poem. If people have control over the levels that are activated, they can influence the kind of feedback they get and, consequently, the effectiveness of the rehearsal.

In addition to variations within a speaker, there are undoubtedly individual differences in the extent to which inner speech is abbreviated. Dell (1978) conducted a small experiment similar to our Experiment 1 and found that inner slips were about as frequent as overt slips. This finding contrasts with the findings reported here, in which inner slips were less frequent. The subjects in Dell (1978) were psychology graduate students, most of whom were studying short-term memory. One could argue that this subject population was either quite experienced with verbal imagery or at least was sensitized to its importance, a condition leading to less abbreviation than would be expected in a less sophisticated population. We believe that the results of the present experiments are more typical, but we must acknowledge the difference. We can, however, predict that, if a group of subjects produces unabbreviated inner speech (as many inner as overt slips), then inner practice should transfer effective to an overt test.

A final point we wish to make concerns the inobservability of inner speech. Despite the electromyographic potentials that may accompany inner speech, its basic nature is mental. We know inner speech by our experience of it. As a result, much research on inner speech uses the methodology of introspection.

Subjects report on the contents of their consciousness. Although introspective techniques are not abjured by today's researchers as they once were, they are, nonetheless, viewed critically. The recent debate about the nature and function of visual imagery has fueled discussion of these issues and has resulted in more sophisticated methods for investigating imagery that go beyond simple introspection (see Kosslyn, 1980, for a review). By focusing on subjects' reported inner slips, we are, to some extent, returning to the bad old days. We are simply taking the subjects' word regarding their slips. Thus, we must acknowledge that differences in the properties of inner and overt slips do not clearly establish differences in the properties of inner and overt speech. We can, instead, appeal only to the plausibility of this assumption and that of our theoretical account of the difference. Ultimately, the validation of our hypotheses must await research that makes use of what Kosslyn (1980) termed the "quantification of introspection," in which the hypothesized mental processes are predicted to have behavioral consequences beyond introspective report. Our second experiment and other research work looking at the effect of inner speech on later overt performance (e.g., Butterworth & Whittaker, 1980; MacKay, 1981) fall into this methodological category and, thus, may help provide better clues to the nature of the voice inside the head.

ACKNOWLEDGMENT

This research was supported by National Science Foundation Grant BNS-84-6886. The author wishes to thank Susan Garnsey and Padraig O'Seaghdha for comments on the manuscript.

REFERENCES

Anderson, R. D. (1982). Speech imagery is not always faster than visual imagery. *Memory and Cognition, 10,* 371–380.

Baars, B. J., & Motley, M. T. (1976). Spoonerisms as sequencer conflicts: Evidence from artificially elicited spoonerisms. *American Journal of Psychology, 83,* 467–484.

Baddeley, A. D., Thomson, N., & Buchanan, M. (1975). Word-length and the structure of short-term memory. *Journal of Verbal Learning and Verbal Behavior, 14,* 575–589.

Bock, J. K. (19820. Towards a cognitive psychology of syntax: Information processing contributions to sentence formulation. *Psychological Review, 89,* 1–47.

Brown, R., & McNeill, D. (1966). The tip of the tongue phenomenon. *Journal of Verbal Learning and Verbal Behavior, 5,* 325–337.

Butterworth, B., & Whittaker, S. (1980). Peggy Babcock's relatives. In G. E. Stelmach & J. Requin (Eds.), *Tutorials in motor behavior.* Amsterdam: North-Holland.

Conrad, R. (1964). Acoustic confusions in immediate memory. *British Journal of Psychology, 55,* 75–84.

Cutler, A. (1981). The reliability of speech error data. *Linguistics, 19,* 561–582.

Dell, G. S. (1978). Slips of the mind. In M. Paradis (Ed.), *The Fourth LACUS Forum* (pp. 69–75). Columbia, SC: Hornbeam Press.

Dell, G. S. (1980). *Phonological and lexical encoding in speech production: An analysis of naturally occurring and experimentally elicited slips of the tongue.* Unpublished doctoral dissertation, University of Toronto.

Dell, G. S. (1985). Positive feedback in hierarchical connectionist models: Applications to language production. *Cognitive Science, 9,* 3–23.

Dell, G. S. (1986). A spreading-activation theory of retrieval in sentence production. *Psychological Review, 93,* 283–321.

Dell, G. S., & Reich, P. A. (1981). Stages in sentence production: An analysis of speech error data. *Journal of Verbal Learning and Verbal Behavior, 20,* 611–629.

Drowatsky, J. N. (1975). *Motor learning: Principles and practice.* Minneapolis: Burgess.

Ellis, A. W. (1980). Errors in speech and short-term memory: The effects of phonemic similarity and syllable position. *Journal of Verbal Learning and Verbal Behavior, 19,* 624–634.

Fay, D., & Cutler, A. (1977). Malapropisms and the structure of the mental lexicon. *Linguistic Inquiry, 3,* 505–520.

Fitts, P. M., & Posner, M. I. (1967) *Human performance.* Belmont, CA: Brooks-Cole.

Foss, D. J., & Hakes, D. T. (1978). *Psycholinguistics.* Englewood Cliffs, NJ: Prentice-Hall.

Fromkin, V. A. (1971). The non-anomalous nature of anomalous utterances. *Language, 41,* 27–52.

Garrett, M. G. (1975). The analysis of sentence production. In G. H. Bower (Ed.), *The psychology of learning and motivation* (pp. 133–177). New York: Academic Press.

Harley, T. (1984). A critique of top-down independent levels models of speech production: Evidence from non-plan-internal speech errors. *Cognitive Science, 8,* 191–219.

Hinton, G. E., & Sejnowski, T. J. (1983). Optimal perceptual inference. *Proceedings of the IEEE Computer Society Conference on Computer Vision and Pattern Recognition,* Washington, DC, 448–453.

Hockett, C. F. (1967). Where the tongue slips, there slip I. In *To Honor Roman Jakobson* (pp. 910–936). The Hague: Mouton.

Hotopf, W. H. N. (1980). Slips of the pen. In I. V. Frith (Ed.), *Cognitive processes in spelling* (pp. 287–307). London: Academic Press.

Jacobson, E. (1930). Electrical measurements of neuromuscular states during mental activities: Imagination of movement involving skeletal muscle. *American Journal of Physiology, 91,* 567–608.

Kosslyn, S. M. (1980). *Image and mind.* Cambridge: Harvard University Press.

Kupin, J. (1979). *Tongue twisters as a source of information about speech production.* Unpublished doctoral dissertation, University of Connecticut.

Landauer, T. K. (1962). Rate of implicit speech. *Perceptual and Motor Skills, 15,* 646.

Lashley, K. S. (1951). The problem of serial order in behavior. In L. A. Jeffress (Ed.), *Cerebral mechanisms in behavior* (pp. 112–136). New York: Wiley.

MacKay, D. G. (1970). Spoonerisms: The structure of errors in the serial order of speech. *Neuropsychologia, 8,* 323–350.

MacKay, D. G. (1981). The problem of rehearsal or mental practice. *Journal of Motor Behavior, 13,* 274–285.

MacKay, D. G. (1982). The problems of flexibility, fluency, and speed-accuracy tradeoff in skilled behavior. *Psychological Review, 89,* 483–506.

MacKay, D. G. (1987). *The organization of perception and action: A theory for language and other cognitive skills.* New York: Springer.

Marslen-Wilson, W., & Welsh, A. (1978). Processing interactions and lexical access during spoken word recognition in continuous speech. *Cognitive Psychology, 10,* 29–63.

Richardson, A. (1965). Mental practice: A review and discussion. *The Research Quarterly, 38,* 95–107.

Rumelhart, D. E., Hinton, G. E., & Williams, R. J. (1986). Learning internal representations by error propagation. In D. E. Rumelhart & J. L. McClelland (Eds.), *Parallel distributed processing: Explorations in the microstructure of cognition.* Cambridge: MIT Press.

Shattuck-Hufnagel, S. (1979). Speech errors as evidence for a serial-ordering mechanism in sentence production. In W. E. Cooper & E. C. T. Walker (Eds.), *Sentence processing: Psycholinguistic studies presented to Merrill Garrett* (pp. 295–342). Hillside, NJ: Erlbaum.

Sokolov, A. N. (19720. *Inner speech and thought.* New York: Plenum Press.

Stemberger, J. P. (1982). *The lexicon in a model of language production.* Unpublished doctoral dissertation, University of California—San Diego.

Stemberger, J. P. (1985). An interactive activation model of language production. In A. Ellis (Ed.), *Progress in the psychology of language* (Vol. 1, pp. 143–186). London: Erlbaum.

Sternberg, S., Monsell, S., Knoll, R. L., & Wright, L. E. (1978). The latency and duration of rapid movement sequences: Comparisons of speech and typing. In G. E. Stelmach (Ed.), *Information processing in motor control and learning* (pp. 117–152). New York: Academic Press.

Thorndyke, E. L. (1898). Animal intelligence: An experimental study of the associative processes in animals. *Psychological Monographs, 2*(4, Whole No. 8).

Vygotsky, L. S. (1962). *Thought and language.* Cambridge: MIT Press.

Watson, J. B. (1919). *Psychology from the standpoint of a behaviorist.* Philadelphia: Lippincott.

Weber, R. J., & Castleman, J. (1970). The time it takes to imagine. *Perception and Psychophysics, 8,* 165–168.

Wells, R. (1951). Predicting slips of the tongue. *Yale Scientific Magazine, 3,* 9–30.

11

Error-Minimizing Mechanisms
Boosting or Editing?

Mark E. Mattson and Bernard J. Baars

Introduction

    1. "This salt is pop ... I mean this popcorn is salty."

Speech errors can have unpleasant consequences. Errors like Example 1 may be a source of amusement, but others may be more costly. Presumably, people have developed methods for minimizing the likelihood of errors and for minimizing their consequences. There are two general ways that errors can be minimized: errors can be edited, or the correct response can be boosted. *Editing* is defined as a reduction in the probability of an erroneous plan or the correction of an error when a mismatch with the planned output is detected. *Boosting* is an increase in the probability of a correct response. Consider an analogy to signal detection theory: The signal-to-noise ratio can be improved by boosting the signal (the intended action plan) or by cutting the noise (competing-action plans that may lead to errors). Enhancing the signal-to-noise ratio either way will lead to fewer errors.

    The goal of this chapter is to analyze the evidence for error-minimizing mechanisms in speech production. First, the basic data on error minimization

MARK E. MATTSON • Social Sciences Division, LL916, Fordham University, New York, New York 10023. **BERNARD J. BAARS** • The Wright Institute, 2728 Durant Avenue, Berkeley, California 94704.

Experimental Slips and Human Error: Exploring the Architecture of Volition, edited by Bernard J. Baars. Plenum Press, New York, 1992.

are presented: people edit their speech overtly, as in Example 1 above. There is also a great deal of evidence for covert processes that influence the likelihood of errors. Several theories that attempt to account for these error-minimization phenomena are reviewed next, concluding with our current approach. This approach is the product of more than a decade of work on these issues.

ERROR MINIMIZATION IN SPEECH PRODUCTION

A number of facts must be accounted for by any complete theory of speech production. Some facts that are specifically relevant to error minimization are presented in this section.

First, people make overt errors, so error minimization is not perfect. This states the obvious: because people make speech errors, error minimization is not error elimination.

Second, people sometimes edit their errors overtly. The most straightforward case for error minimization is the fact that there is overt error detection and self-correction, as in Example 1. Nooteboom (1980) analyzed the overt-self-correction reported by Meringer (1908) for lexical and phonological errors. He found that 64% of the errors were corrected, that the utterance was usually aborted at the word boundary following the error, and that corrections usually began with the word boundary preceding the error. Levelt (1983) performed a detailed analysis of the self-corrections observed when subjects described dot patterns, including detecting the error, interrupting the utterance, and making the repair. Speech was usually interrupted as soon as the error was detected, except that correct words (i.e., words that were not themselves in error) were often completed. Interruption often involved the use of an "editing term," such as "uh," indicating that an error had been detected. More recently, van Wijk and Kempen (1987) argued that there are two mechanisms with different rules for repairing an error: "reformulation," in which a new syntactic structure is constructed, and "lemma substitution," in which a substitution is made without changing the syntactic structure.

As Baars and Mattson (1981) pointed out, self-corrections and expressions of surprise at an error constitute strong evidence that the utterance has violated the actor's intention. There are obviously times when an intention is violated without overt recognition of that fact. But there may be unconscious error-minimizing mechanisms, so that conscious recognition of an error may not be necessary for error minimization.

Third, there are covert processes that minimize the likelihood of errors. It is less obvious that there are processes that cannot be directly observed that influence error probability, but taken together, the evidence that this is the case is compelling. First, Levelt (1983) noted the existence of covert repair (C-repairs), which are cases where a person used an editing term or repeated a correct word when there was no overt error. One interpretation of C-repairs is that the subject noted an error before it was executed, signaled detection of the error by using an editing term, and covertly corrected it before proceeding.

Editing terms without overt errors are only suggestive of error minimization, however, as there are alternative explanations. Speakers certainly pause and hedge sometimes when they have not yet decided what to say, for example (Goldman-Eisler, 1968).

Stronger evidence of covert error minimization comes from studies of speech errors induced in the laboratory. Table 1 summarizes the results of eight experimental studies that illustrate the normal slip-rate advantage (NSRA), that is, the fact that errors that conform to more of the rules of speech and usage are more likely to occur than closely matched errors that violate those rules. We find it convenient to refer to "good" errors (rule-conforming, normal errors) and "bad" errors (rule-violating errors) (without any ethical implications intended). Table 1 shows the references, the tasks, examples of the stimuli and the errors, and the probability of a spoonerism or a word exchange error per trial for "good" and "bad" errors. The stimulus is given first, and the arrow points to the predicted error. For example, Baars, Motley, and MacKay (1975, Experiment 1) presented their subjects with a series of word pairs, some of which were followed by a cue indicating that the previous word pair should be said out loud (see Chapter 6, this volume). Two cued word pairs are shown in Table 1: "darn bore" and "dart board." These were given on two matched stimulus lists, arranged so that, in each list, the matched target word pairs were preceded by the same phonological bias word pairs:

2.	ball doze	(phonological bias pair)
	bash door	(phonological bias pair)
	bean deck	(phonological bias pair)
	List A: darn bore List B: dart board	(cued target pairs)
	RESPOND	(cue to say previous pair)
	*barn door *bart doard	(predicted error)

Subjects made spoonerisms on about 12% of the target trials in this study. Despite the similarity between the matched target stimuli, exchange errors were significantly more likely when the error involved real words like "barn door" ("good" errors) than when it involved nonsense words like "bart" and "doard" ("bad" errors). Dell and Reich (1981) showed the same advantage for naturally occurring spoonerisms. This is our first example of the NSRA: Good errors were more likely than bad errors, so that covert processing seems to be affecting the likelihood of an error differentially in the two conditions. Either the bad errors were sometimes eliminated ("edited"), the good errors were made more likely ("boosted"), or both.

Baars *et al.* (1975, Experiment 2) provided some evidence that bad errors are eliminated. There were two conditions in this study. In one condition *all* of the stimulus words were nonsense, including the targets, and in the other condition, using the same target word pairs, some real-word fillers were added. If the subject made a spoonerism, half the targets produced lexical errors and the other half produced nonsense errors. When *all* of the stimulus words seen by the subjects were nonsense, there was no significant difference between

TABLE 1

Summary of Studies that Illustrate the Normal Slip Rate Advantage

Reference	Task	Good slip		Bad slip		
		Example	Prob/trial (%)	Example	Prob/trial (%)	
Baars, Motley, & MacKay, 1975, Exp. 1	Word pairs with phonological biasing	darn bore → barn door Lexical	17.7	dart board → bart doard Nonlexical	5.6	
Motley & Baars, 1975, Exp. 2 & 3	Word pairs with phonological biasing	Not published High phonological transition probability	38.4	Not published Low phonological transition probability	26.8 13.0	Exp 2 Exp 3
Motley, Baars, & Camden, 1981, Exp. 1	Word pairs with phonological biasing	ker hame → her came Correct syntax	42.0	ker hame → her came Incorrect syntax	18.0	
Motley, Camden, & Baars, 1981, Exp. 2	Word pairs with phonological biasing	tool carts → cool tarts Nontaboo	7.3	tool kits → cool tits Taboo	3.3	
Baars, 1977, Exp. 1	Two-phrase sentences with order confusion and reversal	She touched her nose and cut a flower. → She cut her nose and touched a flower. Socially appropriate	11.1	She rubbed her nose and picked a flower. → She picked her nose and rubbed a flower. Socially inappropriate	2.1	
		The woman heard the melody and remembered the story. → The woman remembered the melody and heard the story. Semantically good		The woman hummed the melody and told the story. → The woman told the melody and hummed the story. Semantically anomalous		
Baars & Mattson, 1981	Two-phrase questions with order confusion	Can you live peacefully before dying happily? → Yes, you can live happily before dying peacefully. Can be true	2.7	Can you live peacefully before dying quickly? → Yes, you can die peacefully before living quickly. Generically false	0.8	
Mattson, Baars, & Motley, 1985	Two-phrase sentences with reversal task	The wizard left the troll and saw the dwarf. → The wizard saw the troll and left the dwarf. Pronunciation normal	17.5	The wizard left the troll and chose the dwarf. → The wizard chose the troll and left the dwarf. Pronunciation awkward	5.5	

good lexical errors and bad nonsense errors. When some of the filler items were lexical, the number of nonsense errors dropped significantly below its previous rate. Apparently, the mere presence of lexical items in the presented list caused a drop in lexical slips.

Using the same phonological biasing technique, Motley and Baars (1975) established that "good" errors with high phonological transitional probabilities were more likely than "bad" errors with lower transitional probabilities. Further, Motley, Baars, and Camden (1981) showed that syntactically "good" errors were more frequent than syntactically "bad" ones; and Motley, Camden, and Baars (1981) showed that "good" socially acceptable errors were more frequent than "bad" socially taboo errors (see Table 1).

Baars (1977) presented subjects with two-phrase sentences, some of which were followed by a cue for the subject to say the sentence aloud with the phrase order reversed (Chapter 6, this volume). For example, if the cued stimulus sentence was "She touched her nose and cut a flower," the correct response was "She cut a flower and touched her nose." Each cued sentence was preceded by identical and reversed versions of itself, to enhance the subjects' uncertainty about the order of the phrases. This task led to exchanges of words between the phrases, as can be seen in Table 1. Baars (1977) found that subjects made more "good" word-exchange errors than bad ones, in which the outcome was anomalous or socially inappropriate. Using variations on the word-exchange-induction task, Baars and Mattson (1981) showed that "good," generically true, errors were more frequent than "bad," generically false or anomalous, errors. Finally, Mattson, Baars, and Motley (1985) showed that "good," easy-to-pronounce errors were more likely than "bad," hard-to-pronounce errors.

In Baars and Mattson (1981), the original analysis did not capture the distinction between true and false outcomes, so we review that study briefly here and present some further analysis. Eleven subjects heard and answered 54 questions, with the constraint that their answer must use the same words that were in the question. Each question had two phrases, and could be answered "yes" or "no" based on general knowledge. There were six variations on nine basic questions. Half the variations of each basic question had rough synonyms in each phrase, selected so that an exchange of these words would not radically change the meaning of the sentence. In Table 1, the "good" slip example has the rough synonyms *peacefully* and *happily*. The other half of the stimulus questions had a single different word, that, if exchanged, would change the meaning of the error answer significantly, mostly by making the answer anomalous. In Table 1, the "bad" slip example has *peacefully* and *quickly*. The analysis in Baars and Mattson (1981) focused on these stimulus categories but did not report whether the actual outcomes were true, false, or anomalous. This distinction is particularly important because, for every question, the answer was false if the main nouns or verbs in the question were exchanged, as in the predicted bad error in Table 1. The example is *generically* false because death does not precede life. Table 2 shows the number of full and partial exchange errors for the two stimulus categories and the two truthfulness outcomes, and it provides an example of each type of error. The errors in

TABLE 2

Exchange Error Frequencies by Stimulus Condition and Truth of Outcome

Outcome	Stimulus condition	Exchange errors		
		Partial	Full	Both
True outcomes	Truth preserving	9	4	13
Is our neighbor Mexico north of our friend Canada? → No, our *neighbor* Canada is north of our neighbor Mexico.				
True outcomes	Truth changing	2	1	3
Can you die quickly before living peacefully? → No, you live peacefully before you die *peace*.				
Total true outcomes		11	5	16
False outcomes	Truth preserving	0	1	1
Do you die happily before you live peacefully? → Yes, you can die happily . . . no, you *die* peacefully before *living* happily.				
False outcomes	Truth changing	2	2	4
Are the intricate roots above the leafy branches? → No, the *intricate* branches are above the *leafy* roots.				
Total false or anomalous outcomes		2	3	5

Table 1 and in the false outcomes in Table 2 are examples of full exchanges, where a pair of words switch places. In a partial exchange, one word moves, but the other does not, as in the truthful outcome examples in Table 2. Of a total of 21 exchange errors,[1] only 5 had false or anomalous outcomes. In some cases (classified as truthful outcomes), the subject avoided an anomaly through overt self-correction. Thus:

3. Do you start dessert before you drink your soup?
   *No, you start your soup before you drink . . . have your dessert.

The normal slip-rate advantage (the higher rate of good or normal slips), then, is a very reliable finding. Some process acts to shift differentially the probability of good and bad errors. The exact character of this process cannot be inferred from the NSRA alone, although Experiment 2 of Baars *et al.* (1975) provided evidence that, under some circumstances, there is editing of bad,

---

[1]In reanalyzing the data in Baars and Mattson (1981), a misclassification of one exchange error and a failure to count another was discovered. This mistake accounts for the difference in the numbers reported here.

nonlexical errors (Figure 1). This experiment showed that nonsense slips appeared to be suppressed *only* when the context indicated that lexical responses might be needed. When *lexical* slips were made either in a nonsense context or in a lexical context, the rate of slips was relatively high, with a median of two per subject. In a third condition, where nonsense slips were made in a nonsense context—that is, where the list of stimuli contained only nonsense items—the rate of slips was not significantly lower. But when some lexical word pairs were added before and after the nonsense slip targets, the rate of slips was suddenly depressed significantly below the other three conditions. It is as if the presence of lexical items created a "mode change" in the operation of the speech production system. It is not surprising, of course, that the speech system is biased toward lexical output. What is interesting about these results is that the rate of nonsense slips dropped only when there was a *mismatch*

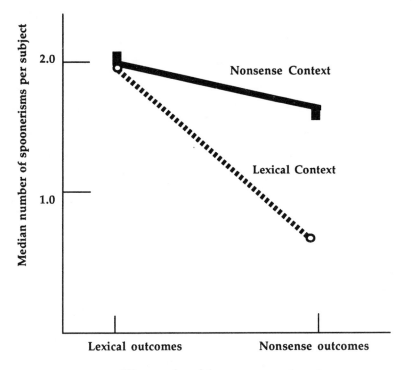

Slips produced from nonsense targets

FIGURE 1. Nonsense spoonerisms drop dramatically when subjects are led to expect lexical responses. The median number of slips per subject stays the same when the slips are lexical and when there is a match between a nonsense stimulus context and the nonsense slips. However, the slip rate is significantly lowered when nonsense slips are elicited from a stimulus list that included normal lexical word pairs, suggesting the existence of some match–mismatch mechanism or editor.

between the surrounding context and the nonsense slip. A mechanism that detects and suppresses mismatches with respect to expected correct outcomes is an editing mechanism.

Physiological measures also suggest that there is some representation of potential errors even when no overt error occurs. For example, in a nonspeech choice-reaction-time task, Cooke and Diggles (1984) found that there were trials in which the electromyographic record showed activation of the wrong muscle, with no overt move in the wrong direction. The galvanic skin response (GSR) changes as a result of novel, attention-getting, and emotional stimuli, among other things (Fowles, 1986). Both orienting and emotional interpretations have been made of changes in the GSR that coincide with slips of the tongue. Initial work established that GSRs occur when subjects make spoonerisms, as compared to correct responses (Motley & Baars, 1976; Motley *et al.*, 1981). The GSR changed more significantly on trials on which subjects had the *opportunity* to make a socially taboo spoonerism, even if they did not actually make the slip (Motley, Camden, & Baars, 1981, 1982). In comparison, the GSR on targets that did not lead to taboo spoonerisms changed much less; the change in GSR when overt taboo spoonerisms were committed was quite large. In these studies, the GSR is interpreted as indicating surprise at the detection of any kind of error, plus an added emotional reaction to the taboo words. Given that there are physiological signs of an error without an error's occurring overtly, it is reasonable to suppose that some covert error-minimization process must keep that internal error from being carried out.

Is this covert error-minimization process conscious or unconscious? Conceivably, the covert slip is conscious, as in Dell and Repka's inner-speech tongue twisters (Chapter 10, this volume). *Covert* does not necessarily mean unconscious, although getting accurate conscious reports of these fast, transient events may be difficult.

Many factors can produce differences in error likelihood. One point underscored by Table 1 is that many rule systems seem to influence error minimization, including lexicality, pronounceability, syntax, semantics, and pragmatics. This observation indicates that a wide range of information sources must somehow be available to minimize the chance of an error. Further, the criterion for error minimization is not fixed. People are known to have some control over error minimization: our ability to trade off speed for accuracy is well established (e.g., Dell, 1986; MacKay, 1982; Pachella, 1974). A shift of criterion can also affect the type of error that occurs, as in Experiment 2 of Baars *et al.* (1975). In that experiment, the mere presence of lexical stimulus words in the list led to an decrease in the number of nonsense errors—apparently, nonlexical errors were more acceptable in a nonsense context. However, the opposite occurred in Experiment 4 of Baars (1977). When the subjects were asked to report on some trials whether or not they had made an error, so that they were encouraged to monitor their performance more closely, "bad," socially inappropriate, and anomalous word exchanges virtually disappeared, and "good" exchanges continued to be made. Error-minimization processes, then, must operate by flexible criteria under different circumstances.

The detection of an error is in part determined by the available resources. Levelt's analysis of self-corrections (1983) indicates that error utterances are more likely to be interrupted at a phrase boundary. This finding was believed not to be a result of a tendency to finish the phrase before correction; instead, Levelt hypothesized that it was due to a greater likelihood of detecting the error toward the end of a phrase, because more monitoring capacity was available. As an independent check, he examined the detectability of errors as a function of where in the phrase the error occurred. As predicted, error detection improved over the course of a constituent. More resources may be devoted to planning at the beginning of the constituent, instead of being assigned to monitoring the output.

In principle, error minimizing may be partially conscious, or entirely conscious and deliberate, or at times it may be entirely unconscious. Introspection, along with the evidence for overt self-correction, suggests that there is often some conscious involvement in detecting, editing, and correcting errors. There may also be cases in which error minimization occurs automatically, without conscious involvement. In experimental NSRAs, introspection suggests minimal conscious involvement in the detection of bad errors. Empirically, this is a weak form of evidence, but as we shall see, there are also theoretical reasons to support this claim.

Generally speaking, when we are aware of a word in inner or outer speech, we are not aware of the criteria or detection processes that determine whether the word is actually in error. People cannot report on the unconscious criteria and correction mechanisms that come into play. Conscious report has its own constraints, but under optimal conditions (i.e., given minimal interference with the limited-capacity system immediately after the target event), people should be able to report whether they were conscious of speech planning, even if they cannot report the details. People can typically report conscious mismatches between the perceived words and the planned utterance, although they cannot specify the exact regularities that may have been violated.

MODELS OF SPEECH PRODUCTION THAT EXPLAIN ERROR MINIMIZATION

Models of speech production differ in their emphasis on editing or boosting to control internal errors. Before we get into specific models, it will be helpful to lay out the space of possible models. The first way that speech production models differ is in their commitment to boosting (no editor), a single editor, or many editors. An editor always involves two distinct mechanisms, in which one (the editor) examines the output of the other in order to detect and correct errors. In order to say that an utterance has been edited, it must be demonstrated that:

1. The error is *represented,* although it may not be overtly carried out.
2. A *mismatch* between this representation and the intention, or between it and generic rule systems, is detected.
3. The detected mismatch lowers the probability of executing the error and enhances the odds that it will be corrected.

In pure boosting models, there is no editor; error minimization emerges from the normal operation of speech production. Models with one editor have a single mechanism (almost always involving consciousness) that allows for the detection and correction of errors, whereas models with many editors involve many processes (typically automatic) that independently detect and correct errors.

The second dimension that differentiates speech production models is of conscious versus automatic error minimization. Models with only conscious error minimization edit speech plans and overt errors without conscious access to the rules and correction mechanisms. Thus, the term *conscious editing* refers to an awareness of the error and the product of the correction process, rather than an awareness of the error detection mechanism, the process of editing, and the criteria for editing. Pure boosting models and models with many independent editors most often stress the automaticity and lack of awareness of error minimization. Finally, there are models that involve a combination of conscious and automatic processes for error minimization.

The final dimension is based on the criteria used for editing: Is the same information that is used to produce the utterance also used to judge its correctness? Perhaps editing is based on the same process that is used to perceive and comprehend other people's speech (e.g., Levelt, 1983). In pure boosting and in "production editing," error minimization is a result of the same processes that produce the utterance. Typically, production editing is associated with automatic processing. In "perceptual editing," error minimization is due to the same processes that evaluate other people's speech, which typically involve consciousness. Finally, some models involve both production and perceptual criteria or suggest mechanisms that are shared by production and perception (MacKay, 1987). With these three dimensions in mind, let us turn to some specific models.

Laver's Neurolinguistic Control Model

Laver (1980) presented a model that specifies the flow of control in speech production using propositional logic. In terms of the dimensions developed in this chapter, his model is a hybrid of automatic production, with many editors and conscious perceptual editing of overt speech. Error minimization is a result of multiple feedback loops. In the prearticulatory stages, the output of each stage of the production process is checked against production criteria through feedback within the stage. When we speak out loud, we also hear ourselves, so that a second feedback system for monitoring errors is provided that uses perceptual targets and criteria. Thus, Laver (1980) argued for two forms of editing and did not discuss boosting. More recent work makes it possible to fill out his abstract characterization of the production process.

Levelt's Perceptual Loop Approach to Speech Repair

According to Levelt (1983), "repairing speech involves a perceptual loop: the self-produced inner or overt speech is perceived, parsed and checked with respect to intentional and contextual appropriateness, agreement of intended and delivered message, and linguistic correctness" (p. 50). In our classification, his model has one perceptual editor that operates on inner speech and overt speech. Presumably, this editor is conscious, as he related it to central control and working memory. Cases like the NSRA, in which errors appear to be minimized with little awareness, constitute a problem for this approach.

Dell and Reich's Spreading-Activation Model of Speech Production

In a series of papers (Dell, 1980, 1985, 1986; Dell & Reich, 1977, 1980), Dell and Reich have laid out a theory of speech production that can account for a great many data on speech and speech errors. The spreading-activation framework, also known as *connectionism* (e.g., Feldman & Ballard, 1982) and *parallel distributed processing* (McClelland, Rumelhart, & the PDP Research Group, 1986; Rumelhart, McClelland, & the PDP Research Group, 1986) has been successfully applied in many areas of psychological theory (in addition to the above references, see also Anderson, 1983; Bharucha & Stoeckig, 1986; Deaux & Major, 1987; Grossberg & Gutowski, 1987; Hunt & Lansman, 1986; Lee, 1984; Norman, 1981; Smith, 1984; Stemberger, Elman & Haden, 1985; and the special issue of the *Journal of Memory and Language:* Just & Carpenter, 1988).

Processing in Dell's model is carried out by the spread of activation throughout a hierarchical network of nodes. There are nodes for morphemes, syllables, phonemes, and features. Every node is connected to related nodes in the layer above and below it. For example, the initial phoneme /s/ is connected to syllables in the layer above it, such as *set* and *sap,* and to features in the next lower layer, such as "fricative" and "voiceless." Every node has an activation value that is determined by its input from all of the nodes connected to it. When a word is to be articulated, the appropriate morphemes are activated, and activation spreads down the hierarchy, eventually reaching the feature level, where the most highly activated features determine the output. Activation also spreads up into the hierarchy, so that a feedback mechanism that is critical to error minimization (as in Laver, 1980) is provided.

To see how error minimization through positive feedback works, some simplification of Dell's model is helpful. Versions of this simplified model have been studied extensively through computer simulation by Dell (1980, 1985, 1986) and by us. Figure 2 depicts part of a network used in some of our simulation work. Two layers of nodes are represented: words and phonemes. Each node has an activation value. In Figure 2, the activation values are based on having the simulation try to say *tool* (the current word), then *kit* (the next word). The current word to be said receives an initial activation of 10, and the next word to be said has 5 units of activation added to its value in order to model anticipatory influences. On each time step of the model, each node sends 0.1 of its activation to all of the connected nodes, each of which sums its inputs to determine its new activation value. Also on each time step, the activation of each node decays. Decay is implemented by multiplying the node's activation by 0.4. The other parameters are the standard deviation of a noise distribution with a mean of 0, so that random noise can be added to each node's activation to simulate the effects of a larger network; the number of time steps activation spreads before articulation; and the value to which articulated phonemes are reset after being said. At articulation, the highest activated phonemes in each group (initial consonants, vowels, and final consonants) are selected for output; then their activation value is reset to 0. The activation amount for the current word and the next word was set arbitrarily, and their value and the phoneme reset value are held constant across our simulations. The activation multiplier and the decay parameter must be adjusted for each network. Generally, we have selected a multiplier in the rough

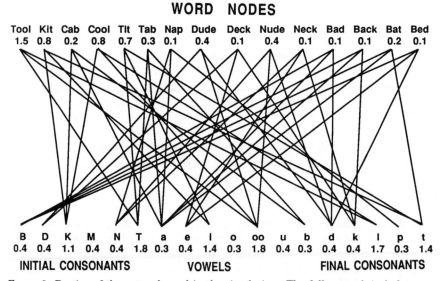

WORD   NODES

Tool	Kit	Cab	Cool	Tit	Tab	Nap	Dude	Deck	Nude	Neck	Bad	Back	Bat	Bed
1.5	0.8	0.2	0.8	0.7	0.3	0.1	0.4	0.1	0.4	0.1	0.1	0.1	0.2	0.1

B	D	K	M	N	T	a	e	I	o	oo	u	b	d	k	l	p	t
0.4	0.4	1.1	0.4	0.4	1.8	0.3	0.4	1.4	0.3	1.8	0.4	0.3	0.4	0.4	1.7	0.3	1.4

INITIAL CONSONANTS   **VOWELS**   **FINAL CONSONANTS**

FIGURE 2. Portion of the network used in the simulations. The full network includes every English word using these 18 phonemes for a total of 126 word nodes and 378 connections. For this demonstration, the current word is "tool" and the next word is "kit." Note the differential activation represented by the numbers under the phoneme and word nodes.

range for a fan effect (Anderson, 1983) and then selected a decay parameter that kept the activation from building up infinitely in the network (Shrager, Hogg, & Huberman, 1987). The noise and the number of time steps were varied according to the purpose of the simulation.

Dell's model (1986) can account for the occurrence and observed frequencies of different error types, as well as for the effect of time pressure on speech errors. For example, exchange errors occur when anticipatory influences and other activation sources cause the wrong phoneme—from the next word—to be articulated. After its activation is set back to 0, it is likely that the correct phoneme from the current word will be the most highly activated node the next time around, the result being a full phoneme exchange.

Error Minimization Works through Positive Feedback between the Levels of the Network

If there is sufficient time, activation that originates at the word level spreads to the phoneme level, and so on. Dell (1985) showed that this feedback creates an advantage for word outcomes, because there are no nonsense word nodes to mediate this feedback. As a consequence of positive feedback, the model produces the lexical NSRA, as found by Baars *et al.* (1975) for laboratory-induced errors and by Dell and Reich (1981) for naturally occurring errors. In terms of our classification, Dell's model (1986) is focused on boosting: automatic error minimization by means of production structures, with no editor.[2] Good lexical outcomes are boosted relative to bad nonsense outcomes, and one can imagine extending this reasoning to syntax and phonology as well: no nodes for rule-violating syntactic and phonotactic constructions means no feedback and fewer bad errors.

Notice that this account of the NSRA works because there are no nodes corresponding to the "bad" outcome in the network. One problem in this approach to error minimization is the case in which there is a real node for the bad error, as is the case for taboo word errors. As seen in Table 1, Motley *et al.* (1981) found that their subjects made fewer taboo errors than matched good errors. Because taboo and good words have nodes at the word level, both kinds of words should benefit from positive feedback. In another study involving targets that could all produce taboo errors, these authors observed significant changes in GSR on trials with long response latencies when the subjects made a correct response. They argued that the GSR and response latency were consistent with the view that the taboo error was represented, detected, and corrected before articulation. Subsequently, Motley *et al.* (1982) observed significant changes in GSR when subjects made "safe partial phoneme exchanges," in which the partial exchange did not include the taboo word. Again,

---

[2]Despite his focus on automatic processes, according to a personal communication (1987) Dell recognizes the existence of conscious error-detection mechanisms.

they interpreted this finding as evidence that the taboo error was edited, as opposed to boosting the matched good error. Based on simulation data, we will show that Dell's model may account for the GSR data, because the taboo word becomes activated, but it does not account for the differential likelihood of good and taboo errors.

The network used in these simulations consisted of 18 phoneme nodes and 126 words. There were six initial consonants (shown in Figure 2 as *B, D, K, M, N*, and *T*), six vowels (*a, e, i, o, oo*, and *u*), and six final consonants (*b, d, k, l, p*, and *t*), making a total of 216 possible phoneme strings, of which 126 were the real words used in the network. The network was designed to include some of the word stimuli and errors used in the taboo word studies (Motley *et al.*, 1981, 1982). Specifically, the network included the taboo words *tit* and *nude*. (We apologize if the reader is offended by the selection of taboo items; with some agonizing, we concluded that staying close to the original study was critical, and that some offense caused by the selection is consistent with the emotional impact of truly taboo words.)

The first simulations examined the covert representation of the taboo error. Because the GSR correlates with emotional impact, it can be argued that any activation of a taboo word will contribute to the GSR, even if the taboo error is never edited. Consider the matched word pair stimuli "tool kit" and "tool cab." As a result of positive feedback, the lexical errors associated with one word pair ("cool tit" for "tool kit") should be more active than the lexical error associated with the other word pair ("cool tab" for "tool cab"). To see how this works, we monitored the activation of 11 target words during four simulations (see the first 11 words in Figure 2). For each time step from 1 to 4, the model "said" 2700 words in 25 blocks. Each block involved attempting to say 25 filler words selected at random from all words except the target words, then saying "tool kit," then 25 more fillers, then "nap dude," 25 fillers, "tool cab," 25 fillers, and finally, "nap deck." Thus, each target word pair was said 25 times at each time step, for a total of 100 repetitions. No noise was added in these simulations. Figure 3 shows the average activation of the taboo error *tit* and the control error *tab* as the model tries to say "tool kit," and Figure 4 shows the activation of the same two-word nodes as the model tries to say "tool cab." Time 1 is the mean activation during the 25 blocks of 25 filler trials before the word pair was said. Time 2 is the mean activation on the 25 trials when the last random word was being said, and the first word in the pair was being prepared. At Time 3 and Time 4, the first word and the second word of the target pair were the current words, respectively. It can be seen that *tit* received more activation than *tab* did when "tool kit" was said (Figure 3), whereas the opposite pattern held when "tool cab" was said (Figure 4). The same pattern held for the target pairs "nap dude" and "nap deck," where there was no node for the error outcome *dap*. According to the spreading-activation model, then, the taboo error is represented and activated (though not as much as the correct word, in most cases). If the GSR depends on the activation of taboo words like *tit* creating an emotional response, the GSR results of Motley *et al.* (1981, 1982) can be accounted for by Dell's model.

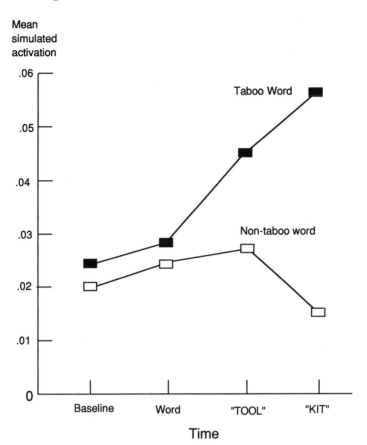

FIGURE 3. Simulated activation of taboo and non-taboo words while preparing and saying "tool kit." "Baseline" refers to the average activation over 25 trials before saying a "word" randomly selected from the lexical set. When saying that word, "tool" receives preparatory activation as does "kit" when "tool" is said.

The second set of simulations assessed taboo error minimization in the spreading-activation model. The network was the same as for the first set of simulations. Random, normally distributed noise with a standard deviation of .4 and a mean of 0 was added to bring the error rate up to roughly 20% of trials at Time Steps 2 through 4 (at Time Step 1, the error rate is always considerably higher). The noise was meant to model the countless outside influences that this network would be subject to as part of a complete cognitive system, including sources of activation like phonological biasing. At each time step from 1 to 4, 2,500 words were selected at random for articulation, and a log was kept for each word, indicating the number of times the model tried to say the word, the number of errors when saying the word, and the number of errors that produced the word. Out of 10,000 trials, *tit* was the error outcome

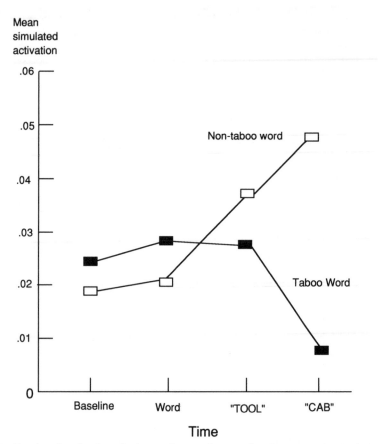

FIGURE 4. Simulated activation of taboo and non-taboo words when preparing and saying "tool cab." "Baseline" refers to average activation over 25 trials before saying a "word" randomly selected from the lexical set. When saying that word, "tool" receives preparatory activation as does "cab" when "tool" is said.

10 times, *tab* was the error outcome only once, *nude* was the error outcome 3 times, and *neck,* 4 times. So spreading activation does not produce taboo error minimization, though the lexical NSRA was replicated in our simulations. The same mechanism that works for lexical error minimization will not work for taboo error minimization, because taboo words have nodes for long-term representation, whereas nonsense words do not. In summary, the spreading-activation approach (Dell, 1986) is a boosting account of error minimization that can account for speech errors and some of their characteristics, but it is not a complete account because it cannot deal with taboo error minimization. In general, the model can also account for other forms of boosting, including phonological biasing, semantic biasing, and Freudian slips (Motley, 1980), because activation from many sources can contribute to making the wrong node the most highly active.

Motley, Baars, and Camden's Editing Model of Language Encoding

The emphasis in the model of Motley, Baars, and Camden (1983) was on prearticulatory editing of speech plans. Although they acknowledged a role for the "conscious . . . process of guarding one's speech," the model details the workings of "an unconscious and relatively automatic process of editing all potential output" (p. 84). Speech production begins with a communication goal; then, appropriate lexical items and syntactic structures are selected. Dell's influence can be seen in the lexicon, which is a spreading-activation network, that permits boosting through positive feedback and activation of words by phonological biasing, semantic biasing, and extralinguistic factors (as in some Freudian slips). After lexical and syntactic selection, the sequence of stages is message formulation, phonological coding, neuromotor coding, prearticulatory editing, and articulation. The prearticulatory editor compares the output of neuromotor coding to the activated nodes in the lexicon. So the Motley *et al.* model has automatic production boosting, automatic production editing, and an unspecified conscious editing process.

The main problem in the Motley *et al.* model is representational incompatibility in the prearticulatory editing process. One might imagine that the output representation of neuromotor coding is very different from the representation of words in the lexicon. If this is the case, how can the two different representations be compared? Motley *et al.* suggested that the output of the lexicon might be neuromotor codes, but if this is the case, why are the intervening stages necessary? This is a general problem in editing models: comparing the intention and its realization requires a common representation, or *lingua franca*. Assuming that the two codes were compatible, Motley *et al.* further suggested that the lexical nodes corresponding to the neuromotor code are checked for activation. If they are active, then no error is detected, so that some errors go undetected. This mechanism would not allow any lexical errors of commission to be detected at all, however, because the reason the error occurs in the first place is that the lexical node is more active than the correct node. Motley *et al.* specified only the representation of the lexicon as an activation network, but networks can also represent syntax, semantics, phonology, and neuromotor coding (Dell, 1986).

Automatic Production with Boosting and Global Workspace Editing

In this section, we develop a model of error minimization that draws on many of the ideas developed by the theorists in the previous section, while also (hopefully) avoiding the problems in their approaches. We propose that error minimization in speech production is carried out by automatic production processes in an activation network (as suggested by Dell, 1986, and Motley *et al.*, 1983) and by using consciousness to edit speech plans and overt speech (as suggested by Laver, 1980, Levelt, 1983, and Motley *et al.*, 1983). These two types of error minimization are necessary to give a complete account of the error phenomena we have discussed.

Consciousness and unconscious processes are intimately intertwined. Actions, including speaking, begin with a conscious intention (Mattson, 1987), which itself is a result of the cooperation of unconscious motivational and goal-directed processes. The conscious intention is underspecified; that is, most aspects of what needs to be done to realize the intention are not spelled out. For example, we are not usually aware of selecting an appropriate syntactic structure, or of activating specific parts of the speech musculature. The conscious intention recruits unconscious specialists that form the intended plan. The intended plan consists of the activated nodes of the speech production system that specify the details of the conscious intention. The highest level nodes of the intended plan are directly activated by the conscious intention (this is the recruitment process), and spreading activation fills out the rest of the plan.

Error Minimization by Automatic Production Processes: Activation Networks

As suggested by Dell (1986), we propose that a considerable amount of error minimization is the result of automatic boosting through positive feedback. The speech production network is clearly structurally hierarchical in some respects (for example, lexical selection precedes phonological specification), and activation spreads down the hierarchy, specifying more and more of the details of producing the utterance. Activation may also spread up the hierarchy, providing positive feedback that enhances the intended plan (as well as related rival nodes). Thus, information can flow up and down the hierarchical network in a flexible way, with 10% bottom-up flow and 90% top-down, or vice versa. Positive feedback leads to an NSRA in those cases in which the bad error has no corresponding node, as in the semantic NSRA, the lexical NSRA, the syntactic NSRA, and the phonological NSRA. People are generally not aware of this influence on error production.

One possible extension of Dell's model (1986) would be the introduction of a competition detector into the speech production network. Errors of commission are thought to result when, for some reason, an incorrect node is more highly activated than the node in the same equivalence class that is part of the intended plan. The higher the activation of rival nodes, the greater the probability of an error. A competition detector would monitor the total activation within a pool of nodes and would respond on the basis of the amount of competition. If competition was over some threshold, then the execution of the response could be delayed and/or a signal of trouble due to competition could be made conscious.

Allowing the initiation of the response to be controlled by a competition detector makes it possible to account for a variety of related findings on response timing and uncertainty. Dell's model produces a speed–accuracy trade-off, in that, when the number of time steps before articulation is only one or two, positive feedback is much less effective because activation has less time to spread. With this mechanism alone, one would predict that errors will have short latencies, because they are more common when the time pressure is greatest. This is a version of the fast-guess model of speed–accuracy relations (Yellott, 1971, as described in Pachella, 1974): Errors have shorter latencies than correct responses because they occur when a person acts before sufficient information has accumulated.

Empirically, however, Baars (1977) and Motley *et al.* (1981) found that the mean response latency for error trials was longer than the response latency for correct trials. This is an example of the speed–accuracy micro-trade-off (Pachella, 1974; Wickens, 1984): within a particular speed–accuracy condition, the latencies of error and correct responses may vary. According to Wickens (1984), when trials differ only in the response criterion adopted by the subject, the form of the micro-trade-off is the same as the macro-trade-off: latency and errors are negatively correlated. When the variability between trials is mainly due to the quality of the signal, then errors and latency are positively correlated, so errors have longer latencies than correct responses. In these error-induction tasks, the activation of the node for the intended plan is the signal, and the activation of rival nodes is equivalent to noise. Increasing the activation of rival nodes reduces the signal-to-noise ratio by increasing the noise, so the quality of the signal is reduced and the error latencies are longer than the correct trial latencies.

The consistent difference in latency between choice reaction time and simple reaction time shows that greater uncertainty is associated with longer latencies. Goldman-Eisler (1968) showed that, in normal speech production, some pauses in speech are associated with uncertainty about lexical selection, which may explain some of Levelt's C-repairs (1983). A competition detector could provide an automatic local computation that would increase latency with competition, providing a mechanism for the speed–accuracy micro-trade-off and the effect of uncertainty on latency. If the conscious intention keeps pumping activation into the intended plan, then delaying execution until competition is resolved will favor the intended plan. If consciousness is directed elsewhere, as when a person is distracted, then the most highly activated node will win out, whether or not it is part of the intended plan.

The other possible function of a competition detector would be to make conscious a potential problem in speech production. Several cognitive psychologists have suggested that conscious involvement seems to be triggered by surprise, or by mismatch with expectations, and that it seems helpful in "debugging" errors (e.g., Baars, 1988; Mandler, 1975). A competition detector can detect mismatches between expected and actual speech and can signal the attentional system to bring conscious attention to bear on the slip, either in inner speech or overtly (Dell & Repka, Chapter 10, this volume). Baars's global workspace (GW) model of the limited-capacity system suggests that consciousness is useful in situations such as this, because the global workspace can broadcast its contents to numerous specialized knowledge sources, which can then cooperatively work on the conscious error (Baars, 1988, and Chapter 4, this volume). Thus, consciousness may be attracted to the problem by means of a competition detector, which detects mismatches with previous expectations. Mismatch detection in turn may cause the "searchlight" of consciousness or, alternatively, the "global workspace" to display the problem, so that many knowledge sources are recruited that are not routinely available, but that can cooperatively solve the unexpected problem. Response delays could occur because the limited-capacity system is being used for several tasks at the same time: it may be involved in mismatch detection, in an effort to stop the plan before execution, in recruiting systems able to correct the error, and so on.

Currently, we are not committed to a particular implementation of a competition detector. One possible modification of Dell's model (1986) would involve adding lateral inhibition within equivalence classes of nodes, and requiring activation to exceed a threshold before the response is executed. This has the effect of leaving the most active node with all the activation (Feldman & Ballard, 1982). Another possibility would be gated inhibition: a competition detector inhibits all nodes within an equivalence class to the extent that it is activated. With little competition, there would be little inhibition, and activation within a class would rise quickly; with lots of competition, there would be more inhibition, and it would take longer to reach the activation threshold for execution.

Error Minimization by Editing of Conscious Targets: Global Workspace Theory

As indicated in Baars (Chapter 4, this volume), GW theory suggests that both the formation of a speech plan and its editing involve a parallel-interactive system, in which details are handled by distributed specialized processors, and novel, nonroutine, or especially significant problems are displayed on a global workspace in such a way that many different processors can interact with the problem. Each step along the way may use a different mix of automatic processing and conscious involvement, depending on the degree to which highly practiced automatisms can be used. Editing—in the sense of error detection, inhibition, and correction—can be done in a very natural way in this system. Global Workspace theory suggests that editing most often involves an—(at least fleetingly)—conscious target containing the error, which is inspected by unconscious systems. The global workspace is like a stage that is lit up, and clearly visible; the audience of specialized processors is watching from the dark auditorium, and the actors are controlled by an equally invisible director and playwright behind the scenes. It may seem somewhat unintuitive to think of conscious events' being controlled and monitored by unconscious systems, but it is in accord with widely shared experience: in speaking, we simply never know the criteria by which we are molding a sentence, and yet we recognize flaws in the sentence by those very same criteria, once we become conscious of them.

Accounting for the Phenomena

In this section, we go back to the phenomena of error minimization and see how our model can account for these data. People make errors, so error minimization is not perfect. Errors may be caused in a number of ways within our model. Mattson (1987) found evidence for five causes of nonspeech action errors of commission derived from an activation network model of action:

1. The conscious intention specifies more than one intended plan.
2. The conscious intention is changed at the last moment.
3. Rival nodes are active because of priming or biasing.
4. Rival nodes are active because of positive feedback.
5. A new goal competes with a well-established goal.

The extension of these causes of nonspeech errors to speech errors is straightforward (for related accounts of the causes of errors, including errors of omission, see Dell, 1986; Norman, 1981; Reason & Mycielska, 1982).

People sometimes edit their errors overtly. Global Workspace theory accounts for overt editing in much the same way that Levelt (1983) proposed: We perceive our own speech, and therefore, we are able to bring to bear the same perceptual processes that we might use for detecting and responding to errors made by other speakers. The principal difference is that global workspace theory allows any relevant unconscious processors—not just perceptual processors—to influence error detection and correction.

There are covert processes that minimize the likelihood of errors. In our model, covert error minimization can result from both automatic production processes and editing of conscious speech plans. The NSRA for bad errors with no corresponding representation is covered by positive feedback (Dell, 1985), as is the GSR response to taboo errors. Cases in which the bad errors are represented, as in taboo errors, require conscious editing via the global workspace.

Many factors produce differences in error likelihood. The variety of factors that influence errors is the result of both the uniform representation of the intended plan as an activation network and the flexibility of consciousness. Activation networks are powerful precisely because they allow many knowledge sources to interact. Positive feedback can operate at many levels because of the uniform activation-network representation. The GW approach allows virtually any factor to influence speech production, providing there is adequate time and limited capacity is not overloaded.

The criteria for error minimization can be shifted. Dell (1986) and MacKay (1982) provided activation network accounts of the speed–accuracy trade-off. The criterion shift observed in Experiment 2 of Baars *et al.* (1975) was probably a result of cutting off conscious editing of nonsense in the all-nonsense condition. Though the difference between lexical and nonsense errors was not significant in the all-nonsense condition, it was in the direction one would expect if automatic positive feedback was still boosting the production of lexical errors.

Baars (1977) observed a shift in criterion when subjects were asked to report on whether they had made a slip. In this case, the subjects were asked to intentionally use conscious processing to detect errors on certain cued trials. In comparison to a control group that did not monitor response accuracy, the self-monitoring subjects made fewer anomalous errors and roughly the same number of normal errors. This seems like the converse of the situation in Experiment 2 of Baars *et al.* (1975): Here, conscious editing was not being done in the control condition, though it was carried out when the subject was instructed to do so, the result being a reduction in the (easier-to-detect) anomalous errors. The subjects may not have consciously monitored their speech as effectively in the control condition because the anomaly was designed to occur in the second phrase of the sentence, when resources were tied up in other aspects of speech production.

The detection of an error is in part determined by the available resources. Resources can influence errors and error minimization in a number of ways. First, if the resources available to activate the intended plan are insufficient, then omission errors are more likely. Second, if a person is distracted or overloaded, then the conscious intention will not keep pumping activation into the intended plan; this lack of activation has consequences for competition resolution. Finally, Global Workspace theory is relevant to resources in two ways: It says that consciousness is the key component in a limited-capacity system, and it suggests that becoming conscious of something inherently brings multiple resources to bear on whatever is conscious, so that, if the problem is conscious often enough, almost any information-processing resource may be brought to bear on it. It is important to keep in mind the immensely complex computational problem of detecting errors at any level of analysis, from acoustic to pragmatic (Baars, Chapters 1 and 4, this volume). This is a non-trivial problem, to say the least, and yet, when we become conscious of any flawed utterance, we do detect errors at any level very quickly. This is one reason why looping back through the entire conscious perceptual system is a viable strategy for monitoring a speech act for errors.

Sometimes error minimizing is conscious and deliberate, and sometimes it is not. We have made the distinction between conscious and unconscious, automatic error minimization central to our account for both theoretical and introspective reasons.

Other Issues.   Another issue is the *lingua franca* problem in editing: in order to detect a mismatch, the representations of output and intention must be compatible. If error minimization is done "locally"—between two levels, as in positive feedback—then, the representations are compatible and the problem does not arise. If error minimization is done "globally"—that is, any way but locally—then the problem becomes acute. Global Workspace theory handles the *lingua franca* problem by suggesting that, in running the output through a conscious perceptual loop (Levelt, 1983) to examine a potentially flawed utterance, one automatically broadcasts to all levels of representation. Then, only those unconscious processors that "speak the same language" as the potentially flawed utterance will respond. We can think about this use of a conscious perceptual analysis as another example of the ability of consciousness to marshal very many information-processing resources in order to solve a focal problem.

One final issue: As we began this chapter by mentioning the potential social consequences of speech errors, we shall conclude with some social mechanisms for error minimization. First, speech errors may be "corrected" by the listener through top-down perceptual processing, which is the analogue in perception of positive feedback. Second, in many cases, listeners may notice the error but may feel that they know what the person meant. Although there is no guarantee that the listeners will not be misled, with many errors this heuristic will work out. Finally, one can always ask the speaker what she or he intended to say, thus bringing a possible error to the speaker's awareness through external social feedback.

Acknowledgments

Some of the research reported here and much of the theory development were supported by National Science Foundation Grant No. BNS-7906024 and National Institute of Mental Health Grant No. 1R03MH3333401 to Bernard J. Baars. We would also like to acknowledge the past collaboration of Michael Motley and Carl Camden, the cooperation of Gary Dell in providing us with information on his computer simulation, and assistance from Gary Felsten in preparing the figures.

References

Anderson, J. R. (1983). *The architecture of cognition.* Cambridge: Harvard University Press.
Baars, B. J. (1977). *The planning of speech: Is there semantic editing prior to speech articulation?* Dissertation Abstracts International, *38,* 5.
Baars, B. J. (1988). *A cognitive theory of consciousness.* New York: Cambridge University Press.
Baars, B. J., & Mattson, M. E. (1981). Consciousness and intention: A framework and some evidence. *Cognition and Brain Theory, 4,* 247–263.
Baars, B. J., Motley, M. T., & MacKay, D. G. (1975). Output editing for lexical status in artificially elicited slips of the tongue. *Journal of Verbal Learning and Verbal Behavior, 14,* 382–391.

Bharucha, J. J., & Stoeckig, K. (1986). Reaction time and musical expectancy: Priming of chords. *Journal of Experimental Psychology: Human Perception and Performance, 12,* 403–410.

Cooke, J. D., & Diggles, V. A. (1984). Rapid error correction during human arm movements: Evidence for central monitoring. *Journal of Motor Behavior, 16,* 348–363.

Deaux, K., & Major, B. (1987). Putting gender into context: An interactive model of gender-related behavior. *Psychological Review, 94,* 369–389.

Dell, G. S. (1980). *Phonological and lexical encoding in speech production: An analysis of naturally occurring and experimentally elicited speech errors.* Unpublished doctoral dissertation, University of Toronto.

Dell, G. S. (1985). Positive feedback in hierarchical connectionist models: Applications to language production. *Cognitive Science, 9,* 3–23.

Dell, G. S. (1986). A spreading-activation theory of retrieval in sentence production. *Psychological Review, 93,* 283–321.

Dell, G. S., & Reich, P. A. (1977). A model of slips of the tongue. *The third LACUS forum, 3,* 448–455.

Dell, G. S., & Reich, P. A. (1980). Toward a unified theory of slips of the tongue. In V. Fromkin (Ed.), *Errors in linguistic performance: Slips of the tongue, ear, pen and hand* (pp. 273–286). New York: Academic Press.

Dell, G. S., & Reich, P. A. (1981). Stages in sentence production: An analysis of speech error data. *Journal of Verbal Learning and Verbal Behavior, 20,* 611–629.

Feldman, J. A., & Ballard, D. H. (1982). Connectionist models and their properties. *Cognitive Science, 6,* 205–254.

Fowles, D. C. (1986). The eccrine system and electrodermal activity. In M. Coles, E. Donchin, & S. Porges (Eds.), *Psychophysiology: Systems, processes and applications* (pp. 51–96). New York: Guilford Press.

Goldman-Eisler, F. (1968). *Psycholinguistics: Experiments in spontaneous speech.* London: Academic Press.

Goldberg, S., & Gutowski, W. E. (1987). Neural dynamics of decision making under risk: Affective balance and cognitive-emotional interactions. *Psychological Review, 94,* 300–318.

Hunt, E., & Lansman, M. (1986). Unified model of attention and problem solving. *Psychological Review, 93,* 446–461.

Just, M. A., & Carpenter, P. A. (Eds.), (1988). (Special issue). *Journal of Memory and Language, 27*(2).

Laver, J. (1980). Monitoring systems in the neurolinguistic control of speech production. In V. A. Fromkin (Ed.), *Errors in linguistic performance: Slips of the tongue, ear, pen and hand* (pp. 287–305). New York: Academic Press.

Lee, W. A. (1984). Neuromotor synergies as a basis for coordinated intentional action. *Journal of Motor Behavior, 16,* 135–170.

Levelt, W. J. M. (1983). Monitoring and self-repair in speech. *Cognition, 14,* 41–104.

MacKay, D. G. (1982). The problems of flexibility, fluency, and speed-accuracy trade-off in skilled behavior. *Psychological Review, 89,* 483–506.

MacKay, D. G. (1987). *The organization of perception and action.* New York: Springer-Verlag.

Mandler, G. (1975). *Mind and emotion.* New York: Wiley.

Mattson, M. E. (1987). Sources of competing activation in action errors. *Dissertation Abstracts International, 48,* 6.

Mattson, M. E., Baars, B. J., & Motley, M. T. (1985, March). *Wrapping up the case against purely top-down models of speech production: Evidence from induced slips of the tongue.* Paper presented at the meeting of the Eastern Psychological Association, Boston.

McClelland, J. L., Rumelhart, D. E., & the PDP Research Group. (1986). *Parallel distributed processing: Explorations in the microstructure of cognition* (Vol. 2) Cambridge: MIT Press.

Meringer, R. (1908). *Aus dem Leben der Sprache*. Berlin: V. Behr's Verlag.

Motley, M. T. (1980). Verification of "Freudian slips" and semantic prearticulatory editing via laboratory-induced spoonerisms. In V. Fromkin (Ed.), *Errors in linguistic performance: Slips of the tongue, ear, pen and hand* (pp. 133–147). New York: Academic Press.

Motley, M. T., & Baars, B. J. (1975). Encoding sensitivities to phonological markedness and transitional probability: Evidence from spoonerisms. *Human Communication Research, 2*, 353–361.

Motley, M. T., & Baars, B. J. (1976). Laboratory induction of verbal slips: A new method for psycholinguistic research. *Communication Quarterly, 24*, 28–34.

Motley, M. T., Baars, B.J., & Camden, C. T. (1981). Syntactic criteria in prearticulatory editing: Evidence from laboratory-induced slips of the tongue. *Journal of Psycholinguistic Research, 10*, 503–522.

Motley, M. T., Camden, C. T., & Baars, B. J. (1981). Toward verifying the assumptions of laboratory-induced slips of the tongue: The output-error and editing issues. *Human Communication Research, 8*, 3–15.

Motley, M. T., Camden, C. T., & Baars, B. J. (1982). Covert formulation and editing of anomalies in speech production: Evidence from experimentally elicited slips of the tongue. *Journal of Verbal Learning and Verbal Behavior, 21*, 578–594.

Motley, M. T., Baars, B. J., & Camden, C. T. (1983). Experimental verbal slip studies: A review and an editing model of language encoding. *Communication Monographs, 50*, 79–101.

Nooteboom, S. G. (1980). Speaking and unspeaking: Detection and correction of phonological and lexical errors in spontaneous speech. In V. Fromkin (Ed.), *Errors in linguistic performance: Slips of the tongue, ear, pen and hand* (pp. 87–95). New York: Academic Press.

Norman, D. A. (1981). Categorization of action slips. *Psychological Review, 88*, 1–15.

Pachella, R. G. (1974). The interpretation of reaction time in information-processing research. In B. Kantowitz (Ed.), *Human information processing: Tutorials in performance and cognition* (pp. 41–82). Potomac, MD: Erlbaum.

Reason, J., & Mycielska, K. (1982). *Absent-minded? The psychology of mental lapses and everyday errors*. Englewood Cliffs, NJ: Prentice-Hall.

Rumelhart, D. E., McClelland, J. L., & the PDP Research Group. (1986). *Parallel distributed processing: Explorations in the microstructure of cognition* (Vol. 1). Cambridge: MIT Press.

Shrager, J., Hogg, T., & Huberman, B. A. (1987). Observation of phase transitions in spreading activation networks. *Science, 236*, 1092–1094.

Smith, E. R. (1984). Model of social inference processes. *Psychological Review, 91*, 392–413.

Stemberger, J. P., Elman, J. L., & Haden, P. (1985). Interference between phonemes during phoneme monitoring: Evidence for an interactive activation model of speech perception. *Journal of Experimental Psychology: Human Perception and Performance, 11*, 475–489.

van Wijk, C., & Kempen, G. (1987). A dual system for producing self-repairs in spontaneous speech: Evidence from experimentally elicited corrections. *Cognitive Psychology, 19*, 403–440.

Wickens, C. D. (1984). *Engineering psychology and human performance* (pp. 362–363). Columbus, OH: Charles E. Merrill.

Yellott, J. I. (1971). Correction for fast guessing and the speed-accuracy tradeoff in choice reaction time. *Journal of Mathematical Psychology, 8*, 159–199.

12

Some Caveats on Testing the Freudian Slip Hypothesis

Problems in Systematic Replication

Bernard J. Baars, Jonathan Cohen, Gordon H. Bower, and Jack W. Berry

INTRODUCTION

This chapter reports on a long-term research program intended to apply the new techniques of slip induction to the classical problem of Freudian slips. We will discuss the program's rationale, early encouraging evidence, and two flawed attempts at systematic replication. These difficulties do not directly contradict the earlier positive results, so far; they do raise important unanswered questions about Freudian slip simulation in the laboratory. They also raise questions about the precise nature of the hypothesis, and about the adequacy of our methodology. Replication problems are rarely published, although methodologists often lament this state of affairs. They seem worth presenting here because, evidently, the earlier reports of "Freudian" results were too optimistic. These very real difficulties are not necessarily unsolvable,

BERNARD J. BAARS and JACK W. BERRY • The Wright Institute, 2728 Durant Avenue, Berkeley, California 94704.   JONATHAN COHEN • Department of Psychology, Carnegie-Mellon University, Pittsburgh, Pennsylvania 15213.   GORDON H. BOWER • Department of Psychology, Stanford University, Stanford, California 94305-2130.

Experimental Slips and Human Error: Exploring the Architecture of Volition, edited by Bernard J. Baars. Plenum Press, New York, 1992.

and a detailed critique may serve to improve future attempts to test the hypothesis. Throughout this chapter, we present the materials used to induce emotionally laden slips, so as to facilitate further research by others who may share an interest in the problem.

RATIONALE

The idea that, in unguarded moments, we may involuntarily allow normally private thoughts to "slip out" is not new. It must be part of linguistic folklore in many parts of the world, and Freud, whom we credit with its modern version, was happy to quote from Schiller and Shakespeare on the subject (Freud, 1901/1938; 1920/1966). Is there any scientific evidence that such significant slips happen?

Consider an actual example from *The Psychopathology of Everyday Life* (Freud, 1901/1938). Freud gave the example of "a young physician who timidly and reverently introduced himself to the celebrated Virchow with the following words: 'I am Dr. Virchow.' The surprised professor turned to him and asked, 'Is your name also Virchow?'" (p. 81). Slips like this are now easy to elicit in the laboratory, as shown in Chapter 6 of this book. We need only create uncertainty between two planned sentences with identical meanings, such as "Professor Virchow, I am Dr. X" and "I am Dr. X, Professor Virchow." Given that uncertainty about order, we will find subjects slipping predictably into "I am Dr. Virchow, Professor X" or some fragment thereof. On this account, in Freud's example only the *first* phrase slipped out, as observed routinely in laboratory studies (Chapter 6). But of course, Freud did not interpret the slip as reflecting a sequencing conflict in the production grammar; rather, he pointed to the young physician's ambition (his wish to be as famous as Dr. Virchow) as the crucial factor in eliciting the slip. But these explanations are not necessarily contradictory. The grammatical uncertainty may simply have created the conditions for the slip, and the young man's ambition may have operated to increase its probability. In Freud's words, much human behavior may be "overdetermined."

Until recently, the only evidence for Freudian slips was anecdotal and unreliable under known conditions. That situation may be changing, now that we have experimental methods for eliciting highly predictable slips in the laboratory (Chapter 6). A variety of slips designed to have a specific meaning can now be elicited. If the meaning of these slips is relevant to some conflictual issue for the speaker, they should, according to the Freudian hypothesis, increase in frequency compared to some control condition. This strategy has now been explored in several studies, with both positive and negative results.

Because Freud's writings on slips are occasionally vague or contradictory, we have suggested several levels of the Freudian hypothesis (e.g., Baas, 1980, 1985, 1987). From "weakest" to "strongest" hypotheses, these are:

1. *The semantic priming hypothesis.* Are slips that express some idea made more often when that idea has been presented before in different words?

2. *The situational priming hypothesis.* Are motivationally salient situations able to increase the rate of slips expressing the motivated state of mind?

These weaker hypotheses, although they represent some aspects of Freud's thinking, do not test his most distinctive and theoretically important claims about slips. They are essentially priming hypotheses, and priming is a very well-established phenomenon in perception, memory, and even action. Thus Hypotheses 1 and 2 would be predicted by most cognitive psychologists. They make the fewest demands on our current conception of the human mental apparatus. Not so for the third hypothesis, however.

3. *The psychodynamic hypothesis.* The very word *psychodynamics* was borrowed from physics to express the idea of human motives as a struggle between mutually antagonistic forces. And indeed, according to Reason (1984), "For Freud, slips were symptomatic of two things. They betrayed the presence of some socially unacceptable impulse, and they revealed the failure, at a moment of reduced vigilance, to suppress that impulse" (p. 45; see also Reason, 1984a). In experimental terms, we can phrase this question as follows: Will a tendency to *avoid expressing* some "primed" taboo thought serve instead, under some conditions, to increase the probability of slips that express the taboo thought? Because this statement assumes two opposing intentions, one tending to inhibit the other, it is a true psychodynamic hypothesis. While psychological theory has not dealt very much with the case of mutually opposing wishes or goals, they are conceptually well within the purview of accepted psychology (e.g., Baars, 1988; Dolland & Miller, 1950; Miller, Galanter, & Pribram, 1961; see Chapters 4 and 11, this volume).[1]

There is a widely made distinction between *supp*ression (as the conscious and deliberate avoidance of a taboo expression) and *rep*ression (as the unconscious and involuntary avoidance of a taboo thought). There are arguments against making this hard-and-fast distinction. Erdelyi (1985) maintains that Freud himself made no distinction between conscious and unconscious efforts to push painful thoughts out of consciousness. Further, one can view repression simply as successful suppression (thought avoidance) that has become automatic and hence unconscious with practice (e.g., Baars 1988, pp. 292–295; LaBerge, 1980; Shiffrin & Schneider, 1977). And finally, as Grünbaum (1984) pointed out, Freud's own examples of tendentious slips invariably involve clear cases of suppression rather than repression. The "Dr. Virchow" slip given above is a case in point. That is, in Freud's examples, the material whose expression is to be avoided is always readily available to consciousness.

In our research program, it seems better to avoid making the suppression-repression distinction for the time being. We do not have the empirical tools at the present time to show the existence of *un*conscious thought avoidance with

---

[1]Notice that conflicted goals may be revealed in contradictions between voluntary (edited) and involuntary (unedited) expressions of the same goal (see Chapters 1, 4, and 11). Further, as we will argue in a later section, the theoretical issue of Freudian competition between alternative goals may be only a special case of the general competition between goals for access to the limited-capacity system (Baars, 1988, Chapter 7).

any degree of certainty (see Baars, 1988, pp. 11–13; Holender, 1986; Holmes, 1974). If this situation were to change, the issue of repression versus suppression would become testable and then, it would be profitable indeed to consider the two ideas separately.

EARLY POSITIVE EVIDENCE

Testing the two weaker Freudian hypotheses (stated above) is quite straightforward. For Hypothesis 1 above, we simply used the phonological biasing technique (Chapter 6) to induce slips like "rage weight—wage rate." A few exposures before the slip target, we added, in addition to the phonological bias words, some word pairs similar in *meaning* to the expected slips. For instance, the words "salary scale" were presented before the target "rage weight" to see if this presentation would increase the rate of "wage rate." The presence of such semantic bias words almost tripled the rate of related slips, consistent with weak Freudian Hypothesis 1 (Motley & Baars, 1976).

Hypothesis 2 was similarly straightforward to test (Motley & Baars, 1979). In order to induce a motivationally compelling state of mind, we made use of the psychologist's last resorts: sexual attraction and fear of shock. Three groups of male college students were used in this task. The first was run on an individual basis by a young female experimenter, who volunteered to dress in a sexually attractive fashion. The second group were told they might receive an electric shock during the experiment and were shown some impressive-looking electrical equipment. (No shock was given.) The third group received neither of these treatments. All subjects were given the identical slip task, with six sex-related slip targets (e.g., "lice legs—nice legs") and six shock-related targets (e.g., "shad bok—bad shock").[2]

As Figure 1 shows, the situational manipulations more than doubled the rate of slips expressing sexual and shock-related ideas, but only for those slips that matched the situation. In the mismatched situation, the rate of slips was not distinguishable from the neutral context, thus, the sexual situation did not increase shock-related slips, nor vice versa. Thus, we may accept Freudian Hypothesis 2: States of mind induced by a motivationally important event may indeed increase the likelihood of making relevant, involuntary slips (Motley, Baars, & Camden, 1979).

What about a true "psychodynamic" slip, reflecting a conflicted state of mind? This is more difficult to test. We need not only to induce a slip express-

---

[2]We apologize for any offense that may inadvertently be given by our use of a female experimenter, and of sexually explicit words. In retrospect, it would have been somewhat better to run female as well as male subjects, with attractive male as well as female experimenters. An unpublished pilot study in the first author's laboratory has shown the expected effect of an attractive male experimenter on female subjects. Needless to say, both versions of the experiment involved objectification of the attractive experimenter of the opposite sex.

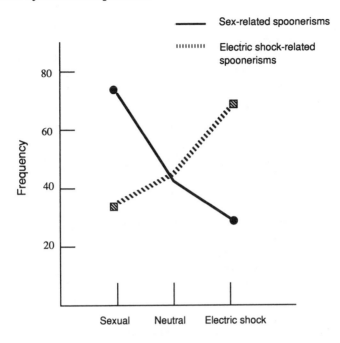

FIGURE 1. Spoonerisms related to sexuality and electric shock primed by the corresponding situations. (After Motley, Baars, & Camden, 1979.)

ing some state of mind, but we must also be sure that the state of mind is in conflict with a contrary goal. Hypothesis 3 predicts that the rate of slips expressing the conflicted state of mind will actually exceed the rate that is obtained without conflict. The problem is, of course, that there are no generally recognized measures of mental conflict: a research program pursuing the psychodynamic version of the Freudian hypothesis therefore inevitably becomes a bootstrapping process. One must develop and validate a measure of conflict in order to test the hypothesis; but the hypothesis itself is part of the network of interacting concepts and observations that may support the notion of inner goal conflict. (We do have at least a plausible conceptual outline of the issues: see Chapter 4; also Baars, 1988, Chapter 7, and the section below on the pursuit of the Freudian hypothesis).

The notion of inner conflict has been familiar to the educated public for about 300 years (Ellenberger, 1970). It is the essence of vast scholarly literatures in clinical theory and, of course, in Western art and fiction over the last several centuries. In experimental psychology, however, the notion has been widely rejected, for apparently good scientific reasons. During the period of behaviorism, though many behaviorists were interested in psychodynamic issues (e.g., Dollard & Miller, 1950; Tolman, 1948), it was difficult within a strict behavioristic framework even to conceptualize the notion of inner conflict (Baars, 1986; Erdelyi, 1985). With the advent of cybernetic theory, the concept of internal goals became scientifically respectable (see Bateson, 1979; Wiener, 1961), and by the 1960s, this approach to goals was already widely known in experimental psychology (Miller *et al.*, 1960). However, internal conflict, in the sense of repressed affect, has continued to have a poor reputation among the core community of scientific psychologists because of the apparent absence of persuasive evidence (e.g., Holmes, 1974).

Conflict has been an important topic in social psychology and personality research. Even there, however, though widely discussed, generally only indirect relationships between explicit, detailed theory and testable observations have been established. It is only recently that scientific psychologists have begun to accept the kind of complex information-processing architecture that can make explicit sense of the role of goals, and of competition between goals in our mental life (e.g., Anderson, 1983; Anderson & Bower, 1973; Baars, 1988). Chapter 4 in this book presents one such theory.

Of course, even a plausible theory is not sufficient in the absence of compelling empirical evidence. And here, we return to the bootstrapping issue: We need to develop and validate measures of inner conflict even as we pursue a test of the psychodynamic slip hypothesis itself. One way is to use existing empirical instruments from personality research, as a first step up the ladder. Existing validation and reliability studies may then be interpreted within a plausible information-processing theory, which may also generate predictions regarding Freudian slips. This was indeed our first approach, as described below. Another way is to take a kind of inner conflict that is so commonplace and consistently reported that it has immediate plausibility to most of us. Good instances are provided by efforts to control stubborn unwanted habits, for example, overeating, smoking, and other automatisms. A third way is actually to ask people to act out a conflictual situation, either under hypnosis or as part of a normal, voluntary task. All three of these approaches are discussed in this chapter.

In our first test of the psychodynamic hypothesis, we chose the Mosher Guilt Inventory, a widely used and well-researched questionnaire of guilt-related beliefs (Mosher, 1966, 1979). In this inventory, subjects are told that other college students gave the following fill-in responses to the capitalized sentence fragments (below). The job of the subjects is merely to indicate their degree of agreement or disagreement. We used only the sex guilt items of the Mosher Inventory, in order to group subjects who scored high, low, or medium on sex guilt. Some examples are:

(1) WHEN I WAS A CHILD, SEX excited me.
(2) SEX RELATIONS BEFORE MARRIAGE ruin many a happy couple.
(3) UNUSUAL SEXUAL PRACTICES are immature.
(4) WHEN I HAVE SEXUAL DESIRES I usually try to curb them.
(5) OBSCENE LITERATURE is detrimental to society.

Note again that this inventory seems to reflect deliberate and conscious conflict about sexually evocative events, rather than deeply repressed material that is not consciously available.

To return to the Mosher Inventory: True and false responses to each item were scored on a scale of −2 to +2 in terms of sex guilt, these scale values having been previously established to have good interjudge reliability. The resulting overall score of sexual guilt itself has good reliability and appears to define a population that has the theoretically expected properties of sexual guilt, so that the measure appears to have construct validity as well. For example, Galbraith (1968) reported that, compared with low-guilt subjects, high-guilt subjects made very few sexual associations to sexual double entendres like *screw*. This finding is consistent with the idea that high-guilt subjects avoid expressing sexual thoughts when they can. Similarly, Morokoff (1981) reported that high-guilt females denied being sexually aroused by listening to erotic stories, even when a physiological measure of sexual arousal showed them to be more aroused than medium- or low-guilt groups. Generally, it appears that high-guilt subjects tend to avoid expressing sexual thoughts, *as long as they have voluntary control over their responses.* But the evidence of physiological arousal also suggests that they may express *involuntarily* even *more* arousal than the comparison groups (see the section below on the pursuit of the Freudian hypothesis; Baars, 1988, pp. 293–295).

If this pattern holds true for slips (which are of course *in*voluntary), we should find *more* sex-related slips in a high-guilt sample than in a low- or medium-guilt sample. This pattern was found. Subjects were given the sexually relevant parts of the Mosher Guilt Inventory during their normal classes, separated from the experimental situation, so that the inventory would not influence their responses in the slip task. Using within-subject comparisons of sex-related versus neutral slips, in a sexually provocative context very much like the one used to test Hypothesis 2 above, we found that high-guilt males made an average of 2.7 more sex-related than neutral slips, whereas medium-guilt subjects made only 1.7 more sex-related slips, and low-guilt subjects made 1.3 more. The difference between the high-guilt group and the two others is statistically significant (Motley, Baars, & Camden, 1979). This result is consistent with Hypothesis 3, the psychodynamic hypothesis. Note again that this hypothesis predicts an increase in the *in*voluntary expression of the conflicted affect, but a decrease in *voluntary* expressions such as free associations, as found by Galbraith (1968). Open expression of taboo thoughts can presumably be avoided in the case of voluntary speech, as discussed in Chapter 11 of this book.

TWO ATTEMPTS AT SYSTEMATIC REPLICATION

The use of the Mosher Guilt Inventory represents the first bootstrapping strategy in relating meaningful slips to the expression of internal conflict. That is, we used a well-established paper-and-pencil test that appears to measure a certain motivational state, as a first step along the bootstrapping ladder. However, motivational and personality measures in general are not explicitly connected with the constructs they are supposed to measure; indeed, they are often said to define the very constructs they presumably measure in a circular fashion (Anastasi, 1988). Certainly, personality measures in general are not connected to a persuasive modern information-processing theory of human mental functions. They do appeal to our commonsense understanding of human beings and often have an implicit psychodynamic basis, which is, however, much more discursive and less precise than the best contemporary theories of mental processes.

Therefore, even if the first test of the psychodynamic hypothesis seemed to work, we are still left with the question: Does the guilt questionnaire really measure what it purports to measure? The question of construct validity makes it important to explore systematic replications, by means of different plausible examples of inner conflict. If convergent sources of evidence seem to support the construct, our confidence in it will increase. Two of these studies have been performed: one focused on a struggle over habit control and the second on hypnotically suggested emotional conflict. Both studies showed some positive results, without however resolving the psychodynamic hypothesis to our satisfaction. They do suggest some ways in which we can learn from our current shortcomings. We will summarize and critique each study. (See also the section below on the pursuit of the Freudian hypothesis.)

Study I: The Effect of Conflict about Overeating on Food-Related Slips

Millions of people experience frustrating conflicts about overeating, smoking, procrastination, or other unwanted habits. We can think of these problems as examples of inner conflict between an impulsive, short-term goal—of eating candy, perhaps—and a contrary goal such as losing weight for reasons of health, appearance, or social acceptance. The great advantage of an inner conflict like weight control is its obviousness: almost every person in our culture has a direct, personal experience of some unwanted habit that is difficult to control. It therefore has a kind of everyday plausibility that makes the relationship between the observable measure (such as self-report) and the inferred conflict quite persuasive. Conflict about unwanted habit control is, of course, largely conscious, although automatic, largely unconscious habits of thought and action do play a role as well.

Method

Twenty-six subjects (ages 17–29, 11 males and 15 females), of whom approximately half appeared overweight, were approached near the campus of the University of California, Berkeley, and asked to participate in a psychology language study at the Wright Institute, located a few blocks away, for five dollars per hour. The subjects who agreed were signed up for an appointed time, when an auditory version of the phonemic biasing task described in Chapter 6 was administered. The task elicited food-related spoonerisms, as shown in Table 1. The stimuli were presented via tape recorder in order to prevent pronunciation difficulties in reading nonsense word pairs, such as "buzzle ghear—guzzle beer." In order to prime thoughts about weight control, some of the word pairs presented were related to it (e.g., "too sweet," "too heavy"). In addition, a bowl of candy was located in front of, and within reach of, the subjects.

After the spoonerism task, the subjects were given an extensive self-report questionnaire about impulse control, embedded within which were questions about overeating and weight control. Of special interest was the subjects' self-reported experience of conflict about overeating. Eleven questions were generated that specifically asked about patterns of conflict between automatic impulses to eat versus voluntary efforts to control those impulses (see Table 2). Each item was to be rated on a seven-point scale indicating its frequency in the subjects' experience. A positive correlation was predicted between this "Food-Related Conflict Scale" and the number of food-related slips. At the end of the

TABLE 1

Food-Related Spoonerisms Used in Study I

1. kurger bing—Burger King	26. mig back—big Mac
2. geet oodies—eat goodies	27 polly lop—lollipop
3. dood ghinner—good dinner	28. soona tandwich—tuna sandwich
4. rork poast—pork roast	29. cripped weem—whipped cream
5. perry chie—cherry pie	30. keys chake—cheese cake
6. kite bookie—bite cookie	31. chibble nips—nibble chips
7. carty pake—party cake	32. ig din—dig in
8. froocy joot—fruity juice	33. kick lone—lick cone
9. haked bam—baked ham	34. sop chewy—chop suey
10. borm wiskitt—warm biscuit	35. tevenly haste—heavenly taste
11. bandy car—candy bar	36. wooger shafers—sugar wafers
12. sudge funday—fudge sundae	37. cheem crease—cream cheese
13. mau chain—chow mein	38. mempting torsel—tempting morsel
14. chish 'n fips—fish 'n chips	39. mot huffin—hot muffin
15. peemey cruding—creamy pudding	40. cummy yake—yummy cake
16. born cred—corn bread	41. stare rake—rare steak
17 tool fummy—full tummy	42. cranana beam—banana cream
18. frot highs—hot fries	43. dot hog—hot dog
19. tutter boast—butter toast	44. gah spetty—spaghetti
20. chied fricken—fried chicken	45. locka chaht—chocolate
21. chato tips—'tato chips	46. saple myrup—maple syrup
22. dobble gown—gobble down	47. metta gheal—get a meal
23. buzzle gear—guzzle beer	48. piant jeetsa—giant pizza
24. shanilla vake—vanilla shake	49. ig pout—pig out
25. crute fake—fruit cake	

TABLE 2

The Food-Related Conflict Scale: Questions about Conflict between Involuntary
Impulses to Eat versus Voluntary Attempts to Control Overeating

---

1. How satisfied are you with your current weight? (On a seven-point scale.)
2. If you have your favorite food in your refrigerator while you are studying, how easily can you resist eating it?
3. When you are tempted by some food or candy, and it is readily available, do you find it hard to resist?
4. Do you eat things you believe you should not eat?
5. Do you sometimes go on binges, where you eat a great amount at one time?
6. Have you ever engaged in any drastic activities to lose weight? (Fasting, purging, etc.)
7. Do you feel that your personal or sexual attractiveness depends on your losing weight?
8. Are you sometimes attracted to people who may be overweight?
9. Do you experience conflict about eating? That is, do you debate in your own mind whether or not to eat something?
10. Do you feel reluctant sometimes to go on a diet, because you enjoy eating so much?
11. Do you ever think that, if you continue your previous eating pattern, eventually it might be unhealthy for you?

---

hour, the subjects were fully debriefed about the study and were given the choice of withdrawing their data without penalty. None chose this option.

Results

In the study, 63 "single" slips (involving only a single word) and 68 "doubles" (showing both words of the predicted spoonerism) were obtained. Of the subjects, 13 reported themselves as being overweight, 10 as the correct weight, and 3 as underweight; 11 said they were on a diet, and 13 said they were not.

Analyses. Spearman rank correlations were calculated between the scores on the conflict scale and the number of single, double, and single *plus* double slips. Only the correlation between the conflict score and single food-related slips was significant ($p < .05$). A Mann-Whitney test was calculated to determine whether the total conflict scores differed according to whether the subjects were dieting (or considering dieting); "dieting" subjects had significantly higher total conflict scores (median ranks of 14.6 vs. 9.9; one-tailed test, Z corrected for ties, $p < .05$). A similar test was conducted comparing subjects who reported they were the "right weight" with those who felt they were "overweight"; this difference did not reach significance, although $p = .095$. (Three subjects who reported themselves as "underweight" were excluded from this analysis.) All of these tests give some support to the notion that the conflict scale was indeed measuring conflict about food.

Multiple Regressions. Multiple regressions were computed for each of the dependent variables: single slips, double slips, and single *plus* double slips. In the first multiple regression, three independent variables were used as predictors: total conflict scores, whether the subjects were dieting (or considering dieting), and whether the subjects reported that they felt overweight. The multiple regressions were not significant, although the beta coefficients correlated with single slips. Further multiple regressions using two of the three independent variables to predict the third were not significant. These results suggest that the prediction of single slips from the subjects' total conflict scores is not strengthened by adding the self-reported overweight or the dieting items to the regression.

Interpretation
The positive correlation between single slips and the conflict score was as predicted, although the lack of result for double slips is puzzling. (Given the latter finding, the negative result for "single *plus* double" is not surprising, just from mathematical considerations.) The positive correlation relating conflict scores to "dieting" or "considering dieting" supports the notion that the Food-Related Conflict Scale did indeed measure conflict about food. Although the relationship between conflict and self-reported overweight did not reach statistical significance, the *p* value of .095 suggests that more sensitive tests, perhaps using more subjects, might well reach significance. Altogether, the data provide moderate support for the predicted results.

Critique of Study I

Study I has some conceptual as well as methodological problems:
1. It is possible that the increased rate of single food-related slips reflects merely some sort of priming of food-related words and concepts. Increased conflict might indeed reflect this of priming; perhaps merely being conflicted about overeating also causes more thoughts about food. But the mere increase in food-related slips may reflect only activation of food-related thoughts, and not necessarily *conflict* about food.

This point brings up the dualistic nature of any conflict hypothesis, which inherently postulates the existence of two opposing tendencies, the impulsive one and the attempt to control the impulse. From this point of view, future studies of this problem should clearly elicit slips expressive of *conflict,* rather than slips that are merely food-related, that is, slips like "foo tat—too fat," or "lust mooz—must lose," rather than "loka chat—chocolate." Such conflict-related slips would help prevent the problem of mere semantic priming by the impulse to eat. This is indeed also a valid criticism of the sex guilt study described above.

2. What is the conflict about? There is yet a subtler critique: Precisely how do we conceptualize the goal that is conflicted? In the case of sexual guilt, the act of speaking freely about sexually attractive people may be inhibited, that is, the inhibition involves *speech* as well as action. This is not so obvious in the case of weight control. Many overweight people can speak unceasingly about their problems with weight control and do so at almost any opportunity. Thus, the question arises: Is the conflict in the case of overweight about *eating* or

speaking? It seems likely that "food conflict," unlike sexual guilt, deals only with the act of eating rather than with speaking. If that is so, we might expect far less effect on the speech system (i.e., slips of the tongue) and a greater effect on slips of action, such as reaching for food (see Chapter 7, this volume).

3. The methodology for eliciting slips also needs to be strengthened. One possibility is that the rate of slips elicited was too low for the "double spoonerisms" to be affected by biasing and conflict. We may have encountered a "floor" effect. In addition, the "double" slips may be more sensitive to editing effects; that is, they may have been avoided because they take about twice as long to say as the "singles" (Baars, Motley, & MacKay, 1975; Chapter 11, this volume). Finally, our priming conditions (the presence of some food-related words and a bowl of candy in the room) may have been too weak. For overweight subjects, the presence of a full-length mirror may be much more evocative of conflict than the mere presence of reminders of food.

4. There is the possibility of adding a concurrent distraction along with the slip task. It is worth recalling Reason's interpretation (1984b) of Freud's hypothesis as involving *two* factors: "[Slips] betrayed the presence of some socially unacceptable impulse, and they revealed the failure, *at a moment of reduced vigilance,* to suppress that impulse" (p. 45, italics added; see also Chapter 1). Notice that this was also postulated in Chapter 1 of this book for the Competing-Plans Hypothesis. This suggests that if we add a momentary distraction to the slip task, the additional loading of limited capacity may help to induce more slips or, more likely, to limit the subjects' ability to monitor, edit, and avoid the pending error. Such a momentary distraction may simply be evoked by a rapid button-press simultaneous with the slip response.

Thus, overall, the results of this experiment are not adequate as a test of the Freudian slip hypothesis. Nevertheless, the study provides some lessons for future research.

Study II. The Effect of Hypnotically Induced Emotional Conflict on Sentential Slips and Double Entendres

If we could somehow "program" an internal conflict into the human nervous system, the issue of validating the construct of inner conflict would be solved. Our third effort to test the Freudian slip hypothesis used one approach to this scientific ideal: the use of hypnosis with highly hypnotizable subjects (in the upper 20% of the population). Such subjects are easy to determine with any of the standard hypnotic susceptibility scales (e.g., Hilgard, 1971), which present a graded series of hypnotic suggestions, beginning with arm raising (which most subjects will do) to more unlikely tasks, such as auditory hallucinations, smelling perfume when presented with ammonia, and obeying unusual posthypnotic suggestions. The last three tasks are not done by the majority of subjects, but highly hypnotizable subjects will do them. Although there has been controversy about the reality of hypnosis (versus social compliance or role playing), there is less controversy about "high hypnotizables." For example, many "highs" will spontaneously show posthypnotic amnesia of the hypnotic experience, without knowing ahead of time that this is a common feature of high hypnotizability. In any commonsense interpretation of role playing or social compliance, the ability to show typical hypnotic behavior without knowing that it *is* typical seems paradoxical, to say the least. (See Baars, 1988, pp. 287–291, for further discussion of these issues.)

This study is distinctive in that *two* separate tasks were administered that may be sensitive to unreported conflict; first, the slip task, and second, a *double-entendre* task, involving multiple-choice items in which one item contained ambiguous words that could be interpreted as reflecting either anger or happiness (see Table 3). Positive results on *either* of these tasks would support the existence of an unexpressed affect, and one could therefore test whether the slip technique *itself* might lack sensitivity to the affective states.

Methods

Subject Selection. The subjects were 31 Stanford students, 13 females and 18 males, who were preselected from an introductory psychology class by their score on the Stanford Hypnotizability Scale (Hilgard, 1971). They were paid $7.50 for 1.5 hours of participation.

General Hypnotic Induction. The induction procedure was a standard one used for many years in the Stanford hypnosis laboratories of Ernest R. Hilgard and Gordon H. Bower. The subjects were relaxed in an easy chair in a quiet room and were given slow, monotonous suggestions that they were growing drowsy, tired, and hypnotized, and that they were concentrating on the voice of the hypnotist. After 5 minutes of such suggestions (long enough for most high hypnotizables), the subject was tested by suggesting that his or her arm would float up of its own accord. If the subject passed this minimal test, the mood induction was given next; if not, hypnotic induction was continued until the subject passed the hand-raising test.

Mood Induction. We will detail the mood induction just for anger, as the happiness induction was entirely analogous:

> In the next few minutes, I want you to begin to feel increasingly irritated and annoyed, and as you work on this annoyance, I want you to become angry, and then more and more angry. I don't want you to get out of control, not into a real fit of rage, so that you actually do anything about it! Keep it bottled up. But I do want you to get quite angry. On a 10-point scale, where 10 is as angry as you've ever been, I want you to get to a 6 or 7 level of anger. Some people find that they can stimulate themselves into anger by recalling a scene or situation from their past when they were provoked to extreme anger. This was perhaps an argument or fight you were in, or a series of extreme frustrations that you had that made you get extremely angry. To help yourself get angry, you should recall one of those anger scenes, close your eyes, and replay it in your imagination, visualizing all the details of the scene, and reexperiencing the frustration, the provocation, and your internal feelings of anger; feel the anger in your body, in your posture, in your clenched fist wanting to strike out, in your

clenched jaws wanting to bite. OK, let's start getting angry now—pull out of your memory an angry scene, annoyance, irritation, frustration. Start to go through this scene slowly in your imagination. You're getting annoyed now, starting to feel the irritation and annoyance. (*These suggestions were continued for several minutes, intensifying the anger.*) You're really angry now, boiling inside.

Posthypnotic Suggestions.   The following posthypnotic suggestions were given:

> I want you to remember this state of anger you are feeling now, because I want you to return to this same feeing of anger later when you start doing the two experimental tasks, that is, when you fill out the questionnaire and also when you do the repeating-sentences task. When those tasks begin, you will begin to get very irritated, annoyed, and increasingly angry at the person running the experiment, and at the silly, stupid tasks she or he will ask you to do. When those tasks begin, you will be able to quickly re-create and reenter this state of strong anger that you're now feeling. Moreover, you will continue to feel annoyed and angered as you continue to work through the parts of these silly, stupid tasks. As you turn each page of the questionnaire, you will be reminded of how angry that stupid task makes you, and you'll be reexperiencing the same level of anger that you're now feeling. During the repeated-sentences task, every time you hear the short beep on the tape recorder, you will be reminded of how irritated and angry this task is making you.
>
> Although you will feel this anger at me and at the tasks, you will nonetheless force yourself to continue performing the tasks and to maintain at least a superficial display of compliance with the experimenter's requests. Although you will be boiling over, keep your anger bottled up inside of you.
>
> OK. Now, I'd like you to turn off your anger; begin returning to a state of neutral, relaxed calm. Let go of your anger, wipe it away, and begin breathing easily, slowly, relaxing. Just relax now. (*Similar suggestions were repeated for 30 seconds.*)

Amnesia and Rehypnosis Suggestions.   These suggestions followed:

> One last thing. You will not consciously remember that I have told you to feel this annoyance and anger at the experimenter and the experimental tasks as you work on these tasks. Rather, you will forget that it was I who suggested that you become annoyed and angered by the tasks. You will simply think of them as very dull, silly, pointless, and irritating, and you will look on them, and on the experimenter, as causing your annoyance and anger. You will forget that this anger is related to this suggestion. You will continue to forget the source of your anger until I rehypnotize you, tell you that you can remember everything, and at that time remove all of the anger suggestions. Do you understand? You will feel angry when we begin the experimental tasks, but you will believe that you are angry because of the stupid, boring tasks.
>
> One more suggestion. After you have finished the two experimental tasks, I will want to rehypnotize you in order to relax you. In order to speed up that process, I want us to establish now a cue that we can use to help you reenter the trance state quickly. That cue will be my saying, "Now, it is time to reenter a deep trance state." When you hear me say that to you, I'd like you to quickly go back into this relaxed, drowsy trance you're now in. Do you understand? OK.

Awakening. The awakening followed:

> Let us begin to awaken you. You have been in a hypnotic trance for several minutes. In a minute, I will wake you up by counting slowly from 20 down to 1. As I count down, you will begin to come out of this deep, sleepy trance and become awake. As I count down, you become more alert; when I reach 5, your eyes will open; and when I reach 1, you will awaken, feeling fully alert and relaxed, as though you've awakened from a refreshing sleep. OK, here we go: 20, 19, . . . 5 (eyes open), . . . 1. You are fully awake, alert, feeling relaxed.

At this point, the two assessment tasks were administered, as follows.

Two Conflict-Assessment Procedures. In addition to the emotionally expressive slip task (Table 3), a double-entendre questionnaire was given to the subjects, designed to tap into either happy or angry affect. Table 4 shows this questionnaire. Note that it has multiple-choice items, in which one choice contains an ambiguity that can be interpreted either in the context of the specific item or in terms of angry or happy affect. Generally, subjects are unaware of these secondary meanings, as assessed by a *post hoc* questionnaire, yet the probability of choosing an ambiguously happy or angry choice increases when subjects are primed for either mood state (for the rationale of the double entendre task, see Baars, 1980; Motley, Baars, & Camden, 1979).

Note that the slip task chosen induced word exchanges in compound sentences (Table 3; Chapter 6, this volume). The major advantage of such sentential slips over spoonerisms is their ability to express a *proposition,* such as "She shot her brother" (Number 1) and "She hit her friend." These slips express an action on an object much more clearly than a two-word spoonerism could. A possible disadvantage of sentential slips is the fact that sentences simply take longer to plan and utter, thus perhaps giving more time for self-correction processes to take place (see Chapter 11, this volume). The slip task was explained as a way of studying prosodic phrasing in speech patterns when people speak rapidly.

The two experimental tasks were administered by different experimenters from those who had hypnotized the subject; these experimenters were blind to the anger versus happiness condition induced in the hypnotic phase of the experiment. This procedure was followed to prevent any contamination, and to ensure that conflict between the role of the hypnotizer and the person who would be the target of anger or happiness would not be confounded.

Rehypnosis and Debriefing. After the two assessment tasks, the experimenter hypnotized the subject again by using the previously suggested cue, "Now, it is time to reenter a deep trance state." Hypnosis was deepened by some further suggestions. At that point, the subject was reminded of the hypnotic mood induction, the angry or happy mood suggestions were removed, and the subject was suggested into a pleasant, calm state of relaxation. He or she was instructed to feel that way when awakening from the trance and leaving the laboratory.

At that point, the previous "awakening" procedure was used to bring the subject out of hypnosis. The posthypnotic cue for canceling amnesia, "Now you

TABLE 3
Sentential Slips Used in Study II

Angry slip items
1. She shot the rabbit and saw her brother.
2. She hit the nail and looked at her friend.
3. I'll shoot the movie and watch the children.
4. He kicked the ball and touched the dog.
5. I work with this person and he argued with them.
6. I pushed the buzzer and waited for the doctor.
7. I threw the ball and caught the man.
8. I whipped the cream and served my brother.
9. I ran to the goalie and booted the ball.
10. I observed my family and picked at my food.
11. I heard my dog and swatted the fly.
12. I covered the baby and pushed the stroller.
13. I left my sister and shoved the cart.
14. He passed my neighbor and grabbed the bundles.
15. I noticed his face and scratched my arm.
16. The garage really stinks and this job is big.
17. They shouted out there and I looked at them.
18. They yelled pretty hard and I thought about this.
19. They want to stop and I wish they would come here.
20. They want to put this down and I'd like to lift this thing up.
21. They want to shut it up but I'd love to open it.
22. He might smash his finger but I want to bend this thing.
23. I can't believe it and he can't stand them.
24. I'm tolerant of this and he's tired of moving.
25. I'm comfortable with this stuff but they're disgusted.
26. This is moving but the movie is nonsense.
27. This suits me but the coat bothers me.
28. This is fair but the food is terrible.
29. This is tasty but the dinner is a waste.
30. This is a risky job and also a lousy corporation.

Happy slip items
1. I am working and my parents are happy.
2. This is boring but the party was fun.
3. Life is all right and the movie was great.
4. I am sitting and she is pleased.
5. I pointed and the light glowed.
6. This is acceptable and the clothes are neat.
7. I am wondering but he is excited.
8. We are working on this job and they are pleased with the car.
9. The ladder is high and I am on the ground.
10. The results are positive and my thoughts are unsure.
11. The weather is fine and this is predictable.
12. The cake is terrific and I feel OK.
13. The radio is turned on and I am working.
14. He enjoys the movie and I remember this.
15. She is glad and I am going on vacation.
16. I'm having lunch and they had fun.

(continued)

TABLE 3 (*continued*)

17. I like seeing this when they're doing that.
18. This is a quick job and that is a great deal.
19. This is OK for me and those are terrific for them.
20. This is easy and later it will be interesting.
21. I'm relaxed with this and my friends are really pleased.
22. This job is acceptable and the old one is very nice.
23. Last year's was super and this is OK.
24. My brother is cheerful and I feel as usual.
25. They're glad to be heard and I'm ready to be doing this.
26. He played a fun game and this is a violin.
27. This book is entertaining and this is very thick.
28. The party was a blast but this is OK.
29. She feels like laughing but I feel so-so.
30. The lecture is fine and this is average.

TABLE 4
Ambiguous Multiple-Choice Items Used in Study II

1. He admired her photo and was most impressed by her _____.
   *a. lashes   b. cheekbones   c. eyebrows   d. lipstick
2. A walk along the windy shore felt _____.
   a. crisp   b. chilly   c. cold   *d. cool
3. After I came back from the laundry room, I gave her the _____.
   *a. sock   b. stocking   c. hose   d. nylons
4. She went to the stove because the soup was _____.
   *a. boiling   b. ready   c. done   d. cooking
5. After talking to him I got into my old _____ and drove off.
   *a. Fury   b. Plymouth   c. Chrysler   d. Dodge
6. I _____ the ball.
   *a. belted   b. tossed   c. bounced   d. threw
7. After working through the problem, I felt _____ I knew the answer.
   a. certain   b. sure   c. very sure   *d. positive
8. The light was _____ at the stage.
   a. aimed   b. pointed   c. directed   *d. beamed
9. Toward the end of the day I still had customers to _____.
   a. attend to   b. help   *c. finish off   d. handle
10. He was standing on a(n) _____ ladder.
    a. extended   b. 10-foot   c. long   *d. high
11. In setting up the party for my friend I prepared the _____ for her.
    a. food   *b. punch   c. snacks   d. drinks
12. The kettle was _____.
    a. calling   *b. hissing   c. gurgling   d. whistling
13. I'm going to eat my hamburger with _____.
    a. ketchup   *b. relish   c. fixings   d. condiments
14. The water was _____.
    a. running   *b. bubbling   c. spouting   d. splashing
15. He made me feel so strong about it, I swore I'd get _____ five o'clock.
    a. going at   b. home at   c. back home at   *d. back at

(*continued*)

TABLE 4 (*continued*)

16. I ironed my shirt so that it's _____.
    *a. neat   b. tidy   c. not wrinkled   d. presentable
17. I should stop always _____ for the best position.
    a. striving   *b. shooting   c. struggling   d. trying
18. Because she was talking too loud, the uncle _____ his child.
    a. hushed   *b. silenced   c. quieted   d. shushed
19. The car was _____.
    a. overheating   *b. fuming   c. smoking   d. stalled
20. He didn't understand my plan, so I gave him an example and _____.
    a. he finally understood   b. it finally occurred to him
    c. it suddenly became clear   *d. it just hit him
21. While playing tennis, my friend hit a high ball to me, and I _____ it.
    *a. smashed   b. played   c. lobbed   d. sent
22. In the past year, he really _____ his net worth.
    a. augmented   *b. appreciated   c. enhanced   d. increased
23. It looked like a(n) _____ big box.
    a. extremely   *b. great   c. very   d. rather
24. If you hold on for a minute, I'll _____ a cup of coffee.
    a. pour   *b. perk up   c. brew   d. make
25. The sun shone _____ on the water.
    a. strongly   b. intensely   c. clearly   *d. brightly
26. This week I have a(n) _____ amount of work to do.
    *a. terrific   b. considerable   c. exceptional   d. large
27. We worked hard all day at the _____ park.
    a. recreation   b. theme   c. outdoor   *d. amusement
28. It took her awhile to _____ the crumpled piece of paper.
    a. smooth out   b. uncrumple   c. unfold   *d. flatten
29. I showed them how to make dough by taking flour and eggs and _____.
    a. mixing them up   *b. beating them up   c. folding them   d. combining them
30. I would have called her but I didn't want to _____.
    *a. tie her up   b. occupy her   c. distract her   d. keep her busy
31. It was four o'clock before they _____.
    a. stopped work   b. quit   c. left   *d. knocked off
32. The painting was _____ brilliant color.
    a. full of   *b. exploding with   c. covered with   d. filled with
33. I think I'm going to join a political _____.
    a. organization   b. meeting   c. group   *d. party
34. I have a _____ for my sister's collection.
    a. bracelet   b. pendant   *c. charm   d. ring
35. I can feel the _____ weave of the fabric.
    a. subtle   b. delicate   c. intricate   *d. fine
36. It's about time for the lights to be _____.
    a. brought up   b. put on   c. switched on   *d. turned on
37. It was a(n) _____ time to get together.
    a. convenient   b. suitable   c. appropriate   *d. good
38. I always lost at cards with him and wanted to _____ more often.
    *a. beat him   b. win   c. triumph   d. succeed
39. There was a _____ on the wall.
    *a. light   b. fixture   c. lamp   d. bulb
40. The water was _____.
    a. glistening   *b. sparkling   c. shimmering   d. rippling

will remember everything," was given. The subject was asked about his or her state of mind and well-being and was reminded of the mood induction again. Any remaining feelings from the mood induction were discussed and explained as part of the hypnotic process. The subjects were then fully debriefed, any questions were answered, they were given the opportunity to withdraw their results without penalty, and they were given the experimenters' telephone numbers to call for any later questions or possible negative aftereffects. Finally, they were paid and dismissed.

Results

Results for Slips. There was no statistically significant relationship between the hypnotically induced affect and the type of slip. Thus the primary hypothesis was not supported.

Positive Results for Double Entendres. Using matched-pairs t tests comparing the percentage of "angry" divided by "happy plus angry" responses, and likewise for "happy" responses, both directions showed significance. The angry subjects marked a higher percentage of angry choices on the multiple-choice items ($t_D = 1.763$, $df = 14$, $p < .005$), and happy subjects chose more happy options ($t_D = -3.945$, $df = 14$, $p < .005$).

Follow-Up Study

In an attempt to probe the issue of role playing in hypnotic subjects, a much-discussed issue in the hypnosis literature, a new group of normal subjects was run, with explicit instructions to pretend to be happy or angry while answering the double-entendre questionnaire. These subjects were able to obtain more happy responses in the happy-pretense condition and more angry responses in the angry-pretense condition.

Discussion and Critique of Study II

Many of the criticism of Study I apply here as well. For example, both slips and double-entendre items reflected the presumed conflictual impulse, rather than conflict *about* the impulse. Thus, any effects could be interpreted as priming by means of the angry or happy condition, rather than conflict about the affect. In this respect, the results from the role-playing subjects are not difficult to explain. Instructions such as "please pretend to be happy while filling out this questionnaire" are likely to inspire bright undergraduates to seek for reasons to express happiness, and perhaps to decode a significant number of choices in the multiple-choice items quite consciously. Even *non*-conscious ambiguities would tend to show the same effect. In any case, in a study like this, it is clearly better to present stimuli that allow subjects to express (conscious or unconscious) *conflict,* rather than the induced emotion. For example, one might attempt to evoke slips like "I'm *not* upset" or even displaced anger, such as "He's mad but I don't care." (Such slips can be easily evoked by means of the techniques of Chapter 6, this volume.)

An even more serious criticism, however, comes from the fact that the slip technique simply did not deliver different results for the happy and angry subjects. Because the double-entendre technique did show results, it seems clear that the slip technique itself was flawed. This is true even if we view the hypnotic subjects as merely role playing: Why, after all, would role playing have an effect on double-entendres, but not on slips?

These largely negative results led us to ask whether the Freudian hypothesis is worth pursuing at all. We discuss this question next.

Is It Worth Pursuing the Freudian Hypothesis?

From some of our findings—such as Study II—the most immediate conclusion might be that the Freudian hypothesis is just plain wrong. But that is too simple. In principle, we cannot know whether the hypothesis is wrong, whether we have some conceptual blind spot in testing it, or whether our slip techniques provide a blunt instrument with which to operationalize the constructs involved.

In this section, we advance some arguments to the effect that the psychodynamic hypothesis is still worth pursuing in future research, in spite of the great difficulties reflected in the two studies discussed in this chapter. Inner goal conflict is inherent in any theory of voluntary control (e.g., Baars, 1983, 1988; Reason, 1984a,b; Norman & Shallice, 1980; Shallice, 1978). The ideomotor theory of voluntary control advanced in Chapter 4 suggests only one mechanism by which different goals can compete for control of the voluntary musculature. Moreover, the Competing-Plans Hypothesis discussed in Chapter 1 can be viewed as a version of the Freudian hypothesis (Freud, 1901/1938), which essentially postulates competition between high-level goals, such as "I want to be as famous as Dr. Virchow," and "I don't want to appear foolish and blatantly ambitious in this distinguished company." This is, in fact, simply another level of competition between plans. In Chapter 1, we pointed out the extensive evidence that plan competition may be involved in the great majority of slips. The Freudian slip hypothesis therefore requires no more theoretical assumptions than are already in place to explain the competing-plans phenomenon (Chapters 1 and 4).

Plan competition, the essence of psychodynamic thought, is not problematic from a cognitive perspective: ever since the cybernetic models of the 1940s, the previously long-disputed notion of an inner goal system has been scientifically quite respectable (e.g., Miller, Galanter, & Pribram, 1961). And it is hardly news that different goals can sometimes conflict. But there are subtler questions that current psychological theory does not address very often: What are the competing goals competing *for?* What is the mechanism by which the "winning" goal system comes to "take charge of" our actions?

The modern ideomotor theory described in Chapter 4 suggests that goals compete for access to something like a global workspace, a "publicity facility" that is closely associated with conscious experience (Baars, 1988). This is similar to the suggestion by Norman and Shallice (1980) that different motor schemata compete for access to a limited-capacity channel associated with consciousness (see also Bower & Cohen, 1982; Reason, 1984a,b). The Global Workspace model suggests a *function* for such competition for access to consciousness: if the "victorious," conscious goals are widely broadcast, they can recruit and control effector systems able to carry out the winning goal.

Among many other implications, this point suggests that the duration of a global goal image may make a critical difference. Highly automatized actions may require only a momentary goal, which may indeed by executed if a set of effectors is ready to carry them out before contradictory goal systems have time to react to them. Novel and conflictual goals may take more time to organize and execute than routine, largely automatized goals (see Baars, 1988, Chapters 7–9).

Our first finding in testing a "true psychodynamic" hypothesis is that subjects who score high on a measure of sex guilt actually make more sexual slips of the tongue, in a sexual situation, than do people who score low or medium. Presumably, high-sex-guilt subjects are in conflict between approaching and avoiding sexually desirable people. This conflict can be modeled as competition for access to a global workspace between goal images for avoidance and for approach (e.g., Dollard & Miller, 1950). Goal images for avoidance do not encounter competition in these subjects and are hence reportable by relatively slow linguistic processors. But goal images for approach do encounter competition from the avoidance goals and are thus limited to very brief access to the global workspace. However, even such brief access may be long enough to trigger highly automatic or otherwise highly prepared effectors that express the consciously unwanted goal. Our slip task presumably provides the kind of highly prepared response expressing the fleeting image of approaching the attractive person. The more these two intentions compete, the more the subject loses control over the unintentional expression of the prohibited goal, because the fleeting goal image cannot be modified as long as it is available for only a short time (see Chapter 11). Thus, the very effort to avoid thinking of the sexually attractive person in the situation paradoxically triggers the to-be-avoided thoughts. Presumably, the same sort of explanation applies to the finding that female high-sex-guilt subjects show more physiological sexual arousal to an erotic audiotape than do low-sex-guilt subjects, even though their *voluntary* reports show the opposite tendency (Morokoff, 1981).

According to Global Workspace theory (see Chapters 1, 4, and 11, this volume; Baars, 1983, 1988), the linguistic processors needed to generate verbal reports of conscious events are also distributed processors, just like the others (Figures 1, 2, and 3, in Chapter 4). If these processors have a relatively long lag time (as one might expect if they are generating a novel description of some conscious content), they may not be able to describe a global goal image that is very fleeting. But a very fleeting goal image may still be broadcast long enough to trigger a well-prepared, highly automatic action.

There is independent evidence that visual images may become automatic (i.e., less available for conscious retrieval and report) with practice (Pani,

1982). Under those conditions, these less conscious events may also become more difficult to control voluntarily. This may account for the differences that Langer and Imber (1979) found between novel and automatic versions of the same task; after automaticity due to practice, subjects could no longer monitor and describe their own performance. In terms of the ideomotor theory, the nonautomatic linguistic processes needed to generate such a verbal description simply lagged behind the automatic processors used to execute the task.

Thus, the very attempt to compete with the faulty goal image for access to the global workspace may paradoxically reduce the capacity of monitoring systems to alter it. This paradox may, in fact, be the origin of persistent involuntary actions of the kind that we see in stuttering, nervous tics, and many other kinds of psychopathology, which have the general property that the more one attempts to control the undesirable action, the less control one has.

This way of thinking about the issues allows us to explain a number of different phenomena involving conscious and quasi-conscious control of action in a very natural way (Baars, 1988, Chapter 7). Many of the resulting ideas have a psychodynamic flavor, at least in the sense that they involve competition between contrary intentions. They are not quite the ideas proposed by Freud, because the theory makes no claim that deep underlying conflicts cause these phenomena; rather, they may result from the normal functioning of the system that normally controls voluntary action by means of consciously available goals.

In sum, in spite of the flawed results described above, there are still important theoretical reasons to continue exploring tests of the conflict hypothesis.

Some Suggestions for the Future

We hope that any future research program can profit from the lessons learned in these studies. It is worth reminding ourselves that we are in a better position to examine the Freudian hypothesis scientifically than ever before, simply because we have the techniques for eliciting an enormous variety of different slips, expressing essentially anything we may wish our subjects to say.

The following are suggestions for future research:

1. The Competing-Plans Hypothesis in Chapter 1 suggests that slips are accompanied by a momentary overloading of the limited-capacity component, which interferes with the detection and suppression of potential slips. Thus, a rapid, limited-capacity-loading task, such as a simple reaction-time button press may have a considerable effect, both on the rate of slips and on the rate of emotionally charged slips. In general, it may be that output tasks like the slip techniques may differ from perceptual tasks simply because the experimenter has less control over short but critical temporal intervals. We can control visual detection tasks down to milliseconds; but a slip task, because the

subject retains some control over the task, can be manipulated only to perhaps the nearest second. Yet we know that 100-millisecond events may make a difference in error rate and so on. Under these circumstances, it may be especially important to have simultaneous overloading of the limited-capacity system, in order to inhibit self-correcting mechanisms.

2. It is important to obtain higher slip rates. Chapter 6 describes a set of principles for developing a variety of slip-induction tasks. Changes in the nature of the task, in the reaction time demanded of the subjects, in the verbal fluency of the subjects, and so on may make considerable differences in slip rates (see, for example, Chapter 9 on the effects of speed and short-term memory loading). One explanation of the lack of slip results in Study II above is that the use of compound sentences allowed the subjects enough time to inhibit or circumvent the impending slip. There may well be more optimal combinations of these factors that will increase the rate of slips in future studies.

3. The most successful work so far has used a real-life motivational inventory, the Mosher Guilt Inventory. It may be a good idea to go back to well-standardized personality or motivational inventories, in order to stay as close as possible to the powerful conflictual goals that may exist in real-life situations, as opposed to possibly weaker laboratory manipulations.

4. For the reasons discussed above, it is important in future studies to have slips expressing inhibitory tendencies directly, rather than expressing the presumed conflictual affect itself.

Altogether, we cannot be satisfied with the results obtained so far: all of the Freudian slip studies have some real flaws, including the original "sex-guilt" study. Nevertheless, we have made *some* progress over and above the mere collection of suggestive anecdotes. This chapter reflects both progress— our ability to elicit conflict-relevant slips, for example—and several remaining obstacles, which clearly require more work. We have made some progress; we may be on the road toward a solution.

ACKNOWLEDGMENTS

The research reported in this chapter was supported in part by the Program on Conscious and Unconscious Mental Processes, sponsored by the John D. and Catherine T. MacArthur Foundation, and directed by Mardi J. Horowitz. The Wright Institute and its president, Peter Dybwad, were also most helpful in the completion of this work.

REFERENCES

Anastasi, A. (1988). *Psychological testing* (6th ed.). New York: Macmillan.
Anderson, J. R. (1983). *The architecture of cognition.* Cambridge: Harvard University Press.
Anderson, J. R., & Bower, G. H. (1973). *Human associative memory.* Washington, DC: Winston.

Baars, B. J. (1980). The competing plans hypothesis: An heuristic viewpoint on the causes of errors in speech. In H. W. Dechert & M. Raupach (Eds.), *Temporal variables in speech: Studies in honour of Frieda Goldman-Eisler.* Amsterdam: Mouton.

Baars, B. J. (1983). Conscious contents provide the nervous system with coherent, global information. In R. Davidson, G. Schwartz, & D. Shapiro (Eds.), *Consciousness and self-regulation* (Vol. 3, pp. 47–76). New York: Plenum Press.

Baars, B. J. (1985). Can involuntary slips reveal a state of mind? In M. Toglia & T. M. Shlechter (Eds.), *New directions in cognitive science* (pp. 242–261). Norwood, NJ: Ablex.

Baars, B. J. (1986). *The cognitive revolution in psychology.* New York: Guilford Press.

Baars, B. J. (1987). What is conscious in the control of action? A modern ideomotor theory of voluntary control. In D. Gorfein & R. R. Hoffman (Eds.), *Learning and memory: The Ebbinghaus Centennial Symposium,* Hillsdale, NJ: Erlbaum.

Baars, B. J. (1988). *A cognitive theory of consciousness.* New York: Cambridge University Press.

Baars, B. J., Motley, M. T., MacKay, D. G. (1975). Output editing for lexical status in artificially elicited slips of the tongue. *Journal of Verbal Learning and Verbal Behavior, 14,* 382–391.

Bateson, G. (1979). *Mind and nature: A necessary unity.* New York: Bantam Books.

Bower, G. H., & Cohen, P. R. (1982). Emotional influences in memory and thinking: Data and theory. In M. S. Clark & S. T. Fiske (Eds.), *Affect and cognition* (pp. 291–331). Hillsdale, NJ: Erlbaum.

Dollard, J., & Miller, N. E. (1950). *Personality and psychotherapy: An analysis in terms of learning, thinking, and culture.* New York: McGraw-Hill.

Ellenberger, H. F. (1970). *The discovery of the unconscious: The history and evolution of dynamic psychiatry.* New York: Basic Books.

Erdelyi, M. (1985). *Psychoanalysis: Freud's cognitive psychology.* San Francisco: Freeman.

Freud, S. (1901/1938). *The psychopathology of everyday life.* In A. A. Brill (Ed.), *The basic writings of Sigmund Freud.* New York: Random House.

Freud, S. (1920/1966). *Introductory lectures on psychoanalysis.* New York: Norton.

Galbraith, G. G. (1968). Effects of sexual arousal and guilt upon free associative sexual responses. *Journal of Consulting and Clinical Psychology, 32,* 701–711.

Grünbaum, A. (1984). Précis of *The foundations of psychoanalysis: A philosophical critique. Behavioral and Brain Sciences, 9,* 217–284.

Hilgard, E. R. (1971). Hypnotic phenomena: The struggle for acceptance. *American Scientist, 59*(5), 567–577.

Holender, D. (1986). Semantic activation without conscious identification in dichotic listening, parafoveal vision, and visual masking: A survey and appraisal. *Behavioral and Brain Sciences, 9,* 1–66.

Holmes, D. (1974). Investigations of repression: Differential recall of material experimentally or naturally associated with ego threat. *Psychological Bulletin, 81*(10), 632–653.

LaBerge, D. (1980). Unitization and automaticity in perception. In J. H. Flowers (Ed.), *1980 Nebraska Symposium on Motivation,* 53–71. Lincoln: University of Nebraska Press.

Langer, E. J., & Imber, L. G. (1979). When practice makes imperfect: Debilitating effects of overlearning. *Journal of Personality and Social Psychology, 37*(11), 2014–2024.

Miller, G. A., Galanter, E. H., & Pribram, K. (1961). *Plans and the structure of behavior.* New York: Holt.

Morokoff, P. (1981). *Female sexual arousal as a function of individual differences and exposure to erotic stimuli.* Doctoral dissertation, Department of Psychology, State University of New York, Stony Brook.

Mosher, D. L. (1966). The development and multitrait-multimethod matrix analysis of three measures of three aspects of guilt. *Journal of Consulting Psychology, 30,* 35–39.

Mosher, D. L. (1979). The meaning and assessment of guilt. In C. E. Izard (Ed.), *Emotions in personality and psychopathology.* New York: Plenum Press.

Mosher, D. L. (1992). Revised Mosher G. Inventory. In C. M. Davis (Ed.), *Sexuality related measures: A compendium.* New York: Davis, Yarber, & Davis.

Motley, M. T., & Baars, B. J. (1976). Semantic bias effects on the outcomes of verbal slips. *Cognition, 4,* 177–187.

Motley, M. T., & Baars, B. J. (1979). Effects of cognitive set upon laboratory-induced verbal (Freudian) slips. *Journal of Speech and Hearing Research, 22,* 421–432.

Motley, M. T., Baars, B. J., & Camden, C. T. (1979). Personality and situational influences upon verbal slips. *Human Communication Research, 5,* 195–202. New York: Plenum Press.

Norman, D. A., & Shallice, T. (1980). *Attention and action: Willed and automatic control of behavior.* Center for Human Information Processing, University of California at San Diego, La Jolla.

Pani, J. R. (1982). *A functionalist approach to mental imagery.* Paper presented to the Psychonomic Society, Baltimore.

Reason, J. T. (1984a). Lapses of attention in everyday life. In R. Parasuraman & D. R. Davies (Eds.), *Varieties of attention* (pp. 515–549). New York: Academic Press.

Reason, J. T. (1984b). Little slips and big disasters. *Interdisciplinary Science Reviews, 9*(2), 3–15.

Shallice, T. (1978). The dominant action system: An information-processing approach to consciousness. In K. S. Pope & J. L. Singer (Eds.), *The stream of consciousness: Scientific investigation into the flow of experience,* New York: Plenum Press.

Shiffrin, R. M., & Schneider, W. (1977). Controlled and automatic human information processing: 2. Perceptual learning, automatic attending, and a general theory. *Psychological Review, 84,* 127–190.

Tolman, E. C. (1948). Cognitive maps in rats and men. *Psychological Review, 55,* 189–208.

Wiener, N. (1961). *Cybernetics: On control and communication in the animal and the machine* (2nd ed.). Cambridge: MIT Press.

V

COMMENTARY

13

The Psychology of Slips

Abigail J. Sellen and Donald A. Norman

> I planned to lock my door but not to put the chain on. I locked the door and proceeded to put the chain on all the while thinking that it wasn't what I wanted to do.

> I planned to call my sister Angela but instead called Agnes (they are twins). What I heard myself say did not match what I was thinking.

> I wanted to turn on the radio but walked past it and put my hand on the telephone receiver instead. I went to pick up the phone and I couldn't figure out why. I searched my mind to think of what I wanted to do before I realized I had intended to listen to some music. (All three examples taken from a diary study of slips reported in Sellen, 1990)

Slips provide compelling evidence of the interplay or sometimes the lack of interplay between reportable intentions and action. As the three examples above illustrate, carrying out actions either in the absence of a conscious governing intention or even contrary to intentions held in the mind is part of our everyday experience. In diary studies of action slips, people often report a temporary detachment from or powerlessness over their actions.

The phenomenon of a dissociation between the conscious observer and the automatic actor has important implications for models of action. According

ABIGAIL J. SELLEN • MRC Applied Psychology Unit, 15 Chaucer Road, Cambridge CB2 2EF, United Kingdom and Rank Xerox Ltd. Cambridge EuroPARC, 61 Regent Street, Cambridge, CB2 1AB, United Kingdom. **DONALD A. NORMAN** • Department of Cognitive Science, University of California at San Diego, La Jolla, California 92093.

Experimental Slips and Human Error: Exploring the Architecture of Volition, edited by Bernard J. Baars. Plenum Press, New York, 1992.

to Baars, and consistent with the conclusions of others in the field, it is this dissociation which, in part, accounts for slips. Slips reveal the potential autonomy of action and goals and are thus, to use Baars' terminology, "liberated automatisms." A model of human action inspired by slips must therefore account for qualitatively different, interactive sources of control.

It is fair to say that there is now some consensus on the basic architecture of human action: most researchers in the field agree on a hierarchically organized system containing multiple levels of representation. At the highest level is the representation of conscious goals and desires. At the lowest levels are representations of the details of the particular actions to be executed. With regard to the issue of control, we have evidence of a broad but important distinction. There are two main modes of control: an unconscious, automatic mode best modeled as a network of distributed processors acting locally and in parallel; and a conscious control mode acting globally to oversee and override automatic control. Automatic and conscious control are complementary: the unconscious mode is fast, parallel, and context-dependent, responding to regularities in the environment in routine ways, whereas the conscious mode is effortful, limited, and flexible, stepping in to handle novel situations.

In conjunction with this emerging picture of the action system come two major changes in the way we view human action, both of which are evident throughout this book. The first trend is a shift away from viewing errors as special events or as the product of special error-producing mechanisms and instead toward a view that characterizes errors as the normal by-products of the design of the human action system. Thus, errors can be characterized as the result of trade-offs in the system—as the costs incurred for benefits gained elsewhere. One example given by Baars in Chapter 1, and elaborated on by Reason in Chapter 3, is the "flexibility–accuracy" trade-off. Actions can be performed accurately and effortlessly because the human processing system has evolved to perform efficient pattern matching. As a result, stored patterns of actions can often be invoked quickly and easily. In part, this is what characterizes expert performance. Experts can recognize familiar patterns or perform skilled responses even when the necessary information is only partially specified. Most of the time, this leads to increased efficiency: decisions are made and actions produced on the basis of partial information and without the need of a precise or complete specification of each action sequence. The cost, however, is the occasional error or slip.

The other emerging trend is a departure from an approach to planning and action in which actions are seen as the end products of a top-down planning process, beginning with a well-specified, conscious intention in the service of some predetermined goal. In the traditional view of planning and problem solving, plans are complete entities that specify how to proceed, given all possible conditions. This view of complete planning is the conceptual opposite of modeling action as being continually responsive to the environment—as being *situated* rather than planned, to use Suchman's terminology (1987). Suchman argued that actions are determined largely through interaction with the environment rather than being planned in advance. Thus, alternative courses of action are often determined when actions are already under way. The role of plans is to provide a way of reasoning about action and of considering alternative choices. This view provides an interesting mix of the behaviorist and cognitive tradition: while the environment exerts continual control, mental activities and judgments evaluate the situation and assess possible responses. Behavior is thus neither purely behavioristic nor purely cognitively determined.

Evidence from the study of slips is consistent with this cognitive-deterministic hybrid view of control, in part, because it demonstrates that some action takes place *in spite of* conscious desires and some takes place even in *the absence of* conscious awareness. However, these departures from desired behavior are still the infrequent case. After all, slips may be common, but they are not the dominant behavior. Appropriate, controlled behavior is the normal mode of action. The study of slips is important because it gives us evidence about the role of consciousness in controlling action. One consequence of the studies reported in this book is that the burden of explanation of skilled action requires mechanisms acting without benefit of a central executive.

It is often with some degree of surprise that psychologists realize the extent to which behavior can be determined and shaped in the absence of conscious control or awareness. A case in point is MacKay's posing of the "awareness puzzle" (Chapter 2). How is it, he asks, that unintended actions accommodate to their surroundings? How is it that factors of which we are not aware increase the frequency of certain kinds of slips? Such questions are reminiscent of similar issues that are now the focus of a growing body of research in the field of human memory. Recent work has shown that even if we cannot consciously recall something ("explicit memory"), other kinds of behavioral tests (e.g., word-fragment-completion tests) can show the existence of "implicit memory"—memories that exist despite our inability to access them consciously. This analogous situation elsewhere in psychology speaks to a larger issue. Perhaps instead of being surprised by the extent to which unconscious events shape our behavior, we should be more inclined to question our conscious abilities, and to view the intervention of awareness and will in behavior as exceptional, rather than as the rule. In our doing so, the challenge becomes one of understanding and modeling a system in which the details of action can be specified without appealing to some type of all-knowing executive controlling agency. This is not to say that we can ignore the role of "volition," "will," "consciousness," and "intention." In many ways the study of slips forces us to confront these elusive concepts head-on, a task begun by Reason in Chapter 3 and Baars in Chapter 4.

The book raises many theoretical issues central to an understanding of the psychology of action. We discuss some of these issues under four general subheadings: unconscious mechanisms of control; the role of conscious control; the relationship between verbal and nonverbal slips; and error detection and the evaluation of action. We comment first on theory and follow this discussion with an examination of some of the methodological issues that arise in slip research.

UNCONSCIOUS MECHANISMS OF CONTROL

Two observations recur throughout the book that bear directly on the nature of the mechanisms for the unconscious control of action. First, the form of errors is lawful: the erroneous components of actions tend to conform to the constraints of the immediate context within which the error appears. This point can be illustrated both by the manner in which erroneous components accommodate to the constraints provided by the structure of the action, and by the fact that there tends to be a lawful relationship between substituted and intended components in action (in speech referred to as *sequential class regularity*). Both Baars and MacKay (Chapters 1 and 2, respectively) discuss these issues. Second, erroneous actions are sensitive to the constraints of the external world. For example, even when a person reaches for the wrong object, the hand configures itself appropriately for the unintended object. In both cases, it seems that some levels of control can do their jobs properly even though something has gone wrong at other levels in the system. The first observation shows that the rules governing action *production* are generally intact when actions are unintended. The second case shows that the rules governing the *reactive* component of the action system are also intact when slips occur.

There are two views of the lawful nature of slips: that they are a natural result of action formulation or that they result from the covert editing of actions. This issue is the central concern of Mattson and Baars in Chapter 11 and reappears throughout this volume and elsewhere (e.g., Levelt, 1989). Connectionist models of speech and action production by Dell and MacKay (Dell, 1986; Dell & Reich, 1980; MacKay, 1987, and Chapter 2, this volume) support the notion that the lawfulness is a natural result of the process of action formulation. Their models account for "sequential class regularity" in slips by appealing to the underlying structure of the action system. Categorical constraints built into the models ensure that substitutions, blends, and exchanges in action components occur within the same sequential class. In essence, the notion is related to the more general idea of *slot filling* in schemata—a notion discussed by Reason in Chapter 3. Errors are lawful because the "slots" determined by schemata are specialized to or connected to certain classes of candidate action components. Priming or activation thus spreads among a restricted set of possibilities all of which belong to the same class, and the result is substitutions only within that class.

Baars, Motley, and others (Baars, Motley, & MacKay, 1975; Mattson & Baars, Chapter 11, this volume; Motley, 1980; Motley, Baars, & Camden, 1981) have proposed a very different notion. These authors have suggested that covert, specialized editing mechanisms are responsible for checking different aspects of the about-to-be-produced action (e.g., lexical, syntactic, and semantic aspects). Incipient actions that violate any of these rules are suppressed or preempted. These editing processes may occur consciously or unconsciously.

There is good evidence for both the action-formulation and the editing models. Action-formulation models have the virtue that they have been tested through computer simulation, where they produce many of the kinds of slips observed in real life. Mechanisms for unconscious or conscious editors have not been made so explicit. However, we know that editing mechanisms must exist. After all, people often correct their speech and actions just after speaking or acting, and this could not be done without some sort of error monitoring and correction mechanism. That these mechanisms may operate on internally represented actions just before their emission would neither be surprising nor revolutionary. Subjective experience also tells us that we can become internally aware of slips before they occur (the basis of Dell and Repka's study, Chapter 10). Moreover, there is good evidence (see Chapter 11) to indicate that slips are indeed represented and edited before the emission of the overt action.

The fact that both approaches seem viable may simply mean that both exist, that they are not mutually exclusive. What this suggests is that slips are the result of an organized action system not only predisposed to rule-governed output but also containing editing mechanisms.

Contemplating the existence of unconscious editors implies the existence of unconscious control systems operating on *internal* feedback. The fact that unintended actions are often modified for external constraints implies the existence of unconscious control systems using feedback from the *external* world. Attending to the environment and using perceptual feedback effectively can be accomplished at a level independent of our conscious intentions. A model of action must therefore account for perceptual-motor feedback loops that operate locally as opposed to being driven from higher, conscious levels of control. It is a difficult problem because, in some sense, we must describe how we can be "aware" of and process external information in order to operate on it without this awareness making contact with our intentions. To date, this problem has not been examined empirically, nor has it been incorporated into models of action.

THE ROLE OF CONSCIOUS CONTROL

To what extent is conscious control involved in initiating, guiding, and terminating action? Generally speaking, we can think of goals as the specification of desired world states. This is different from intentions, which are the means by which desired world states are achieved. The power of goals as the driving force behind behavior is convincingly demonstrated by the Chevreul pendulum as described by Baars (Chapter 4). In this demonstration, consciously imaging the desired world state both initiates and determines the course of action. Termination of the action can also be characterized as a deliberate conscious act, occurring when the goal state specified by the original plan is perceived to be satisfied.

Although it is important to describe this kind of goal-driven action, clearly there are other kinds of behaviors to be accounted for in a model of action production. Consideration of different definitions of the term *goal* led Mandler

(1985) to describe a range of other kinds of goal-driven behaviors. He pointed out that in some situations, actions may be done for their own sake, and although they may accomplish certain "goals" because they are executed, they need not have been invoked by anything conscious. (This is similar to Searle's concept of "intentions in action," in which actions may express an intention without having held that intention consciously in mind; Searle, 1980). Further, actions need not be terminated by the satisfaction of some predetermined goal state. Some behaviors are consummatory acts in themselves and have inherent "stop rules" that cause termination. In other cases, actions may be terminated because their goals are not or do not appear to be reachable. Thus, the view of goals as conscious cognitive states that determine the course of behavior is overly simplistic.

The existence of the class of slips known as *capture errors* shows that complex action sequences may be initiated automatically by familiar environmental cues without any conscious envisioning of goals. There are many examples in diary studies of external cues inciting routine actions. In one case, a person carrying a loaf of bread to the freezer threw it instead into an open washing machine (Sellen, 1990). In another, a person passing through a garage spied his gardening boots and proceeded to put them on (Reason & Mycielska, 1982). Consciously entertaining the wrong end state before initiating these actions in these instances is very unlikely or, at least, is never reported in examples of capture errors in diary studies.

Slips also show the extent to which affordances in the outside world rather than predetermined plans can be responsible for *guiding* actions. Description errors are one class of slips that are presumed to occur precisely because plans for action are ill specified or ill described. Thus, I may intend to put the milk back in the refrigerator and my empty glass in the sink but do the opposite, in part because the objects afford these actions, and in part because the objects have not been well specified in advance. A similar point is made by the example at the opening of this chapter, where a person reported reaching for and picking up the telephone when the original intention was to turn on the radio. Affordances of objects in the outside world may be more influential in guiding actions than plans. Other examples of slips, however, illustrate the fact that affordances may trade off with plans. In one example from Sellen's diary study, a person tried to light a cigarette with the lid of an aerosol can, going so far as to bring the lid to the end of the cigarette before realizing the error. Clearly, in this instance, the original plan was strong enough to override the lack of affordances until a critical action was prevented.

The study of slips leads us to the conclusion that much of behavior is reactive rather than preplanned, that many of the details of action are determined during action. Birnbaum and Collins's chapter (Chapter 5) suggests that not only are low-level details determined in this way, but goals themselves may be autonomous, computational agents "looking out for themselves" and taking advantage of opportunities as they arise. This view of action as "opportunistic" is therefore consistent with a view that downplays the importance of the role of planning in action. The reactive nature of behavior is understandable when we consider the complexity and unpredictability of the environment: we cannot possibly know all that is happening, and even what we do know is of limited accuracy, partial completeness, and subject to change. It is understandable that animals have evolved to take advantage of and react appropriately to circumstances as they arise.

What, then, of the role of consciousness? There is much agreement that the primary roles of conscious control are to handle departures from routine actions, to oversee and monitor action, and to step in and evaluate actions when things go wrong. Norman and Shallice (1986) suggested that conscious mechanisms, including volition (will), can bias the course of action only by activating or inhibiting the underlying control elements. In this model, most action does not need conscious control. Consciousness is needed only in carefully circumscribed circumstances, such as when the task is not well learned, unexpected events occur, something goes wrong (troubleshooting), or the situation is considered critical or dangerous. But even in these cases, conscious control exerts a directional bias on action but cannot control it completely. Consciousness and willful direction of one's activities are simply among the many factors that interact in the formation of action sequences. This view is consistent with many of the observations of slips, especially the conditions in which one observes oneself performing actions that were not intended.

Explaining just how conscious redirection and intervention occur presents some difficult problems. Both Baars (Chapter 1) and Reason (Chapter 3) suggest that conscious control steps in when the choice points in action are underdetermined. Suppose we plan to depart from our normal routine at some point in the future. Is there any way, apart from mental rehearsal that we can remind ourselves of this intention when we need to? How are internal reminders set up in advance? What mechanisms are responsible for signaling the need for conscious control? These have not yet been adequately described. Clearly, though, there must be something that directs and triggers the conscious control system. In Chapter 11, Mattson and Baars recognize this need in suggesting a "competition detector" in spreading activation models to signal the occurrence of competing activations to the conscious control system. Until we begin to model these metacognitive mechanisms, our understanding of action will be sadly lacking.

THE RELATIONSHIP BETWEEN VERBAL AND NONVERBAL SLIPS

A third important theoretical issue is to separate the influence of language from slips. To date, the majority of the literature has concentrated on slips involving language (e.g., Cutler, 1982; Fromkin, 1973, 1980). The question is to what extent there are common governing principles underlying language-based and pure action errors.

Language has a number of special properties that may make it quite different from most other actions. Among the characteristics are:

1. *Level of practice.* For human adults, language is a very highly practiced

skill—among the most practiced of human skills. Most language understanding and generation are done without conscious control or even awareness: authors are fond of stating that they often do not know what their characters will say or do until they read for themselves what they have written in their manuscripts.

2. *Few natural constraints and arbitrary action patterns.* Both writing and sound patterns are unrelated to meaning. Instead, associations between them result from a long historical development period in which certain arbitrary sounds have come to be assigned to the words of a language and certain arbitrary shapes to the basic written symbols. As a result, there are very few natural constraints on language production.

3. *Strong rule-based constraints.* Although there are few natural constraints, grammatical constraints are very strong. Language has evolved so as to require reasonably strict adherence to constraints at many levels of the utterance: pragmatic, semantic, grammatical, phonological, and phonetic, with only the phonetic constraints having any basis in physical structure.

4. *Rapid behavior, short time units.* Language is spoken rapidly, requiring movement times measured in milliseconds and interpretation times equally fast.

5. *A cooperating, forgiving recipient.* Many physical actions interact with an inert, unintelligent world and must therefore be precise and accurate in both spatial and temporal aspects. Language is directed toward cooperating, intelligent recipients, who can compensate for most deviations. Action slips are often noticed because the environment fails to respond appropriately to the action or prevents further action. But ungrammatical and even nonsense utterances are often naturally compensated for by the listener, so much so that, as a result, they are not noticed by either party.

Clearly, slips in different domains involve different units of representation, and these must be considered in attempting to compare data across domains. As pointed out by Mattson and Baars (Chapter 7), analysis of the units involved in speech slips has been used as an argument for the "psychological reality" of the underlying units of representation for speech production. In speech, we find evidence for migration, transpositions, substitutions, omissions, and insertions for many different kinds of units ranging from single letters and phonemes on up to words. In typing, Mattson and Baars (Chapter 7) argue for units at the level of keystrokes; hand, finger, and position specification; and serial position. Other studies of typing errors (e.g., Grudin, 1983; Rumelhart & Norman, 1982; Sellen, 1990) confirm this finding. In addition, there are cases of substitutions at the lexical level where one word is captured by a related word (e.g., *father* for *mother,* or *Hugh* for *huge)* as well as capture by common letter clusters such as *ing* and *th.* This suggests that units larger than keystrokes are also represented in the system. (See Dell, 1986, for a model of speech production which, in part, is based on this phenomenon.) One of the only studies to examine the issue of units for non-speech-based action is that reported by Mattson and Baars (Chapter 7). Their finding is that we can speak of the natural units of action in terms of direction of movement, the particular action involved, the object of action, the number of times the action is repeated, the effector involved, and the amplitude of movement.

Despite the special nature of language, there is much in common between the mechanisms that produce language and other forms of action. Many speech slips seem to be mirrored in the slips of other modalities of action. Omissions, transpositions, insertions, and substitutions of natural units can be described in a variety of verbal and nonverbal domains. Recency and relative frequency seem to affect both classes alike. Plan competition and cognitive overload seem to play similar roles. The problems of action sequencing plague both speech and nonspeech actions. The many chapters of this book attest to the common mechanisms underlying all actions, whether they involve language or not.

ERROR DETECTION AND THE EVALUATION OF ACTION

A final major theoretical topic is the detection of slips. The topic of error *evaluation* has received far less attention than error *generation*. The exception is in the sense that error detection processes have largely been taken to refer to detection of slips *before* the emission of an action, and almost exclusively with respect to speech errors. This is quite different from the detection of errors in overt action, although the form of some kinds of covert slips may be similar, in some instances, to overt slips (as Chapter 10 by Dell and Repka suggests).

Detection of slips in overt, *nonverbal* actions has so far received little attention. Very few controlled studies designed to elucidate the mechanisms involved can be found in the literature. The laboratory studies that do exist involve a range of tasks: typing (Long, 1976; Rabbitt, 1978; Shaffer & Hardwick, 1969; West, 1967); simple perceptual-motor tasks (Adams, 1971; Adams & Goetz, 1973; Schmidt, 1987; Schmidt & White, 1972); key-pressing tasks (Rabbitt, 1966a,b, 1967, 1968, 1978; Rabbitt & Phillips, 1967; Rabbitt & Vyas, 1970); natural speech (Miyake, 1982; Nooteboom, 1980); statistical problem solving (Allwood, 1984); and use of a computer data base (Rizzo, Bagnara, & Visciola, 1987). Other studies have focused on simulated or natural settings in order to gather error detection data. Among these are a study of a hot strip mill (Bagnara, Stablum, Rizzo, Fontana, & Ruo, 1987) and nuclear power plants (Woods, 1984). Finally, diary studies have provided data on a wide range of everyday errors. Diary studies by Norman (1981) and Reason and Mycielska (1982) include some detailed descriptions of the circumstances surrounding detection. Sellen (1990) provided the first diary study to focus specifically on this aspect.

One conclusion from an examination of this literature is that slips can be caught either before action, during the execution of the overt action itself (through visual, kinesthetic, or auditory feedback, for example), or afterward, on the basis of the *outcome* of the error. The ability to detect errors on the basis of outcome is important because slips often go undetected at the time of com-mission. Detection occurs because the slips may cause changes in the world from which they can later be inferred. Other times, constraints in the external world limit or prevent the erroneous action or following actions from occurring, thus leading to the detection of the slip. This is detection by a "limiting func-tion" (or "forcing function," to use Norman's, 1988, terminology).

Different still from the detection of self-produced slips are the processes involved in the detection of slips either produced by other people or otherwise contrived and deliberately introduced into stimulus material. Such studies have been mainly concerned with proofreading tasks (Healy, 1980; Levy & Begin, 1984; Monk & Hulme, 1983) and detection of errors in speech (Cohen, 1980; Cooper, Tye-Murray, & Nelson, 1987; Lackner, 1980; Tent & Clark, 1980). The detection of errors produced by other people has also been examined in the field, within an actual navigation team onboard ship (Seifert & Hutch-ins, 1989).

Finally, it is helpful to distinguish error "detection" from error "identification." *Detection* is discovering—whether consciously or subcon-sciously—*that* an error has occurred, without necessarily knowing what the error was. *Identification* is determining *what* was done wrong. Both detection and identification differ from "correction," which requires knowing *how* to undo the effect of the error. Correction requires detection, but not necessarily identification.

The cognitive processes involved in the various aspects of error evaluation may be very different indeed. A variety of these error detection mechanisms have been proposed that can be classed as error matching, closed-loop feed-back, editing, and spreading-activation mechanisms.

Error Matching.   Models containing "error-matching" mechanisms pro-pose that detection occurs because we have stored representations of errors that can be matched to emitted performance in working memory. In a model of writing, Hayes and Flower (1980) describe these "error representations" as productions specific to different kinds of errors. Once triggered, ongoing be-havior is interrupted and the appropriate correcting procedure is automat-ically activated. Allwood's model of statistical problem solving (1984) also alludes to such a matching mechanism. There are obvious limitations to this approach, not the least of which is that they fail to describe how novel errors may be detected.

Closed-Loop Feedback.   Another class of mechanism is based on the notion of *closed-loop feedback*. This type of mechanism tends to arise primarily for low-level processes in the context of tasks such as moving the arm some criterion distance (e.g., Adams, 1971). The "error" in these tasks is the differ-ence between the desired state and the state actually achieved, usually specified as a continuous variable. This "error signal" is the basic control signal for all servomechanisms and, in fact, is an essential aspect of the operation of these systems: the "error" is the driving force for continued behavior rather than an unintended choice of action. The term *closed-loop* refers to the fact that the measured value of the actual behavior is brought back to the input of the action system, where it is compared with the intended value, the discrepancy then "closing the loop" by being used as the controlling input for further action. The discrepancy is called an *error* in the sense of this chapter only when its value exceeds some arbitrary threshold (much as an arrow aimed at the "bull's-eye" is not a miss as long as the variation in end point remains within the painted circle of the target).

The closed-loop system is important in that it points out the necessity of defining three components of an error detection system: the system's feedback, the reference value against which the feedback is compared, and the monitoring mechanism that does the comparison. Closed-loop models have inspired more complex, multilevel models of action such as that of Miller, Galanter, and Pribram (1960), though how slips are represented in such a system or how they would be detected has never been made explicit.

Editing Mechanisms. Editor models focus on the detection of errors *before* the actual production of actions. Editor theories assume that a component of the system external to the processes responsible for production monitors the correctness of action execution, as in theories of prearticulatory editing (e.g., Baars *et al.*, 1975; Mattson & Baars, Chapter 11, this volume). Editors have been suggested for the lexical, semantic, syntactic, and social appropriateness of utterances. Freud proposed a variant of an editor, a "censor" that monitors for socially or personally sensitive material and prevents its expression, often preventing it from reaching conscious awareness. To Freud, many slips were expressions that escaped the censor's operations, thus revealing to the skilled observer (if not to the perpetrator) the nature of the underlying, repressed material. Thus, Freud's editor primarily operated between subconscious operations and conscious ones, although it could also serve to edit behavioral acts. The point is that many different specialized editors have been proposed to evaluate production at many levels in the control structure.

There have been a variety of criticisms of editor theories, some of which are pointed out by MacKay in Chapter 2. Complexity or lack of parsimony is the most common. It is not easy to figure out a plausible mechanism. As Levelt (1989) pointed out, in order for an editing system to work, the editing devices must contain all the knowledge that the production components possess in order to evaluate the correctness of the internal representations. This results in reduplication of knowledge in the system as well as the danger of suggesting a "watchful homunculus" at each level in the system. Further, if there is a system powerful enough to detect and prevent errors, why is it not used to generate the action in the first place? In the face of such problems, alternative mechanisms for covert editing such as Levelt's "perceptual loop" seem more feasible. However, as yet, none of these alternatives seems wholly adequate in accounting for all the data, as Mattson and Baars point out in Chapter 11.

Spreading-Activation Mechanisms. A final class of detection mechanism falls within the category of spreading activation, often within neural network models of speech and action. One benefit of such models is that they can be generalized beyond speech to incorporate action slips. However with regard to detection, only MacKay's "node structure theory" (1987, and Chapter 2, this volume) has been explicit about how the detection of slips might occur. MacKay discusses the fact that internal mechanisms in node structure theory can trigger awareness, thereby invoking conscious error-evaluation processes. Although it provides a possible explanation of the detection of slips below the level of awareness, this theory does not account for the phenomenon of the conscious examination of slips internally, such as in inner speech. This is symptomatic of the fact that, in general, the role of supervisory or attentional mechanisms in error detection has not been well described.

The General Problem of Error Monitoring

There can be little doubt that attention is central to the problem of slip detection. Slips can occur at many different levels in the system, in both verbal and nonverbal actions. Because so many different levels of behavior can be monitored for correctness, the place where attention is focused becomes critical. Similarly, the amount of available attention is important. Baars (Chapter 1) showed that increasing subjects' sensitivity to their own errors altered the production of semantically anomalous but not of semantically acceptable errors, a finding suggesting that an increased allocation of attentional resources to detection can result in the better internal detection and correction of some errors.

Data from the area of the detection of *overt* speech errors suggest that a person's goals are important in determining what aspects of behavior are monitored. For instance, one finding is that listeners are more likely to detect errors affecting meaning (word level) than phonetic errors (sound level). Speakers, on the other hand, detect meaning and phonetic errors about equally (Cutler, 1982) or detect phonetic errors only slightly more often (Nooteboom, 1980). This finding probably reflects the fact that listeners are intent on extracting the meaning of the speech stream whereas speakers are concerned about both proper pronunciation and the content of communication.

A person's knowledge of a topic can also affect attentional allocation and, thus, error detection. Miyake (1982) studied the interaction between pairs of people attempting to discover and understand how sewing machines work. Speech errors were most likely to be detected when they occurred in a discussion relevant to the current level of understanding of the sewing machine. They were not as likely to be detected when they referred back to previous levels of understanding. Miyake proposed that people detect fewer errors when they are contained within known information. Findings such as these suggest not only that attention is necessary for detection, but also that the focus of attention determines what *kinds* of errors are detected. Further, the focus of attention depends on a variety of factors, including goals and task-specific knowledge.

Finally, note a fundamental distinction between detection mechanisms that leads to a testable hypothesis. Some detection mechanisms may act unconsciously and *evoke* awareness, whereas others may *require* awareness for detection. We propose that slips involving low-level mismatches (between the motor plan and the executed actions, for example) are apt to invoke conscious awareness rather than to require it. Because the detection of low-level slips invokes awareness and because information about the mismatch is available to the processing system, it is relatively easy to determine the nature of this kind of error. On the other hand, slips at higher levels occur because intentional control is temporarily absent. High-level slips typically do not involve problems in executing or triggering the components of action; they involve the unintentional activation of entire sequences of routine actions—problems in schema selection rather than schema execution. The detection of high-level slips therefore requires that intentional control (awareness) be reestablished. High-level slips are thus both harder to detect and harder to identify.

The suggestion is that the level at which the mismatch is signaled has implications for the role of conscious control and the amount of information available. Simply put, detecting mismatches at higher, conceptual levels of action representation is more effortful than detecting mismatches at lower levels of control, where it is the *production* of action that is represented.

TWO UNEXPLORED AREAS OF RESEARCH

As a final comment on theory, we point out two areas of research that have so far received very little attention: the distribution of slips in time and the effects of slips on subsequent action.

The Distribution of Slips in Time

The chapters in this book have almost exclusively been concerned with the *form* of errors as a clue to the underlying mechanisms responsible for action. Besides data on the frequency and probability of error occurrence, there is very little research that attempts to describe the time characteristics of slips. How are slips distributed in time? Is it possible to predict *when* a slip will occur?

One experiment suggests that the time of error occurrence for key-pressing slips in a forced-choice, self-paced task is random (Sellen & Senders, 1985). In this experiment, the majority of errors appeared to be emitted with a constant probability per unit of time. In other words, such errors were distributed according to a Poisson distribution with respect to the number of errors occurring per unit of time and also were distributed geometrically with respect to the distribution of intervals between the occurrences of errors. This finding was consistent across individual subjects even though the subjects differed in their overall rates of errors and exhibited different speed–accuracy trade-offs. Thus, changes in overall error frequency did not affect the fit of the data to the Poisson and geometric distributions. These results are consistent with the notion of a random error process governing the time of slip emission.

One possible explanation is that there are some kinds of errors that are "uncaused" and endogenous in the sense that they are internally and spontaneously generated. A more mechanistic account is that distractors are responsible for causing this subset of slips.[1] This view assumes that correct performance requires a minimal number of attentional resources for the control of actions, and that distractions disrupt the attentional process. Therefore, errors are distributed randomly in time because distractors, whether internal or external, occur randomly in time. Whatever the internal mechanisms involved, the existence of random errors means that, although we may be able to predict the form of an error and its overall frequency, we cannot hope to predict exactly when an error may occur.

Although the timing of some errors may be described as random on a moment-by-moment basis, there is evidence that people use errors to adjust their overall frequency of error occurrence. In studies of sequential reaction times for discrete, self-paced tasks, Rabbitt and Vyas (1970) found that, below a certain reaction time, as reaction time is decreased, the probability of an error increases. Further, the reaction time for the response immediately following an error tends to be significantly longer than the median reaction time. Rabbitt and Vyas proposed that people adjust their own speed–accuracy trade-off functions in order to optimize their performance by slowing their rate of responding on the hypothesized detection of an error.

Many other aspects of the timing of slips remain uninvestigated. It remains to be seen whether errors in tasks beyond simple forced-choice key-pressing tasks obey a different set of laws with regard to their distribution in time. Some kinds of errors may, in fact, be cyclical in nature. We know very little about how the frequency of error changes during the course of a day, although the data do indicate that the relationship between circadian rhythms and errors is systematic (see Queinnec & de Terssac, 1987). For that matter, we know very little about the distribution of errors in the course of a lifetime. Reason (personal communication, October, 1989) has found that older people report fewer errors in diary studies, a finding that tends to go against our intuitions about errors and aging. Whether they actually *commit* fewer errors is unclear. A number of alternative explanations are possible, including the possibility that, with age, we are less efficient in *detecting* our errors.

---

[1]This alternative explanation was offered by Neville Moray (personal communication, May, 1983).

The Effects of Slips

The systematic study of the effects of slips on various aspects of the cognitive system, from affect down to the disruption of low-level processes, is also badly neglected. Baars (Chapter 1) suggests that one of the most important criteria for the definition of a slip is that it creates the reaction of surprise on detection of the error. What are the implications of this response? Mandler (1989) suggested that errors not only result in negative affect but also interfere with ongoing cognitive processing. He suggested that errors may interfere with cognitive processing for at least three reasons: the detection of errors preempts conscious processing; the detection process requires cognitive resources; and the negative affect resulting from the detection causes interference through autonomic arousal. Moray and King (1984) found that the detection of errors increased subjective ratings of work load, emotional stress, and time pressure. This effect was found to be greater when an error led to more work. Even telling a person that an act was in error increased the subjective difficulty and effort required of the task.

The effects of errors on ongoing performance can be seen in other ways. There is the phenomenon of "posterror slowing"—an increase in reaction time for responses immediately following errors—commonly found in studies of reaction times. Rabbitt (1966a) showed that there are longer than average latencies for responses following error correction responses in simple forced-choice tasks. This is also true in transcription typing: the keystroke following an error tends to be longer than the average keystroke or the keystrokes leading up to the error (Salthouse, 1986; Shaffer, 1973).

The common interpretation of posterror slowing is that it occurs because the actor is detecting and reflecting on the error before resuming the task. Unfortunately, posterror slowing has not been measured separately for detected and undetected errors, so the assumption that conscious detection causes the slowing has therefore not been explicitly tested. A more recent study that does make this distinction (Sellen, 1990) actually found greater slowing for undetected errors than for detected errors. Posterror slowing can therefore be attributed to factors other than conscious detection. The exact nature of the disruptive effects of errors needs to be examined in more detail with regard to both the cognitive and the emotional consequences of realizing an error.

METHODOLOGICAL ISSUES

The study of slips poses some unique problems, many of which are attested to by Part III of this book. With the exception of the techniques developed by Baars, Motley, and co-workers (and summarized in Chapter 6), there is a dearth of techniques for systematically studying and inducing slips. We need to extend and supplement these methodologies in different domains and for other kinds of errors. Meanwhile, there are a variety of methodological issues still to be addressed, and many obstacles still to be overcome.

Defining and Classifying Slips

Difficulties begin even with the definition of a "slip." There are a variety of definitions. Norman (1981) and Reason and Mycielska (1982) defined them to be a deviation of the action performed from what was intended. Baars (Chapter 1) offers the operational definition of "actions that people quickly recognize as unintended, once they become aware of them" (p. 4). However, as Dell and Repka demonstrate (Chapter 10), actions do not need to be overt to be classified as slips. Not only do people readily report making slips of the tongue covertly, but the slips are qualitatively similar to overt slips of the tongue.

If we accept that covert slips are truly slips, then some interesting questions are raised: Can we make nonspeech slips covertly? Do we have to be aware of covert slips in order for them to be slips? The postulation of unconscious covert editing processes presupposes that internal errors do in fact occur. If we are willing to accept the existence of these internal monitoring processes, then it is reasonable to accept that the errors themselves may occur below the level of awareness.

Ascertaining the existence of such errors becomes a difficult problem, however. Rabbitt (1978) showed that erroneous keystrokes in a typing task on a manual typewriter were more likely to be emitted with a weaker force than correct keystrokes. He suggested that this effect was due to a "pulling back" on the realization of an incipient error. If this is in fact a valid explanation, it seems very likely that these errors are realized unconsciously in high-speed typing. Physiological measures may be a possible approach to measuring covert errors, but the validation of such measures presents a challenging problem.

The diversity in the form of slips leads naturally to the task of classification. There is no consensus in the literature about how this task is to be done objectively and systematically. A fundamental difficulty in developing taxonomies is that there is no simple correspondence between the form of a slip and its underlying cause. Situational and task variables may disguise the cognitive mechanisms at work. In the psychological literature, the form of a slip is often described phenomenologically at a generic, context-free level of description. Thus, in typing and speech error taxonomies, we find slip categories such as omissions, repetitions, insertions, and substitutions.

To deduce the mechanisms responsible for different slip forms, we need to know the context in which the error occurred. A good example of how this can be done is found in the domain of typing errors, in which the error data are supplemented by measures of keystroke latencies and high-speed photographs. A case in point is substitution errors in typing that involve striking the key adjacent to the intended key. By using videotape analyses, Grudin (1983) showed that some substitution errors involved the correct finger embarked on an inaccurate trajectory. Other substitution errors were the result of incorrect keys' being pressed by the fingers that normally strike them rather than by the "correct" finger. Grudin suggests that this indicates two underlying processes: one in which there is faulty execution of an action (the first case) and one in which there is faulty assignment of the finger (the second case). Without the supplemental data, there would have been no basis for this discussion using the phenomenology of the errors alone.

A valid interpretation of any data based on slip taxonomies requires that we also be able to determine the relationship between error form and the possible causal factors. Unless we can make statements about the underlying mechanisms, comparisons of error frequency data can be meaningless. Mattson and Baars (Chapter 7) make a comparison of error rates across entirely different task domains: spoonerisms in speech are compared with spoonerisms in gesture. The fact that similar slip-inducement techniques resulted in similar error forms is some basis for making such a comparison. However, this kind of analysis assumes not only common causal mechanisms, but comparable units in different domains. Whether we can equate transpositions of speech units with nonverbal actions harks back to earlier discussions of the relationship between verbal and nonverbal slips.

Frequency versus Probability

Another basic problem involves the use of error frequency data. Error frequency may be very different from error probability. *Frequency* refers to the absolute number of occurrences of an event, whereas *probability* refers to the relative rate with respect to the number of opportunities. The validity of laboratory-induced errors is often addressed by comparing the relative frequencies of different kinds of slips within a sample. The use of frequencies rather than probabilities can lead to invalid conclusions, as can best be illustrated by the controversy (now resolved) over whether there is a lexical bias effect for naturally occurring slips (see Chapter 8). The lesson is that it is important to take the opportunity rate for errors into account in order to draw valid inferences. A failure to do so can lead to erroneous conclusions. After all, an infrequent error (one that is low in frequency) may in fact represent a high-probability event, but in the observed situation, there may be few opportunities for the event to be expressed.

It is usually difficult or impossible to measure probabilities in naturalistic situations because of the difficulty in determining the number of opportunities. Opportunity rates in the laboratory can be determined *a priori,* and thus, probabilities of error can often be estimated under these controlled situations. Even so, it can still be a problem to decide what constitutes an opportunity. For example, in Chapter 7, Mattson and Baars compare the percentage of errors on a per trial basis across different task domains. One problem is that it is probably not the case that trials in different tasks contain the same number of opportunities to err. Even within a task, determining the appropriate unit for an opportunity is difficult. Consider a typing task. The keystroke, as the basic unit of action, could reasonably be equated with one opportunity. Alternatively, the word or the phrase could also be considered an opportunity, depending on the type of error involved. Some errors are expressed over the course of larger response units. In complex, multiple-level tasks, the choice of the appropriate unit is theory-bound, and in the absence of an agreed-upon theoretical structure, it may be impossible to determine the appropriate units and hence the number of opportunities in a given task.

The Ecological Validity of Laboratory-Induced Slips

The various techniques for producing slips described in this book are effective ways of producing blends, transpositions, and other kinds of errors resulting from various combinations of competing plans. The assumption is that competition between incompatible plans occurs naturally in the course of speech, accounting for spontaneous slips. Baars (Chapter 6) gives a phenomenological argument for the ecological validity of such induced errors based on a comparison of error form, antecedent conditions, and the correlation between these conditions and the errors they produce. Shared phenomenology is also the basis for the argument developed by Chen and Baars in Chapter 9 for the underlying mechanisms responsible for transformational errors. But slips that result from limits in time to respond or from attempts to resolve competing plans represent very limited classes. Many slips result when we are absentminded or distracted. Typically, such slips are not blends of alternative plans but instead are manifested as entire automatic sequences of actions.

The laboratory environment is probably inherently unsuited to the study of these absentminded slips. They are usually produced when a person is internally preoccupied or distracted, when both the intended actions and the wrong actions are automatic, and when one is doing familiar tasks in familiar surroundings. Laboratory situations offer completely the opposite conditions. Typically, subjects are given an unfamiliar, highly contrived task to accomplish in a strange environment. Most subjects arrive motivated to perform well and, in an environment free of normal distractions, are not given to internal preoccupation, despite the best efforts of the experimenter. In fact, distractions are likely to be interpreted as deliberate attempts to thwart their performance. In short, the typical laboratory environment is possibly the least likely place where we are likely to see truly spontaneous, absentminded errors.

The best warning of these difficulties comes from the attempt to measure performance difficulties due to fatigue in the laboratory. These measures are notoriously difficult to get, and whereas the experimenters may find their own performance suffering if they attempt to keep up with the subject, the subject's performance may remain at high levels. One anecdote tells of a subject performing brilliantly through several days of forced wakefulness, but then (when no longer being monitored by the experimenters) having an automobile accident on the drive home. If the measurement of performance difficulties with such a controllable manipulation as lack of sleep proves to be so difficult, what hope do we have with the variables thought to affect error?

Forcing subjects to be preoccupied turns out to be very difficult. One can create extremely boring tasks so that subjects distract themselves. The drawback is that the kinds of errors that result from these tasks will be rare, will be limited in form, and may not be generalizable to many other tasks. Giving subjects multiple activities or imposing too many distractions on them often has the opposite and undesired effect of making the subjects more motivated and causing them to commit fewer errors.

Another difficulty inherent in laboratory-induced errors is the low frequency of errors in artificial tasks. It is often impossible to obtain a large enough sample of errors in a reasonable time to conduct statistical tests. This is especially true when one is looking for a particular kind of error. There are simple ways of increasing error rate. Subjects can be stressed, given too many things to do at once, distracted, bothered, made tired, or given little time to respond. The problem is that we cannot be sure when we impose such conditions that, with the change in the nature of the tasks, the nature of the underlying mechanisms is also not changed.

A second issue with regard to error rate has to do with the ratio of error to opportunity. Very simple tasks mean more opportunities to err because they can be accomplished more quickly. The trade-off is that there is a low probability of erring on any one trial. Complex tasks may yield a higher probability of erring on a per trial basis but usually take a longer time to complete. The result is fewer trials or opportunities on which to err per unit of time. A side effect of manipulating task complexity in order to change the error rate is that it will also affect the kind of error one is likely to observe. Simple tasks tend to yield a large percentage of slips, whereas complex tasks result in more errors of intention, planning, and judgment.

Because of the extent to which conditions may be contrived in order to induce errors in the laboratory, the problem of demonstrating ecological validity is an important one. It is simply not enough to assume that the differences between laboratory and field do not affect the internal processes that generate errors. With regard to errors, there is good reason to believe that such an impoverished environment may result in the action of different mechanisms. We should not haphazardly attempt to boost error rates or to contrive experimental tasks. The point is often made that there needs to be a closer correspondence between laboratory tasks and real-world situations. We concur with this opinion and feel that the development of paradigms for slip inducement must rely on a closer scrutiny of the real-world conditions under which slips occur. One promising line of research is to capitalize on the fact that, in the natural world, people usually do more than one task at a time. Often, natural errors happen because people are engaged in multiple tasks, with multiple goals. Under these conditions, the demands of one task often interrupt or distract from those of another.

CONCLUDING REMARKS

The study of slips has made great advances over the years, as indicated by the studies in this book, but we are still far from understanding their nature. In part, the reason is that slips are only a small part of the entire story of action production, a topic little explored within cognitive science. Action production is actually an entire cycle, including the formation of goals and intentions, the execution of an overt act, and the perception and evaluation of the action and its outcome. This means that a full understanding of human action—and thus of slips—can come about only when we truly understand the entire cycle from motor skills, to perception, to the relevant internal processing and decision making.

Although slips are not uncommon events in daily life, they are infrequent enough to make their study difficult. When one brings slips into the laboratory, the benefit is that their conditions can be better controlled and the resulting behavior better measured. The deficit is that the laboratory environment is apt to distort the nature and kind of slip that is observed.

There are still many factors that need to be studied about slips, especially the nature of conscious awareness and its relationship to action in general, how action is monitored and how slips and other deviations from intentions are monitored, and how the inappropriate behavior is modified.

Slips provide a unique window through which to view human behavior. The processes of normal behavior are usually best revealed through the study of abnormalities, which makes the study of slips an important and essential aspect of cognition. Slips are also a component of human performance in critical tasks, especially in industrial situations that can lead to serious accidents. Thus, the laboratory and theoretical studies of human slips and human error in general can have an important impact on application. It is for all these reasons that the study of slips must be encouraged and expanded. But slips should not be studied in isolation, nor should they be thought of as a specialized field of study. The study of human error is in reality part of the study of human behavior, and as such, it belongs in the forefront of studies of human cognition.

REFERENCES

Adams, J. A. (1971). A closed-loop theory of motor learning. *Journal of Motor Behavior, 3*(2), 111–149.

Adams, J. A., & Goetz, E. T. (1973). Feedback and practice as variables in error detection and correction. *Journal of Motor Behavior, 5*(4), 217–224.

Allwood, C. M. (1984). Error detection processes in statistical problem solving. *Cognitive Science, 8*, 413–437.

Baars, B. J., Motley, M. T., & MacKay, D. (1975). Output editing for lexical status from artificially elicited slips of the tongue. *Journal of Verbal Learning and Verbal Behavior, 14*, 382–391.

Bagnara, S., Stablum, F., Rizzo, A., Fontana, A., & Ruo, M. (1987). Error detection and correction: A study on human-computer interaction in a hot strip mill production planning and control system. *Preprints of the First European Meeting on Cognitive Science Approaches to Process Control,* Marcoussis, France.

Cohen, A. (1980). Correcting of speech errors in a shadowing task. In V. A. Fromkin (Ed.), *Errors in linguistic performance: Slips of the tongue, ear, pen, and hand.* New York: Academic Press.

Cooper, W. E., Tye-Murray, N., & Nelson, L. J. (1987). Detection of missing words in spoken text. *Journal of Psycholinguistic Research, 16*(3), 233–240.

Cutler, A. (1982). The reliability of speech error data. In A. Cutler (Ed.), *Slips of the tongue and language production* (pp. 7–28). Amsterdam: Mouton.

Dell, G. S. (1986). A spreading activation theory of retrieval in sentence production. *Psychological Review, 93,* 283–321.

Dell, G. S., & Reich, P. A. (1980). Toward a unified model of slips of the tongue. In V. Fromkin (Ed.), *Errors in linguistic performance.* New York: Academic Press.

Fromkin, V. (Ed.), (1973). *Speech errors as linguistic evidence.* The Hague: Mouton.

Fromkin, V. A. (Ed.), (1980). *Errors in linguistic performance: Slips of the tongue, ear, pen, and hand.* New York: Academic Press.

Grudin, J. T. (1983). Error patterns in novice and skilled transcription typing. In W. E. Cooper (Ed.), *Cognitive aspects of skilled typewriting.* New York: Springer-Verlag.

Hayes, J. R., & Flower, L. S. (1980). Identifying the organization of writing processes. In L. W. Gregg & E. R. Steinberg (Eds.), *Cognitive processes in writing.* Hillsdale, NJ: Erlbaum.

Healy, A. F. (1980). Proofreading errors on the word "the": New evidence on reading units. *Journal of Experimental Psychology: Human Perception and Performance, 6,* 45–57.

Lackner, J. R. (1980). Speech production: Correction of semantic and grammatical errors during speech shadowing. In V. A. Fromkin (Ed.), *Errors in linguistic performance: Slips of the tongue, ear, pen, and hand.* New York: Academic Press.

Levelt, W. J. M. (1989). *Speaking: From intention to articulation.* Cambridge: MIT Press.

Levy, B. A., & Begin, J. (1984). Proofreading familiar text: Allocating resources to perceptual and conceptual processes. *Memory and Cognition, 12*(6), 621–632.

Long, J. (1976). Visual feedback and skilled keying: Differential effects of masking the printed copy and the keyboard. *Ergonomics, 19,* 93–110.

MacKay, D. G. (1987). *The organization of perception and action: A theory for language and other cognitive skills.* New York: Springer-Verlag.

Mandler, G. (1985). Scoring goals. *CC-AI, 2*(4), 25–31.

Mandler, G. (1989). Affect and learning: Causes and consequences of emotional interactions. In D. B. McLeod & V. M. Adams (Eds.), *Affect and mathematical problem solving: A new perspective.* New York: Springer-Verlag.

Miller, G. A., Galanter, E., & Pribram, K. H. (1960). *Plans and the structure of behavior.* New York: Holt, Rinehart, & Winston.

Miyake, N. (1982). *Error detection in natural conversations.* Unpublished manuscript, University of California, San Diego.

Monk, A. F., & Hulme, C. (1983). Errors in proofreading: Evidence for the use of word shape in word recognition. *Memory and Cognition, 11*(1), 16–23.

Moray, N. P., & King, B. (1984). *Error as a cause and effect of workload: Mental workload as a closed loop system.* (Working paper 84-11). University of Toronto, Department of Industrial Engineering.

Motley, M. T. (1980). Verification of "Freudian slips" and semantic prearticulatory editing via laboratory-induced spoonerisms. In V. A. Fromkin (Ed.), *Errors in linguistic performance: Slips of the tongue, ear, pen, and hand.* New York: Academic Press.

Motley, M. T., Baars, B. J., & Camden (1981). Syntactic criteria in prearticulatory editing: Evidence from laboratory-induced slips of the tongue. *Journal of Psycholinguistic Research, 10,* 503–522.

Nooteboom, S. G. (1980). Speaking and unspeaking: Detection and correction of phonological and lexical errors in spontaneous speech. In V. A. Fromkin (Ed.), *Errors in linguistic performance: Slips of the tongue, ear, pen and hand.* New York: Academic Press.

Norman, D. A. (1981). Categorization of action slips. *Psychological Review, 88*, 1–15.

Norman, D. A. (1988). *The psychology of everyday things.* New York: Basic Books. (Also published in paperback as Norman, D. A. (1990). *The design of everyday things.* New York: Doubleday.)

Norman, D. A., & Shallice, T. (1986). Attention to action: Willed and automatic control of behavior. In R. J. Davidson, G. E. Schwartz, & D. Shapiro (Eds.), *Consciousness and self regulation: Advances in research,* (Vol. 4). New York: Plenum Press.

Queinnec, Y., & de Terssac, G. (1987). Chronobiological approach of human errors in complex systems. In J. Rasmussen, K. Duncan, & J. Leplat (Eds.), *New technology and human error.* New York: Wiley.

Rabbitt, P. (1966a). Errors and error correction in choice-response tasks. *Journal of Experimental Psychology, 71*(2), 264–272.

Rabbitt, P. (1966b). Error correction time without external error signals. *Nature, 212*, 438.

Rabbitt, P. (1967). Time to detect errors as a function of factors affecting choice-response time. *Acta Psychologica, 27*, 131–142.

Rabbitt, P. (1968). Three kinds of error signalling responses in a serial choice task. *Quarterly Journal of Experimental Psychology, 19*, 37–42.

Rabbitt, P. (1978). Detection of errors by skilled typists. *Ergonomics, 21*(11), 945–958.

Rabbitt, P., & Phillips, S. (1967). Error detection and correction latencies as a function of S-R compatibility. *Quarterly Journal of Experimental Psychology, 19*, 37–42.

Rabbitt, P. M. A., & Vyas, S. M. (1970). An elementary preliminary taxonomy for some errors in laboratory choice RT tasks. *Acta Psychologica, 33*, 56–76.

Reason, J. T., & Mycielska, K. (1982). *Absent minded? The psychology of mental lapses and everyday errors.* Englewood Cliffs, NJ: Prentice-Hall.

Rizzo, A., Bagnara, S., & Visciola, M. (1987). Human error detection processes. *International Journal of Man-Machine Studies, 27*, 55–570.

Rumelhart, D. E., & Norman, D. A. (1982). Simulating a skilled typist: A study of skilled cognitive-motor performance. *Cognitive Science, 6*, 1–36.

Salthouse, T. A. (1986). Perceptual, cognitive, and motoric aspects of transcription typing. *Psychological Bulletin, 99*(3), 303–319.

Schmidt, R. A. (1987). The acquisition of skill: Some modifications to the perception-action relationship through practice. In H. Heuer & A. F. Sanders (Eds.), *Perspectives on perception and action.* Hillsdale, NJ: Erlbaum.

Schmidt, R. A., & White, J. L. (1972). Evidence for an error detection mechanism in motor skills: A test of Adams' closed-loop theory. *Journal of Motor Behavior, 4*(3), 143–153.

Searle, J. R. (1980). The intentionality of intention and action. *Cognitive Science, 4*(1), 47–70.

Seifert, C., & Hutchins, E. (1989). Learning from error. *Proceedings of the Eleventh Annual Conference of the Cognitive Science Society,* Ann Arbor, MI.

Sellen, A. J. (1990). *Mechanisms of human error and human error detection.* Unpublished doctoral dissertation, University of California—San Diego.

Sellen, A. J., & Senders, J. W. (1985, May). *At least some errors are randomly generated (Freud was wrong).* Paper presented at the NASA 21st Annual Conference on Manual Control, Columbus, OH.

Shaffer, L. H. (1973). Latency mechanisms in transcription. In S. Kornblum (Ed.), *Attention and performance* (Vol. 4). New York: Academic Press.

Shaffer, L. H., & Hardwick, J. (1969). Errors and error detection in typing. *Quarterly Journal of Psychology, 21*, 209–213.

Suchman, L. (1987). *Plans and situated actions: The problem of human-machine communication.* New York: Cambridge University Press.

Tent, J., & Clark, J. E. (1980). An experimental investigation into the perception of slips of the tongue. *Journal of Phonetics, 8,* 317–325.

West, L. J. (1967). Vision and kinesthesis in the acquisition of typewriting skill. *Journal of Applied Psychology, 51*(2), 161–166.

Woods, D. D. (1984). Some results on operator performance in emergency events. *Institute of Chemical Engineers Symposium Series, 90,* 21–31.

Index

Local theories of speech and action, insufficient explanation of slips, 4
Loss of voluntary control, 105

MacKay theory of speech production, 240–244
Memory, implicit vs. explicit, 319
Mental practice, 104, 110
Mental workload, 104, 217, 223, 227–230
Methodological issues in the study of errors, 331–336
Momentary overload, limited capacity, 99, 117, 141
Mood induction, 301–302
Morphological accommodation, 202
Morphological errors, 197, 207–209
Motivational priming, 292–293
Motor cortex, 157
Multiple levels, 4
Multiple tasks, 335–336
Muscle movement, 42

Naturalness, 138, 144–147, 148
Negative attributions, 105
Neurolinguistic control model (Laver), 272–273
Node structure theory (McKay), 42–46, 64, 328
Nodes
  content of, 46, 240–242
  sequence of, 47, 240–242
  mental, 42
  motor, 242
Nonqualitative state of mind, 98
Nonverbal slips, 130, 151–193
Nonvoluntary, 94, 95
Normal slip rate advantage (NSRA), 265–271
Novel access, 99
Novel problems, 76
Novelty, 73, 99, 102, 103, 112, 114
Novice, 114
Null hypothesis, 144

Oak-yoke primes, 78
Object manipulation errors, 152, 172–193
Omissions, 153
Operating models, 22
Opportunistic planning system, 36, 121–125, 322–323
Options, 124
Order reversal, 197

Ordinal conflict effect (OCE), 136, 137, 138, 142, 148, 154–193
Ordinal conflict slip induction techniques, 131, 133, 134, 135–139
Orienting reaction, 59
Overdetermined nature of slips, 290
Overloading, of limited capacity, 6, 13, 18, 26–31, 132, 143, 310–311
Override, 75

Parallel distributed processors (PDPs), 89, 97, 98
Parallel processing, 75
Parallel search process, 73, 75
Partial-opacity hypothesis, 244, 248, 250
Pathology, 75, 113
Perceptual biases in detecting speech errors, 196
Perceptual feedback, 41
Perceptual loop model, Levelt, 273, 328
Pertinent novelty, 58, 61–64, 66
Phonemic bias, 132–135
Phonological bias techniques (phonological priming), 131, 197, 292
Phonological errors, 198–207
Phonological fusion, 132
Phonological level, 240, 241
Piano playing, 154
Plan competition, 16, 26–31, 127
Positive feedback in activation networks, 275–282
Post-error slowing, 331
Practice, mental and physical, 41, 110, 252–258
Priming, 35, 42, 56, 63, 66, 77, 78, 80–81, 104, 134, 142–143, 148, 240
Prior practice and probability of speech errors, 40
Prospective memory, 75
Psychodynamic hypothesis, 291, 292–293, 309
Psychopathology, 310
Publicity organ of the nervous system, 99

Question-answering technique, 137, 145

Rapid memory scanning, 107
Rasmussen, 75
Recall, 81–82
  cued, 197
Recency, 82, 84
Recruitment, 99, 100